A Twilight of Centaurs

A Twilight of Centaurs
The Opening Campaigns of the
First World War as Witnessed by an
American Volunteer Driver With
British Cavalry on the Western Front

From Mons to Ypres With General French
and
With Cavalry in 1915

Frederic Coleman

A Twilight of Centaurs
The Opening Campaigns of the First World War as Witnessed by an American Volunteer Driver With British Cavalry on the Western Front
From Mons to Ypres With General French
and
With Cavalry in 1915
by Frederic Coleman

FIRST EDITION

First published under the titles
From Mons to Ypres With General French
and
With Cavalry in 1915

Leonaur is an imprint
of Oakpast Ltd

Copyright in this form © 2013 Oakpast Ltd

ISBN: 978-1-78282-239-4 (hardcover)
ISBN: 978-1-78282-240-0 (softcover)

http://www.leonaur.com

Publisher's Notes

The views expressed in this book are not necessarily those of the publisher.

Contents

From Mons to Ypres With General French   7

With Cavalry in 1915   297

From Mons to Ypres With General French

THE AUTHOR

Contents

Preface	13
The Retreat Begun	17
"Proper Rearguards"	40
Into the German Lines	66
End of the Great Retreat	90
The Winning of the Marne	104
Wine From a Mountain Cave	124
Cavalry in the Trenches	139
Diary Under Howitzer-Fire	151
A German Attack	168
Night Marches	179
Fall of Antwerp	188
A Visit to Ypres	206
A French Attack	236
The Battle in the Salient	258
The Christmas Truce	267
Appendix	284

Dedicated in Affectionate Recollection
and Unbounded Admiration
To the Splendid Troopers
of the
Second Cavalry Brigade, 9th Lancers,
4th Dragoon Guards and 18th Hussars
The World has seen no finer Soldiers
in all its
Pageantry of Wars

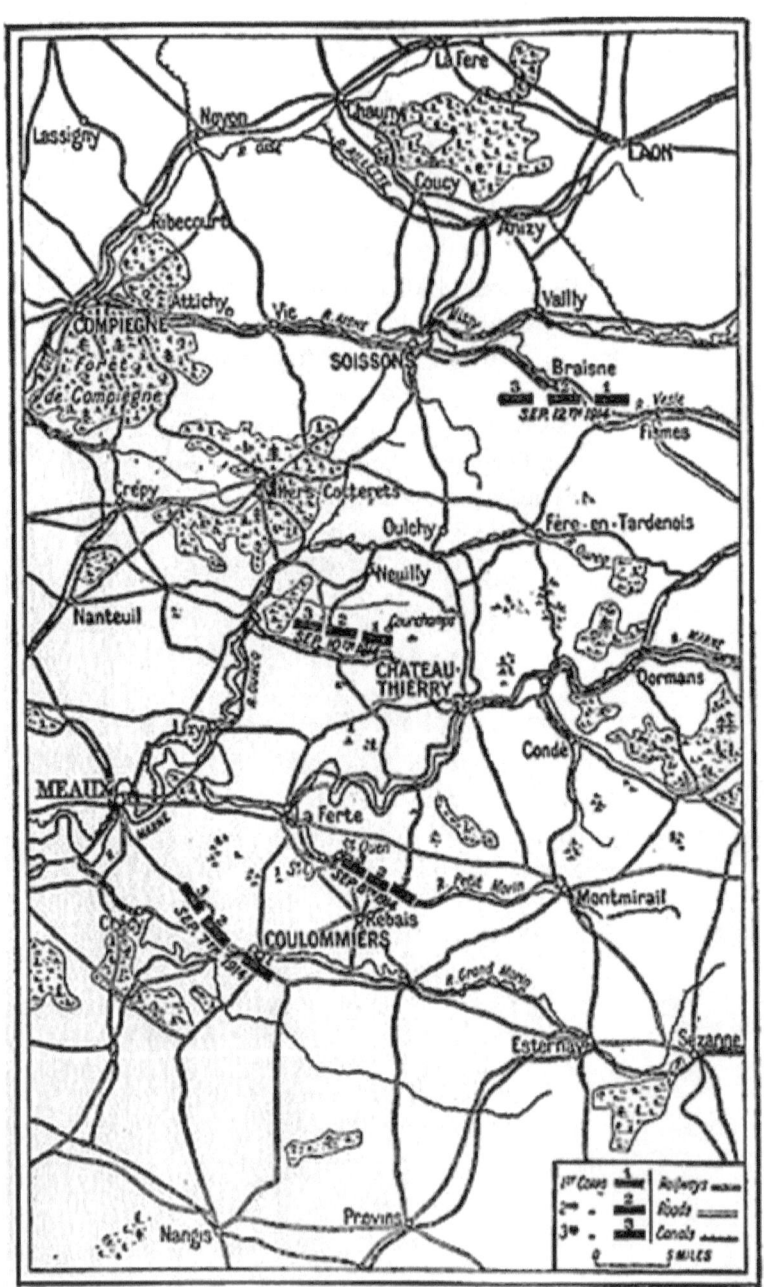

Preface

This is a plain tale.

I am an American, and I have believed from the commencement (1914) of the war that the Allies' cause was just.

I am an admirer of brave soldiers, and willing to pay tribute to good work, from a military stand point, by men on either side.

For ten months I was with the British Expeditionary Force in France and Flanders.

I am so greatly indebted to many units of the British Army for the opportunity afforded me. to undergo experiences which form the subject matter of this somewhat rambling narrative, that I must make my acknowledgments, for the most part, collectively.

At the hands of Sir John French's Headquarters Staff I met unfailing kindness and courtesy throughout my sojourn in their midst.

Of General Smith-Dorrien I can sincerely speak as all speak who have met him, with profound recognition of his high attainments as a military leader, and of his great heart. Truly, a kinder man I have never met.

During the months I spent with the British Cavalry I felt an ever-increasing pride to have been attached to that branch of the Service. The officers and men of the 2nd Cavalry Brigade could not have been more friendly had I been of their own number.

My work with the 1st Cavalry Division brought me into somewhat less personal touch with the individual units, but I was most cordially treated on all sides.

To General Allenby and his Staff I have ever been grateful for the cheery welcome that made tired hours invariably brighten when I had the good fortune to come into touch with that efficient and energetic coterie.

The 2nd Cavalry Brigade Headquarters Mess, and later the 1st

Cavalry Division Headquarters Mess, of which I was a member for so long a time, contained good fellows to a man. Among them I formed friendships which are the most cherished of all my priceless mementos of the most wonderful year of my life.

It is, however, to General de Lisle, personally, that I am under the deepest obligation. I have been brought, at one time or another, into close contact with the Field Forces in time of war of half a score of nations. Among them I have never met an army officer more keen upon his work than is General de Lisle. My personal affection for him, my admiration of him, and my sincere good wishes run hand in hand.

To Julian W. Orde and his efforts the Royal Automobile Club Corps owed its existence. To him I owe a great personal debt. No matter what the issue or how difficult of access that which was required, Julian Orde never failed a member of the R.A.C. Contingent—that hurriedly organised little band of whom Sydney Green (with General Hubert Gough from the beginning of the campaign) is the sole remaining active member.

Friends galore have given me those invaluable suggestions and opportunities whereby one gains a close insight into affairs, and oftentimes a pictorial record of them.

To none do I tender more sincere acknowledgment in that connection than to my old friend Percy Northey, a sometime member of the R.A.C. Corps.

Many gallant gentlemen mentioned in the following pages have gone on before, but, thank God!, many have "come through."

Friends and readers, do not forget that most Americans feel much the same as I feel about the war.

An overwhelming majority of those of my countrymen who know the truth would do what lies in their power to further the success of the Allies and their righteous cause.

Frederick Coleman.

1st Army H.Q.Qrs.
Cambridge
27. Aug. 15.

Dear Mr Coleman

You ask me to give you a letter which will be certain evidence that you were with the fighting troops of the British Army from the commencement of this great war —

I very gladly write such a letter for throughout the time I was with the Army in France from the 19th Aug 14 to 7th May 15. I frequently came across you — & always pretty close to where the shot & shell were flying pretty merrily — The first time we met was in the Square at St Quentin during the great retirement, the morn'g after the battle of Le Cateau, the 27th Aug (12 months ago to-day) when Lord Loch introduced me to you & you kindly gave me a lift in your car —

Yrs sin'y
H Smith-Dorrien

29th Division
Dardanelles
31st August 1915.

My dear Coleman.

I was so pleased to get your letter of August 5th containing the announcement and outline of your proposed lectures. The latter brings back vividly the interesting as well as dangerous journeys we spent together in your wonderful Car from August 31st, just a year ago today, until the end of May following, when I was transferred to this Division. My Cavalry never went into action without your car moving backwards and forwards from the firing line to my Head Quarters, and I hope you will make it clear to your audiences that you did not view the fighting from positions miles in rear, as is necessarily the case with Correspondents.

I see you have reproduced the photograph of the car after our H.Q. were blown up outside Messines, but I wish I had a picture of your face when you missed your gears the morning that shell burst in our faces and smashed the radiator & wind screen.

Well, goodluck my dear Coleman. Whatever life may bring you; & I hope it will be all prosperity and Success, you will always admit that you never spent a more wonderful time, one that can never be forgotten, than the months you spent in the front line with my 1st Cavalry Division.

I need not say how much assistance you were to me during all this time; but you may not know that I reported more than once that without your car at my disposal I could never have kept in close touch with my Brigades across the Aisne, at Ypres and Messines.

With all good wishes and kindest regards to Mrs Coleman & Ruth.

Yours ever,
Beauvoir de Lisle

Chapter 1

The Retreat Begun

On a pleasant August evening in 1914 I embarked on a troopship at Southampton. I was one of twenty-five members of the Royal Automobile Club who had each volunteered to take his motor-car and proceed at once to the General Headquarters of Sir John French's Army. That Army, the original British Expeditionary Force, was in France or Belgium, we knew not exactly where. It was generally anticipated by all and sundry that, if not actually fighting on that Friday evening, August 21st, it would soon be engaged with the Germans advancing towards France through poor Belgium.

The day before, Brussels had fallen. At the time I left Southampton the British 1st Corps and 2nd Corps, with a cavalry division, were in Belgium entrenching a position from Condé east to Mons and on to the eastward as far as Binche, on the road to Charleroi.

The twenty-five volunteer motorists who composed our party had been sent officially from London by the War Office to drive officers of the General Headquarters Staff at the Front. Our troopship arrived in Havre at an early hour on Saturday, the 22nd, but owing to lack of facilities for disembarkation of the cars night had closed in before the little band was ashore and ready to proceed across the North of France to the Belgian Line. Sunday morning the twenty-five cars were *en route* for Amiens. Three of the party ran ahead with General T. D'O. Snow, commanding the 4th Division, and his staff, and the remainder lunched at Neufchatel, and reached Amiens at teatime.

Here the majority of the party remained, to be assigned on the morrow to various duties. Six of us pushed on that night to Le Cateau. Arriving after dark, we found that Sir John French's Headquarters were in a chateau near the town, and G.H.Q., as General Headquarters proper was termed, was located in a large school in the centre of the town. The drive had been long and dusty. After a late and meagre dinner at the Hotel du Nord, a hostel of modest pretensions, we spread our blankets underneath the trees of the schoolyard and were soon wrapped in sound slumber.

That Saturday and Sunday had seen part of the German invading army under Von Buelow take Charleroi from the French 5th Army and win the crossing of the Sambre. The Sunday had seen the first clash between the German and British armies. By the middle of the day the first great German attack against the British force had developed, and Von Kluck, with his German 1st Army, was outnumbering and, at one or two points, beating back the British troops before night had fallen. On Sunday night Sir John French had learned that the retirement of the French 5th Army on his right had rendered the Mons line untenable, and orders had already been given to fall back.

The great retreat had begun.

I awoke at daybreak on Monday, the 24th, to the sound of the guns. Drummond's 19th Infantry Brigade had disentrained at Valenciennes the night before. A new line from Jenlain, a few miles from Valenciennes, eastward through Bavai to Maubeuge was to be our new front, and we were retiring under cover of an attack by our 1st Corps.

I was asked to take two medical officers and two male nurses from Le Cateau to Landrecies. British wounded were being hourly brought into the town, where French wounded had arrived in some numbers already. At the door of one of the improvised hospitals, formerly a school, I had a chat with a wounded gunner. He was a corporal in one of the batteries attached to Haig's 1st Corps and had a shell sliver through his right knee, another through his arm, and a flesh wound in his hand. He had little idea where he had been except that the fighting had been in Belgium. Four of our batteries of field-guns had been placed near each other on a hill, and the men told that the position was to be held at all costs. The German infantry and some of their cavalry had come within range and been badly cut up until the German guns got the range of our batteries.

> Their shells burst well up in the air, throwing out dense clouds of smoke in three colours. The fumes of the shells were overpowering and bullets the size of marbles rained all about. Two of our lot were killed and thirty wounded while we were serving the guns. Finally, we had to leave the position, taking away our wounded. We had to abandon the guns, as the enemy's fire

THE CONGESTION OF THE ROADS BY THE FLEEING COUNTRY FOLK

BELGIAN REFUGEES ON THE ROAD BETWEEN MONS AND BAVAI

was too fierce to allow of our removing them.

High explosive shell made him and his fellows "go hot all over" when struck. These pieces of shell burnt him when they struck him, he said, a quick burning pain following the contact with the hot bits of projectile.

In the afternoon I ran from Le Cateau to Inchy, on the Cambrai road, to pick up General J. A. L. Haldane, who was in command of the 10th Brigade. While waiting in a lane by the road I spent an interesting hour watching a Battalion of Dublin Fusiliers, a part of the newly-arrived 4th Division, which had that day disentrained at Le Cateau, break camp in the adjacent field. Their eagerness to engage the enemy and their thirst for information were both great. The tension was high, for the significance of the French retirement on the right of the British Force was sinking in. I encountered a number of English officers from time to time who openly reviled a retirement the strategical needs of which had not been explained to them, the plain necessity of it not as yet having become apparent.

I was back and forth between Inchy and Le Cateau several times during the afternoon. General Henry H. Wilson used my car to drive slowly and carefully over the road in order to reconnoitre the surrounding country. He explained to me his dislike of the best available ground in that vicinity as a defensive position.

During the afternoon stories of the day's fighting had begun to come into Headquarters. Le Cateau had seen but few wounded men until that Monday evening. In spite of the exaggeration which accompanied the tales of casualty from the Mons and Condé fighting, I gathered that Haig's Corps had effected a successful retirement and reached the protection of the guns of Maubeuge on the right, whilst Smith-Dorrien's 2nd Corps had retired cleverly during the afternoon and reached the vicinity of Jenlain. The retirement as a whole, therefore, difficult as it was, had been carried out admirably. A jumble of reports poured in regarding an action at Audregnies, where rumour persisted that the 2nd Cavalry Brigade under General de Lisle had been well-nigh wiped out. One dust-covered subaltern told me that the Brigade was going out of the village in column of sections when it was attacked by German infantry, with the result that but 240 men out of the original 1,500 remained. Ninety of the 9th Lancers, eighty of the 4th Dragoon Guards, and seventy of the 18th Hussars were, he said, all that was left of the command. Close on the heels of this

FOUR GENERATIONS OF FRENCH REFUGEE FAMILY IN ONE FARMCART

FRENCH REFUGEES DURING THE RETREAT ON PARIS

first report was a more intelligible and infinitely more reliable one, brought in by Captain Francis Grenfell, of the 9th Lancers, who had been shot twice through the leg. He told me that the cavalry had charged a German infantry division well supplied with machine-guns, and never reached a point closer than 800 yards to them. Grenfell and some of his lancers had that day saved the guns of the 119th Battery of R.F.A., for which he was subsequently awarded the V.C.

I spent several hours gathering a coherent story of that fight at Audregnies, which had covered the retirement of Sir Charles Fergusson's 5th Division as he was falling back not far south of the canal line between Condé and Mons. The Germans were working round the 5th Division left. Unless they were checked it appeared to Fergusson that his force would be cut off. General Allenby with his cavalry division was on the left rear of the 5th Division. When Allenby received word of Fergusson's danger the 2nd Cavalry Brigade was in and near the little village of Audregnies.

The German infantry could be seen coming south in considerable numbers and heading straight for the town. A couple of squadrons of the 18th Hussars were a bit north of Audregnies and to the east of it under the shelter of a railway bank. The 9th Lancers and 4th Dragoon Guards were in and back of the village proper. Away on the left, to the west of Audregnies, was the 1st Cavalry Brigade, the 11th Hussars occupying a walled farm practically due west of the village, and the Queen's Bays in support a bit to the south. Still further west, in Baisieux and in front of it, was General Hubert Gough's 3rd Cavalry Brigade, which had to deal with another German infantry column coming down from the north.

Thus the 2nd, 1st, and 3rd Cavalry Brigades were facing the German advance, which was in two distinct sections. The Germans appeared to be in such numbers in front of Audregnies that de Lisle gave orders to Colonel David Campbell, commanding the 9th Lancers, to hold the Germans at all costs and to charge if necessary. One of our batteries was not far from the village, and the noise made by the German shells searching for it, and by our guns firing a reply, was incessant.

By some slight misunderstanding of the verbal order given by de Lisle, Colonel Campbell took it that he was to charge the enemy at once. The 9th Lancers pushed on through the village and galloped down a lane which converged into an open field in plain sight of the enemy. When the 9th Lancers had passed through the lane as fast as they could get through it, for it was narrow, tortuous, and thick with dust, they had not far to ride across the field when they were confronted with a stout wire fence. The 4th Dragoon Guards were coming on after them. The enemy's shell fire was at once directed at the approaching horsemen. The German infantry opened with machine gun and rifle fire at points variously estimated at from 500 to 800 yards distant. There was no getting across the wire. The only thing left to be done was to wheel to the right and gallop for safety to the eastward across the German infantry front, thus affording the enemy such a target as infantry rarely obtains.

Swinging around to the right past a sugar mill, then out from the momentary protection of its adjacent piles of slack and cinders, they kept on to the eastward, then turned south, some seeking the cover of the railway embankment, others making for a cemetery which lay to the east of Audregnies, or scattering to the high ground to the south. Captain Francis Grenfell, who had been wounded, found himself under the railway bank with what he was convinced was the sole surviving remnant of the 9th Lancers. In fact, it was not until next morning that it was realised how many had escaped. The 9th Lancers lost in killed, wounded, and missing about seventy-five all told. The 4th Dragoon Guards' casualty list included two officers and fifty-four men.

The great value of the Audregnies charge was that it accomplished the object in view. It stopped the advance of the German infantry and allowed the 5th Division opportunity to retire southward. The German line did not make a further move forward from that position for at least four or five hours after the charge. The troopers themselves, as more than one of them told me, "could not see what we were charging either going or coming." The field across which they had to gallop was so plastered by all sorts of fire that to do more than simply gallop and keep clear of fallen and falling comrades was all that the men could do. De Lisle issued a special Brigade Order at Le Plessis on August 28th, which read as follows:—

> I wish to express to the 2nd Cavalry Brigade my extreme pride and satisfaction with their conduct in the severe engagement at Audregnies on Monday, August 24th. The fight was necessary to save the 5th Division from an organised counter-attack during their retirement, and the object was achieved by the steady and gallant conduct of the brigade. Major-General Sir Charles Fergusson, commanding the 5th Division, thanked me

personally for saving his division, adding that but for the cavalry brigade his division would have been destroyed to the last man. I especially wish to commend the true cavalry spirit of the 9th Lancers in daring to charge unbroken infantry in order to save neighbouring troops, and that of the 4th Dragoon Guards in the effective support given without hesitation or thought of danger. I intend to bring to the notice of high authority how greatly I value the devotion of my brigade. This to be read to all units on parade tomorrow.

I was first shown this order by one of the troopers of the 9th Lancers who had been with Captain Grenfell in the charge. He had become possessed of one of the original copies of the order, and proudly showed it to me as a souvenir of the event. "It was hell, that charge," he said with a grin, "but I suppose it had to be done. Anyway, to read over that order made it seem to have been worth while."

I slept in my car on Monday night, and before dawn on Tuesday, the 25th, was aroused from pleasant dreams by a sharp request to get under way. The driver who left his car opposite the door of G.H.Q. and slumbered in his seat was apparently considered fair game for early risers. Before I was thoroughly awake I was tearing off to the northeast along the Roman road that led to Bavai. The Forest of Mormal looked cool and refreshing in the early light as we spun past it along the dusty road. I was told that General Smith-Dorrien's 2nd Corps, the 4th Division, and the 19th Brigade were to retire on Le Cateau, and General Haig's 1st Corps was to move south on the eastern side of the Forest of Mormal to a position about Landrecies and Maroilles. As we neared Bavai troops were already on the road. After delivering a message we turned and were soon back in Le Cateau.

Following the example of a couple of Tommies in the stable-yard of the school, I negotiated a bath under a water-tap and treated myself to a shave. I then departed in search of breakfast. I found the Hotels du Mouton Blanc and de France completely sold out of food, and in but little better case for drinkables. A glass of coffee and a bottle of beer were all I could forage for breakfast. The Royal Automobile Club drivers had arrived in the thick of things and been put so continuously to work that no one, they least of all, had thought of how they were to be rationed. Events of such great import were crowding so fast on one another that so trivial a matter as breakfast or dinner was not to be worried about.

The lady of the house wherein I had been billeted volunteered to wash some clothing for me. I accordingly left a goodly proportion of my wardrobe in her charge, where, so far as I know, it may be still. By eight o'clock all was bustle and movement. I drove General Henry Wilson to Sir John French's Headquarters and sat for a time listening to the German guns. British losses of the day before were reported to have been heavy—heavier than, later, they really proved to be. A staff officer told me that the Worcester regiment had been practically wiped out. A feeling of pessimism was creeping over us and becoming universal. Even General Wilson, imperturbable and invariably of good cheer, said to me, "We are not doing any too well!" General officers, of whom there seemed to be an unusual number about, all wore a worried look on their faces.

The early morning was hot, and the sun's fierce glare promised a scorching day. The British troops, tired, had far to go, with no chance to obtain needed rest before their start. There was a general lack of understanding as to why we should be leaving the line Jenlain-Bavai-Maubeuge. Few of us were cognisant of any details of the situation. The inhabitants of Le Cateau were very badly worried. Stories became circulated throughout the countryside to the effect that the British had suffered a crushing defeat and were being driven in full flight before a remorseless enemy. Tales of *Uhlan* atrocities were to be heard on every side. The French folk had seen the British Army marching northward in the full pride of its strength, and had wrapped themselves in quiet satisfaction, confident that their Allies from Albion would save them from the horrors of invasion. The British retirement came to them at first as an unbelievable thing. Before midday on that Tuesday, driven by mad rumours of any and all sorts, the whole community was in full flight to the southward.

Between eight and nine o'clock Le Cateau was treated to the sight of long lines of Sordêt's French Cavalry, 14,000 of whom were moving from our right to our left rear. I was not very favourably impressed by their appearance, although I heard that in the earliest part of the campaign they had used their sinister-looking black lances to good effect. From their yellow helmets and blue tunics to their red breeches they appeared more campaign soiled than one would have thought likely at so early a stage of the proceedings.

The Duke of Westminster drove up in his big car, and we chatted for a few moments. Interesting tales of a car-load of Germans shot to bits and a German aeroplane brought down at Dinant helped to pass a cheerful few minutes. As we stood in the headquarters yard young Robert Rothschild strolled up in the uniform of a French Staff officer. Colonel Seely, ex-Minister of War, wandered about, apparently waiting for someone, and looking lonesome.

Before ten o'clock I had a run to the village of Croix, on the Bavai road, with Lieutenant-Colonel Lord Loch of the Grenadier Guards, who was attached to Sir John French's Staff. Running along the roads in that part of the world was getting to be quite a business at this time. French cavalry, British cavalry, British infantry, and no end of supply columns monopolised every square inch of the roadway. French lines of *vedettes* crossing the hills stretched away to right and left. A German aeroplane sailed by us and over Le Cateau, and then sailed back again. Rifle fire from the Tommies rose and fell in waves of sound as the graceful monoplane soared high out of range in the clear sunshine.

Seeker, one of my R.A.C. comrades, came into Le Cateau from Haussy, a village north of Solesmes, with the report that the Germans were there. At six o'clock in the morning he arrived in Haussy from Jenlain. He had been told to await one of the transport trains of the 19th Brigade. He found the market-place full of people who were preparing to leave the town. The Germans were reported to be four kilometres distant. A bit later someone came in with the report that the *Uhlans* were only two kilometres away. Finally the postmistress came to him and informed him that she had received telegraphic instructions to close her office and take her departure. Seeker was inclined to disbelieve the reports as to the proximity of the Germans.

Entering an *estaminet*, he ordered a cup of coffee. The good woman of the house provided him with the coffee quickly, and then disappeared. A strange stillness seemed to settle on the village. Rising, he strolled to the door. No one was in sight. The town had been absolutely evacuated. Seeker confessed to feeling a peculiar nervousness on finding himself the sole occupant of the village, and decided to take his car to the top of the hill which led away to the southward. Mounting the hill, he brought the car to rest at the top of it and dismounted. As he did so he described a troop of *Uhlans* riding into the town from the other side. He jumped into his car and tore away for Solesmes, leaving the transport train of the 19th Brigade to whatever fate may have overtaken it.

Before noontide I took Lord Loch eastward from Le Cateau to Reumont, the headquarters of Sir Charles Fergusson's 5th Division. The evidence of my eyes discredited the stories in which the 5th

Division troops had been described to me as badly hammered. The infantry seemed in good shape, except for tired feet, and the artillery, horses and men, in fine fettle. Scars of battle were here and there apparent. Now a wounded officer would pass mounted, and now and again I saw a bandaged Tommy in the line. Battalions, regiments, and Brigades streamed by, interspersed with lorries loaded with ammunition. Long trains of motor-wagons full of provisions, sacks of flour, meal, and potatoes, boxes of biscuit, half beeves, bales of horse fodder—the food of the army, horse and man.

As I sat by the roadside one battalion turned into a wheat field on the right of the road and another battalion into an adjoining field on the left. The boys pulled down the shocks of wheat and made beds of the bundles. The sky had become mercifully clouded, though the day was hot and the countryside dry and dusty. Water was at a premium. I soon found that distributing a swallow of water here and there from my canteen met with great appreciation. At the further side of the field, soon spread thick with khaki-clad figures was a farmer busy harvesting his shocks of grain on a couple of wagons. Just after noon we heard a very heavy cannonade towards Cambrai. A report reached Divisional Headquarters that the Germans had rushed the French in Cambrai and taken the town.

Many refugees mingled with the columns of troops along the road. A cartload made up of two or three families from Maubeuge told us frightened tales of German atrocities. Touring cars loaded with French staff officers tooted madly in an endeavour to pass the lines of big wagons on the narrow road. Family wagonettes filled with well-dressed people were in the line. Now and then a lady of well-to-do appearance passed, walking behind a carriage loaded with goods and chattels. At one point the road was blocked with a lorry containing printing stores, with all the presses and other accessories of a headquarters staff office. More refugees, and then more Tommies trudging along, dusty and begrimed, but all cheerful and strong; hot and tired, but with very few stragglers in evidence.

I began to notice a striking difference between British cavalry at the halt and their French comrades. The English troopers always dismounted, and were more likely than not busy attending to some wants of their cattle. To see a French cavalryman dismounted, no matter for how long a time he might be halted, was indeed rare. French horses showed the strain, and in contrast the British horses looked in the best possible condition. Thus for an hour or so we slowly pushed

FRENCH CAVALRY ALONG THE ROAD NEAR MEAUX DURING THE RETREAT

FRENCH RESERVISTS AT WORK ON THE FORTIFICATIONS OF PARIS

our way here and there along the country roads, their fields fair with shocks of standing grain waiting for the harvest. We were doomed to spend the day in the middle of lines upon lines of troops with equally long lines of refugees filing by, and the air ever full of dust. Ox carts, horse carts, and a donkey cart with six little children in it, crawled along, then a tired mother with her three-year-old girlie on her back, some refugees with bundles, more without, all the men elderly or very young, but women of all ages and children in droves—a never-to-be-forgotten sight. Wonder, despair, patience, pain, apathy—the drifting faces made a heart-breaking picture. Now and then, but rarely, some French refugees would pass in a private motor-car, usually of ancient type. The number of mothers carrying babies through the dust and heat seemed out of all reasonable proportion to the rest.

When we returned to Le Cateau at two o'clock we found that G.H.Q. had moved back to St. Quentin. I requisitioned a half loaf of bread and a tin of bully beef from a passing supply lorry and made a splendid luncheon. A brain wave resulted in application at the chemist's shop for bottled waters. Half a dozen of Vichy were produced and at once stowed away in the car for future use, as water was precious. Aeroplanes sailed overhead and refugees drifted southwards until neither attracted further attention. Westminster told me that our soldiers brought down one of the German aeroplanes that were reconnoitring, its petrol tank punctured by a rifle bullet. The pilot and observer were shot as the machine began to descend.

A report was prevalent that the Russians had had a success, and the good news was eagerly seized upon and passed from lip to lip.

In mid-afternoon I ran to Bertry, General Smith-Dorrien's headquarters, with Lord Loch. Women, children and girls, the only inhabitants remaining, were in the streets in force and greatly excited. A battalion of Jocks had come into the town, and every native was vastly interested and amused by the brawny kilt-clad men from the North. The local baker disposed of his stock of huge round circles of bread in as short a time as it took for him to exchange it for the modest sum it brought him. Pretty girls at the roadside with tempting pitchers of beer were catering for the wants of the soldiers. We came round a corner upon a W. and G. taxi, which brought a smile and a fleeting thought of the contrast between its former service and its present occupation. The 2nd Army Corps was well in place by evening. Some of the brigades were in the towns, some in camp in the fields, the rest going into position along the roads as fast as they arrived. The first battalions were divided into working parties, and while trenches were being dug, kettles were singing merrily over roadside fires.

As we returned to Le Cateau our passage was blocked by a crowd of country-folk rotating about a German prisoner in the midst of a corporal's guard of stout Tommies. A mere lad in grey, smooth-shaven, with downcast eyes and pale face, he seemed absolutely overwhelmed by the threatening cries of the rabble that filled the road and ran alongside him screaming imprecations in a very pandemonium. If he remembered how some of his German comrades had killed our wounded as they lay on the field of battle—if such tales could be believed—I wondered whether that mild edition of the Hun was expecting a speedy execution at the hands of his captors. He certainly looked it.

At Le Cateau a staff officer told me that though some German cavalry had penetrated into Cambrai in the morning, it was still in the hands of the French in the afternoon, and that Sordêt's cavalry was not far from the town. At six o'clock a cool, refreshing rain started. This later developed into a cold drizzle, which was anything but welcome. The Le Cateau townsfolk had another spasm of excitement over a German bicycle scout who had been caught near Beauvais, a village half-way between Le Cateau and Cambrai. This German youth was thin and lantern-jawed, adorned with a straggling blonde moustache, and of most anaemic appearance. Painfully fearful of the hostile crowd, and, oh, so thankful for his round score of guards, he heaved a great sigh of relief when brought within the gateway out of the sight of the vociferous French crowd. His knees shook beneath him as he was marched off upstairs to encounter the Intelligence officer.

At this moment Westminster was arranging a departure with a couple of staff officers for a run in his car along the front. He placed in the car a couple of rifles and a belt of ammunition taken from two of the soldiers. A very youthful Tommy, closely observant of every detail of the proceedings, connected the arrival of the spy and the arming of the car, and said to me in an awed whisper, "Where are they going to take him to shoot him?" The youngster was almost disappointed when I explained that an enemy's scout in uniform was entitled to all the privileges of the most respected prisoner of war. "*I* would not let him go sneaking around spying. I'd shoot him," he insisted. A couple of minutes after I saw him sidle up to the German boy who had been returned from his interview with "Intelligence," and furtively offer him a cigarette.

Ten minutes later I asked the British boy if he still thought the juvenile German should be summarily executed. My Tommy grinned sheepishly and said grudgingly, as though ashamed of the sentiment expressed, "Oh, well, I suppose the poor beggar has to do just the same as we do." I found the British Tommy was more often than not annoyed when discovered at some kindly action.

That night I ran to St. Quentin. The rain had set in doggedly. Passing provision and ammunition trains, with artillery and cavalry occupying a considerable share of the roadway, the slippery pave played all sorts of tricks in the way of unusual and unexpected skids. The one and a half hours of that run south seemed to occupy a much longer period. In passing a motor-cyclist at good speed, the back part of a car in front of us brushed him off his machine. He slid thirty feet, coming to rest in front of my car and in the full glare of my headlights as I skidded sideways to avoid passing over him. We picked him up, straightened his handlebars, and bent a pedal into place. Finding him by no means incapacitated, we mounted him and started him off again. I was surprised he was able to ride. But that was before I had come to know that the motor-cyclists with the British Expeditionary Force bore charmed lives.

G.H.Q. in St. Quentin was in a big barracks of a place. When I arrived it was late and wet, and too much bother altogether to try to get a billet, and I was too tired to care for dinner.

At three o'clock on the morning of Wednesday, August 26th, I was so fortunate as to encounter a staff officer with a moment to spare, from whom I could gain some concrete idea of the situation.

The British Expeditionary Force had been dispatched from England with such secrecy, and I was in any case so unfamiliar with the general make-up of the British Army, that a careful explanation as to just what troops composed Sir John French's command was most welcome. It was easy for me to remember that Haig's 1st Corps was composed of the 1st and 2nd Divisions, with the 1st, 2nd and 3rd Brigades in the 1st Division, and the 4th, 5th and 6th Brigades in the 2nd Division. Smith-Dorrien's second army contained the 3rd and 5th Divisions. In the 3rd Division were Brigades 7, 8 and 9, and in the 5th Division Brigades 13, 14 and 15.

The fact that General Snow's 4th Division (10th, 11th and 12th Brigades) of the 3rd Army and the 19th Brigade, which was not attached to any particular Division, were in evidence I knew from having been told of their detraining when they had arrived at Le Cateau

A Bivouac of a Brigade Headquarters on the Great Retreat

Cavalry at the end of the Great Retreat resting in the forest S.E. of Paris

and Valenciennes respectively. My informant told me that General Allenby, commanding the cavalry division, had under him the 1st, 2nd, 3rd, 4th and 5th Cavalry Brigades. With great patience my mentor sat in the car and drilled into me the composition of first the cavalry units and next the units of the 2nd Corps, and finally the 1st Corps.

But my best bit of luck was to come. The fact that my car was available at the moment a car was required to run "up front" provided me with a journey which put me in much better touch with the trend of events. The morning dawned clear and cool. I was asked if I knew the road to Le Cateau. I replied that I had come over it the night before, and was quite familiar with it. Thereupon I was ordered to proceed to Le Cateau with as little delay as possible. As the sun rose it was evident that the day would be a scorcher. The air was clear after the rain of the night before, and in front of us the increasing sound of guns told of strenuous battle. I do not know the name of the officer who was my passenger, nor do I know whether he was constitutionally moody or whether some strange presentiment of the day's events came over him. In appearance he was a confirmed pessimist.

I questioned him as to the general situation, and he told me that he was not clear as to what was taking place in front of us. The officer—a major—told me Haig's Corps had been attacked in Landrecies the night before, and a severe all-night battle had resulted. The major was under the impression that the retreat of the whole British Army, carried on with such speed on the day before, would be continued to the southward. As we drew nearer to Le Cateau our progress was rendered increasingly difficult by congestion of traffic by all manner of horse and motor transport. The battle in front of us was gradually developing, and soon the sound of guns became a continuous roar. Apparently the further retirement of Smith-Dorrien's command had been rendered impossible by an impetuous German advance.

At the edge of Le Cateau a cavalry officer told us the 19th Brigade were holding the town and General Briggs and his 1st Cavalry Brigade were at Catillon, a village four or five miles to the east of us. Briggs' force, said he, was our only protection on the right flank. He did not know where Haig might be with his 1st Corps. We told him of Haig's fight at Landrecies, and the three of us pored over my map long enough to make up our minds that somehow a gap had been left between Le Cateau and Landrecies, a matter of seven or eight miles.

We were right. That gap existed. It was through that gap that the German forces were to be poured in mass after mass that day, driving back the small cavalry force in front of them, and compelling the retirement of the right of Fergusson's 5th Division, and the consequent retreat of the whole line.

Already the air was tense with the reverberations of battle. The sound of the fighting came from in front and to the west of us.

We ran to Bertry and stopped by the railway-station. A sergeant who stood beside the car told me the Germans had the day before enfiladed a trench full of South Lancashires of the 7th Brigade and "wiped out every one of them, except one subaltern and five men, with machine-gun fire."

That story was the forerunner of half a hundred similar ones I was to hear during the next few days of commands completely annihilated, or nearly so. I have often wondered if I missed any one battalion of the 2nd Corps from out this category of disaster. If the rumours had been true, only a handful of British troops would have crossed the Marne away to the southward a few days later. As soon as the retreat was in full swing I heard the most extraordinary stories of contingents wiped out, destroyed to the last man—save always the sole survivor who told the tale. The tendency to exaggerate casualties was by no means confined to the lower ranks.

Just after seven o'clock a car drove up and General Sir Horace Smith-Dorrien alighted. He had come to the station to telephone to Sir John French, away to the south at St. Quentin. General Smith-Dorrien was as cool and self-possessed as though the battle pounding away in front of us were a sham fight.

I gathered the "situation" in Bertry as it could have been gained nowhere else that morning.

General Smith-Dorrien had under his direct command the 2nd Corps only. The 4th Division, which was falling back from Solesmes as his 3rd and 5th Divisions retired southward, and General Allenby's Cavalry Division were under the orders of G.H.Q. With the 2nd Corps was the 19th Brigade, having on arrival at the front been pushed up hurriedly to the Condé-Mons line, and still more hurriedly pulled away from it.

Fighting rearguard actions all day long, the 2nd Corps had reached the Le Cateau position on the 25th with the idea that a stand would be made on that line. When Smith-Dorrien came into Le Cateau in the evening he found Sir John French had moved to St. Quentin. The chief of staff, General Murray, told Smith-Dorrien that the plans were changed. "You are not to fight. You must keep on retiring," were the instructions.

Smith-Dorrien said:

> But, I cannot retire further. My men are just coming in. They have been on their feet all day and are too tired to go on. My rearguards have been at it all day, and there is no other way out of it. I *must* fight.

Murray could only say that the orders to continue a retirement and avoid a conflict were definite and in writing. Sir John had been most explicit.

But General Murray could not change the conditions any more than he could change the orders. General Smith-Dorrien knew he could not get his men further south without some rest. Von Kluck was pressing on. Three extra corps had been swung round from the eastward to crumple and turn, if not envelop, the Allied left. A smashing blow at the advancing enemy might hold him off till nightfall of the 26th and allow retirement then. So the smashing blow was delivered.

It was two o'clock on the morning of Wednesday before Sir Horace had learned the location of the units which were to be thrown into the fight. His battle line from east to west was the 5th Division, 3rd Division, and 4th Division, with the 19th Brigade in Le Cateau on the right rear of the 5th Division. Briggs with his 1st Cavalry Brigade and a bit of another Cavalry Brigade was on the right flank, and the rest of Allenby's five Cavalry Brigades on the left rear of Snow's 4th Division. All of them were informed of the battle that was to take place and the part they were to play in it. Smith-Dorrien also sent word to General Sordêt, with his French cavalry, that the fight was toward, and any help he could give on the extreme left would be of great value.

Sir John French had during the previous day (Tuesday) sent to General Sordêt more than once asking his assistance, and each time received the reply that his horses and men were so worn out that Sordêt could not come up and join issue with the enemy. General Smith-Dorrien's message to Sordêt was, "I am going to fight, and hope you can help cover my left flank."

At last, between two and three o'clock in the morning, the dispositions of the troops were made, and the tired men caught such sleep as they could before the coming of the dawn.

At break of day the conflict began. Five hundred German guns were hailing shell on that front before the day was over, and the sound of them was deafening before the morning was well advanced.

In response to a request to telephone Sir John French, Sir Horace had come to the station at Bertry. He found General Henry Wilson at the other end of the wire. Wilson said:

> Sir John wants you to retire at the earliest moment possible. He is anxious you shall not continue the fight a moment longer than is absolutely necessary. He is of the opinion that in not falling back you are risking a Sedan.

Smith-Dorrien explained that he could not break off the fight at any moment he might desire:

> The only thing we can do is to give the Germans a smash, and we are going to do it. The men are too tired to walk further. They can't use their feet. The only thing for them to do when they can't stand is to lie down and fight. Both my flanks are in the air. I don't know where Haig is on my right. At least, I am not in touch with his left. I hope for some French support on my own left. My instructions to the divisions are all clear, and I have arranged lines of retirement south in case we are forced back. All we can do under the circumstances is to see if we can't hold them off until dark.

Someone who heard General Wilson told me long afterwards that he said to Smith-Dorrien in conclusion, "Well, General, your voice is the only cheerful thing I've heard for three days. Give 'em hell!"

And he did.

After a short stop in Bertry I flew back to St. Quentin and G.H.Q. with my pessimistic major.

In St. Quentin I saw Toby Rawlinson, a member of our R.A.C. Corps and a brother of General Sir H. S. Rawlinson. He told me of the fight at Landrecies the night before. Haig's 1st Corps had come into position along a line from Landrecies to Maroilles about dark. They were very tired. The Germans swooped down in force through the Forest of Mormal in motor buses, and by nine o'clock were in position in front of the town of Landrecies in great numbers. Landrecies was held by the 4th Guards Brigade, consisting of two battalions of the Coldstreams and the Irish and Grenadier Guards. The first German officers to approach our pickets were dressed in French uniforms and came in crying "*Vive l'Angleterre!*" They rushed our thin line of outposts in mass, and were actually in the streets of the town before the Guards had time to complete any brigade or even regimental formation.

One Guards captain placed his men on either side of the roadway, crouching on the pavement with their backs to the houses. When the stream of Germans had filled the street between them the Guards rose with a yell and gave the enemy the cold steel. Down one street and another British machine-guns went into action and mowed down lanes in the German ranks. Rawlinson's carburettor went wrong in the dark and in the middle of the attack, and his motor-car refused to move. After the fierce German onslaught had been thrown back to the northern edge of the town with severe loss, the German field-guns poured shell into all quarters of Landrecies, setting fire to the houses. With his car pushed to the side of the pavement, in the pitch dark, a galloping battery of artillery just missing him by inches, Rawlinson took down his carburettor, effected his repair, and put it up again.

On the edge of the fierce night fight, in which the Guards lost eighty to ninety of their number killed and thirty to forty wounded, and the Germans left between 800 and 900 dead in the streets—in one place so crowded that corpses were propped against each other in a standing position—in the dark and rain, by the fitful light of bursting shells or burning houses, truly that was motorcar repair under difficulties.

Rawlinson left Landrecies at four o'clock in the morning. The fight had developed strenuously on the east towards Maroilles, but had ceased before daybreak. The German onslaught had been repulsed and the Guards enabled to get well away. Haig's retreat was continued on the main road south to Guise.

We heard but little of what was taking place at Le Cateau as the morning wore away. I was asked to take Major Thresher, the camp commandant, to Noyon to establish G.H.Q. there. A French major accompanied us. We ran to Noyon *via* Ham and Guiscard. At the latter town some argument between the French officer and the French reservist sentry, the former wishing to proceed without being bothered about the production of passes or other machinery for delay, resulted in our finding ourselves gazing into the muzzle of a French rifle with orders to stop until the Officer of the Guard was satisfied of our *bonâ-fides*. As I had no part in the argument, most of which I did not understand on account of the rapidity with which opinions were expressed on both sides, I felt that the sentry was taking quite an unnecessary view of my importance when he insisted upon keeping the muzzle of the rifle pointed directly at me instead of covering the other occupants of the car. He gave me a nervous sixty seconds.

In Noyon the work of arranging offices for G. H.Q. and billets for those attached to it bid fair to occupy Major Thresher for the rest of the day, so I returned to St. Quentin in quest of further adventure. When I arrived most of G.H.Q. was being shifted from St. Quentin with a considerable amount of bustle. No effort was made to disguise the fact that the battle along the Cambrai-Le Cateau front was going against our 2nd Corps. There was no actual panic, but on all sides was that obvious effort to be cool which bespeaks strain. Running north in the direction of Le Cateau I found the roads becoming blocked. As I turned the car with difficulty at a point near Renancourt I realised that to remain there would be to become involved in the maelstrom of southbound transport.

At that point four roads in a radius of less than a kilometre debouched from the north with but one main outlet to the southward. Running back towards St. Quentin I picked up an Army Service Corps subaltern who was considerably the worse for wear. He was in charge of a column of transport on what he described as the Le Cateau-St. Quentin road. He was moving southward with his lorries and an escort of 150 men, who were scattered along the train, and neither ready nor organised for attack. As the lorries came up a hill a couple of hundred *Uhlans* dashed over the top and charged the train with a rush. The subaltern said four men and himself were all that got away, the rest being taken or killed. He was dashed against one of the lorries in the *mêlée* and was suffering from a broken rib. I dropped him where headquarters had been to report his experiences.

By evening all sorts of rumours were afloat in St. Quentin. G.H.Q. had moved to Noyon. My car was standing in front of the *mairie* with two or three others when a number of officers came out, and jumping hastily into the cars, started away. It would be foolishness to allege that the general tendency was one of composure. I was the last to leave, and had not proceeded twenty feet before a rear tyre burst. The *mairie* was on the north side of St. Quentin. The officers in my car left it for a passing lorry with the idea of picking up some staff car in the centre of the town. Time drags under such circumstances, and as dusk was approaching I managed in replacing the burst tyre to bungle one or two simple operations which spelled delay.

A motorcyclist stopped for a moment and told me that the road from Le Cateau would thenceforth be impassable for cars owing to the lines of troops and transport coming over it. Considering where he had been and what he had seen he was not over-pessimistic, though he was frankly of the belief that very little of Snow's 4th Division remained, if indeed much of Smith-Dorrien's army would get away. The retirement on the right he thought would result in the 4th Division on the left being surrounded and cut off.

With this unpalatable news I finally got under way for Noyon, which I reached at a late hour.

Chapter 2

"Proper Rearguards"

Just before midnight as I was turning in, Borritt, the member of the R.A.C. corps who usually transmitted orders from Major Evans of G.H.Q. Staff to the R.A.C. drivers, came to my billet and told me that a volunteer was required for a precarious piece of work. Borritt's insistence that the driver must volunteer for the job, and the general air of mystery in which he wrapped it, roused my curiosity. I could only elicit from him at first that whoever drove the car which was required for the mission in hand would be called upon to dash through one or possibly more towns that were in German hands. Pressure elicited the further information that no news had come to G.H.Q. from General Smith-Dorrien during the evening, and just how much of the left wing of the army remained, and where it was, was unknown. Therefore, if a message did not come from the 2nd Corps by three o'clock in the morning a staff officer was to be sent by car to establish communication with whatever might remain of Smith-Dorrien's command.

When I learned that Loch was the staff officer who had been chosen for this mission I was glad to volunteer to act as his driver. I had cut away the exhaust of my car and rendered it unusually noisy. As this did not appear to be an advantage in such circumstances, I awoke Jimmy Radley, an R.A.C. comrade, and obtained his permission to use his Rolls-Royce car for the journey, in case I should be called upon to make it. Before retiring I spent an hour in becoming familiar with any little eccentricities of Radley's car and putting in its tank twelve precious gallons of petrol which I had conserved in the tonneau of my car against emergency.

It was after one o'clock in the morning when I got to sleep, and before three Lean, a cheery young Scots subaltern attached to G.H.Q., awoke me and told me I was to dress and proceed at once to Headquarters. I lost no time in turning out, thinking I was in for an interesting experience in the way of a somewhat perilous early morning excursion. Upon reaching the street I found that news had come from the 2nd Corps, brought by General Smith-Dorrien himself. My trip with Loch was "off" and my twelve precious gallons of petrol gone.

We had news that the fight had been a severe one and that we had suffered many casualties. Our infantry had held the German advance splendidly throughout the morning. Their losses were slight compared with those of the enemy, whose attacks, hurled with persistent valour, could make no headway against our devastating fire.

With four or five German guns to our one in action our artillery had fought valiantly, but with fearful loss.

At about two o'clock in the afternoon word had come to General Smith-Dorrien from Sir Charles Fergusson that the German fire on his right flank was so hot that the men of the 5th Division were beginning to dribble away from the trenches. Investigation showed that the Germans were taking advantage of the Le Cateau-Landrecies gap and pouring through it. Nothing remained but to fall back. The order for a gradual retirement, beginning on the extreme right, was given. The troops on the left were to leave their trenches when they saw the line on their right retiring. When the 5th Division had left the line the 3rd and 4th Divisions, to the westward, were gradually to come back in turn.

Up to the time of retirement the casualties had not been great, but as the men left the cover of the trench line the German gunners peppered the fields with shell. It was marvellous that no greater casualties were inflicted. General Smith-Dorrien had worked indomitably to secure an orderly withdrawal from the position and prevent a rout. Had the Germans been a few hours later on our right much of our subsequent confusion might have been saved.

Fergusson's retirement commenced by 2.45 p.m., and before four o'clock the whole line was falling back.

Reaching St. Quentin at half-past eight in the evening, and finding that Sir John French and G. H.Q. had gone south to Noyon, Smith-Dorrien came on to Sir John's headquarters, after an effort to arrange for railway trains for his wounded and exhausted men, arriving between one and two o'clock in the morning.

He soon woke up his chief and reported the situation, then hurried back to the work of getting his scattered forces together again.

The need for staff officers at St. Quentin being imperative, every available man was hurried to some point where he could assist in the directing of the entangled units. A convoy of three or four cars was soon speeding away to the north, and not long after dawn had reached St. Quentin.

I suffered an annoying delay *en route*. Before leaving London I had requisitioned a couple of German-made metal-studded tyres as spares. The metal tread of one of these, which I had put on a back wheel, came adrift and fiendishly wound itself about a mudguard, so I had to chisel away the entire guard to get it loose, the metal being bent down and buried in the side of the tyre. The wheel refused to revolve until I had removed the obstruction. When one is in so great a hurry as we were that morning an operation of this kind, performed in the dark, has its disadvantages. The country of origin of that tyre was more than once casually mentioned during the stop.

The morning of Thursday, August 27th, found us in the direct path of what in the early hours of the day we believed to be but the remnant of the shattered left of the British Army. Like the dawn of the day before, the morning broke clear and warm, promising a hot summer day. The perfect mornings on the retreat were some compensation for our short hours of rest.

St. Quentin on Thursday, August 27th, saw rare scenes and strange sights.

An orderly, well-disciplined army had been through a great fight. Its infantry, unbeaten by the infantry that opposed it, had been ordered to retire. "Gawd knows why," hundreds of Tommies were saying. The vastness of the scale of operations, the uncertainty of the General Staff itself as to just what was happening in some quarters of the field, and the universal ignorance of the rank and file as to what had happened elsewhere than in their own immediate vicinity, all tended to discouragement.

After inflicting such terrible losses as the German foot soldiers suffered at Cambrai-Le Cateau, the British Army had taken a hammering which seemed to many of them totally unnecessary.

To fight stubbornly and victoriously against an advancing enemy, hurling back his masses as fast as they are poured forward, is soul-inspiring. To leave such occupation for a scamper over a shell-swept field, comrades falling to right and left as they run, is not. Units that had just proven to themselves their invincibility were smashed and disintegrated in the very obeying of an unwelcome order to retire.

Jumbled together, inextricably mixed, each group convinced that their little remnant contained the only survivors of their individual command, confusion worse confounded was only to be expected.

The work of sorting out the men from the steady flowing stream of humanity as it moved southward, of re-forming an army that had lost most semblance of form, was the task set before the British officers in St. Quentin that morning at sun-up. It did not take them long to set about it. Stationed here and there along the main route through the town, each officer of staff became an usher, urbanely advising each little knot of stragglers where to proceed to find the nucleus of their particular unit, and obtain food, drink, and news of their comrades.

The wounded were in considerable numbers. Ambulances drew up at the railway-station and unloaded. A couple of sweet, little, old French ladies bustled about on one side of the station square, giving out tea as fast as they could make it.

Moving about St. Quentin in a motor-car that morning was slow work, as the roads were full to overflowing. Not far from the *mairie* a wounded officer, his vitality all but spent, was placed in my car. I took him as quickly as possible to the station. Badly wounded in the chest, he said with a pale smile, "I've been about a hundred miles, it seems, since I was hit, and in pretty well every sort of conveyance *except* a motorcar. Two miles on a limber nearly finished me."

He looked, poor chap, as though he had reached care and attention none too soon.

For a time I was to act as usher at a point a bit north of St. Quentin. Placed on the road by a staff officer, and told where the men of the various units were to be directed, I chose to stand by a French lady, who, with her daughters, was supplying coffee, steaming hot, to the passing Tommies.

Never shall I forget that staff officer's parting instructions:

Cheer them up as you keep them on the move. They are very downhearted. Tell them anything, but cheer them up. They've got their tails down a bit, but they are really all right. No wonder they are tired! Worn out to begin with, then fighting all day, only to come back all night—no rest, no food, no sleep—poor devils! Yes, they are very downhearted. Tell 'em where to go, and cheer 'em up—cheer 'em up.

Of all the jobs that have ever fallen to my lot, I thought, this promises to be one of the most hopeless. Cheer them up, indeed! A fine atmosphere this, for cheer. Ragged and muddy and footsore they looked, straggling along.

The first individual who caught my attention particularly was a tall captain, an old acquaintance. He showed me his service cap, through the crown of which two neat bullet-holes had been drilled. Both of the vicious little pellets had missed their intended mark, though one had ploughed a slight furrow along his scalp, leaving an angry red welt.

No one had examined his head to find what damage had been caused, and he asked me to investigate. He bent over, and I poked my finger here and there, asking "where it hurt "and how much—in short, doing the best I could to accommodate his thirst for information.

As I was intent on my amateur probing a voice from behind commented, "A close shave the little divil made that toime, shure." Turning at the soft brogue, what was my surprise to see a Jock, in a kilt that looked as if its wearer had been rolled in the mud. Hapless, his shock of red hair stood on end, and a pair of blue Irish eyes twinkled merrily. I was genuinely surprised. It was before I had learned that an Irishman in a Scotch regiment is no *rara avis*—nor a Cockney in a battalion dubbed Irish on the rolls, for the matter of that.

As if entering himself in a competition of close shaves, the Irishman held his right ear between thumb and finger. "And what do ye think o' that?"he queried.

Right through the lobe of his ear, close to his cheek, a Mauser bullet had drilled a clean hole. "Close that, I'm thinkin'," said the proud owner of the damaged member, "and I niver knew how close me ear was to me head till that thing come along."

A burst of laughter from the group that had gathered was infectious. The boys trailed off together, chatting over further stories of close shaves, leaving me thankful the Irish lad had come by, cheered *that* lot up, and so saved me the task.

The next group to reach me contained a sergeant and a dozen or so Tommies, of most disreputable exterior.

"To what lot do you belong, sergeant?" I asked.

"We're Riles, sir," said the sergeant.

"You're what?"

"*Riles!*" with decided emphasis.

With a spasm, I remembered the Royal Fusiliers were in the 9th Brigade of the 3rd Division, and directed the group accordingly.

"You oughter know who *we* are," said the sergeant, somewhat haughtily. "We're the lot what was first in Mons and last out, *we* are."

"That's right," piped up a squeaky voice that came from a diminutive member of the squad; "buck, you beggar, buck. Tell 'em the tale."

A grin on half a dozen faces told that the small one might be expected to produce some comment when occasion permitted. The sergeant turned. "What's ailin' *you*, Shorty?" he demanded.

"Tell 'em the tale," croaked the little man. "Fust in Mons and last out. In at three miles an hour and out at eighteen. That's us, you bet," and he snorted as the squad roared in appreciative mirth.

So they drifted on, anything but downhearted, if one could judge from the running fire of banter between Shorty and his sergeant, which kept their comrades in continual chuckles as they toiled on.

Truly I thanked Shorty for his assistance in the "cheer-'em-up" department.

Detachments went past at times in step, whistling or singing. Some were obviously too footsore to walk normally, but they heroically tried to keep pace with the rest, and made a brave show of it.

One big, lantern-jawed chap, as he caught sight of me, insisted on his score of companions forming single file. They brought rifles to shoulder and stepped out in style with an indescribable swagger. The Sphinx would have broken into a smile at the sight of them. As the leader, much begrimed, came up I explained that hot coffee was to be had from jugs held by three little pig-tailed French schoolgirls under a tree hard by.

As the boys drank, the leading spirit chatted. I gathered from casual remarks, if they were to be believed, that talking was a habit with him. In fact, remarks were proffered, *sotto voce*, that he had not ceased talking, except to sleep, since leaving England. The comments of his soiled band seemed meat and drink to his soul. He fairly revelled in them.

"Pals we are, all right," he said with a grin, "though no one would think it to hear 'em, would they? Know how to fight, they do, but can't talk—that's their drawback. Don't know no words."

A hot strong draught of good black French coffee gave him pause, but a moment later he was at it again. I told him where to go. As he tramped off he said, "Come on, you blighters! Don't block the road. You ain't no bloomin' army now. You're a forlorn 'ope, that's what you are. Nice-lookin' lot o' beggars. 'Op it!" And they "'opped it" to the music of his cheery abuse. God bless him!

Not long after, a very woebegone procession hove in sight. But few were in that squad, and they seemed very worn and tired. Red-eyed from lack of sleep, barren of equipment, many a cap missing, and not a pair of sound feet in the lot. Every man had his rifle, but they looked very "done."

"Here are the pessimists at last," thought I. "It will take something to cheer *this* bunch."

I discovered their regiment and informed them of the whereabouts of their fellows. "Yes," said I, "three streets on after you get to the fountain, then to the right, and there you'll see a big building on the left—that's the one."

"We've been rear-guardin'," said a cadaverous corporal who acted as spokesman. "We're proper rearguards, we are. Been doin' nothin' else but rearguardin'."

"Right," said I; "don't forget. Third turning after the fountain. Plenty of food there."

"Rearguards, we are," from the lugubrious one. "Proper rearguards. Ain't done nothing else for three days."

"Cheero!" I insisted; "three streets on after the fountain, and then—"

"*Proper* rearguards "he started again.

"But," I interrupted in turn, "I'm telling you where there's *food*, my boy."

"And *I'm* tellin' you, sir, if you'll not mind," he continued gravely, "that we're *proper* rearguards, we are. And we 'ave learned one thing about *proper* rearguards in this 'ere war right off, and that is that rearguards ain't expected to eat. So we 'ave give it up, we 'ave. It's a bad 'abit any'ow. Ain't it, boys?"

Off they trudged, grinning. The funereal visage of the spokesman turned and indulged in a sombre wink, whereat they laughed to a man, and I with them.

"Proper rearguards *don't* eat." He had had his joke, and played it out to his heart's content.

Ah, well, it was an experience!

I had not been long on that roadside when I realised that many of us had been labouring under a great delusion. It was not that someone was needed to cheer up the Tommy; it was that most of us needed the Tommy to cheer *us* up.

The indomitable pluck of the soldier in the ranks and his effervescent cheeriness were to save that retreating army of Smith-Dorrien's as no staff work could have saved it had the Tommy not possessed those characteristics to such remarkable degree.

Many an officer whose hair had grown grey in the service said that day that Tommy was of finer metal than he had ever dreamed it possible of any soldier. The very air was full of unostentatious heroism.

One grizzled brigadier, seated on his horse, watched that straggling army pass, tears dropping now and then unheeded on his tunic, his lips pressed hard. One of his staff heard the old warrior mutter, as one detachment passed, soiled, but with bold eye and shoulders well back: "Ah! they may be able to *kill* such men, but they will never be able to *beat* them."

I began to look at the men with new eyes as the morning passed. If the thousands straggling by but continued to come, I thought, many more must have been saved than any of us imagined. Beneath the grime and dirt and weariness I saw clear eyes and firm jaws, even when men were almost too worn out to walk further. Those who appeared to be positively unable to go on were, stopped at the St. Quentin station, to be sent south by rail.

I realised that in front of me was passing a pageant such as man had rarely seen in the ages. It was a pageant of the indomitable will and unconquerable power of the Anglo-Saxon.

Early in the day I was relieved and sent back to the station. Horse wagons full of wounded jostled the ambulances in the station yard. Even the motor transport lorries, as they rolled past, paused to drop off their quota of maimed and bandaged men in khaki.

One young subaltern passed, sound asleep in his saddle and unmindful of all about him, his horse following the human current.

At times a pitiable group of refugees went by, though for the most part the refugees had been crowded off the main roads by the retreating army or diverted to other routes.

A sergeant of the East Surrey regiment, of Fergusson's Division, came up. His face was haggard. He reported two hundred and fifty men, with five officers, were all that was left of that battalion.

Standing near the bridge, close by the station, I saw General Smith-Dorrien a few feet distant. He turned, and I caught his eye. He was speaking to a passing officer. I hardly remember his words. Something about plenty more of the same command being down the road a bit, I think. It was good to see Smith-Dorrien's face and hear his voice. I had heard much of him during those days, and never was he spoken of save in terms of affection. As he looked my way he smiled, with the sort of smile that everyone within range takes to himself as his own property. It was of inestimable value that morning in St. Quentin—

Smith-Dorrien's smile. It put heart into many a man.

I was struck with the number of guns going by. Battery on battery wheeled past, most of them battle-scarred in some way. They had passed through a rough time, our guns, and one could hardly see an artillery unit without wanting to cheer them.

Scores of ambulances poured down from the north, filled with exhausted men as well as wounded. The prevailing note was query as to where someone else might be. Most men seemed to consider themselves "lost" and utterly unaware of the whereabouts of those of whom they were in search. The bakeries opened, and the Tommies, all hungry, some painfully so, as more than one had been without food for twenty-four hours, proved good patrons. The sight of fat rings of bread around the neck or over the arm of a passing soldier looked peculiarly cheery.

A drowsy fit struck me. The hot sun and the continually-moving columns affected me like an opiate. I was roused by Lord Loch and presented to General Smith-Dorrien, who said he had neither car nor horse with which to get about. Loch, to my great delight, put my car at Smith-Dorrien's disposal. It was a treat to watch the general. Kindly and cheery, his personality pervaded everything about him. At the station, he was much interested in an ambulance load of wounded who had just arrived. He spoke to many of the men personally.

Soon after I took the general to the *mairie*. He was very cordial and chatted with me *en route* just as he talked to all of us in St. Quentin that morning. Staff officers, soldiers, everyone—all were parts of the whole. It was a lesson, watching him saving the scattered pieces of his corps and welding them into a fighting force that would be all the better for the awful experience through which they had passed.

"Not very comfortable times," he said with a smile. "This part of the world as one would have seen it if touring hereabouts a month ago and the situation in which we find ourselves today present an immense contrast, do they not? "

He commented on the strenuous character of my work. I remarked that the more I saw of the sort of thing we were going through, the more thankful I was to be there, if I could be of any use.

I was naturally pleased when he replied, "You gentlemen with your cars are certainly of use, of great use—of that you may be sure."

"Well, General," I said, "no able-bodied man who can get here should want to be anywhere else, if that is the case."

He laughed and added: "A man certainly wants to be able-bodied for this sort of experience."

As we crawled slowly past long lines of motor lorries, many of which had been reported lost, we chatted of the power and make of my car, and of cars in general. Smith-Dorrien not only put one perfectly at ease with himself, but acted as a tonic. One could but borrow some of his cool assurance.

A French staff officer called at the *mairie* from General Sordêt.

At half-past four on the previous afternoon, when the battle was still raging in front, our rearguards fighting like mad to protect the retreating army, General Smith-Dorrien heard a furious bombardment on his extreme left. Mounting, and accompanied by one of his staff, he galloped away to the westward towards the sound of the guns. He thought the Germans had gotten round his left. Through the line of the retreating 3rd Division and on beyond them to the 4th Division he rode, only to discover that the guns were further westward than he had thought. Then he realised that the noise of battle told of Sordêt "helping cover the left flank" of his hard-pressed British Allies, in spite of the fatigue of his troops.

The French officer at the *mairie* the next morning told us of a strenuous conflict in which the tired French cavalry and some French Territorials had gallantly pitched into the Germans' right with a good will, inflicting severe losses and driving back the oncoming enemy.

Corroboration of this had reached Smith-Dorrien the night before, when he had found two of his Royal Flying Corps officers in the station at St. Quentin. During the battle they had been flying over the German line in front of our left flank. Between four and five o'clock in the afternoon they flew through a veritable storm of bullets, some of which disabled their engine and forced a descent. They were able to land safely, two or three miles behind our lines, but found the aeroplane so damaged that it had to be abandoned. They procured a couple of bicycles and made their way to St. Quentin. These officers told Smith-Dorrien that, before descending, they had seen the French troops, cavalry and infantry, engaging the Germans on the extreme left.

Naturally, Smith-Dorrien expressed his thanks to Sordêt's staff officer in unmeasured terms. Asking him to convey his appreciation to General Sordêt, Sir Horace said he would there and then "make a special report on the subject to the field-marshal"—Sir John French.

The Frenchman, apparently the happiest man in St. Quentin that morning, after many adieus to us all, and wishes of good fortune to everyone, rode off post haste to rejoin his chief.

Later I was given a new job. I was to accompany Captain Cox, of the G.H.Q. Staff, to a point to the north of St. Quentin, and there to wait with him and again direct stragglers. Cox was instructed to stay in that position as long as it was advisable for him to do so—from the standpoints of usefulness and safety. As he was the nearest Staff officer to the enemy, we judged, from what we had been told, that it was quite possible we might have to "run for it "before the day was over. We could not understand why the Germans had not followed up their victory at Cambrai-Le Cateau, and were not enveloping St. Quentin and the scattered 2nd Corps at that moment.

Cox explained to me that in case the Germans pushed ahead, and it became impossible for us to remain longer where we were, we would proceed to the square where the *mairie* was located, pick up Lean, our Scot, then scoot for it to the southward, past the railway station. A subaltern named McLean, with his motorcycle, was attached to us. I learned later that he was Marconi's secretary before the world-war. He had given the alarm of the oncoming Germans at Landrecies. We made a compact to the effect that he should be allowed to keep ahead of the car in case of a scamper, so that he could get in with us in case he fell off his "bike."

The congestion of traffic was so great along the town's main thoroughfares that I started off by myself to reconnoitre a new way round in case we wanted to get to the station in quick time. Down a side road I passed a museum which was being utilised as a hospital. A doctor asked if I would take a load of wounded men to the station. I took three Tommies, all badly wounded, into the car. Occupying the front seat with me was one of the Royal Scots, with a nasty hole in his shoulder.

> We were quite all right in our trenches. The bullets were dropping like rain, but we were keeping well out of the way of them. Then all of a sudden we got the order to retire, the Lord knows why. When we began to retire we got it very bad.

That feeling seemed fairly universal.

They hated so to come back.

It was a fine thing—that splendid fighting spirit. Magnificent soldiers they were, every one of them.

I landed my trio at the station, where they all shook hands with me and wished me luck. One could not walk, and all three were in great pain, but bearing it as soldiers should, without any undue fuss.

When I got back to him Cox had his hands full. Before I rejoined him I had a cool wash in a tiny provision shop of sorts. The day was a lovely one, warm and sunny.

While I was laving myself a couple of South Lancs, men entered the shop and ordered tea and bread-and-butter. One of the pair was voluble enough for both. He was eager to explain the whole battle. He drew the 2nd Corps' position in line and placed the Germans in a half circle, the ends flanking the British right and left.

We were well entrenched, and the Germans opened on us from five hundred to six hundred yards. They fire in absolute masses. Never was anything like it heard of. One row of them lies down, behind them a row kneels, and back of them again a third row stands. You couldn't imagine such a target. It seemed *too* easy. You could just pump the bullets into 'em like smoke, and never miss a shot. You have no idea how it seemed, lying there firing into that grey bunch of men and thinking all the time what fools they were to stand there and take it. And the funny thing was that they couldn't shoot for nuts either. The standing lot didn't even raise their rifles to their shoulders, but fired from the hip. They must have sent an awful lot of pills our way, but they couldn't hit a balloon.

The quieter soldier took up the narrative. "As fast as we would knock over a German another would take his place."

That had impressed both of the South Lancs, men. They spoke of that feature of the fight with obvious respect for the men, fools and Germans though they were, who could stand such punishment.

"Our men must have hit at least ten of them to everyone of us that got it," said the quiet one.

Both men were loud in the praise of our guns, the fire from which had been splendidly accurate.

But that battery back of us got it like hell afterwards.

At one time in the forenoon we drove the Germans in front of us back quite a bit. They came on again thicker than bees. The Bedfords retired on our right not long after three o'clock, and then we were ordered back. As we went the Germans got some machine-guns up and enfiladed our trenches. When we once got out into the open the shrapnel followed us all the way. One, two, three, four in line, and then one, two, three, four in line again, further over, and so on. Lord, but we had plenty hit then! I think their guns were mounted on motorcars the way they got 'em about.

"Yes," chipped in the quiet one, "so do I. And as if it wasn't bad enough scampering across those fields like rabbits, our lot bunched after a bit, and then we did fair get what for!"

And I left them to their tea, fighting the battle over again with great gusto, revelling in reminding one another of how various of their comrades had "got it."

Tired? Well, they should have been, and no doubt they were. But in the memory of that awful battle it was easy to forget their fatigue.

I stood by Cox for a time and helped "hearten them up." One young lad from the Royal Irish Regiment was woefully tired and hungry. He was helping a comrade who had strained his knee and was in no little pain. I asked him if he thought he could get on another mile or so, and he grinned and replied, "Sure. My lot have been in action Sunday, Monday, Tuesday, and Wednesday, and after that I can do anything you like on Thursday."

It was sad to see some of the lame ones come in. Now and then one would go by gingerly and slowly, every step a bit of exquisite torture.

After a number of smaller groups of stragglers, quite decent-sized detachments came through. A really very small percentage of the men were without rifles.

All were astonishingly cheerful. Many a group went by whistling in chorus. The majority of them looked full of fight, and only now and again would a broken one go by.

The French women were splendidly helpful. Steaming bowls of coffee, little boxes of food, bits of cake, pitchers of tea or jugs of milk, matches, cigarettes, anything they thought would help to cheer or comfort, they brought to the roadside for the Tommies.

A good-sized contingent swung by in step, singing. Stopping for a drink of coffee, a sergeant told me every one of them had been marching continuously all night long.

Twos and threes strolled down the road at intervals leisurely, as though interested spectators. Good-natured banter was flung from one group to another. Questions confirmed what I had been told, to the effect that most of our casualties had been from shrapnel, after the retirement had begun. Very little damage had been inflicted on our troops by the German infantry fire. All testified to that.

By noontime we wondered that we had no news of stragglers being taken up, or *Uhlans* cutting them off as they came ambling down the road. A subaltern told us of Renancourt. The chaos there was maddening. A battery of enemy guns or a strong force of cavalry could have piled up thousands of casualties at that point. The roads thereabouts were full of abandoned trains, and here and there an abandoned gun, he said.

But still no news of the enemy's further advance, which we had so confidently expected all the morning.

Guns could be heard to the north and to the west. Sordêt's French Cavalry and our own gallant cavalry brigades were efficient rearguards.

A French reservist force was not far from us, to the north of St. Quentin, but in no great numbers, and not, to my mind, particularly formidable.

A German monoplane put in an appearance, but created little stir.

We began to theorise. Had Haig's lot turned, after all, and struck Von Kluck's left flank? No, we would have heard the guns. Rumour came, too, that Haig had been fighting severe rearguard actions in front of Guise.

Had the Germans been so unmercifully hammered at Cambrai-Le Cateau that their troops were unable to follow? Unlikely. Then, there were plenty more of 'em. That we knew.

How those German first line regiments had stood the gaff! Losses of thirty to forty *per cent,* demoralise all but the finest commands, we argued. Von Kluck's stalwarts have been through the mill for days now—has our punishment stopped the rush of their onslaught at last?

So we theorised.

And we were not far wrong, after all. Von Kluck had tried hard to smash and envelop the British Left, and had failed. He had knocked back Smith-Dorrien, in some confusion, but only after enormous losses had been inflicted on the German forces. The backbone of the movement against French, the attempt to wipe his "contemptible little army" off the map, was broken by the fight put up by the British Left that Wednesday at Cambrai-Le Cateau.

Our British Cavalry was doing wonders unbeknown to us. Briggs and de Lisle with the First and Second Cavalry Brigades were covering the 2nd Corps' retreat, and Gough and Bingham, with the Third and Fourth Cavalry Brigades, were protecting the retirement of Haig's First Corps. Chetwode, too, with the 5th Cavalry Brigade, was in front of Haig and delivering stinging blows to the German advance.

By one o'clock so many of our men had passed that all thought of a demolished army had left us. Dirty, tired, and hungry though they were, they were cheery and fit. They wanted rest and, above all, food. But no one could imagine them in the least beaten. The British Tommy and his indomitable spirit had saved the day. His good temper and pluck had survived the awful experience between the commencement of the retirement from the battle line in the middle of the afternoon until dark had ended the fight. More, it had lived through the awful night of confusion and retreat with its hunger, thirst, and utter weariness. The morning had brought little respite, but the sun was shining, and with the warmth of the day Tommy came back into his own and up came his head and his heart.

He had saved himself!

Dozens of times little groups reported to us that they were "all that were left "of such and such a regiment. Almost invariably we could tell them of others of their command whom they would find further on at the point of rendezvous, where they could be sure of food and a brief rest.

Early in the afternoon word came to us from mounted scouts that the *Uhlans* were about three miles out and coming on in force. Cox sent me to Headquarters to see if there was any truth in the report. From what I could gather, it seemed that a *Uhlan* force was heading south, a bit to the east of us.

Cox considered it advisable that we should run out eastward toward Guise and search for information about the German advance. Accordingly we picked up Lean and with our cyclist pounded away. A mile or so out of St. Quentin we ran across the 16th Lancers, who were in Gough's 3rd Cavalry Brigade. They were dismounted in a nicely-sheltered field surrounded by trees, and were very well concealed. As Cox was talking to the commanding officer of the 16th a mounted scout rode up in blue overalls, old brown coat, and a brown cap. Had I not heard him speak English I would have thought him of some other nationality. He reported a detachment of German cavalry just outside St. Quentin on the north. The order "Fall in in squads "was given, and the 16th mounted and started away northwards. I wondered if they would find two thousand German infantry that had been reported not long before by some French reservist scouts as coming on towards St. Quentin from the north-west.

On we ran at a good pace to the east, and before long crossed the Oise at Origny. Here we met the advance guard of Haig's 1st Corps *en route* from Guise. Haig's line of retreat was to be to the south to La Fère. Cox wanted to find Sir Douglas Haig himself, so we passed well-nigh the whole of his command to reach him. This operation, on the country road, was at times trying. Finally, not far from the village of Jonqueuse, a few kilometres west of Guise, we saw Haig on a little hilltop by the roadside, chatting with his staff and a handful of French officers, as they kept their glasses on the rolling country stretching away to the northward.

A brigade staff officer, with whom I had a moment's talk, told me that on the previous morning two battalions of infantry of the 1st Corps had been ineffectively picketed, with the result that the Germans had rushed them and inflicted severe damage. "Only two officers of one of the battalions were left," he said. That was the first version I heard of the story of the Munster Fusiliers. Another staff officer told me a few minutes afterwards that the Munsters were at the rear of the corps, and a messenger from headquarters with orders for their retirement failed to reach them. They stayed where they were, even though attacked by overwhelming numbers, and fought until they were completely surrounded. Even then they refused to surrender until they had fired their last round. Their losses were terrible. During the next hour I heard the same story with half a dozen variations, but that one appeared to be the most correct. I climbed up alongside General Haig's staff, and stood there for an hour or more listening to the sound of the cannonading. North of Guise on our right and away to the left and to the north of St. Quentin the guns were hard at it.

Samuels an R.A.C. driver, showed up at an opportune moment with a Bologna sausage, a bottle of villainous *vin blanc*, and some quite decent Russian cigarettes. They disappeared instanter, to our very material benefit.

At last we started for Noyon and G.H.Q. Cox was anxious to get there as soon as possible, so I chose a cross-country route to La Fère down small roads through the smiling and fertile valley of the Oise.

Even the smallest winding roads were good ones. While still near Guise we passed a wagon-load or two of refugees. Before we were out of earshot of the gunning, however, the countryside took on its usual appearance. All day long we had been in the midst of scenes of war. Here, a very few miles away, one could hardly imagine war existed in the same valley. Perhaps the women and children, with an old man or two, gathered more eagerly in the doorways of the village houses as we dashed through, but the men-folk not at the front were hard at work in the fields and about the farmyards. The crops were generous and the land fairly blossomed with plenty. A commercial traveller in his cart was selling his wares in front of a village store as if never a German had crossed the Rhine.

As we neared La Fère a barricade had been formed by pulling a couple of farm carts across the road. A trio of reservists were on guard, one armed with a nickel-plated 38-calibre revolver of the old "bulldog" type, the sole visible weapon of the outpost. The sentry with the bright bit of ordnance smilingly apologised for the necessity of examining our passes, waving the pistol about airily in emphasis of his urbane remarks in a manner that badly scared me. I began to get the idea that given a combination consisting of a French reservist, a firearm of sorts, and me, I would invariably be in line with the muzzle of the weapon. And I am of too nervous a temperament to enjoy that sort of thing.

La Fère was full of French troops and was the rail base of the 2nd Corps. Smith-Dorrien's headquarters, so one of our Flying Corps told us, were first located at Ham, and then moved to Guiscard. The broad road from Le Fère to Chauny and thence to Noyon was soon covered. We reached G.H.Q. by dinner-time. I was thoroughly tired, so after a hurried dinner in a restaurant of sorts, was soon fast asleep in a most comfortable bed.

I was still in the arms of Morpheus on Friday morning (August 28th) when Captain Cox wakened me to borrow my map, a rather better one than those provided by G.H.Q. Cox told me I was on that day to drive Lieut.-Colonel J. S. M. Shea (35th Horse), attached to General French's staff as a liaison officer. I count the day a lucky one that I met Jimmy Shea, for he is of the salt of the earth.

After breakfast we reconnoitred the different roads through Noyon. The 2nd Corps was continuing its retreat southward. The units were still somewhat scattered and required general collecting together and organising. The army was to drop back to the line Noyon-Chauny. We were more concerned with the 2nd Corps units which were passing through Noyon, as our own work lay with them. The 4th Division, 19th Brigade, and some of the cavalry units were also passing through our hands. Most of the morning we stood by the roadside watching provision trains, ambulances, lorries laden with ammunition, and all the transport of an Army Corps file past us. Batteries of guns and detachments of infantry all were working slowly southward. G.H.Q. had moved to Compiègne in the morning.

I heard a great deal of general gossip during the forenoon from staff officers and officers of various contingents that were on the road. It was fairly well known by this time that three German Army Corps had been diverted from a point further east and swung around to reinforce Von Kluck's 1st Army. We heard but little authentic news of the French, but Dame Rumour was busy with all sorts of general reports of German successes at Dinant and further east.

Once in a while a block came in the traffic, and then we had an awful job working up and down the packed lines straightening out the transport and the troops. It was a fine day and very hot. The troops were cheery and good-natured. I was particularly impressed by the kindness of the men to their horses. Not only the cavalry troopers, but the men in charge of horse transport were invariably considerate of their cattle. The roads in the vicinity of Noyon were lined with trees, the cool shade of which was most welcome. In the afternoon the 2nd Army proper began to swing through in real earnest. For three hours a steady stream of infantry in different detachments passed. All were wonderfully cheery and looked particularly well, sleepy some of them, and here and there a swollen foot gingerly treading the hard roadway. Considering the distance they had come, marvellously few of the men limped. Stragglers grew hourly fewer in number, which showed that the detachments were getting together again. Frequently a regiment came swinging along in step, singing or whistling in unison.

We had news of a peculiar order issued by G.H.Q. to the effect that the officers' kits should be taken from the wagons and destroyed, to provide accommodation for footsore infantry. The 4th Division carried out this order before it was countermanded, and eleven wagonloads of kit were burned by the roadside—by no means a reassuring sight.

A big Scot saw me take a letter from one of the staff officers, and asked me if I would perform a similar service for him. No sooner had I agreed to do so than his entire regiment, which had halted for a moment, grasped the opportunity and began scribbling notes home. It was indeed touching to see these hurried missives written on all sorts of scraps of paper. There was no chance to pick or choose as regards form. Most of the letters were to wives, and many to mothers, with now and then one to a sister or a sweetheart. The majority of them

Algerian Cavalry going into action on the Vesle near Braisne

"I" Battery R.H.A. firing on the La Tretoire, which was being attacked by the Coldstreams

were just a line to say all was well. Few indeed could be called illiterate, and I saw none that were illegible. What most impressed me was the cheery vein that ran through them. No note of despondency crept into that wayside postbag. It was one more evidence of the stout heart of Tommy Atkins that makes him the finest soldier in the world.

Among the troops a couple of spies came, led between two French soldiers. One was short and swarthy, with coal-black moustache and hair. He looked a Greek, and was dressed as some small shopkeeper might have been on a Sunday outing. The other prisoner wore a knit cap and big khaki-coloured coat that had apparently come from our quartermaster's department at some time. He was tall, of light complexion, and furnished the greatest contrast possible to his companion. They both wore a look of abject misery as they trudged along in the dust to their death. Spies or suspected spies had short shrift with the French in those days.

We raised some coffee from a wayside house in the afternoon, but could get no milk. The town was thoroughly emptied of eatables, and most of the private houses were closed. Later in the afternoon we got some eggs at one house and a bit of bread-and-butter at another; and finally found an *estaminet* where we could buy some wine. Discovering a countrywoman at a drinking hall who would cook for us, I arranged quite a dinner for Colonel Shea, Dudley Carleton, Jimmy Rothschild, who was acting as Carleton's chauffeur, and myself. After dinner Rothschild went to the post office to send a telegram. I was sceptical about his ability to do this, for the utmost secrecy was being preserved as to our whereabouts in France. Rothschild offered to get a wire through for me. He wrote a brief message in French, addressed to my wife in England, assuring her that I was fit, well, and happy. Great was my surprise when the postmaster agreed to send it. Subsequently I was still more surprised to find that the wire had arrived in London in good time. Moreover, the telegram clearly stated that it had been despatched from Noyon on that Friday evening.

Late that night we left Noyon for Compiègne. Owing to the congested nature of the roads we lost our way and wandered in the forests of Ourscamps and Laigue till past midnight. Arriving in Compiègne, we could find no empty beds in the hotels, but finally were lucky enough to discover a couple of empty cots in a college dormitory, used as a temporary hospital.

The German pressure on our rearguards had visibly slackened on Friday, the 28th, and by night the British Expeditionary Force had made good its escape from anything in the nature of annihilation. I had seen almost all of the 1st Corps, and on the 27th and 28th had watched a large number of the 2nd Corps, 4th Division, and 19th Brigade. I had no hallucination about the army being a beaten one. The spirit of the men alone made it impossible to describe them as beaten. The moment I realised that things were better than they had at first sight seemed, I watched eagerly for signs of a further stand. The more I saw of French's Army the more convinced I became of its invincibility, and longed for the day when we could "get some of our own back."

At an early hour on Saturday, the 29th, Colonel Shea and I proceeded to a large hotel in Compiègne and foraged for breakfast. Most of the servants had left, but resourceful Toby Rawlinson hied himself to the kitchen and cooked a splendid breakfast for Shea, Jimmy Rothschild, and me.

Cox told me the Germans had left off hammering after the British Expeditionary Force, and were turning their attention to some of the French contingents on our left. I did not know at the time that General d'Amade was in touch with Von Kluck's right in the direction of Arras. French troops were east of the line between Guise and La Fère, and were engaging the attention of Von Kluck's left. On that Saturday our cavalry fought a rearguard action at Ham, and subsequently a more determined one at Guiscard. After the two or three hours' fighting at Guiscard that afternoon the German advance was satisfied to draw off and leave us alone.

I spent the morning running to Noyon and back, and later took a couple of G.H.Q. staff officers to a *château* near Cuts, south-east of Noyon, where General Smith-Dorrien had his headquarters. Arriving at the chateau, which was a very handsome one, I found my car short of lubricating oil. In my endeavour to borrow some I drew an undue amount of attention to my improvised uniform, which had not improved in appearance. My efforts might have proved fruitless but for the fact that General Smith-Dorrien came out at the moment. He stepped into a big car, and was about to be driven away when he saw me. Bowing, he asked me with a smile how I was standing the campaign. Considering the circumstances under which I had met him a couple of days before, and the short time I had been in his company, I was surprised he remembered me, and naturally felt the warm and genial touch of his recognition. As he drove away, the lubricating oil which I had begged in vain before was thereafter immediately forthcoming.

On our run to Cuts, through the Forest of Laigue, we had passed many transport trains on the move to or from rail bases. Every nerve was strained to get the 2nd Corps mobilised, rested, fed, and well supplied with ammunition at the earliest possible moment. A 2nd Corps staff officer told me that the General Orders of the Day announced that a division or more of the enemy were advancing from St. Quentin to Noyon, and that the cavalry, which had been fighting rearguard actions since Mons, had orders once more to block the way. A subaltern in charge of an ammunition column begged for news. I asked him if he had seen anything of interest. He said:

> It has been interesting enough for me. My column has had four hours' sleep in three days in addition to what they could snatch here and there on the move. No sooner had I got them to one place in response to orders which it seemed impossible to carry out, than I have been cursed for getting them there, and hurried away to some other point to find someone waiting for me there with more cuss words. I am a wandering Jew, for ever on the move, and don't ever expect to stop again as long as I live.

While at General Smith-Dorrien's headquarters I was introduced to General H. de B. de Lisle, commanding the 2nd Cavalry Brigade. General de Lisle wanted to get back to his command. He had come for a conference with General Smith-Dorrien. We ran to Guiscard or near it. The 2nd Cavalry Brigade had been attacked at nine o'clock in the morning at some point to the north of Guiscard. The position not being as satisfactory as desired, de Lisle had retired from Guiscard at eleven o'clock to a point about two and a half kilometres south of the town. There, with the support of the guns, which they had lacked in the position further north, they withstood the German attack for over two hours, and eventually compelled the Germans to retire. We passed a couple of lorry loads of wounded before reaching the 2nd Cavalry Brigade. I had not before had an opportunity of coming into contact with the British cavalry, which had been performing wonderful feats of valour, and whose existence for the past week had been one continual rearguard action.

I was much impressed with their splendid quality throughout. I heard that afternoon of a couple of magnificent cavalry actions of the day before by General Gough's 3rd Cavalry Brigade and General Chetwode's 5th Cavalry Brigade between St. Quentin and Le Fère. They had met and routed a couple of columns of German cavalry, and demonstrated their absolute superiority as cavalry over the enemy's mounted forces. That the 2nd Cavalry Brigade should have fought so successful an action when dismounted, after the splendid mounted work that it and its fellow brigades had been doing for days past, showed its marvellous adaptability. A staff officer came by and told us that heavy fighting had taken place on Von Kluck's right and left flanks, the French being driven back in the west and having held their own in the east.

The 2nd Cavalry Brigade was billeted that night at Ourscamps, a village a few kilometres south of Noyon. I drove General de Lisle and Captain "Rattle" Barrett (15th Hussars), who was de Lisle's staff captain, about the village and the grounds of the old *château*, selecting bivouacs for the three regiments of the Brigade—the 4th Dragoon Guards, the 9th Lancers, and the 18th Hussars. In the beautiful summer evening we watched a long-drawn-out fight between a German aeroplane and two British aeroplanes which were chasing it back to the north. Apparently the faster British plane was the speediest of the trio, but the German was clever in his manoeuvring. We could see puffs of smoke from time to time as one or other of the airmen fired. They wheeled and dipped and dived, circling now up and now down, drawing steadily away, until they finally passed out of sight. We would have given much to have known the result of the contest.

I compared notes with one and another of the cavalry officers who had been in closest and most continuous touch with the enemy from the beginning.

Haig's 1st Corps, they agreed, had the best opportunity to get away without heavy loss, as the brunt of the German attack was further west, on Smith-Dorrien's 2nd Corps. The splendid fight put up by Smith-Dorrien's threatened left saved it from casualties to a greater extent than was yet realised.

How comparatively few casualties had been inflicted by Von Kluck's smashing attack we did not know until the official reports told us that on the retreat and the advance to the Marne the total for the three Corps and the Cavalry division was 64 officers and 212 men killed, 1,223 of all ranks wounded, and 13,643 missing, and most of them of course either killed or wounded, and not unwounded prisoners. Only 15,142 from a force of over 100,000. When one takes from that number the casualty lists of Audregnies, Landrecies, Guiscard, Néry, the fighting near Villers-Cotteret, La Ferté Jouarre, and the conflicts that took place near the Grand Morin, Petit Morin, and the Marne itself, one realises that Sir John French's army not only escaped annihilation at Mons and Cambrai-Le Cateau, it escaped great loss, and that in the face of circumstances which made it seem impossible it could do so. At least, it seemed impossible to us, a day or so later, that it *had* done so.

Sordêt's cutting in on the left of the line at Cambrai with his guns, and letting us get away from the Cambrai-Le Cateau line, was freely commented on by the cavalry. They knew how greatly Sordêt's cavalry had helped us.

Most engrossing to me was meeting those who had been last in St. Quentin. On Wednesday, the 26th, the great battle of Cambrai-Le Cateau had been fought. Thursday I spent in St. Quentin, leaving it in the afternoon, when reports of oncoming Germans within a couple of kilometres of the town were brought in by both French and English scouts.

Friday I had spent in Noyon. The cavalry had been in and about St. Quentin most of that day. The German occupation of the town had been delayed until nearly every straggler who reached it from the north, if not all, had been gotten away.

Major Tom Bridges, of the 4th Dragoon Guards, had been sent into St. Quentin on Friday afternoon to see if more stragglers could be found. In the square near the *mairie* he found a couple of hundred or more men of various detachments, who were seated on the pavement in complete exhaustion and utter resignation to what appeared their inability to rejoin the army which had retreated far to the southward.

They, too, expected the Germans momentarily. A couple of half-crazed, irresponsible chaps had preached some rot to them that made them think themselves abandoned to their fate. Bridges needed but a moment to see how far gone they were, how utterly and hopelessly fatigued. No peremptory order, no gentle request, no clever cajolery would suffice. With most of them the power to move seemed to themselves to have gone with ceaseless tramping, without food or sleep, for the thirty-six hours past.

A brilliant idea came to the big, genial major. Entering a toy shop, he bought a toy drum and a penny whistle. He strapped the little drum to his belt.

"Can you play 'The British Grenadiers'?" he asked his trumpeter.

"Sure, sir," was the reply.

In a twinkling the pair were marching round the square, the high treble of the tiny toy whistle rising clear and shrill:

> *But of all the world's brave heroes,*
> *There's none that can compare,*
> *With a tow, row, row, with a tow, row, row,*
> *To the British grenadiers."*

Round they came, the trumpeter, caught on the wings of the major's enthusiasm, putting his very heart and soul into every inspiring note.

Bridges, supplying the comic relief with the small sticks in his big hands, banged away on the drum like mad.

They reached the recumbent group. They passed its tired length. Now they came to the last man. Will they feel the spirit of the straining notes, rich with the tradition of the grand old air? Will they catch the spirit of the big-hearted major, who knows so well just how the poor lads feel, and seeks that spot of humour in Tommy's make-up that has so often proved his very salvation?

The spark has caught! Some with tears in their eyes, some with a roar of laughter, jump to their feet and fall in. The weary feet, sore and bruised, tramp the hard cobbles unconscious of their pain. Stiffened limbs answer to call of newly-awakened wills.

> *With a tow, row, row, with a tow, row, row, to the British grenadiers.*

They are singing it now, as they file in long column down the street after the big form hammering the toy drum, and his panting trumpeter "blowing his head off" beside him.

"Go on, Colonel! We'll follow you to hell," sings out a brawny Irishman behind who can just hobble along on his torn feet.

Never a man of all the lot was left behind.

Down the road, across the bridge, mile after mile towards Roye. The trumpeter, blown, subsides for a while, then, refreshed, takes up the burden of the noble tune again.

At last Tom Bridges turned and said: "Now, boys, ahead of you is a town where you can get food and drink and a bit of rest before you go on. It isn't far. Good luck!"

But not they. They were not going to lose their new-found patron. Clamour rose, shrill and eager. "Don't leave us, Colonel," they begged. "Don't, for God's sake, leave us! They all left us but you. We'll follow you anywhere, but where to go when you leave we don't know at all."

So Bridges toiled on to Roye with them, got them food and billets, turned them over to someone who would see they got on to their commands in some way, and went back to duty with his regiment, arriving at two o'clock in the morning.

Big Tom Bridges! Indeed, he had more than once earned the name, but never more gallantly and wisely than on that afternoon in August in the turmoil of the great retreat.

CHAPTER 3

Into the German Lines

On Sunday, the 30th, I rose early and put in a busy morning in Compiègne on messenger work, at noon time returning to G.H.Q. for further orders. The day was frightfully hot, the sky a very clear blue, quite pale in the heat. In a group under a shady tree I found Captain Kirkwood, good fellow and soldier of fortune, who had been in South Africa, big game shooting, when the war cloud gathered over Europe. Hurrying back, he reached Paris in the early days of the retreat, and after some difficulty managed, owing to the fact that he was an ex-officer of British cavalry, to get permission to report himself to Sir John French's Headquarters.

At first it seemed unlikely that he would be given a chance to join up with the Expeditionary Force, but he had been told that morning that if he would report to General de Lisle he would be given work to do as a Captain of the 4th Dragoon Guards, who had lost heavily in officers. Kirkwood was in a quandary, wondering how he could obtain transportation from Sir John French's Headquarters in Compiègne to General de Lisle's Headquarters, wherever they might be. This was an undertaking that bristled with difficulties owing to the scarcity of motorcars.

He told me his troubles, and I at once saw an opportunity to be released from more prosaic duty at Compiègne, obtain a run up to the front, and possibly see something of the rearguard fighting.

A brief explanation of the situation to Major Bartholomew, one of the officers in charge of the motor-cars attached to Headquarters Staff, was sufficient to obtain permission to take Captain Kirkwood to 2nd Cavalry Brigade Headquarters. Knowing that the 2nd Cavalry Brigade had billeted the night before in Ourscamps, I thought our most interesting plan would be to run to Ourscamps and then beat south along the road they had taken to reach the Compiègne-Soissons line.

I had gathered at G.H.Q. that the whole of the British Force was to fall back on the Aisne. Some rumour was about which told of a conference between General Joffre and Sir John French on the Saturday afternoon, and that the advantage gained on our right by the French 5th Army was to count for naught as the whole line was to retire not only on our immediate right, but away to the east where the German centre was dealing sledge-like blows in an effort to hammer through the French centre. Though we did not know it, that Sunday morning was to witness the German occupation of La Fère and Laon to the east of it. The retreat of the British Expeditionary Force had begun again, as had the consequent advance of the Germans.

It was difficult for us, at that time, to understand the lull in the operations of the 27th and 28th of August, and the renewal of the chase on the 29th and 30th. It was long before we realised that the operations on the British front during those days were of slight importance relatively, when compared with the great battles that were taking place to the eastward. Naturally we were entirely concerned with our immediate surroundings, and the fact that the whole line to the westward had to move back to conform with the stubbornly-resisted advance of the Germans bearing down on Rheims and Châlons was as yet unknown to us.

I started off gaily for Ourscamps with Kirkwood just after midday.

Some cheerful individual had assured me that the French cavalry were still at Noyon, and I had taken his word for it with childlike simplicity.

Running to Choisy, we crossed the Oise, and, gaining its western bank, passed through Ribecourt. Pushing on with a clear road and invigorating sunshine to spur us, it would take but a few minutes to cover the eight kilometres to Noyon. The *pavé* of the main road was in such bad state of repair that a temporary path had been utilised under the trees by the roadside. It was rough, but not so bad as the *pavé*, except that here and there great ditches made one pull up rather sharply.

Groups of country folk along the highway waved us on. Once Kirkwood remarked that we had best be careful, as we were surely running very close to enemy country, but I thought we were certain to have warning from the country folk if any German had been seen in the vicinity. No sooner had I expressed an opinion to this effect, than a peasant at the roadside, a bright-eyed, bent, little old chap, indulged in a lively pantomime in an endeavour to attract our attention. As I was running well over forty miles per hour I required a few yards for stopping, the little man in the meantime using the fore fingers of each hand to describe as best he might above his head the appearance of the *Uhlans'* horned helmets, and alternating this bit of sign language with unmistakable motions indicating pointed moustaches of the Kaiser type.

As we slowed down he ran to us, and in answer to Kirkwood's questions, informed us that the *Uhlans* were just ahead of us. I suppose we looked somewhat incredulous, and the idea may have come to him that he had not sufficiently explained himself, for again he went through his antics, picturing the pointed moustaches and the horned *Uhlan* helmets. As he was somewhat incoherent, we beckoned to another peasant, who approached and told us quietly and with great conviction that thirty *Uhlan* had but a few moments before passed along the road in the direction in which we were travelling. This was alarming information. If we had run sufficiently far into the German lines for *Uhlan* patrols to be passing along the road in both directions, there was great possibility that we would not again see Compiègne.

As an American in khaki the Huns might be expected to make short work of me if I fell into their hands. My uniform, procured at a few hours' notice from a London theatrical costumier, was of a nondescript sort, not calculated to insure my being treated by the Germans as a member in good standing of the British Army.

I had good reason, therefore, to wish to avoid capture at all costs.

The point at which we had stopped was but very few kilometres from Noyon, and at that point the road from Passel joined the main pike, giving me ample opportunity to turn the car without backing it.

While we were talking with our informants a mounted *Uhlan* rode out in full view in the roadway ahead of us, not more than 500 yards distant. He halted and apparently called to his companions under the trees by the roadside, for a dozen joined him immediately. For a moment they made no movement, inspecting us with the greatest interest. Kirkwood had got out of the car to have a look with his glasses and to make sure that they were foes and not friends. I swung the car around in a twinkling and Kirkwood jumped to his seat with a remark that the *Uhlans* were on the way.

We flew back over the road, a cloud of dust rising behind us. A few shots were fired. The car clattering over the terribly broken road made such a din one could hear little else. All sorts of possibilities passed through our minds. A puncture or a burst tyre would have meant a wheel pounded to pieces in no time: another *Uhlan* scouting party on either side of the road was more than probable and might have spelled disaster. All went merrily, however, and we were in Ribecourt again almost before we knew it. My forehead was covered with perspiration—in anticipation, I suppose. At Ribecourt we met a British officer in a car and a motorcyclist with him, from our Intelligence Department. They were bound for Lassigny. We warned them in due time and they proceeded cautiously by a side road, to the west of the point at which we had encountered the *Uhlans*.

Leaving Ribecourt we passed a British cavalry patrol of eight troopers. We again reported the presence of the *Uhlan* outpost on the main road. The sergeant in command of the patrol told us that in Chiry, a town between Ribecourt and Passel and only a quarter of a mile or less to the west of the main road, the *Uhlans* had been quartered in some strength all the morning. The patrol had been in the woods not far from Chiry watching the *Uhlans* for an hour or more, and in their opinion there were at least 200 of them in and about the town. That we should have thus rushed past so large a force and come back again without their intercepting us was a matter of pure luck, and turned what might have been a serious matter for us into an amusing adventure. We must have been within but a few hundred yards of them both going and coming.

We had, beyond a doubt, been well within the German advance line, and out again without being in the least the worse for it.

Crossing the Oise we ran to Le Plessis and Brion, and there encountered a party of French engineers who were waiting to blow up a line. They told us all the bridges were destroyed south of Noyon. We met one of our own engineer officers who told us that the Ourscamps bridge was blown up early that morning. If we had planned a hasty retreat by the route originally selected we would have been nicely caught in a trap.

I gained some information as to the obstacles we were putting in the way of the advancing Germans by destroying railways and bridges. Everything in the nature of a bridge which could be destroyed had been rendered impassable. This had no inconsiderable effect on checking the impetuosity of the German forward movement.

We ran to G.H.Q., and I reported the fact that the *Uhlans* were well south of Noyon. We again took the road for 2nd Cavalry Brigade Headquarters, planning to run through the Forest of Laigue to Tracy-le-Mont. At the fork where the roads for Noyon and Soissons branch a handsome Rolls-Royce landaulet was piled up against a telegraph pole at the side of the road; Jimmy Rothschild was standing despondently beside it. Approaching the fork, Jimmy had suddenly been confronted by a French sentry, who had emerged from the undergrowth and called upon the approaching motorist to halt, at the same time throwing his rifle to his shoulder and pointing it very directly, so Jimmy said, at the driver—who happened to be Jimmy. Realising that he must stop at all costs, he turned the car to the roadside, where the front axle struck the telegraph pole—with dire results. We took everything removable from the car, piled it into a cart, sent it to Compiègne, and, taking Rothschild in the back, we started again for Tracy-le-Mont. We were told the forest was full of *Uhlan* scouts, who had been seen crossing the road, but we were apparently in quite as much danger from Jimmy Rothschild's Mauser pistol, which he loaded and carried at the "ready," until both Kirkwood and I demanded that he should keep it pointed in the direction of the enemy rather than towards the back of our heads.

Down some of the long wooded aisles we could see moping horsemen in the afternoon light. If they were *Uhlans* they were undoubtedly quite as shy of meeting us as we were of encountering them. We passed French soldiers in trenches along the way, ready and waiting for the oncoming enemy.

Tracy was a beautiful place. There we found our cavalry, and passed squadron after squadron and battery after battery of guns on the way southward to Attichy. From Attichy we doubled back to the village of Vieux Moulin on the south of the Aisne where we found General de Lisle.

My run back to Compiègne was made in quick time as I had been told on leaving Headquarters that G.H.Q. was to be moved at 10 o'clock to Villers Cotteret. At 10 o'clock, however, orders were changed, and we stayed in Compiègne. Someone had annexed my room in the hotel, so I sought the cot in the college where I had slept my first night in Compiègne. I was alone in the dormitory and overslept. I turned out on the morning of Monday, the 31st, at half past seven and found everyone attached to G.H.Q. gone, except one or two tardy ones. G.H.Q. took "some watching" in those days. If one turned around it was likely to disappear to the southward. Picking up a couple of staff officers as passengers I was soon headed for Senlis, *en route* for Dammartin, the next town to which G.H.Q. was to lend the dignity of its presence.

Near Senlis we went by columns of French infantry. For the first time during the campaign I saw the sturdy little French foot soldiers on the march. With a goodly interval between each company, in loose marching order they scattered all over the road. Their heavy kits included the inevitable tin pots packed on their backs. It seemed cruel to garb a soldier in such clothes on a hot day. I little realised how much I was to admire them before the end of the campaign. None of us knew what we were yet to owe to the French Army, and in what high regard we were one day to hold it. Near St. Vaast the road wound upwards through the woods.

All the way up the ascent we passed the toiling legion in long blue coats over heavy red breeches, pattering along, uncomplaining, always on the move, covering the ground with most wonderful rapidity in what seemed to me a most unorthodox manner of doing so. From Senlis to Dammartin we skirted the Forest of Ermonville, running through wonderfully beautiful country. Here a silver-clad hillside, there a rare *château*, and by it a lovely village. Evidences of war were there, carts full of refugees generally so occupying the road that one had little space for passing. I had a fast run and arrived at Dammartin in advance of G.H.Q.

The parts of my car known to the mechanically-minded as universal joints needed grease. Nice accessible things, universal joints. Taking my car to a point on the road where I seemed sure of isolation for a time, I crawled under the brute, and with many irrelevant remarks proceeded to unlace the leather boots which covered the parts to be doctored. Plastering them with what part of the soft grease I could keep from dropping down into my eyes, I at last, sweating at every pore, and "fed up" with chauffeuring, rested, self-satisfied with my conscientious efforts. Then I tried to withdraw from beneath the car. There was the rub. I lay head down, the curb preventing escape on the lower side. I was so nice a fit between the bottom of the step and the paving-stones, that to wriggle uphill on my back was impossible.

Consequently, after fruitless labours to extricate myself, I lay for half-an-hour until a couple of doughty Scots passed. When they had recovered sufficiently from the humour of the situation, they put down their rifles, and each taking firm hold of a leg hauled me forth,

CHOISY, ON THE MARNE

THE BRIDGE OVER THE MARNE, NOGENT

even more disreputable in appearance than before.

A French limousine car reached Dammartin, an object lesson for timid motor drivers thereabouts. It was riddled with bullet-holes and the seats were covered with blood. Four Frenchmen were coming from Montdidier to Compiègne that morning and were ambushed by *Uhlans* along the road. The driver was shot through the body, but managed to keep the wheel and get the car well away to safety a mile or so further on, when he succumbed to his wounds. Beside him his brother had been shot dead. Taking the driver's place when he collapsed, one of the occupants of the car had brought it on to our headquarters—a gory spectacle.

An engineer officer told me of a little tragedy in his corps. Two R.E. officers and half-a-dozen men had been sent back to blow up a bridge near Compiègne. They set rapidly about their work, and were but half through it when a volley from cover near by hit the officers and five of the men, one only escaping.

Jimmy Radley, in describing what he called a "real day's work," incidentally showed of what value the motorcar has become in military operations.

On the day before—Sunday—he had taken a staff officer from Compiègne to Soissons, and thence as far north as Laon. Pushing still north to Nouvion, near La Fère, they reached the Headquarters of the French general commanding the extreme French left. There they learned that the big fight at Guise had been followed by severe fighting at Renansart and Mayot, not far to the northward. In spite of the report that the Germans were even then coming into La Fère, in order to get to St. Gobain, Jimmy's staff officer dashed through Danizy and past La Fère, sighting no Germans, though evidently all but in touch with them. Next they visited Coucy-le-Ctâteau, *en route* for Soissons. At Coucy they were warned that *Uhlans* had been seen at Bagneux, some distance south.

The Soissons road was the line of retreat of our 1st Corps, and passage of it was difficult. From Soissons, the car turned northward again, and for the second time visited Laon, soon to be evacuated in the face of the rapid German advance. The road from Soissons to Laon was full of Belgian soldiers and refugees from Namur. Leaving Laon, Radley sped south to Bourg, then through Braisnes, back to Soissons, and finally home to Compiègne, his starting-point. Truly, work enough for one day.

Some charming French folk insisted most hospitably upon my

joining them at *déjeuner*, which in Dammartin was all the more a blessing as the sole village inn was unspeakably dirty and uninviting—an exceptional French hostelry.

Continuous work at high speed had depleted my stock of spare tyres. I found myself without one remaining spare cover or tube. As none were available about headquarters nor seemed likely to be, and the Gates of Paris were less than thirty kilometres distant, I asked permission to run to Paris that evening to replenish my stock of pneumatics and return before daybreak. I was told that no official permission could be granted, but that I would not be required before morning if I chose to take upon myself the responsibility of the journey. Prince Murat, who was at that time attached as a French soldier interpreter to G.H.Q., was anxious to run into town to get his motorcar, and I gladly agreed that he should bear me company. We reached Paris by dusk, passing a number of French troops scattered here and there in the towns on the way.

We were frequently challenged, and, in fact, through some districts went pass in hand. At first sight, Paris seemed quite unaffected by the proximity of the fighting, but as dusk came on, and we entered the central part of the city, it assumed a very different aspect. A visit to the Invalides obtained an order for the necessary covers and tubes from the French War Office. Armed with the official order for our requirements we repaired to the Grand Palais d'Automobiles, which was the supply depot for all motor requisites. We found the great hall full of cars, and plentiful supplies of tyres and petrol available. All was bustle and hurry, but every deference was paid to our requests, and we were soon supplied with our needs. It was dark by this time, and headlights were denied us. Paris at night in war time was no place for a motorcar.

A visit to Murat's flat in the Avenue de Monceau necessitated a journey that more than once nearly proved my undoing. How I escaped the excavations in the streets, which seemed for ever to be in front and upon all sides of me, I never knew. As we returned, the great semaphore arms of the searchlights on the tops of some of the buildings down town waved back and forth across the inky sky. We reached the Ritz with a sigh of relief, and sat down to a civilised dinner. Only eight or nine tables in the dining-room were occupied. The Spanish Ambassador was at one table and Sir Francis Bertie, the English Ambassador, at another. I had a chat with Sir Francis, telling him some general news of the retreat, and obtaining from him some idea of the general operations in return. He told me that the day before bombs had been dropped on Paris from German aeroplanes, and a couple of people had been reported killed thereby. At one table was a group of Americans in golf clothes.

Paris was rife with rumours. Two French staff officers told of a big engagement on that day, but they had no details. At ten o'clock I suggested returning to Dammartin, but Murat and other French friends declared that such a project would be suicidal. It was bad enough, they argued, to traverse the roads inside the fortifications in the day time. French Reservist sentries were a bit jumpy at that season. One of my French staff officer acquaintances retailed a story of one of the Reservist sentries who had turned out a whole regiment to meet the onslaught of a German force, which proved to be an inoffensive herd of cows, two of which the sentry had accounted for before the arrival of reinforcements. Yielding to pressure of sound counsel, I ran out to Murat's flat and accepted his hospitality for the night. We would have enjoyed the picture of the continually playing searchlights but for the game of hide-and-seek between excavations and hoardings along the *boulevards* in the pitch darkness.

On the morning of Tuesday, September 1st, I was away with the first light. Many features of daily Parisian life were in quite normal evidence. The streets were being washed as usual, and the early morning market carts were rolling along in quite their customary leisurely fashion. Crowds of people were already surging to the railway stations. Cabs or such conveyances were notable by their absence. Sentries along the road, particularly at railway crossings or bridges, looked me over interestedly, and once or twice stopped me to afford closer inspection but peculiarly enough, I was not required to show a pass of any sort until I was quite 18 kilometres out of Paris. The 6th Corps under Maunoury was already beginning to move northward from Paris, and the road was lined with marching troops. Reservists were busy digging trenches here and there, and I heard and saw the smoke of one or two explosions where houses were being cleared away to afford a better line of fire for the guns around Paris. Further north, through towns in which French troops were garrisoned, my pass was in constant demand. In one small village I had to show it to three different sentries.

Arriving at Dammartin I found Sir John French's Headquarters were in a quaint little *château* faced by a circular drive lined with beds of beautiful flowers. G.H.Q. officers were located in the coach-houses

THE RIVER AISNE NEAR BOURG

A VIEW OF THE AISNE AT ONE OF THE POINTS WHERE THE BRITISH ARMY CROSSED THE RIVER

and the adjoining servants' quarters of the *château*. Outside the gates, in a lane of truly rural appearance and dimensions, were all sorts of motorcars. G.H.Q. was just turning out when I drove up, officers and men busying themselves with hurried toilets in whatever receptacle they could find that would hold water. All asked eagerly of news from Paris.

I called at the G.H.Q. Post Office for a letter, and Major Warren, in charge of all questions relating to the post, delivered a homily on the disappointments and delays in that department. Letters had arrived the night before which had been posted in London fourteen days previously. Letters outbound from the Expeditionary Force were first carefully censored and had most of their contents deleted. Once prepared for despatch they awaited a supply train, and were then taken to our supply base, sometimes a day or two after being turned in to G.H.Q. At the supply base they were again censored, subsequently to proceed leisurely to the rail base. There they were censored once more. They were then considered ripe to be forwarded to England.

On arrival in London they were held for four or five days to ensure that any news they might contain would be sure to be stale. This procedure we accepted as a matter of course without complaint. We had little time for letter writing and little desire to transmit any information except the news as to our bodily welfare. I was not nearly so much concerned with what manner of communication I could send to England as with the failure to obtain news from London. The short notice which preceded my departure made me all the more anxious to obtain word from home, but I was destined to be a long time without it. One authentic story that I heard during the retreat, *re* the censor, is quite worth repeating.

The address which we were required to give to our friends at home was simply General Headquarters, British Expeditionary Force. If we indited this cabalistic formula on the outside of an envelope containing a letter to England the communication was instantly destroyed. If we headed a letter with this superscription it was torn off. If we embodied the address in the body of the letter, however, it was let through. One day a number of us were comparing experiences and these facts were undeniably set forth and evidence produced as to their authenticity.

We would have given much to have had the censor present at that *séance*, and to have expressed to him, collectively and individually, our opinion as to his methods.

The early part of the morning I spent watching a never-ending stream of supply lorries and ammunition wagons. Dozens and dozens and dozens of wagons of horse transport passed through the town. For half an hour I was engrossed with the field wireless service, which was working steadily. A Scottish company was guarding a Silesian officer, who had a wound in his right arm. He was a fine-looking young fellow in a smart grey uniform and handsome grey shako.

At 10 o'clock I met an officer who wanted to obtain conveyance to Soissons to join the 3rd Cavalry Brigade. I expected to find that the Germans had crossed the Aisne and were south of Soissons, but I offered to run up that way. I was anxious to see what was happening to Haig's Corps. We ran by way of Nanteuil to Betz.

The refugees along the road were pitiable. A handsome girl, well dressed, rode by on her bicycle sobbing bitterly. Loads of women in farm carts went by crying. One mother with her baby asked anxiously for news of the Germans. When told they were undoubtedly moving southward she made a strenuous effort to be brave. The baby raised its little hand, and touched her face and cooed to her. Kissing it fondly, she burst into torrents of tears. The women had heard such stories of German atrocities that they were well-nigh frantic. There was no complaint and no reviling of the British for dropping back, but it was clear that many of the poor folk could not understand the continual retreat. There seemed no end of the refugees, cartload after cartload passing by filled with women. It was indeed rare that we saw a man among the refugees.

A light touch was given by a gracious lady and her young son, who were just about to depart from Betz in their motorcar. With true French politeness she explained to us that she wished to give her *château* to the British in case it would be of use to them. The likelihood that night would find the Germans in it made this seem almost a joke.

We started for Villers Cotteret for lunch, and shortly after one o'clock reached the outskirts of Ivor. Heavy rifle firing could be heard in front, and the enemy was evidently well south of Villers. A bitter fight was in progress in the woods in front of us. The 4th Guards Brigade were hard at it. They suffered severe losses, although they scored off the Germans in the hand-to-hand fighting in the forest.

Giving up the idea of going to Villers, we worked southward, passing the 5th Brigade of the 2nd Division, consisting of Worcesters, Highland Light Infantry, and Connaught Rangers. It was a hot day, and the Tommies were very tired and feeling the heat. The enemy were not many kilometres behind and pressing on rapidly. We found the Germans had been in Crépy for some hours, and were moving south in considerable strength. Our rearguards were in position between Betz and Crépy.

Having delivered the officer as near to his command as possible, I called at General Haig's Headquarters at Mareuil, a town on the Ourcq, to see if I could take back a message to Dammartin. It was evening before I was again on the road. Running south on the Meaux road, I found it filled with refugees in all sorts of vehicles. Big wagons half loaded with straw and piled with country folk ambled along, pulled by four oxen. Hordes of women and children were walking, trudging along in the dust beside heavily-laden vehicles.

I arrived at Dammartin just after 7 o'clock, and while waiting outside G.H.Q. encountered Captain O'Mahoney, of the Army Service Corps. He had been captured by the Germans, and made good his escape. I gathered some of the details from him, but he was so sleepy, that to obtain a careful account of his experiences was difficult. After awakening him three or four times as he sat in my car telling me the story, I gave it up as a bad job and let him slumber in peace.

The incident of O'Mahoney's escape is well worth relating. I give it just as it was told by his driver.

> One night we were poking along in a low-lying mist. The armies were retreating, and we knew we were making for the southward. I did not know where we were. I was driving the captain's car, and we had one chap in the tonneau with us. The captain told him to keep a good look-out behind and see that the three lorries, which were following us, kept close together. We numbered about a score all told, besides the captain. He had told me to go slow, as we were sure to butt against French or English sentries before long, and the slower we went the more likely we would be to avoid trouble. We knew the enemy were not far away, and heard all sorts of stories about their being in one town or another, close behind us or to one side. We had learned by then to disbelieve half what we heard.
>
> We crawled along with sidelights lit, without headlights, as we had run out of carbide days before.
>
> The mist grew thicker and the road blacker. Once or twice I thought I was off it altogether, but managed to save myself and

the car just in time.

Someone sang out in front of me, and as I pulled the car up I could see a sentry by the dim light of the side lamp. The radiator was almost touching him, and he was holding his rifle at the ready. The captain rose beside me and said, 'English,' just as I heard a voice in front saying, 'Get out of that car.'

With those five words I knew we were up against it, for they were spoken with a sure-enough German accent.

I stood up, and the captain dismounted from the car. He was told to unload his pistol and hand it over to a German officer who came from behind the sentry. I could see several Germans by that time. They were big chaps, and wore enormous helmets with great spikes on the top, which made them look very tall in the mist.

I heard the engines behind us still running. The driver of one of the lorries had enough presence of mind to ditch his machine. That put it out of commission as far as the Germans were concerned, for no one could bother in that sort of a night with that sort of a road to pull the lorry out of the mud and water. The lorry behind the one that was ditched was so close to it that it had to be backed to get it round. A little ingenuity got a back wheel of that one into the ditch as well. That caused some swearing by the Germans, but they had bagged the car and one lorry and twenty-one prisoners, so I suppose they thought they had done well enough. They disarmed us all, and started us off by the road, surrounded by cavalry.

I talked with the captain about the fix we were in, but he saw nothing for it but to drive on as ordered. We passed at least a division of cavalry. The captain thought we had seen four brigades. They were a fine-looking outfit, splendid horses, and fine-looking men.

At daybreak we were brought before some sort of commander. The captain was told to dismount from the car, and was taken over into the field to talk to the German chap, who gave him a cigarette as he came up. I could hear the conversation. The German spoke good enough English to pass as an Englishman. The first thing he said was, 'Why are you fighting us?'

The captain was wise in his answer. He said, 'Because I am ordered to do so.'

'From where were you coming when caught?' asked the German.

The captain threw back his shoulders, looked the big chap straight in the eye, and said: 'That is not a fair question, sir.'

The German smiled, but his 'Perhaps not' sounded very gruff. He talked a moment in German with an officer by him, and, finally, turning to the captain, said: 'We do not want you with us. We are a flying column and cannot be bothered with you; but we shall have to keep you with us until we can hand you over to the first supply train we meet. You will have to accept the situation, and do your best to do just as you are told, and make your movements conform with our wishes in every particular. If last night had not been an occasion for the greatest secrecy, the sentries would probably have fired upon you instead of taking you prisoner. As it is, you are an inconvenience to us, and you must bear that in mind.'

With that, the captain came back to the car. I could see he was downhearted. We moved along a bit further, still surrounded by plenty of cavalry, and before the sun was well up firing commenced in front. I pulled up when I heard the bullets cut way through the trees overhead. A big mounted chap near me pointed his lance up the road and motioned to me that I had better get on. So I did. No German near us at that time spoke any English, or at least none would talk to us; but they had no difficulty in getting me to go right on.

The firing grew rather hot, though the bullets were going pretty high. A lane led away to the right, and we were chased down that and then sent to the left. Finally we were made to come back again, and then go still further to the left. Every little while we came into the line of fire, and more than once the bullets whistled uncomfortably close to us. The captain said that it was becoming quite plain to him we were being purposely exposed.

We waited about fifteen minutes at a corner, and a German officer rode up and told us in English to go on down the road. The captain spoke up then, and said that he considered we were being put into the way of the fire of our troops with the idea of getting us shot by our own lot. The Hun officer only shrugged his shoulders and gave no answer. A moment later he rode back, and said, 'Give me that map case.'

The captain replied: 'I have no objection to giving up my pistol and field glasses, but when it comes to taking my map case, particularly as it is empty, it looks to me more like robbery than anything else. The map case is my private property.'

The German officer looked very sour at this, and gave another shrug to his shoulders, and tossing up his head went away mumbling something in German.

We were with a fine regiment for about half an hour after this, when finally the fight drifted round our way again. Someone told the captain that the British cavalry were immediately in front. Apparently the regiment who were looking after us was not expected to make a stand, for it started away, a squadron at a time, at the gallop—a very fine sight as they tore through the woods.

We were taken from the car and the lorry, and marched through the woods a bit, and finally put in a deep ditch in charge of an officer and twelve men. A stiff lot of rifle fire went over our heads. The officer in charge of us seemed a rather decent sort of German, and spoke a few words of English. His men were firing regularly, but were keeping down behind the top of the ditch safely, so they could not have been doing much damage. The German came over to where the captain was lying, and sat down there for a few minutes, every little while repeating two English words, which seemed about the only thing he could produce in the way of talk. 'Very hot, very hot,' he would say, and grin.

The attack drifted round to the left a bit and lulled down, then became more fierce again. One or two bullets began to sing down the ravine rather than across the top of it. We had all been safe enough up to this time so long as we lay low. When the firing worked round to the left, however, the officer came over to the captain and shook hands, and said 'Goodbye.' He evidently did not intend that all his men should leave, for only two or three went with him, and then two or three more a bit later.

The captain got it in his head that it was more than likely we would be shot before the last of the Germans left us, and the next few minutes of waiting were mighty tough. The suspense nearly made me ill.

At last all the Germans had gone except one evil-looking private. I never saw such a villainous face on any man. No one out of the whole German Army could have been picked for a murderer whose looks would have better fitted the part. A low

The Black Watch crossing the Aisne at Bourg

forehead, narrow slits of shifty eyes, a mean thin-lipped mouth, with chin just square enough to show you that he was stubborn enough to carry through a job if it took his fancy. I shall never forget his face.

The firing had died down again, and the stillness was awful. For the first time I counted our boys and found four were missing: there were fifteen left besides the captain and myself, and we were all lying together in a bunch. Most of us had our eyes on the German. I could not keep my eyes away from him: the evil look on his face fairly mesmerised me. He handled his rifle in a threatening manner for a minute, and actually went so far as to finger the lock and trigger. The captain said afterwards that it was all he could do to keep from jumping at him and downing him, but he was just far enough away for such a move to have meant a bullet, sure.

Suddenly the firing came on again, and our guard paused for a moment as though undecided what to do. At last, with an oath he turned and bolted up the ravine in the direction in which his fellows had disappeared.

The relief was so great when he went we almost forgot the way we were fixed. One or two of the boys jumped up and began to cheer, but this drew a storm of fire at us and over us, and the captain's remarks were more pointed than polite. There seemed no safe way for us to attract the attention of our own troops immediately in front, so we decided to hook it. We managed to get back to the motor and lorry without getting hit, though how we did it I don't know. No Germans were in sight. We started up the machines and drove along the road to the left until we got a turning up which we could run in a general southerly direction. A mile further on we came in touch with one of our cavalry patrols, and half an hour later we were well within our lines.

The captain was all for going back and getting the two lorries which had been ditched, but the retreat was still on, so that was out of the question.

Whatever happened to the four men that became separated from us I don't know, but none of the rest of us were any the worse. The captain was a bit sore, and I think all the rest of us were, that they wouldn't let us go back after those two lorries we had lost.

Bad news came of a surprise attack by the Germans between St. Vaast and Néry at daylight that morning. Spies had apparently located the camp of the 1st Cavalry Brigade to a nicety. L Battery of the Royal Horse Artillery was attached to Briggs' Brigade and bivouacked with it.

In the mist of the grey dawn the Germans, who had brought up eight guns in the night, and numbered several thousand, opened fire at 400 yards.

In the first few minutes, so accurately did the enemy gunners have the range, three of the six guns of L battery were smashed. Two of the battery officers were killed and three wounded. The cavalry brigade did not escape, the Queen's Bays, 5th Dragoon Guards and 11th Hussars suffering a number of casualties, and General Briggs' brigade major being killed by a shrapnel bullet.

To the hail of shells was added a storm of machine gun fire at close range. In a few minutes every officer and nearly every non-commissioned officer in L Battery was wounded, and it was threatened with total annihilation. Only one of its guns remained in action and two men of its crew were all that were left to serve it.

By this time the cavalry brigade was engaging the Germans, and Colonel Ansell was leading a couple of squadrons of his 5th Dragoon Guards around their flank, and Colonel Tommy Pitman's 11th Hussars were fighting hard in front. Some of the Middlesex Regiment, too, of the 19th Brigade, hearing the firing, were coming up rapidly in support, as did the 4th Cavalry Brigade.

So fierce was the onslaught of the dismounted troopers, that victory was snatched from the enemy. The Germans were completely routed with considerable loss, and their eight field guns were taken. Colonel Ansell was killed and the 5th Dragoon Guards suffered heavily. L battery was, of course, the greatest victim, its losses being over eighty *per cent*, of its strength. The story of the capture of the German guns after so great an initial advantage had been gained by them ran over the army like wild fire, and had a most cheering effect.

The following detailed account of the fighting at Néry by the 11th Hussars is taken from a diary kept by an 11th Hussar officer:—

On August 31st, the 1st Cavalry Brigade arrived at Néry just before dark and billeted. At 4.15 a.m. on the morning of September 1st, a patrol, under Lieut. Tailby, was sent out to the high ground to the north-east, and the regiment stood to arms at

4.30 a.m. The morning was misty, and it was difficult to distinguish objects at a distance of more than 150 yards. At 5.30 a.m., Lieut. Tailby galloped in carrying a German cloak, and reported that his patrol had ridden in the mist right up to a regiment of German cavalry on the ridge northeast of Néry, and had been chased back as far as the ravine.

The squadrons were immediately placed into position, B Squadron sending one troop to the southeast corner of the village, one troop to the church overlooking the ravine to the east, one troop to the north-east corner of the village, and one troop being kept in support. C squadron defended the farm immediately to the south of the church, and A squadron was kept in reserve.

Scarcely had these dispositions been made when an extremely heavy artillery and machine-gun fire opened from the ridge to the north-east of the church.

As soon as the situation was clear, A squadron was placed at the disposal of the G.O.C. Brigade and sent to fill the gap between L Battery, and the right troop of B squadron, where it remained in action until the conclusion of the engagement. The German guns were in position to the south-east of the village and within 400 yards of L Battery. The wagons with their escort were left on the ridge immediately to the east of the church, but owing to the mist and a report that the French cavalry were coming up, fire was not opened on them until a dismounted patrol had been sent across the ravine to clear up the situation, and a good opportunity was thus lost.

Meanwhile the enemy had been gradually working round to the south and occupied the sugar factory.... Here they captured the owner and his workmen, whom they used when retiring as a screen against a party of the Bays under Lieut. de Crespigny. Several of the civilians were wounded, and the Germans escorting them made off toward their own guns. These unfortunate civilians took cover in a beet field until they were eventually rescued by us at the end of the action. At about 8 a.m. the 4th Cavalry Brigade arrived in support and opened a heavy artillery fire on the German guns.

The enemy then tried to man-handle the guns out of action, but being under close range of the Bays' machine-guns (which were most admirably handled all through), and of the two machine-guns of the 11th Hussars, which had been brought round to the road at the south-east corner of the village, most of the enemy withdrew. Eight guns were left upon the field.

Our infantry now arrived from the North and passed through the village. C squadron were ordered to mount and follow up the German retreat. They crossed the ravine and worked round the left flank towards the German guns; Bell-Irving's troop dismounted and opened fire on some thirty Germans who were retiring. Norrie's troop galloped through the German guns only to find them abandoned, and the advanced infantry closed upon them, the squadron pushed on to Varrines, capturing a number of prisoners and horses, and made good a farm about a quarter of a mile beyond that point; here they captured about thirty led horses and more prisoners. The squadron was recalled as the brigade was ordered west.

The whole action had lasted about two hours, during which the enemy kept up a heavy fire of guns and maxims. The regiment kept up a heavy fire throughout, except during the short period as stated above. The casualties in the Bays, 5th Dragoon Guards and L Battery were large, owing to their position at the moment of attack. Those in L Battery were especially heavy, as they gallantly attempted to bring their guns into action under a murderous machine-gun and artillery fire at a range of 400 yards. Several of their guns succeeded in opening fire, but were inevitably silenced by the superior hostile fire.

All the officers and men with the guns had been put out of action. Captain Bradbury, who died of wounds the same day, Sergeant-Major Dorrell and one other received the V.C. for their gallant conduct. There is little doubt that the attackers suffered very heavily, and the loss of their guns probably accounted for a German wireless message which was intercepted later in the day, which ran as follows:—

'Attacked by English at dawn, unable to fulfil mission.' The attacking force consisted of a Cavalry Division of six regiments, with machine guns and a battery of twelve guns. It looks from the above message as if they did not originally intend to attack Néry, but suddenly finding themselves in the fog within 400 yards of a British force in billets, decided to attack.

The brigade was ordered to join the cavalry division about five miles west, remained in position there about five hours, and eventually retired south to Borest.

Sept. 2nd. 1914.
Moved at dawn through the forest of Ermonville; glorious weather and glad of the shade. On crossing one of the rides, came on the tracks of horses and sent a troop to follow them up. They found the ride strewn with German kit of all kinds, lame horses, etc., showing a hurried retreat. They had gone by five hours previously and turned out to be our Néry friends, the cavalry division, who had bumped into one of our columns and retreated rapidly, leaving their four remaining guns.

At half past seven on the evening of September 1st, panic orders came for a sudden movement of G.H.Q. The driver of a car came in with word that a body of six or seven hundred *Uhlans* had been seen in the vicinity. A never-to-be-forgotten scene was staged in the leafy lane. The big lamps of the cars sent long shafts of light through the gathering dusk. Hurried packing was done by everybody. Groaning lorries were forced up the steep drive. A detachment of cavalry and the Bicycle Company attached to G.H.Q., some few foot soldiers, and a couple of lorry loads of Tommies hurried off together. No time was given to obtain food. Everything was helter-skelter. My car was the last out but one, and I left Dammartin with a sad realisation that my last remaining linen had been deposited that morning in Dammartin's sole laundry, and I had again left behind me goods and chattels which I was more than likely destined never to see again. I asked permission to go and retrieve my clothing, but was told that departure was a matter of the greatest urgency and I could not possibly be spared.

No one who took part in that inglorious scamper will forget it. We raced away in the night, the moonlight throwing deep shadows along the road. A few shots rang out—a dozen or so—which increased the general tension. Never was so much dust distributed over a flying column. The right side of the road was filled with slowly moving supply trains. French cavalry rode past, and French reservist infantry were occupying trenches along the roadway. A dozen aeroplanes loomed white and ghostly in a field as we swung by. Motor cyclists dashed in and out around the swiftly moving cars. We were white with dust from head to foot. G. H.Q. sped on through the night as though all the German devils were on our trail. After what seemed an interminable time we reached Lagny.

Such hurried departure from Dammartin produced confusion on

our arrival at Lagny. Our entry into the town was made through lanes of cheering crowds, who were to see the Germans enter the town not many hours afterwards. No cheering then, I imagine.

At one hotel only—the Hotel de la Renaissance—food was available, and there most of us got some sort of a dinner before the night was over. I was fortunate in dining off an omelette made from the last couple of eggs at 11.30, and straightway thereafter turned in on the floor of a hairdresser's shop facing the square, in which the G.H.Q. cars were drawn up in the pale moonlight.

CHAPTER 4

End of the Great Retreat

Sleeping in one's clothes on the hard floor of a shop and rising to a breakfast of lukewarm coffee and dry bread, the best available breakfast, is not the primrose path to a day of light-heartedness and good humour, but, nevertheless, I have rarely enjoyed myself so much as on that Wednesday, September 2nd, in Lagny.

Sir John French's army was piling south as fast as it could come. Past the Marne and on toward the south-east of Paris it was to file in hurrying columns.

All day long my car stood in the square at Lagny, save for a short journey or two about the town.

At 8.30 in the morning a big explosion near at hand, and a huge column of black smoke, followed by another fifteen minutes later, told of the French engineers who were blowing up the bridges over the Marne. All the morning they were at work demolishing bridge after bridge in and near the town.

At an early hour I encountered an old friend of cheery personality in Colonel Reggie Ford, the Deputy-Director of Supplies, and with him General King and General Gilpin, the Director of Transport.

A pleasant chat gave me some rough idea of our lines of retreat. That both our armies and the French were falling back steadily was about all the news at that time. The front of our line was to be south of Dammartin by nightfall if all went as planned. G.H.Q. was to move southward during the day, its next stop being Melun.

The sun was scorching down on us in earnest before the morning was well advanced.

I sat in my car and gossiped. A fortunate purchase of a goodly stock of red and white wines, as well as a couple of dozen bottles of mineral water made the cool shade of my hood and the soft, comfortable seats of my car all the more a port of call. The rich orchards of the surrounding valleys were groaning with delicious fruit. A countrywoman sold me a whole basket of luscious peaches and pears for a couple of francs. Life took on a brighter hue.

Some of the stories I heard that morning at Lagny were illustrative of the little that was known of the general plan of the campaign that was proceeding. Most of the corps commanders drove up during the day and called on Sir John French. The town was full of rumours of all sorts from every part of the line.

One G.H.Q. Staff colonel told me of one of our motorcyclists who had been found dead with lance holes in his hands and his body partially burned. I searched in vain for any corroboration of this report, though it was retailed to me in great detail and with absolute seriousness.

Another officer thought we had lost most of our guns. He could count thirty-seven to thirty-eight we had lost to his personal knowledge. One command that originally had twenty-four guns was left with but one, he said.

A General Staff officer who had been in touch with the staff of the French 5th Army on our right chatted for a long time about the disappointment of the French who had been fighting between La Fère and Guise on August 29th.

The French had a terrible hammering at Guise, he said. In spite of it they sprang a night attack on Von Kluck's left and won an unequivocal victory. Next morning they battered the Germans with 200 guns and almost had them on the run. The enemy retired, and the French were eager to follow up their advantage, sure of capturing no end of guns, which could not have been gotten away. Just then came the order to retire to Sains and Vervins. This, alas, was due to Sir John French having dropped back from Ham and Guiscard, in spite of the strong French force on his left which had come out from Amiens towards Peronne and Nesle. "All the French wanted us to do was to hold the centre. They begged us to do this, but back we came, and the opportunity was lost."

How bad my pessimistic friend felt and how little he knew of the great conflicts to the eastward that were preventing a stand being made in the western theatre!

Another ill-informed strategist explained that orders from Whitehall to keep a way open to the sea had forced the retreat to continue and Paris to be sacrificed. Our base at Boulogne was to be shifted to the mouth of the Loire, away to the southwest. Von Kluck was to gain his objective after all, and Paris streets would soon echo to the tramp of German legions!

Still another alarmist told strange tales of German *Uhlans* successful south of Dammartin and near at hand, but Borritt of the R.A.C. lot had just come from there, and declared such a rumour to be without the slightest foundation. Borritt had been compelled to leave Dammartin on the previous evening in such haste that he had no opportunity of collecting the bag containing his kit. He returned for it during the early morning. Conflicting rumours made him wary. Leaving his car south of the town he crept up the road stealthily, prepared to bolt if he saw Germans in Dammartin, as report said they were. After a careful reconnaisance he saw a khaki-clad soldier cross the road ahead of him, and on entering the town he found General Haig's Headquarters there. He told me the 4th Division and 19th Brigade had been formed into a 3rd Corps, with General Pulteney in command. They were in action, as a rearguard, on the extreme left rear of the retreating army.

Of the many stories that were rife in Lagny that day, none took account of the fact that Von Kluck would leave Paris to itself and swing to the southeast to smash the French 5th Army, as he was to endeavour to do during the next forty-eight hours. All were greatly concerned with the fate of Paris, which seemed doomed.

At noontide I was asked to take a sorry-looking German prisoner and his grimly cheerful guard, a splendid, big Cameron Highlander, to the railway station. One could hardly imagine so meek a German. Not a sound escaped him. Not a look did he give to right or left. I gave the Highlander a couple of apples from my store and he promptly handed one to the subdued Hun, who took it mechanically with not even a look of thanks. While detained at a level crossing, French soldiers, brimming over with good humour, crowded around the car to see the captive. They were kindly enough, in a rough way, and tried to cheer the poor beggar, but to no effect. Sadness radiated from him. He oozed despondency at every pore. I was glad to turn him over to the Railway Transport Officer.

The roads through Lagny were packed with fleeing refugees. White oxen in fours and fine big draught horses drew load upon load of them. Tandems of three pulled most of the great carts, and blocks in the traffic were numerous. Whole families were piled on wagons full of grain, three generations frequently in one party. Now and then a quartet of milk-white oxen lumbered along pulling a clumsy wagon crowned with a score of women and children huddled together under a dozen huge black umbrellas, an odd sight indeed.

All the afternoon tales of the fighting and explanations of and reasons for the retreat, coupled with prophecies of all sorts came from one quarter or another.

Late in the evening I had a moonlight run to Melun over a grand road. Dozens of sentries along the way stopped us and carefully examined our passes. Once we were held some time on account of our ignorance of the password, but finally allowed to proceed on the strength of my own French pass.

Refugees and columns of motor transports made slow travelling, and it was nearly midnight when we pulled up at G.H.Q. at Melun. I was not long in finding the Trois Monarques, and a drink wherewith to remove some of the dust I had been breathing for miles along the way. There I found Seeker, of the R.A.C. He had lost his car when *en route* to Senlis two days before. Crushed between two lorries and towed into Senlis, he hoped to effect a repair. News of the oncoming Germans emptied the garages of the few remaining workmen on September 1st, however, and the troops evacuated the town by eleven o'clock that morning. Seeker stayed until two o'clock, when the Germans were reported to be not far north, so there was nothing for it but to leave his car to the enemy and come sadly away on foot.

He was off to Paris at daybreak, he said, to purchase another car to take its place.

No room being available in the hotel, I obtained a billet in the Ecole Jeanne d'Arc, where the motherly old sisters provided me with a clean and comfortable cot.

September 3rd saw me in a new job, which was to last me for many interesting months to come.

The French Government had the day before left Paris for Bordeaux, and Headquarters of the French Armies and the French War Office were to move to Bordeaux that day.

The capitulation of the French capital seemed to most of us to be a foregone conclusion.

General Gilpin had purchased three motor-cars, which were to be assigned to Allenby's Division for intercommunication between cavalry brigades. I was asked to take the trio to Allenby's headquarters at Gournay, a village on the south bank of the Marne, a few miles east of Paris.

Anxious to see more of the actual fighting than I could possibly do if attached to G.H.Q., I applied to be assigned to the brigade work for which one of the three new cars had been purchased. My request was granted, and I was off and away from Melun in short order.

The run north on the main road to Meaux found even that broad highway well-nigh impassable owing to the lines of transport and columns of refugees. The hot days and long marches were telling on the poor fleeing country folk in sad fashion. On every side were sad sights—weary mothers wheeling poor little prams; one pathetic peasant woman seated on a bank by the roadside, rocking her dead baby and crooning over it; aged *grandes dames* tottering on the hot way; one well-dressed old lady, with shoes in hand, limping along, her bruised feet showing red through great holes in her thin stockings; and more than once some worn-out women, exhausted, lying prone in the ditch in merciful insensibility.

I lost one car en route, the driver being delayed and separated from us by a stop for a puncture.

Turning over his fellow to Colonel Ludlow, A.A.Q.M.G. of the 1st Cavalry Division, whom I found in a fine *château* at Champs, I slept the night in a stable, and was off at daybreak to find the lost sheep.

It was night on Friday, September 4th, before I returned with him. Back to Melun, then to our rail bases at Mormant, Guignes, Verneuil, and Chaumes, on to General Smith-Dorrien's headquarters at Maisoncelle, and at last to Sir Charles Fergusson's headquarters at Bouleur, I ran before my mission was accomplished. A spare car was fair game for all and sundry in those days. Each headquarters would gladly annex it should opportunity present.

At Champs, Major MacAlpine-Leny, 16th Lancers, on General Allenby's Staff, had the apportioning of the cars. Learning that I was keen on being sent to General de Lisle and his 2nd Cavalry Brigade, he very kindly arranged matters thus. I found General de Lisle and his staff in a deep wood near Champs. He at once welcomed me into his mess, presenting me to the other members of it, of whom I was to see much during the weeks that followed.

Captain Hamilton-Grace, 13th Hussars, was at that time Brigade-Major of the Second. Captain "Rattle" Barrett, of the 15th Hussars, who had captained the team that brought the International Polo Cup back from the United States, was staff captain. Lieutenant Fairclough, R.F.A., was signals officer, and Lieutenant Jeff Phipps-Hornby, of the 9th Lancers, the well-known gentleman rider, and Lieutenant Pat Armstrong, 10th Hussars, were *aides*.

Dinner by a camp fire in the woods, surrounded by the troops of cavalry, was picturesque to a degree. Rolling ourselves in our blankets, we were not long in wooing slumber, warned of an early start on the morrow.

So thick was the foliage under which I was sleeping, that a heavy rain fell in the night. without wetting or waking me.

We breakfasted by firelight soon after three o'clock on the morning of Saturday, the 5th, and were soon on the road for Limoges, eight kilometres north of Melun. The ghostly files of French and English cavalrymen had commenced their southward trek long before daybreak. The smaller roads to the west of the Forest of Armainvilliers were full of troops on troops of cavalry, so I chose a route straight south through the beautiful forest.

Each little town near the Aisne had its guard and quaint little fortifications. Here ditches, flanked by barrels of stones, there carts minus wheels and filled with bricks and cement. Now and again hastily-improvised stone walls, sometimes covered with branches, but always barricades of some sort at each entrance to each village, and all most conscientiously manned by a local guard.

The 4th Division and 19th Brigade, composing the newly formed 3rd Corps, were on the march south through the Forest. The Welsh Fusiliers and Scottish Rifles, unshaven and unshorn, tramped on in the early morning, already hot, looking fit in spite of their tattered array.

Arriving early at Limoges, I had time to run to Corbeil and back on a foraging expedition before the Brigade made an appearance. The three regiments were billeted in the farms about us, and a dear old woman in one of them cooked a splendid dinner, chiefly consisting of an omelette and a fat duck, for the headquarters' mess. Borrowing a small hand basin after dinner and repairing to a well in an orchard hard by, I indulged in a bath and general clean up.

The day was hot and clear. Most of the brigade were engaged in cleansing the dust from themselves and their kits and accoutrements, or in taking a midday *siesta*.

Suddenly, at four o'clock, came word that the brigade was to move at once to Chaumes, away to the eastward. We lost no time in moving. My work was to take Captain Barrett there at once to proceed with the billeting. This was concluded only to find orders were changed, and the brigade was to proceed still further eastward, through Mormant to Ozouer-le-Repos.

I slept on the grass under a great tree that threw a deep shadow in the bright moonlight. We all closed our eyes in different mood than on any night in the previous fortnight. We were moving to the east and the Germans were coming westward. At last we were advancing to meet the enemy. I felt a new life had begun. The very air seemed sweeter, the moonlight softer, the whole world a better place to live in.

Little, indeed, we knew, but that little was much to us.

Dawn of Sunday, the 6th of September, found me awake. The battle with the advancing enemy was to commence at last. At the breakfast table General de Lisle said to Hamilton-Grace, "See that the fighting men are in front today." Gastins, due east, was the first objective, and the Second Brigade was to lead the van.

That Sunday morning was to see history made. General Henderson's airmen had marked the eastward swing of Von Kluck's forces. Joffre was ready to strike, and, on Friday, had conferred with French. Maunoury was on our left, and Conneau's cavalry on our right, with d'Esperey's 5th Army east of him. At that hour the Germans—having reached the Petit Morin—were to find the river would mark the limit of their great advance.

Before the day was over Sir John French's order was to "call upon the British Army in France to show now to the enemy its power, and to push on vigorously to the attack."

The retreat was over—the advance begun.

We never doubted the outcome.

Early the order to form up was given. Through the wide village street the troopers in double column led their chargers, greeted by the rising sun.

Past the big stone barns and prosperous farm houses, past the grim old square-towered church, tramped the troopers. Now they were in saddle and in another moment away, a gallant sight indeed.

Again we had a day of dust and sweltering heat. Our line of advance was north-east, in the general direction of La Ferté Gaucher and the Petit Morin. When between Gastins and Pécy we were informed that a considerable German force was but a few miles ahead, and soon our advance guard was in touch with them.

Back and forth along the roads from time to time with various officers of staff, or standing by the general watching operations through field-glasses, new sights and scenes unfolded themselves during every hour of the day.

Regiments and batteries coming up through the fields, or pushing their way under orchard trees, bands of pickets riding in with reports and tearing away again at a gallop—all was never-ceasing movement.

While the morning was young a German shell burst in a farmyard near me, a score of geese and chickens its only victims, though it set a grain stack on fire.

The *whizzy-pop* of the shrapnel from the enemy's field-guns was to grow familiar before the day was over. One such shrapnel, unluckily placed, burst over a group of three officers and ten men of the 9th Lancers, hitting every one of them.

A message took me well to the front, to the gates of a big *château*. As we pulled away, a bang, followed by another, told of a couple of shell-bursts close behind us. A few minutes later, on another visit to the *château*, I saw six or eight troopers burying a still form wrapped in a rug. A quickly-dug grave by the gate was made, and the body laid in it without delay. Killed by the shells that had come as we left, they said, and killed at the very spot where the car had stood. Two wounded men, hit by the two shells, were lying near, and a sergeant showed me where a piece of shrapnel had torn away an ammunition packet on his breast, without inflicting other hurt than to bruise the skin.

Wounded came back, often supported by a comrade as the day wore on, and the fighting was sufficiently close to the point from which the general was directing operations, so that the merry popping of the rifles through the woods echoed all about us.

Scared inhabitants fled to the rear. Once or twice hysterical women in madly careering carts rushed past, threatening to smash into oncoming guns. Villagers who remained at home, old folk, looked awed and sombre on us as we passed. Colonel Seely materialised during the afternoon, and gave us news that Pulteney's 3rd Corps was fighting hard on our left, and the French on our right were fiercely engaged and foraging slowly forward.

We bivouacked that night in the fields, dining in the stubble by the headlights of the car, and sleeping in the open. A chilly night after the hot day, and wet with a heavy fall of dew.

Four o'clock on the morning of Monday, the 7th, saw us up and warming ourselves by the welcome fire, over which breakfast coffee was boiling.

Moving on, the objective of our column, one of three lines of cavalry, was in the general direction of La Ferté Gaucher again, leaving Croisy on our left. Conneau's cavalry was close at hand on our right, and keeping line with us.

A wrong turning at a crossroad put me in advance of the 2nd Brigade. I ran into a bit of sniping fire, but it soon ceased as our advance guard went forward. We were in touch with the enemy every foot of the way, though we had not as yet found him in force. Seven or eight *Uhlans* rode from behind a cluster of stacks, less than a thousand yards from us, and galloped to the north, a handful of our troopers hotfoot after them. Then heavy rifle fire in front, and, soon after, our guns.

Oh, the fascination of it! The glory of a galloping regiment of cavalry, flowing over a green field in line of squadrons! On we pushed. Past a little village in a valley, tucked away so cleverly one came upon it unawares, then on to a rise of ground, another dip, then a steep hill, and suddenly a shell burst right in front. I pulled up short. The fascination of it was like to run away with me when our own cavalry was chasing the German cavalry. Also it was like to run away with my judgment. A car might get further forward than necessary, perhaps even further forward than was wise.

Bang! bang! Two German shrapnel. *Whizz*, over and beyond, with a bang behind. *Crash!* One fell to the right, between two squads of galloping troopers. The horses reared and shied, but not one fell. The second group rode through the white shell-cloud, and dashed on.

Rifle fire ahead, and bang came a shell, bursting over me. Bang! Much too close!

I went into the village of Montcel to seek the protection of its buildings, leaving the car.

I passed up the wide street, deserted except by a dead German officer in front of a cottage, and gained the further edge of the cluster of mean houses that composed the village.

Behind a friendly stone wall, I stopped and took out my glasses. The stubble stretched away towards a line of woods.

Diagonally, across the broad road that led north from the village, came a line of horsemen.

Magnificent in the morning sun they rode, a solid line rising and falling with regular cadence, as though mechanically propelled.

The 1st Garde Dragoner Regiment of Berlin, of the Garde Cavallerie Division of the Garde Corps, the proudest, finest cavalry of the German Army—over one hundred of them, seeming double the number to me—were charging across the fields.

On they came, like machine-made waves on a machine-made ocean.

Then from the left shot other horsemen, one well ahead, another not far back, and a scattered scurrying bunch of two score behind, riding like mad, full tilt at the ranks of German pride and might bearing down upon them.

Colonel David Campbell, of the 9th Lancers, close on his heels Captain Reynolds, his adjutant, and forty-five of his gallant regiment were charging more than double their number of the flower of the enemy's horse.

The Germans quickened appreciably, and their lances waved downwards to the rest. Their pace was slow compared with the whirlwind rush of the smaller band.

I was on the wall when the impact came. *Crash!* went the 9th into the Garde. Colonel Campbell and Captain Reynolds were down, and horses reared and staggered. I wondered that none of the chargers funked it. Each horse seemed imbued with the spirit of his rider. Not one charger "refused."

No sooner had the smash come than I realised the wall was no place for me, so off I dashed to my car and safety.

The 9th scored heavily off their more numerous foes. A few fell, but more than double the number of Germans bit the dust. Crack British troopers proved their undoubted superiority, man for man, by the number of German dead and wounded we found on the field. Galloping on, the 9th circled round the village and away to the rear.

The Germans stopped, and many of them dismounted. One of them went coolly through the pockets of Reynolds, lying with an aluminium lance through his side. A farrier-sergeant lay dead near a pond at the village end. The Germans knocked in his head and tossed his body into the pool.

All this happened in the twinkling of an eye. Some of the Garde penetrated the village street, but returned after a gallop down and back.

By this time Colonel Burnett, of the 18th Hussars, with a dismounted squadron, had worked round to the left with a machine-gun. When he opened on them, the Germans mounted and swung by him and into the full line of fire.

That squadron of the 18th had a splendid target. The result was a field strewn with many German dead. The rest galloped away, leaving their wounded behind them.

One of the 9th, running out from the village to pull the lance from Reynolds's side, was shot dead by a wounded German lying near.

Strange sights were seen by some of the men in that charge. A non-

TROOPS GOING INTO BIVOUAC ON THE NORTH OF THE AISNE
THE DAY THE PASSAGE OF THE RIVER WAS WON

commissioned officer of the 9th ran his lance full through a German officer, who, thus impaled, stuck at the lancer and severed his hand at "the" wrist. One trooper of the 9th ran his lance straight through a German till his hand touched the doomed man's breast. A German horse was seen galloping away with a corpse pinned to its back by a lance.

Colonel Campbell, who so gallantly led the charge against such odds, received a nasty lance-wound through the shoulder.

I brought my car into the village. Entering a cottage in search of a sheet to throw over the disfigured face of a dead German officer, I found two women, who had been in the house during the fighting. They told me the Germans had spent a night in the village, and had treated them quite well. The German cavalrymen had food, said the elder woman, and left money therefore. She showed me a ten-cent Netherlands piece and a ten-cent Belgian coin, with a hole in the centre, with which the Huns had paid her.

In an orchard, around which ran the stone wall on which I had stood, we found two Germans hiding. One was the trumpeter of the Dragoner Garde, with painful lance holes in both his legs. A 9th trooper gave a German a cigarette and politely struck a match for him. The other prisoner was unwounded, and had been concealed near us, loaded Mauser in hand, for an hour or more. His discovery led to the orchard being thoroughly beaten, but no more game materialised.

By 9.30 the heat was as fierce as that of the average summer noonday. The general and his staff were scanning the country round from a stack not far in front. After I had delivered the papers taken from the prisoners found in the orchard, the general suggested I should break the lances of the dead German troopers who here and there dotted the field. I had not visited half a dozen before I found that some of the supposedly dead Germans were still alive. This necessitated a journey to advise our medical officer of quarry for him. Thereafter I mounted the stack in the heat and watched I Battery of the R.H.A. shell the wood in front of us.

A fine fight, Montcel. A fair charge, the smaller force scoring off the larger one by pure merit in handling of horses and weapons. The crack cavalry regiment of the Prussian Army met one of the best British cavalry regiments that day to the bitter cost of the former. Its casualties must have reached well-nigh one hundred all told. The Second Cavalry Brigade lost 8 killed, 22 wounded and 5 missing during the whole of the morning.

The wounded trumpeter of the Berlin Dragoner Garde after the charge of the 9th Lancers at Montcel.

So the forenoon passed in heat and inaction after the stirring events of the earlier part of the day. G.H.Q. had sent instructions that the cavalry were, until further orders, to keep the Dagny line. French aeroplanes reported the enemy in force at Choisy. Our brigade was to send patrols there, and to Chartronges and Leudon.

An *al fresco* luncheon, under a tree by the roadside, was interrupted by a French officer, whose motorcar panted up to us in a flurry. He brought the good news that the French were in line with us on both right and left, and that our British infantry had that morning taken Coulommiers, on the Grand Morin.

At two o'clock we were on the move. For half an hour I had the experience of being well shelled in Choisy, where a smart fight developed.

Every road about us vomited infantry, horse and guns. We were hard after the right wing of Von Kluck's army, pressing on as fast as orders from G.H.Q. would permit.

That night we slept in the village of Feranbry, just south of La Ferté Gaucher, which was in the hands of our infantry.

CHAPTER 5

The Winning of the Marne

Clean straw strewn on the stone flags of a farmyard made a bed fit for the gods, and at four o'clock on the morning of Tuesday, the 8th, I was as fresh as a daisy and ready and eager for further push to the north.

Feranbry was a woebegone sight on that lovely September morning. The Germans had dirtied the town inconceivably, smashing and looting the little shops and the dwelling houses. Many dead horses were scattered about the town.

We were treated to a wonderful surprise. As we started for La Ferté Gaucher the sky along the eastern horizon showed salmon pink and palest blue. The fields by the roadside were full of cavalry units and batteries of guns. Regiments advancing over the meadows in line of squadrons, an imposing array; batteries, belated, galloping into position with an inspiring rattle and bang over any and all obstructions; motorcycles dodging and panting past less swift users of the road; and even the push-bicyclists putting every ounce of energy into their pedalling—it was good to be alive that morning as the salmon in the east changed to pale gold and the blue to turquoise.

Over the brow of the steep hill leading down into La Ferté a splendid panorama was spread below. The white buildings, red-capped with roofs of tile, nestled in the valley and the rolling hills, well-wooded, rose beyond in myriad shades of green. Away to the right we could see French cavalry mounting the far rise. The morning air was heady as wine. The sun mounting upward, gathered all the rainbow hues of the sky into one great flaming ball, that gave promise of scorching heat when the delightfully cool morning breezes had left us.

La Ferté was cruelly smashed; the bridge over the Grand Morin blown up, but repaired for our passage. By the roadside at the top of the steep hill to the northward were slight trenches full of sleeping Tommies, lying rifle in hand.

Dense woods opened out into fields covered with signs of German bivouacs. Broken bottles were strewn everywhere. Dead Germans in ones and twos by the roadside, and dead horses in numbers, already fouled the pure air.

A German aeroplane soared above us. We were used enough to see enemy aircraft, but that morning the numerous troops were in the mood for action of some sort, and the appearance of the air scout was the signal for every man with a rifle to have a shot at the aerial target. The machine-guns began it, and when the infantry joined in a roll of sound swelled about us like the roar of a battle. On came the aeroplane, sailing high above in apparent safety. When it came over us our troopers took up the challenge. The bugles were ordered to sound "Stop firing," but were unheard in the din. Higher and higher soared the plane, and the rifles behind us popped intermittently, then settled into a rattle and roll as ours had done.

But all to no effect, as far as one could see.

On to the north we went through Rebais, more war-scarred than any of her sister towns to the south. Houses burnt and burning on either side of the street, dead Germans and dead horses so numerous they failed to attract more than a passing glance, the marks of shell-fire here and there—Rebais had seen a hard fight and bore the traces of it.

The Germans had been in Rebais two days, the townsfolk said.

I had orders to proceed to La Tretoire, but a kilometre from the town I found the 1st reserve line of the 4th Guards Brigade lying on the grass and waiting orders to move up and join the stiff fight the Coldstreams were having in the town in front of us.

Our field-guns on left and right were in action, and German shrapnel were bursting just ahead. The 2nd Division of Haig's Corps was spread along the road from Rebais, the tired men asleep by the roadway in all postures and positions.

The wounded from the fight in La Tretoire trickled back in increasing numbers.

Clouds had gathered and the day became suddenly cool. The reserve line moved up where the rattle of small arms told of the thick of the battle and our guns hammered away like mad.

One of General Haig's staff officers told me 100,000 Russians had come through England via Archangel, and were in Ostend. The story spread like wildfire, and I heard it from a score of others before the day was over.

The 2nd Cavalry Brigade had crossed the fields to the right. Putting the car at the stubble, I left the road and followed.

Watching batteries for a time, then moving on after the advancing squadrons, I reached the tiny village of Mont Vaudron, opposite the Petit Morin from the town of Sablonnières. Leaving the car in the shelter of a stout stone house, I crept down the hill to a point of vantage from which I could see the bridge below and the town to the right across the little river.

The German shrapnel were bursting on my right and behind me. Our shells were singing overhead, and bursting on the hill across the stream.

Down the wooded hill went the 4th Dragoon Guards and into the thick foliage. For a moment they flashed into sight as they dashed across the approach to the bridge. Straight on they rode, full into and over a mud parapet that the enemy had hastily thrown up across the further end of the bridge. After them ran the kilt-clad forms of a battalion of Jocks, who charged the town in the face of a heavy fire from in and behind the buildings. Sooner than it takes to tell it, the Scots, who, I later learned, were the Black Watch, had put to rout those of the enemy that were not killed or captured. Unable to catch more than fleeting glimpses of the fighting, I could see we had won the bridge and the town. Gaining my car, I wound down the roadway past a number of our dead, along the steep descent, and over the bridge to a group of thirty German prisoners, who had been taken in the town.

Pushing on up the long, winding, wooded hill to Hondevillers, I reached the town with our advance patrols, the last German disappearing over a farmyard wall and into the cover of the woods as we hove in sight.

Searching for General de Lisle, I ran to Le Petit Villers. There a couple of batteries of 1 8-pounders, soon to be reinforced by a couple more, were sending shrapnel as fast as they could fire into the retreating enemy.

A cloud of dust on the roadway on a distant hillside would tell of a line of enemy transport chased by our shells, while in the nearer distance a dozen shrapnel, well-placed in a cluster of houses, sent the Germans scurrying up the hillside like so many rabbits.

General Monro, commanding the 2nd Division, stood by the batteries, and watched the fleeting enemy with intense interest. All were engrossed with the work of the gunners, the noise being incessant and deafening. Suddenly, from a wood 800 yards to the left of us, a volley of Mauser bullets came. The Germans had crept into the edge of the trees and let fly at short range. There was a quick scamper for cover. Backing the car down the road into the protection of a wall, I found myself in a lane that had been chosen as an avenue for the battery horses and limbers.

A detachment of the Highland Light Infantry was on the double for a point where they could stop the fire on the batteries, which were spattering away merrily. Rain started to fall. I raised my hood, getting a bullet through it a moment later. Told in strenuous language that I was in the way, I dashed down a lane that ended in a ploughed field. Fortunately it was dry, so I made my way back to Hondevillers, and from there to Basseville, our night quarters. Fairclough and I made a night journey to La Tretoire in search of our Brigade cyclists, but could not find them.

After a late and meagre dinner, I tried to sleep in the tonneau of the car, which proved cramped quarters for my somewhat ample proportions, and when called at 2.45 on the morning of Wednesday, the 9th, I woke stiff and cold. An egg, a cracker, and a cup of black coffee warmed me, and we were soon on the road in the dark, headed for the Marne.

The crossing of the River Marne promised, we thought, a hard and costly fight. The rapid retreat of the Germans, withal we were hard on their heels, was more orderly than might have been expected. Little, indeed, did they leave behind except their dead. At La Tretoire we heard that the 1st Corps had captured men and guns, but that portion of the enemy's rearguard with which the cavalry had to deal succeeded in keeping his guns well out of our grasp.

Challenged every few minutes by sentries guarding sleeping detachments along the lesser lanes, twisting here and there in a vain endeavour to find anyone who knew the general route of any particular unit save his own, I lost the 2nd Cavalry Brigade before dawn that morning. Proceeding straight where I should have turned, I pushed past regiments of slowly moving cavalry until a peremptory order to put out the sidelights of my car, accompanied by the information that not even a cigarette was allowed thereabouts, led me to ask where I was.

"On the road to Nogent, and but a short way from it," was the reply, "and not far from the head of the 1st Cavalry Brigade."

Truly, thought I, a bit of luck. Briggs, I knew, had been assigned the attack on the bridge across the Marne at Nogent-l'Artraud, which lay midway between La Ferté St. Jouarre, which was to be taken by Pulteney's 3rd Corps, and Château-Thierry, where the 1st Corps was to force the passage of the river.

The line of the Marne, many of us thought, would be stubbornly held by the enemy.

Briggs, his Brigade confirmed, was to take, the Nogent bridge at daybreak. We waited on the hill above, the tall trees looming taller still in the dim light of the earliest morning.

Straining our ears, we heard no sound of firing. Daybreak came and passed, and still no guns. Not even a rifle-shot sounded from the valley below us.

It was an eerie vigil. We wondered what had gone wrong, when the show would commence, and whether the enemy would shell the main road on which we were waiting, in what was no doubt fair range of his guns across the river.

A French liaison officer chatted cheerily. He told us Maunoury had a strong line from Meaux north along the Ourcq, and would soon be across it and endangering the existence of Von Kluck's right and rear. He told us, too, of a savage battle for Montmirail the night before—he had just come from somewhere down that way—and how d'Esperey had taken the town at the point of the bayonet, and was ready to push forward on our right.

As five o'clock came without noise of battle, I drove on. Just above the town of Nogent, which is on the south bank of the river, a bicycle orderly stood panting from his exertions in coaxing his machine up the hill. He was the bearer of good news. The Germans had prepared the bridge for defence in a most careful manner, and guarded it till 4.30. Some said it was mined. At all events it was well-nigh impassable. At 4.30, for some inexplicable reason, the enemy evacuated the position, and fled without firing a shot, just as our advance guard reached the approach to the bridge.

I thereupon lost no time in reaching the bridge. Our troops were still crossing it. Briggs was swinging a regiment up the hill preparatory to getting our guns on the higher ground without delay.

Colonel Tommy Pitman, of the 11th Hussars, who had started for Nogent at half-past one in the morning, showed me the evidences of the thorough manner in which the enemy had blocked the way. The railway-gates at the south end of the bridge had been wound about with wire. Carts and obstructions all the way across had been woven into barricades with lengths of wire.

Colonel Pitman said his men were hard at work for three-quarters of an hour cutting their way through. And that without molestation from the Germans, the last one of whom was seen departing by motorcar in the distance, as the 11th came through Nogent. Walking over the bridge I strolled down the steep bank to the river's edge, meditating on the ease with which we had crossed the Marne, and with difficulty realising that I then stood on its northern bank.

The ground was strewn with bedding and miscellaneous loot. A mess of potatoes, pared and washed to an inviting whiteness, sat in a pot of water placed on carefully prepared twigs waiting the match. Just before daybreak, said an aged riverman, the Boches had moved all the barges and boats from the south bank and moored them on the opposite side. A novice could see the German departure from Nogent was a surprise to the enemy rearguard.

Regaining the bridge I watched long lines of our 2nd Corps infantry file past. Guns had begun long since, away to the west, and told of an argument over the crossing of the river at La Ferté St. Jouarre. There the 3rd Corps was to fight well through the day without winning the passage of the Marne until the German defenders of the town were compelled to retire by other 3rd Corps troops, who had crossed the stream further west at Changis.

At 7.30 our guns on the hill behind us dropped a couple of shrapnel on the ridge in front. A couple of minutes later the air was full of the sound of whistling shells as they sped high above the valley, bursting over the wooded crests to the north. White clouds in miniature lined the heights.

I was admiring the picture when a horseman came down the road and up to the bridge at a gallop. It was General Briggs.

"That your car?" he questioned sharply.

"Yes, sir."

"Go like the devil to that battery and stop its firing. It is shelling my men."

I went up the hill road, blocked with two descending lines of ammunition trains and regiment on regiment of foot soldiers, at a speed which would have caused a Surrey magistrate to search the statute-books for the extreme penalty of the law, had I been driving at such a rate on the Brighton road.

Luckily I found General Findlay, of the Royal Artillery, without delay and delivered my message, which I was told to repeat to a Brigade C.R.A. further to the rear. That mission accomplished I proceeded more leisurely down to Nogent again, and thence to Romeny, on the Château-Thierry road, searching for news of the 2nd Cavalry Brigade.

Dippers of delicious fresh milk, proffered by charming French lassies, were ample excuse for a momentary halt. Stories of the fleeing Germans were on every lip. For two days and nights the hated invader had been pouring north in two lines through Charly and Chezy. The Germans, but few of whom passed Romeny, laughed at the villagers, they said, some of them crying out as they passed that they were *Anglais, et bon amis*. Whereat the French girls chattered their disapproval. The German smiles fell on barren soil in Romeny, where the true French hearts beat hot with hate of the Boche, be he ever so genial to the non-combatant by the way.

"Rattle" Barrett, with an echelon of the 2nd Brigade transport, put in a welcome appearance, and suggested my looking for General de Lisle toward Chezy, to the westward. By half-past nine I had found him with General Allenby, at a farm south of Chezy. We pressed on the north, our objective being the village of Le Tholet, a few kilometres west of Château-Thierry, which had seen a stubborn fight.

The valley of the Marne afforded a beautiful view. White, fleecy cloudlets sailed lazily in a perfect blue sky. Chezy took the romance out of the panorama round about, however. Its churchyard was littered and its buildings smashed. The Germans left what had been a quaint, clean little town, dirty and foul with their passing. We climbed slowly up Mont de Bonneil after crossing the Marne. At noontide the heat was intense.

I followed Generals Allenby and de Lisle and the Divisional and Brigade Staffs across country. The dry stubble and hard meadows, free of fence or hedge, allowed ample scope for scouting a point of vantage whereby to cross the few ditches, and my progress was watched with interest by the mounted officers. A halt was made when the main Paris-Château Thierry road was reached.

News came that Baker-Carr, one of the R.A.C., leading half-a-dozen other cars, had declined the cross-country run and pushed on to Coupru. Approaching the village at a smart pace, a rifle volley stopped them short at a thousand yards. Such a competition in rapid backing and quick turning ensued as is rarely seen at the most lively gymkhana. Good luck for the little cavalcade of cars that the Germans opened fire at a distance, instead of waiting till their quarry had reached a sure range. Fortunately, none of the occupants of the cars were hit, though more than one of the vehicles bore marks of Mauser bullets.

A squadron of the 18th Hussars was sent to round up the enemy, and soon returned with a couple of dozen prisoners in tow, having killed the officer in command of the detachment and four or five of his men.

A strong, fine-looking lot, the prisoners. From Schleswig-Holstein, they said. Looked more like Danes than Germans. They were frankly glad to be out of the further fighting.

I spent the afternoon watching our gunners smash away at retreating columns of enemy transport, tearing northwards from Château-Thierry, where the 1st Corps had captured a number of prisoners, we were told, and a gun or two after a stiff fight.

Our night quarters were a near-by farm. I awoke on the morning of Thursday, September 10th, with a dawning realisation of the fact that the passage of the Marne was gained, and a great strategical victory had been won by the Allies.

We were well across the river as far east as Château-Thierry, where our right had been reached by d'Esperey's left. The news from further east was vague, but rumours of a great victory on the far right were afloat.

The Germans were on the run in earnest, and all was going well. Exactly what Maunoury on our extreme left and Foch in front of Châlons had accomplished was as yet unknown to us, but rumour was persistently cheerful.

So good was my bed of straw in the great yard of the farm that the rain at half-past two in the morning well soaked my clothing before I wakened sufficiently to realise the advisability of changing my billet for the drier, if less comfortable, shelter of the tonneau of the car.

There I slept so soundly that at four o'clock, when a member of the staff called me, breakfast was over, and I was told I had best be ready to depart instanter. A good-hearted woman of the household gave me a quart or so of milk in lieu of the breakfast I had missed.

An attempt to move my car was utterly abortive. At that most inconvenient of seasons I learned much of the theory of construction of a French farmyard. Built as it was in the form of a square or quadrangle, the centre devoted to an accumulation of manure and general refuse, one was wise to keep to the stone paved roadway round the sides.

Barrett and I had arrived "home" tired out at 11.30 p.m., and I had run the car well off the firm, stone-paved portion of the farm courtyard. The morning found it a couple of feet below the surface of the surrounding fringe of roadway. I enlisted the sympathy and assistance of the farmer, and the car was brought to firm ground by a team of fine French draught horses. This badly bent the car's back axle. Later, a cyclist informed me that this was a blessing in disguise, for, if ordered to follow my car, he could always depend on marking its passage by its peculiarly unorthodox wheel tracks.

Some 1st Division troops filed through the farm while the rescue work was in progress. Proceeding to the Paris-Château Thierry road, I was ordered by General de Lisle to take charge of our two-seated brigade car, the motor cyclists and the common or garden cyclists, and keep on to the right of the Brigade, which was to proceed across country to the northward. I obeyed these orders until I was informed I was leading my mixed, if small, command over somewhat new territory in the sense that no patrols had preceded us, when I changed my plans, and returned whence I had come with all my following.

Starting again, I followed the advance of the 1st Division to the left of the cavalry. Passing the long lines of infantry and many batteries was trying work. It was seven o'clock before I reached the head of the division. Past Lucy and Torcy we went discussing at times with passing officers the wonder we felt that the retreating enemy took no advantage of such splendid positions. Just north of Torcy I reached the head of the Sussex Regiment, which was in the lead. In front was Captain Nicholson with a squadron of 15th Hussars, Divisional Cavalry to the 1st Division.

Up a long steep hill into the village of Courchamps, the Scouts informing us of Germans just ahead and then a halt for a moment and a chat with the villagers.

"For five days and nights," said a woman, who was busy filling bowls of fine, fresh milk for the soldiers without a thought of remuneration, "the Germans have hurried northwards." The bulk of the retreating invaders had passed two days before, but some infantry went by later. The German cavalry were in the village an hour and a half before us. The villagers said many guns were with the German columns.

A drizzling day. Shortly after eight o'clock we halted in front of the town of Priez. On our left a transport column of the enemy raced northward, and shortly afterwards we could see a line of motor lorries away on our right tearing along at high speed, as though belated to a point of great danger and in full realisation of it.

A fierce cannonade on our left told us of the 3rd Corps at La Ferté-Jouarre.

General Bulfin, commanding the 1st Brigade, asked me to what I was attached. On learning I was with the cavalry he bemoaned the fact that the cavalry were not on his left, as the fast disappearing transport of the enemy would have fallen an easy prey to one of our cavalry brigades on that flank.

Major Frazer, of General Allenby's staff, drove by at nine o'clock, and asked why I was making no progress toward joining the cavalry division. I explained that the only available road to the east had but recently been reached by the infantry advance, and was even then being fired over by the machine-guns dinning away a few hundred yards in front of us.

Priez lay in a valley. The top of the slope beyond was plainly visible from where we stood. Bulfin's brigade was advancing up the far hillside as we chatted, and nearing the crest. An ideal spot, I thought, for a stiff German rearguard action.

Frazer suggested our proceeding as far as the village. I accompanied him, leaving my convoy of cycles behind. We dismounted from our cars in the hollow, after passing the village proper. The deployed lines—consisting of Sussex and South Hants Regiments—had reached the crown of the hill in front. Their arrival was the signal for the commencement of a very pretty little fight.

The rifle fire grew in volume until singing bullets were so frequent at the point we had chosen that I took cover in a roadside ditch. My attention was arrested by the frantic efforts of a scared woman to close the shutters of an adjacent house, the side of which was being well peppered.

Turning from my momentary aberration, I discovered that Frazer's car had returned from whence it had come. A lonesome feeling coming over me, I left the ditch and the car, and ran across the road to the shelter of a bank, behind which a number of the Sussex Regiment were taking cover. I found the detachment was A Company, Captain Bond commanding.

After a quarter of an hour of enjoyment of good shelter from the increasing Mauser pellets, an order came to A Company to advance up the hill to the firing line. They started off to the right, taking such

Melinite shrapnel bursting above the Chavonne ridge

2nd Life Guards in the straw-filled reserve trenches on the Aisne heights

cover as the low bank afforded. A disinclination to be left alone in such a warm corner led me to accompany them.

The enemy had succeeded in driving back the left of the British line, which enabled them to cover our advance up the hill from our left flank. A number of our party were hit, particularly at an open space fifty feet in extent, where the bank at the roadside was quite unnecessarily low. The two men immediately in front of me and the man just behind me were hit, all three being wounded in the head.

The German guns opened on the village behind us and the slope away to the rear. Our guns replied, but their range was short, some of the shells bursting over us.

To me the situation seemed somewhat bizarre. Our enjoyment of our surroundings was by no means augmented by one of the Sussex men from the line in front, who came running back with the news of a general retirement. Rifle fire in front, rifle fire from our left, and shrapnel from both front and rear, made us wonder whether retirement was not less wise than staying where we were. But orders are orders, so we headed down the slope for the village.

Reaching the fifty-foot gap, a couple of bold ones rushed at it, only to fall before they had got across. That part of our journey must, it seemed, be taken in full sight of the enemy. While pausing and contemplating this fact, a herd of a score or more cows galloped, bellowing, down the hedge-side in the field by us. Suddenly blessed with an inspiration, we sprinted down the road in the lee of the barrier thus providentially imposed between us and our friends the enemy. "We're all right so long as the beef holds out," panted a Tommy, as the bullets went "*puck-puck*" into the cattle.

In a matter of seconds I had reached the car, and was mentally consigning it and its contents to the Boches, when a major of the Sussex battalion asked me if I would take it back with as many of the wounded as we could pack on it. I was of the belief that any occupant of a car that tried to pass through the village and up the slope in plain sight of the enemy, and in the direct path of his shrapnel, would stand little chance of escape, but the wounded were tossed into the tonneau, into the front seats, on the folded hood at the rear, and all about, wherever space could be found. I jumped into the driving seat, and backed the car to the cross-roads in the town, suffering a collision with a wall en route.

The car's steps were lined with soldiers, and one was mounted on a front wing.

"Now, boys," I said, as I headed the car round for the dash up the hill, "the rise is steep, and this is no 'General' omnibus. All that are not wounded hop off, and I'll see if I can get the rest out of it."

With a cheery word they jumped off, except one, who stood on the step at my side.

"Are you hit?" I queried.

"No, but I'm all right. I won't fall off, guv'nor," he replied with a grin.

"If you are bound to come with us," said I, "vault up behind me and stick on."

He did so, and as I felt his hand on my shoulder I looked up at him and remarked, "I've got you between me and the Germans whatever happens."

But we found that ride no joke.

Up the hill we crawled. My load was eleven, some badly hit. Two cyclists in front gave promise of blocking the way as we gathered speed, but a shell burst over us that knocked one of the pair off his wheel. He careered into his fellow; the pair rolled into the ditch together. *Bang!* went another shell, seemingly a few feet over us. Four men from a group ahead of us were hit, so falling that they almost blocked the roadway. Bullets sang all about. Someone hanging on one of the steps was hit, and cried out as he dropped off. As the slope became less steep I overtook an ammunition limber, the team—minus driver—in full flight toward the rear. Off the road and into the dry stubble field I guided the groaning car, past the tired horses, galloping their poor best, and into the road again, urged, by a quartet of shrapnel that seemed to burst—oh!—so close to us!

A mile or so in the rear, we found a hastily improvised hospital, in a field by the road, where I delivered my load. An orderly came to me as I drove up, saying laconically, "Wounded?"

"Yes," I answered, "all but one." Turning, I sought the persistent one whom I had mounted at my back.

"*I* stopped one, coming up the hill," said the object of my remark, with a grin—"I stopped one proper, I did!" And as he disentangled his feet from those of a sadly wounded comrade on whom he had been supporting himself, he opened his tunic and showed me a blood-soaked side. "Through," he explained. "Might have got you if I hadn't been there," he added, "So maybe it was just as well. I couldn't have brought the others back in this thing." And he grinned again as I put him down where the orderlies could get him.

"Good luck, son," I said, with a lump in my throat. His teeth were set as he was borne by two hospital men to where the doctors could attend to him.

As they took him down the bank the corners of his mouth twitched in another half-smile, and he said, "Thanks. Don't you worry about me; I'm all right. It's nothing!"

I have often thought of him, and hoped he came through in good shape. His spirit was so very, very fine.

Wiping some of the red off the cushions of the car, I turned it again towards Priez, and ran as far as a haystack, to the right of the road. The rain had ceased. I sat with some of the King's Royal Rifles in the lee of the stack for a time. Shrapnel was bursting near by. Two big high-explosive shells went over us, and lit not far behind. Some of General Lomax's staff and a number of 1st Division officers were in front of the stack. I joined them and distributed some chocolate I had in the car, which was very cheerily greeted. Shells came closer. As an excuse to get back for a breathing space, I picked up three or four passing wounded, to take them to the dressing station. No sooner had I started than a blinding flash in front, and a black smoke cloud in our eyes and nostrils, told of the arrival of another high-explosive shell. It had lit in the road, striking two mounted orderlies. The horses and men were literally blown to pieces, and the road scarred with a huge hole.

One poor chap in the car was so near gone when we arrived at the hospital that his chances were declared by the doctor to be one in a thousand.

Through the middle of the day and into the early afternoon our guns hammered at the enemy. Another infantry Brigade was sent up and forced the Germans to retire. The action was only a rearguard fight, but the considerable number of wounded in the dressing station, and all along the road, told of the efficiency of it. A constant procession of stretchers went past. General Findlay, seated beside the road, not far from the haystack that gave me shelter for a time, was hit by shrapnel and killed.

The Sussex Regiment lost heavily. Not only were their casualties considerable, but among the list were some of their best officers. Altogether, Priez cost us between three and four hundred killed and wounded.

Shortly after mid-day one of General Lomax's staff asked me to take a message to General Allenby.

A COUPLE OF BATTERIES OF 18-POUNDERS BEHIND THE AISNE HEIGHTS

This required my going south, and then turning east and north again. The left of d'Esperey's 5th Army was in touch with our right. Passing Grisolles and Rocourt, and proceeding north toward Oulchy-le-Château I saw many French troops, but could get no word of Allenby. I watched a couple of batteries of 75's shell Oulchy. The French officers were very friendly. As the white shell clouds burst against the dark green foliage in front we chatted of prospective victory. They were pleased when I told them that one of our Divisions, checked for a moment at Priez, had taken it and pushed on to shell Neuilly-St. Front. Soissons and Braisnes were *their* objectives, the French officers said.

I pushed on to a high point, and at last met General Allenby, whom I had almost despaired of finding. I delivered my message, and mounting a haystack watched the French infantry attack north of Oulchy, supported by French and English batteries.

In the evening, with General de Lisle, I visited Grisolles, Latilly, Nanteuil and Rozet-Ablin. These little towns in the valley of the Ourcq were charming in their simple beauty. The Germans had not stopped long nor done much damage thereabouts. The coming of the Allies had restored confidence in the twinkling of an eye. Already the peasant folk were at work digging their hidden stores of flour from out their straw stacks.

Captain Barrett and I spent most of the night searching for our Brigade transport, which had gone astray. Discovering it at last, and providing the officer in charge with a map, we ran back to our night quarters at Rozet. There we slept on couches in the partially dismantled drawing-room of a house which a villager described as the property of a French field-marshal. Dinner having been consumed in our absence, Barrett and I made a hearty meal off cold soup, bread and jam, and slept soundly until four o'clock the next morning.

The first hours of the next day we spent in careering about the country for news of horse transport, which had gone stubbornly astray in spite of maps and instructions. Through village after village we searched for a time to no avail. Three small detachments had spent the night in the same little village without any one of them being in the least aware of its proximity to the others. At daybreak the three had left, still unconscious that their fellows were hard by, each to go in a different direction. We found them all at last, after unravelling Gilbertian blunders on the part of thoroughly muddled "non-coms." It is easy to laugh at such "Mix-ups" when they become disentangled, but truly difficult to do so until the trouble is over. Horse transport trains breed short tempers more often than not.

Our course bore eastward, and then north for Braisnes. Close to us on the right Conneau's French cavalrymen were advancing. They bore signs of campaign wear. Our appearance was far from prepossessing. A wash was a luxury and a shave unknown. Dirty as we were I think the French were dirtier. Their rusty *cuirasses* helped to give one such an impression, as did the once white bits of trimming on their uniforms. The *Chasseurs d'Inde* looked a wiry lot. Their baggy blue trousers, red jackets, and red *fez* on yellow turban looked still gay, though well-begrimed. Their dapper little Arabs stepped gingerly, aware all eyes were on them.

We passed several groups of German prisoners. General de Lisle told me our 1st and 2nd Divisions captured over 1,000 of the enemy the day before, and with them seven guns. Later reports swelled this to double the number of prisoners and guns, and rumour told that machine-guns and transport had; also been taken.

Breakfast in an open field found us munching bully and dry bread with true ardour. For luncheon we brought similar appetites to an identical menu. Blinding downpours of rain fell for most of the afternoon. Our forward movement was curtailed by orders from above. The 9th Lancers had pressed well on toward Soissons. De Lisle sent me to Maast to recall them. Major Beale-Browne, commanding the 9th, said Lucas Tooth's squadron was beyond Nanteuil, and well up the Soissons road. Would I run on and pass the order to reassemble? Certainly. Reaching them in the rain Lucas Tooth told me they had chased the *Uhlans* just over a ridge beyond. One of his troopers saw three or four of the enemy and rode at them with a yell. They dashed back and soon overtook seventy of their comrades.

Catching sight of the larger body the 9th trooper turned and galloped for assistance. The *Uhlans* came on slowly behind him. Gathering together the troop of which he was a member, the handful started full tilt for the enemy. The moment the troop came over the brow of a rolling hill, and in sight of the Germans, the latter, disregarding their greatly superior numbers, turned and fled. Our cavalry was gaining a sinister reputation.

We spent the night of Saturday, the 11th, in Arcy, where a good dinner cheered us all. A hot bath in a wash-tub, and a blanket-bed on the clean tiles, made for solid comfort.

On the morning of Sunday, the 12th, a French officer told us how well the Allied Forces were succeeding. Foch had pressed on and might soon be at Rheims, he said.

I was with the extreme advance during the forenoon. Rifle shots close at hand; pools of fresh blood in the roadway; dead horses, not yet cold, and scared peasants, all told of cavalry patrols in collision at daybreak. We stopped on a line of hills. Down the slopes in front lay Braisnes and the crossing of the Vesle. We were afforded a splendid view of the field-gun battle for the river. The horizon in front and away to the right, as far as the eye could reach, was one long line of black or white shell-clouds. Dozens, scores, hundreds of cloudlets, ever changing, new ones born with every second, yet no two alike in form.

Before eleven we lunched. A big round loaf of bread, to obtain which a kindly native walked two miles, a tin of sardines, two tins of bully beef, a tin of marmalade and a tot all round of wonderful Army rum, provided a hearty meal, not only for our own staff but for General Allenby and many of the divisional staff as well. Rain fell in sheets while we were lunching, our dining-room being the shelter, more imaginary than real, of a small haystack. The fight for Braisnes was within earshot. The Germans had barricaded the bridge and the main street of the town, and were putting up a strong rearguard action.

Some of the 3rd Division Infantry Battalions trudged by at a good pace unmindful of the downpour or the mud underfoot. Many of the Tommies had ponchos, some had overcoats, and here and there a blanket or brown gun-cover kept off the wet. Only a few of them were without protection of a sort. By noon-time the bridge was taken, and a couple of hours after we moved up. The Queen's Bays had been in the lime-light, and greatly distinguished themselves. From the winding wooded road down into the valley the hills across the river loomed grey-green in a rain-mist.

On the bank by the way lay the dead body of Bertram Stewart of the Intelligence, who had taken a rifle and gone down to lend a hand. Beyond him a wounded trooper sat propped against a milestone gasping with pain. Across the bridge we came upon a broken bit of loop-holed wall, then a barricade of sand-bags in the street, a score or more of German prisoners, a crowded ambulance, and behind it an old rickety one-horse landau, creeping slowly so as not to jar the wounded soldier stretched on a door laid crosswise over the carriage superstructure. The main thoroughfare was full of infantry. The 1st Cavalry Brigade that had taken Braisnes was on ahead, winning the

German positions on the slopes beyond the town.

Shops were emptied in short order of what little the Germans had left untouched. A dear old Sister of Mercy, not five feet tall, found me endeavouring to make a purchase of *viands* of some sort and took me under her wing. Calls on storekeepers proving futile she guided me to a pretentious dwelling. Here we found an old lady who gave me a half a loaf of bread, a small pat of butter, and a bottle of wine for our mess. She could not be induced to take any remuneration. A shell hole had ruined the grass plot in the centre of her dainty garden, having first passed through her bedroom. The Germans had demanded her keys at the point of a pistol and had well ransacked her house, she said. She was a sweet old lady. How a human being could maltreat her I could not imagine.

The fight for the hill north of Braisnes was not over, but after half-an-hour's wait behind a haystack outside the town I was allowed to proceed. At the base of the hill our shrapnel had played on the roadway with deadly accuracy. The ditches were full of dead and wounded Germans. The steep slopes were lined with well-made trenches one above another. On up the winding road that mounted the slope we toiled, three lines abreast, squadrons of cavalry, lines of ammunition wagons, motorcars and horse-guns all together.

The rifle and rapid gun-fire from the crown of the hill was still telling of the stubborn fight while we were crawling round the lower curves of the ascent. As I gained the crest I saw a group of over 100 German prisoners and piles of broken German rifles by the road. Still more lines of trenches disfigured the fields on either side.

Our billet for the night was the quaint village of Longueval, less than two miles from the Aisne. I was alone in the car with General de Lisle when we entered the village. We were well ahead of our troops. Personally, I felt some qualms at such a reconnaissance, but we found no Germans thereabouts. The people were most cordial in their welcome, and told us the enemy's troops had been billeted on them for the past ten days. A big stone farm with an ample yard housed the headquarters' contingent. After dinner, I took Raymond Hamilton-Grace to General Allenby's headquarters for orders. That run in the dark, rain, wind and mud, was a veritable nightmare. Several times carefully-followed instructions as to the localisation of Divisional Headquarters were proved to have been utterly wrong.

Once we went past our last outpost and into the light of the still burning ruins of farms beyond it. When we at last located the head of the division, we found it planted in an awful hole, approachable only through a sea of mud. Our quest for orders was in vain, as no orders had yet been issued. I had hoped for a letter from home, as not one line from London had reached me since my departure nearly a month before. But no letter awaited me. It was late when we returned to Longueval, and a bundle of straw on a stone floor made a tempting bed.

CHAPTER 6

Wine From a Mountain Cave

On the morning of Sunday, the 13th, no less an undertaking than the crossing of the Aisne was to fall to the lot of the cavalry. Orders had come for a general advance. The 1st and 2nd Cavalry Brigades were to move north. The 2nd Cavalry Brigade was to reconnoitre the river crossings from Villers to Pont-Arcy.

The item of the greatest interest to me in the daily orders was the point given as the general objective of the Brigade. No matter how impossible for motorcars the country which de Lisle would traverse with his troopers, if I knew the objective, I would be there before his arrival, or close after it. The point given as the 2nd Cavalry Brigade objective that 13th of September, was Chamomile, a village some ten kilometres due north from Bourg, on the road to Laon. Night did not find us at Chamomile. True, we were to cross the Aisne on that day, and to do so in unexpectedly good time. Chamomile, however, we were not to see that day, nor the next. Nor have English or French troops set foot in that village yet, though another 13th September has come and gone.

At 4.30 a sergeant came in with the report that the bridge across the Aisne at Villers had been found destroyed, and a pontoon bridge had been had been constructed within fifty yards of it. A bit later came a report from Bourg. The bridge there also was destroyed, but a nearer bridge over a canal that ran parallel to and south of the river had been left intact. More important, a third bridge in the vicinity, by which an aqueduct was carried over the main stream of the river, was still standing. If that bridge could be rushed, the passage of the Aisne would be secured and a way made for the advance of the troops of the 1st Infantry Division behind us.

Daylight struggled through the haze just before five o'clock, and showed us a lowering sky. A sharp burst of heavy rain fell.

The 9th Lancers and the 4th Dragoon Guards were ordered to take the Bourg bridge at five o'clock, and effect a crossing of the river.

Why we were allowed to get over the Aisne with so comparatively little opposition at Bourg will probably never be known. Some German had blundered, and blundered badly. A couple of batteries of our field-guns gave the town a sound shelling, and the dismounted troopers surged across the canal bridge. At the far side the damaged river bridge gaped before them. On their left was the aqueduct bridge. Behind its embankment were German infantry with a machine-gun. Their position rendered them safe from our shells, and gave them opportunity to pour a fire into the flank of our attack, almost into its rear. Nothing remained but to rush the enemy, which was done most gallantly, and with gratifying success.

The 4th D.G.'s lost Captain Fitzgerald and four or five men killed at the bridge, and the 9th Lancers suffered some casualties, but, considering the advantage gained and the importance of the crossing, the resistance was absurdly slight. When the aqueduct bridge was finally won, and the Germans who defended it dislodged or killed, great was our amazement at the weakness of the force which had been left to guard it. The German guns from the heights north of the river began shelling Bourg as soon as we had taken it, but for the most part they were busy protecting the broken bridge at Pont-Arcy and the pontoons at Chavonne, both to our left. At these points the 2nd Infantry Division met stubborn resistance, but eventually won their way across the river.

Showers came and went. The roads were deep with mud. I crossed after the guns. The main bridge over the river being impassable, my only alternative was the aqueduct bridge. The half towpath, half lane beyond was not meant for car traffic. The artillery had ploughed through, however, so on I went. Axle-deep in thick mud, slipping, sliding, skidding slowly forward, I at last came to the point where the guns had made a path up the steep bank to the main roadway beyond. No choice remained but to charge it at such speed as one could muster. Near the top the whirring wheels refused to bite, and back the car slid towards the river. At the edge of the bank the driving wheels luckily encountered some obstacle that gave them a grip, and the straining, striving car slowly crawled upwards, eventually to force its way, back wheels revolving at full speed in the ooze, up to and over the crest of the bank and on to safety beyond.

THE FAMOUS SUGAR MILL TRENCH ABOVE TROYON

HIDING CHARGERS BEHIND THE ROAD BANK
FROM THE ENEMY OBSWERVERS

The 2nd Cavalry Brigade advanced north towards the town of Vendresse, three to four miles distant. The 1st Infantry Division tramped along in their wake.

Towards noon I encountered an orderly who said General de Lisle wanted me to come up front and bring the luncheon basket, to carry which had now become a daily duty. As I passed detachments of cavalry on the Vendresse road I asked if the general had gone on in the direction I was pursuing, and invariably was answered in the affirmative.

As the road became free of lines of Tommies and ammunition waggons I quickened my pace. At the side of the road the 4th Dragoon Guards stood, dismounted. Someone at the head of the column waved as I sped by, and gave a friendly shout. I waved in return, slowing to pass a squadron of that regiment proceeding in column of twos towards Vendresse. I had lowered the hood, encouraged by a glimpse of the sun, but as I reached a sharp bend in the road not far from the town a sudden shower pattered down, the big drops promising a quick drenching. Mindful of the lunch in the tonneau I stopped the car and jumped out to raise the hood. Before I had done so the squadron overtook me and passed on the trot. First I was tempted to hasten and precede them, but a refractory nut delayed me, so I let them pass, tailing an affable sergeant at the rear, who threw me a cheery word as he jogged by.

A moment later a sharp rattle of fire directly in front, and the whirr of bullets all about, made me pull up in record time, throw in the reverse, and back frantically for the shelter of the bank around the turn. The scattering shots became an angry roar, and a storm of whistling missiles sped overhead. The horsemen left the road at the first volley, and disappeared into the scrub on the left, some of their number falling before they could escape from the path of the fusillade. A bullet tore through the canvas of the hood and gave one of the sticks a nasty smack, but in less time than it takes to tell it I was out of harm's way behind the shoulder of the hill. Backing to the 4th D. G.'s, Colonel Mullins greeted me with a sarcastic question as to whether I was trying to get killed. "Playing at advance guard with a car," he termed it.

What I had taken as a friendly wave in passing had been an effort on his part to stop me, as General de Lisle had left the road at that point, and climbed a hill to the left. The fire grew hot again in front, and stray pellets spattered round, so I turned the car in the narrow road and ran further to the rear. Our batteries began the game of dislodging the enemy from Vendresse and the slopes beyond.

An officer from G.H.Q. drove up and chatted for a time. We were not the only part of the army across the Aisne, he said. The passage of the river had been won by the 3rd Corps to our left and by the 2nd Corps beyond them. All along the seventeen miles allotted to the British front the north bank of the stream was ours save at points of exceptional strength, such as Condé, which was, it proved later, to remain in German hands for many a long month. He told me the sum total of official casualties to that date. Out of 15,800 the number of killed, wounded, and missing, 12,500 were missing, most of the latter being killed or wounded of course. This intimated a sad jumble of reports due to the confusion of the retreat.

By two o'clock I found the chief and his staff, who welcomed the luncheon-basket. Before our repast was over the German shells were searching thereabouts, two disquieting visitors coming close over us. Orders came to move back. As I had headed the car forward I was told to turn again and make for a safer position. As I backed to do so two more shells fell in the road not far distant. My consequent effort to rush matters resulted in my back wheels becoming embedded to the hubs in soft earth at the roadside. *Whizzy-bang* went two more big ugly fellows just beyond. No one was in sight along the way. What to do I did not know. Reckless efforts to jerk the poor car out by its own power drove the rear wheels deeper in their soft bed.

Bang—bang—bang—bang!

Four shrapnel burst over the trees across from me and rattled and crashed through the branches with a terrifying din. I was at a loss for a solution of my difficulty, and became apprehensive of results.

Down the road from the rear came a two-seated car. The driver pulled up, took in the situation at a glance, dismounted, and producing a stout rope, tied it to my car, and coolly towed it on to the roadway. No sooner had he done so than a very rain of shells fell over the road fifty yards ahead.

Thanking him and admiring his coolness, I explained that the headquarters of which he was in search was further to the rear, and we pulled out without delay to a safer locality. I never learned the name of my benefactor. His pluck saved me. The next day I examined the spot and found two good-sized shell-holes had been made in the road not ten yards from where I had been so ignominiously stuck.

The brigade went to the high ground between the Bourg-Vendresse road and Verneuil. A battery was shelling the Germans from that position, and soon the German guns replied. The 9th Lancers suffered on the ridge, losing Captain Lucas Tooth, a splendid cavalry officer. Before dark we were relieved by the Rifle Brigade, and our troops went into billets at Oeuilly. A *château* there had been left in a filthy state by the Germans, but piles of clean straw in the ransacked drawing-room made a comfortable resting-place.

On Monday, September 14th, I was called at a quarter-past two in the morning, and asked to be ready to start at 3.30. We were still inclined to wonder by what good fortune we had been allowed to force a way across the Aisne at Bourg, the day previously, with such great success and so few casualties.

Our passage of the Aisne and our pressing forward to Vendresse and up to the Chemin des Dames, a great east-and-west highway beyond, was so important a move, and bore such prospect of result, that it was but natural we should be in ardent expectation of a sight of the Rhine within the near future.

The winning of Bourg, and the consequent following up by Haig's 1st Division of the advantage thus gained, gave Sir John French an opportunity to quickly develop the situation by a general push along our whole front on that Monday morning. We learned that Maunoury, with his French Sixth Army, had crossed the Aisne between Compiègne and Soissons. We knew the French were across the Aisne on our right and we were expected to advance to a new line from Laon, due north from Bourg, to Fresnes, which lies practically due north from Soissons. The 2nd Cavalry Brigade was ordered to move off at once *via* Troyon and Courtecon. Our route from Oeuilly led to Bourg, then north. Between Bourg and the Chemin des Dames the road lay through beautiful country. Well-wooded heights rose on the left, and the way ran along a deep valley until reaching Vendresse, then wound upward past the little village of Troyon. Just before it reached the Chemin des Dames the road passed a large sugar mill. The town of Courtecon, our objective for that day, lay beyond. Courtecon was at that time, and has always been since, in German hands.

We started full of hope of pressing on to further success, the Battle of the Marne fresh in our minds.

In the dark and the rain, without any lights, the road full of cavalry regiments and attendant batteries of artillery, progress was slow. Ahead of the brigade, I found a detachment of infantry, which challenged in the dark in so truculent a manner that I decided to wait and allow some of our own command to precede me. I brought the car to rest at a point where the road from Bourg forked, one branch leading to Vendresse, the other to Moulins. As I waited in the rain a single shot rang out on the ridge, the dark woods of which towered above. The brigade advance guard came up, de Lisle and his staff close behind. The general directed me to follow after him, preceding the advance squadron of the 9th Lancers, which was under command of Captain "Rivy" Grenfell.

Passing through the dark gorge before the road curved round to the right and left as it entered the first scattered houses of the village of Vendresse, I lost touch with the advance party and the general. Slowing down, I had a chat with Captain Grenfell. I told him that my orders were to push on, but that I thought it would be wiser for me to keep out of the way of his advance squadron and follow behind it. I was not sure of the road, had lost the advance guard, and manoeuvring the car without lights, with no one preceding me in the roadway, might cause some delay and confusion. Grenfell agreed that I should be less in the way if I would follow his squadron. This decision undoubtedly saved my life.

We toiled along in the dark, when suddenly from the front came the rattle of machine-gun fire and a storm of bullets. The road was sufficiently wide for me to turn the car. I sped away towards the other squadrons of the 9th Lancers, which were coming up. The leading squadron, behind which I had been crawling, scattered off the road when the machine guns in front opened fire. The first volley shot Captain "Rivy" Grenfell dead, a bullet striking him in the forehead as he was riding up the road.

The Germans were bent on holding the crest of the hill. General Bulfin's 2nd Brigade, the Sussex, the Northamptons, and 60th Rifles, were on our left front. The 4th Guards Brigade were further to the left, but what troops, if any, were on our right I could not discover. The machine-gun and rifle fire grew increasingly heavy in front. The enemy were in greater strength than we had anticipated. For a time I sat in the valley with but little information. Stories were told me of Captain Grenfell's squadron, one being that the Germans had allowed our advance guard to pass through their lines before opening fire. Later we learned that the advance guard had left the road, and Grenfell's squadron was acting as the point.

A motorcyclist was sent up to get information of the situation on the crest. On his return he reported that our brigade was well under cover, and we were holding our position but not advancing. Later an orderly from the front, with a moment to spare, told me our troops were no further forward than the point we had reached the day before. A captain who had a scouting party along the crest during the night joined our conversation. He said he saw no Germans above Vendresse, evidence that some of the enemy had advanced at dawn. Some Scots Guards came down the hill wounded, and reported that the fire from the enemy in the vicinity of the sugar-mill was very heavy.

It was a rainy, dreary morning. By seven o'clock a number of wounded had come to the dressing station at the foot of the hill. Our batteries had begun firing, but so far no enemy shells had disturbed us. Another of our batteries dashed up towards Vendresse, a most inspiring sight. Major Beale Brown, of the 9th Lancers, told me more of Captain Grenfell's death. His squadron had proceeded under the impression that they were following the advance guard, and bumped right into the German picket. Captain Grenfell was the fifteenth officer of the 9th Lancers killed during the campaign. The 18th Hussars and a battery went by. Our field-guns opened with increasing frequency in positions to the right and left.

The Welsh Regiment and the Gloucesters passed, the former followed by its handsome white goat. Stout chaps the infantry men, bearded like a bard, except for sundry hairless youths. Their firm step in the muddy road as they swung along at a good four miles an hour was evidence of their fitness and the spirit that was in them. Their faces showed great contrast, and I was struck by the youthful ones among them. In the dull, lowering, apprehensive weather, swinging forward grimly in the drizzle to face the German machine-guns on the crest, one could well be proud to be fighting under the same flag. A short mile away many of them were to meet their death. They were not going towards it carelessly, or thoughtlessly, but were pressing forward with the eagerness of splendid fighting stock, when the battle is within sight and hearing. A heavier roll of rifle fire, or an increase in the *staccato* of the rapid fire guns, seemed a signal for a quickening of their step. I never saw finer soldiers.

General de Lisle took me down to the headquarters of the 1st Division at the cross-roads outside Vendresse, where we learned that the infantry had definitely captured the ridge, and on the right were through Paissy, which was taken the day before, and had got well beyond it. The numbers of wounded increased every minute. Batteries continued to be sent up the hill and off to the right. The German shells came closer to us. Three shells fell on the roadway not far ahead of a dozen couples of stretcher-bearers, who had started for the front. They trudged on stolidly. Our guns behind us, right and left, were hammering away so pertinaciously that it was likely we would soon come in for a severe return fire. A heavy infantry engagement commenced in front of Paissy. The shots echoed down the glen in an increasing din. The General returned to the 2nd Cavalry Brigade headquarters. We passed the North Lancashires on their way to the firing line.

De Lisle's formula when starting on our little expeditions by car was, "I would like to go on now, President, if you do not mind going under fire again." "President" was my nickname, bestowed to mark my nationality. De Lisle was always cheerful. He had an increasing amount of enjoyment that morning watching my nervous jumps when the "Black Maria" shells exploded in our vicinity. The big howitzer shells caused me an unusual amount of nervousness. Just before ten o'clock a couple of messages were passed by word of mouth down the troops along the roadway. The first one, thrown from detachment to detachment, was, "Pass the word back that no notice is to be taken of the white flag." Sinister message that, telling its own story. Someone had trusted the white flag as a signal of surrender, to his cost.

The next few days were replete with such instances, but the first of such stories that came to our ears made the greatest impression.

The next message said, "Pass the word that German prisoners are going by." Fast on its heels, as we looked up the road in anticipation, came another message, "Pass the word back that no rude remarks are to be made as they go by." How many budding gems of scorn were nipped by that last order.

Prisoners drifted past, half a hundred of them, dejected in appearance, but sturdy and well-fed. They looked little like members of an army that had been pressed so hard in retreat as had Von Kluck's. At ten o'clock we ran up a crossroad, a mere lane, to Moulins, and climbed the steep hill to Paissy, a mountain village. Its cave dwellings and its one roadway nestling in the shelter of the high cliff-side were full of picturesque Algerians and *Zouaves*. Leaving the car we walked up to the top of the cliff, and were afforded a wonderful view. English cavalry of another brigade galloped by on the skyline.

We could see but few troops, but the general explained that in front of us some of the 1st Corps infantry were getting into touch with our 2nd Cavalry Brigade. As we stood at the top of the ridge it was most inspiring to feel that one of the greatest battles of the world's history was in progress in front of us. No one was at so good a point

COLONEL STEELE'S HEADQUARTERS (COLDSTREAM) ABOVE VENDRESSE

COLONEL SERROCOLD'S HEADQUARTERS (60TH RIFLES) ON THE AISNE

of vantage as we were to witness it. Yet we could see but little of it. If our First Army and d'Esperey's French troops on our right could succeed in forcing a way through the German line, and drive a wedge separating the seven corps in front of us, a great victory might result. French motorcars filled with eager officers had been pushing about all morning in search of our divisional generals. Events seemed to be marching rapidly towards the consummation of our desires.

Once let us break through and pivot the line on our left, swinging our right up the road to Laon, great things might be expected. Our anticipation of success in this huge battle for position between armies of somewhat equal numbers, and our enjoyment of the magnificent view of the high hills and deep valleys, were interrupted by the continual searching in our vicinity of the German high-explosive shells. Their increasing frequency made me wish to cut short our visit to Paissy, in spite of the vantage afforded, for the longer we stayed the closer they came. Running down the hill and to Moulins, I turned up a cross-road, when the engine of the car began to miss fire, and finally stopped. Of all the positions in which I had been during the morning, that was the most awkward in which to repair a balky car. A battery was stationed forty-yards distant in a field. It was firing steadily, and the German guns were returning the compliment with equal persistency.

I detached the pipe leading to the carburettor, and blew out the petrol line with the aid of the tyre pump. To hurry the operation was impossible. A couple of shells dropped in the field at my side, and made me bungle the work. The banging of our guns, the smash of the German high-explosive shells near-by, the rattle of the rapid-firers and the roll of the rifles all round us as the great fight drifted to the left, made the air seem charged with electricity. I steadied myself, made a careful examination of the petrol line, and at last got it cleared. The general had walked on. I lost no time in leaving that unpleasant position. Passing over the same road a few days later, I marvelled to se the holes on either side and on the edge of it, where hundreds of German shells had fallen that morning.

We returned to our wayside headquarters and made a good lunch of bully beef and bread and butter. General Bulfin's 2nd Brigade had been held up at the sugar mill, and the North Lancashires had been sent up through Vendresse in support. The 4th Guards Brigade, advancing in front of Chavonne and Soupir, with Ostel as their objective, had experienced wicked fighting, but reached the Ostel ridge. The struggle for the sugar factory and the Chemin des Dames position was still proceeding. Our troops that had passed Paissy had not yet reached the Chemin des Dames on their side. The Moroccan troops, on the right of the British line, had not brought their line far forward.

We received a report that the French had taken Craonne, further to the right. We were destined to receive numerous reports to that effect within the next few days.

That lunch was the first meal I had eaten to the sound of heavy artillery fire in close proximity. I have breakfasted in a boiler factory, and dined to the accompaniment of an equatorial thunderstorm. That luncheon had elements of both. I went with General de Lisle to Major-General Lomax's headquarters and heard our batteries sent up the hill to assist the attack on our left front. I was sent to move back our transport, as the 2nd Cavalry Brigade had been ordered to the left. The counter-attack of the Germans to the west of the 4th Guards Brigade had threatened to drive back the 3rd Division, who were in front of Vailly. A staff officer told me that the 3rd Division had been unable to reach Aizy, and that the enemy counter-attack in that quarter might turn our left flank.

After I had delivered my message to our transport I waited at a fork in the road, watching 300 German prisoners, including four officers. Nearly double this number of prisoners were taken that morning. The 300 gathered at that point had been captured in the trenches above Troyon by the Sussex Battalion, in a direct charge, in which Lieutenant-Colonel Montresor, of that regiment, was killed. By noon the German counter-attack in front of Chivy, north of Verneuil, developed strongly. Half an hour later, the fight still drifting westward, the 2nd Cavalry Brigade left the road to mount the hill toward Verneuil, winding up the steep ascent in column of twos. Squadron after squadron and regiment after regiment disappeared in the undergrowth at the top of the rise.

A lame horse left behind refused to be abandoned, and hobbled along in the rear of his regiment in pathetic testimony to his willingness to go with the others, no matter where they were bound. The rain ceased and the sky cleared, a fresh wind springing up to dry the muddy road. I walked up the slope, and, gaining a good point of observation, lay and watched the artillery duel on the far hillside. Clouds of black smoke and white bursts of shrapnel against the varying green of the thick foliage made a fascinating picture. A dispatch rider showed me a message from General de Lisle to General Lomax stating that I Battery was in action one mile northwest of Bourg, that the shelled Germans were running from their trenches, and that our 1st Division troops could be seen advancing. Red Cross attendants, doctors and ammunition supply passed frequently. At 3.45 I ran to General Lomax's headquarters to enquire which road I should take to rejoin General de Lisle.

I was told to go to Verneuil, and there ask for information. Returning to Bourg, which I found full of 1st Division wounded, I passed on to Verneuil, the streets of which were littered with dead horses and men. I counted thirty-five dead horses from where I stopped. I was told General de Lisle was further to the right, but the shell-fire was so continuous over the road that I returned to a point near Bourg. High explosive' shells fell before me, behind me, and on both sides of me, as I made the return journey. At times I ran through clouds of black smoke from the big howitzer shells. In front of Bourg a battery of our 60-pounders was in action, and I stopped by them some little time. Fifteen empty ambulances passed *en route* for Verneuil, and shortly afterwards another dozen followed. One of the hospital men told me three hundred of our wounded were in the town.

A German aeroplane hovered over a battery of our guns to the left of Verneuil for a moment. Immediately afterwards a very tornado of the enemy's shells were hurled at the battery. We expected to see it put out of action, but, to our surprise, it continued firing.

Seeing the cavalry moving west across country, I drove to Soupir, and from there to Chavonne. On reaching Chavonne I found that the General had gone up the steep road to the heights north of the town, where the Coldstreams and the Guards had entrenched themselves on the crest. Shells were dropping with monotonous regularity between Chavonne and Soupir.

At lunch we had discussed the desirability of annexing something in the nature of drinkables. Lieutenant Rex Benson, of the 9th Lancers, told me that in the quaint hill town of Pargnan, not far from Oeuilly, I would find a woman at a tiny hotel, from whom I might obtain a bottle or two of wine. I left word that I would return before dark, and drove hurriedly to Oeuilly and up the winding ascent to Pargnan. The proprietress of the hotel was most hospitable. She could let me have two bottles of wine at one *franc* each, she said. The production of a twenty-*franc* note and a request for a good supply led to a journey with *Madame*, an old retainer, an emaciated youth and a pair of infants.

Down the cellar stairs we went, moved a pile of large empty casks from a further corner, then down a black hole, stooping low and stumbling against each other in the darkness. At the end of the passage a candle showed we were in a good sized cave in the hillside, with low ceiling of damp rock and floor of soft sand. A walk into the further blackness, and the boy was told to dig. The woman had buried her wine to keep it away from the Germans. Dig the lad did most valiantly for some time, but in vain. One of the toddlers was despatched for a larger shovel. After its arrival, by dint of our combined exertions, we exhumed four bottles of champagne and fourteen of a very passable red wine, which had been buried four feet below the surface. My offer of twenty-five *francs* for the lot was eagerly accepted.

I arrived at Soupir after dark, finding our headquarters in a small tumbledown barn at the corner of the grounds of a *château* which had belonged to Calmette, the editor of the *Figaro*, not long before shot by Madame Caillaux. General de Lisle ran to the *château*, where we found General Briggs' headquarters. After a consultation, we returned to our humble quarters and turned in for the night. I was so tired I went to sleep in the car. The firing in front of us began vigorously in the early part of the night. Another message to Briggs became necessary. Captain Barrett wakened me, and asked me to run to General Briggs' headquarters. There was a strict order against any car lights. The road was in a frightfully slippery condition and deeply ditched on either side. So it seemed better policy to walk.

As I had been the only one to accompany the general on his previous visit, Barrett asked me to act as guide. Cavalry and artillery filled the beautiful parks. The dull light of the camp fires showed picturesque groups here and there under the trees. We were challenged several times. More than once the challenge was accompanied by the ominous click of a bolt, always disconcerting when the challenging sentry is so close to the line. One never knows just how jumpy sentries may be under the stress of circumstances.

We found General Briggs seated on the steps of the *château*. He explained the situation carefully. The left of the cavalry was to rest on the river, its right to be in touch with the left of the Guards. We returned to our own headquarters by eleven o'clock to find that the mess wagon had come up. A slice of ham and a piece of bread made a good dinner, and I immediately afterwards "turned in" on a blanket spread beside the car. Firing became incessant towards midnight, but I slept soundly until a sharp rainstorm drove me under shelter. I tried the floor of the barn. The general was sleeping in the manger. The staff were spread about here and there on the earthen floor. I chose several positions in turn, all of them being impossible from the standpoint of comfort. Hummocks and hollows of exasperating shapes seemed to protrude themselves upon me wherever I might lie. Withal, I spent one of the most uncomfortable nights of the campaign.

So the day ended, with our hopes of piercing the German line shattered, and with the dawning realisation that we were facing a splendidly prepared and dangerously strong position. It began to filter into our minds that the German retreat was over and that we had best prepare ourselves for fierce counter-attacks to hold the lines we had gained. We were well across the Aisne. We heard that Maunoury at Vic had done well and was not unsuccessful at Soissons. Our 3rd Corps were reported to have a strong position in the direction of Chivres and Vrigny. The 3rd Division was still in Vailly. Our Chavonne-Soupir line leading away north of Verneuil and on to Troyon, thence to a point north of Paissy had been maintained, if not advanced materially. Good news came from the French in front of Craonne, and again we heard they had taken that town, although subsequent reports invariably came after news of Craonne's capture to tell us that the Germans still held it.

Promise of a hard fight to maintain our positions was sure on the morrow. Sleep was of inestimable value, so we slept as best we could.

Chapter 7

Cavalry in the Trenches

Typed reports from G.H.Q. began to bear universal interest about this time. One that reached us during our first days on the Aisne collected evidences of German discomfiture, due to the pressure we had given their hurried retreat. Enemy shells were thrown into the Vesle at Braisnes. We captured German cavalry orders crying for aid to their infantry, admitting that their horses were worn out and the roads so congested they could not get their transport away. Some half-starved Huns were taken prisoners, and others found who were nearly dead of fatigue and exhaustion. Diaries from the bodies of enemy dead testified to the horror of our continual shrapnel fire. A bomb that one of our airmen dropped on a party of *Uhlans* killed fifteen of their number.

We called these reports the *Cheer-up Journal*. The Chavonne-Soupir ridge was definitely ours by dawn on Tuesday, the 15th. Earliest light was the signal for the enemy to commence shelling our hard-won positions. A blue-grey smoke pall hung over the woods on the crest in front of us all the morning. The air was rent with the sound of continuous battle, in which all arms, from rifles to big howitzers, played their part.

No morning ablutions these days. We were an unwashed, unshaven lot.

German gun-fire meant business on the Aisne. Shrapnel was hurled at the hill-tops by scores. I spent some time watching the shell-bursts twenty to thirty at once. Salvoes of sixes and dozens burst together in the tree-tops. Thick clouds of greenish-yellow massed and drifted in the clear light. The early sun, fighting through hazy clouds, painted the floating smoke-balls a pale heliotrope.

The general took me to Soupir, and up the steep mountain road

A CAVE HEADQUARTERS ABOVE THE PARGNAN

GENERAL FITZCLARENCE'S CAVE HEADQUARTERS (15TH BRIGADE) ON THE AISNE

toward the trenches. Our shells screamed over our heads, and enemy shells as well, the latter bursting in all directions, in front of us, behind us, on every side. As the road changed to a mere track, de Lisle left the car and proceeded on foot. A wounded Tommy sauntering past volunteered the information that the wood near by was full of dead Germans. In a cottage beside me was a dressing-station—a sad sight. Worn-out men, bandaged, were sitting about it, heads drooping, broken, weary, many in awful pain, yet not a word of complaint. Coldstreams, Irish Guards, and Connaught Rangers were among the wounded. The Irish Guards suffered heavily in taking the woods. Four of their captains were killed, one wounded, and a subaltern wounded as well. Lord Arthur Guernsey and Lord Arthur Hay were among their dead.

Someone had noted a couple of officers shot from behind. One of the wounds was in the back of the neck, the bullet ranging down the spine. A search resulted in the discovery of German sharpshooters hidden in the thick foliage of tree-tops in the rear.

One of our gallant officers stooped to give a wounded Prussian officer a drink. The shattered German looked up, recognised that the would-be Samaritan was one of the hated enemy, and shot him dead.

A group of Germans in the wood surrendered, waving a couple of white flags in token of their submission. As our men ran out to take their arms, another enemy detachment, coming suddenly upon the scene, opened on friend and foe alike, and mowed down scores.

Returning to our barn near the Calmette Château, we were stunned by the shock of two big howitzer shells, one fair on the roadway beyond us and the other close beside it. Pushing on, we found one of the two had killed nine battery horses and five men, wounding fourteen of their comrades. One horse had fallen across the road, and had to be moved to allow our passage.

Before we left the vicinity of that *château*, Black Marias and dead horses became so common as to fail to excite remark.

After a run to General Allenby's headquarters, we again climbed the Soupir ridge. The cottage that had been a dressing station a couple of hours before had been found to be too directly in the line of fire, and the wounded had been moved to some point below. As we went past, shells were bursting close to us, several landing less than one hundred yards distant. Down the road trickled a procession of wounded, an unusual percentage of them hit in the face and head.

A pathetic little sight came under my eye as a quartet of shattered soldiers—two British Tommies and two Germans—walking abreast and evidently communicating with each other with difficulty, came to a halt. They turned, each German extending a hand, and each Tommy grasping it. After a moment's handclasp, they plodded their bandaged way, one limping badly. Stretcher parties were numerous.

A message to the headquarters of General Monro, commanding the 2nd Division, took me from Soupir to Moussy-sur-Aisne. Dozens of dead horses lined the road and the town was full of them. Moussy proved a veritable shambles. Blood had been spatted everywhere. General Monro's headquarters were beside a haystack outside the town.

Before noon, while I was resting on the Chavonne road, Major Hugh Dawnay and Westminster drove up, asking for the Guards Brigade. As they left for Soupir, four high-explosive devils lit a couple of hundreds yards away with a crash. Then four more, only little beyond us. Westminster and Dawnay returned a few minutes later.

"Pretty hot in Chavonne, isn't it?" said one of them. "Two shells lit in the trees just above our heads as we started back."

The sky-line was white with shrapnel. Someone joked about a recent G.H.Q. report that told of a shortage of German ammunition. It seemed the enemy must stop searching in our vicinity for batteries or the general must move headquarters, at least, if he wished to have any staff left to him. But close as the shells came not one of us was hit. We even became in a measure accustomed to them as the day wore on. I lay in a ditch and took snapshots of the bursting shells above me.

After lunch I strolled past the imposing gates of the Calmette Château and through the beautiful grounds. A fairy lake, covered with pond lilies and lined with a rare rockery, was tucked away in a bower of trees. The clear, cool water provided a refreshing bath.

At General Haig's headquarters in Bourg, later in the day, Hugh Dawnay outlined the strategic situation to me most lucidly. He gave me a simple explanation of Von Kluck's plans and the state of affairs generally. I jotted it down and retailed it to more than one interested listener during the next week. No one would imagine how little the regimental officers, or Brigade commanders, for that matter, knew of the broad plan of operations at that time. The fact that the line of the French 5th Army on our left stretched from Noyon to Soissons was news to us. To the east the French held from our British right at Paissy to Rheims, thence to St. Menehould, and on to Verdun and beyond. Dawnay gave me my first definite news of Foch's great victory on the advance north, when the enemy left 9,000 dead on one battlefield.

The French, ever thorough in all matters of scientific detail, have made *post-mortems* on dead German soldiers. The data thus obtained confirms the report of the Intelligence Department that the invaders are subsisting off the country.

Our night stop was Oeuilly, and for the second time we were sheltered in the ravished *château*.

Rain set in—the sort of rain that soaks into one's system—and by the time we reached Oeuilly we were thoroughly wet.

Wednesday bade fair to be one continual drizzle. Our brigade was ordered into the trenches on the Chavonne ridge. I ran the car to the very top. As the road wound above the village the ascent became quite steep. The valley of the Aisne stretched away in panorama below. Cave dwellings lined the way at frequent intervals. The inevitable convoy of stretchers met us as we mounted upward, many of the wounded pale and drawn from hours of suffering while waiting for daylight to permit their being moved. The path was in no condition for night traffic. At the top of the hill were our trenches, and those of the enemy in plain view a few hundred yards in front of us.

The 4th D. G.'s, 9th Lancers and 18th Hussars spent the morning "taking over" from the Queen's Bays, 5th D. G.'s and 11th Hussars. As the men came out of the trenches they looked tired and worn but splendidly fit.

Brigade headquarters were located in a house on the hill, a poor place, but affording shelter.

Just afternoon we sat down to lunch. Hardly had we done so when word came that the enemy was advancing all along the line. At the same moment news reached us that the German shells had rendered Bourg uninhabitable, and Haig had found it advisable to move his headquarters.

Increasing shrapnel fire in front made the echoes resound. We were off through Chavonne and up the road that led to the trenches. A battalion of Jocks had made a wall of good-sized stones which barred the way. A few moments' work by a score of them cleared a path. While we were waiting shells burst near, and hot bits of shrapnel fell in the car. On we climbed. As we passed a cottage a shell hit it and tiles showered down in armfuls, some of them rattling against the metal panels of the car. Horse ambulances had found their way up and down from the valley to the crest during the morning, and had made the road so slippery that de Lisle left the car in the shelter of a bank

Eighteen-pounder hit by a "Black Maria"

and trudged on foot. The 2nd Life Guards came up and occupied the shallow straw-filled reserve trenches beside me. Our guns took a hand with increasing fury. I began to like the sound of our own shells on their flight overhead—a song I was to learn one day to love.

An hour passed. The general came down from the line and told me our batteries had smashed the enemy attack in splendid style.

I took Hamilton-Grace to Haig to report. As we left our headquarters a shell struck it, but only tore off a bit of roof and hurt no one. Before we had gone one hundred yards a big black chap smashed a tree in the road in front of us. Soon after we passed another one fell in almost the same place. "Close work," said Grace with a laugh.

Beside the wall of the Calmette Château we sped, mindful that we were traversing an unhealthy locality. The 1st Brigade were along the roadway, the 11th Hussars at the further end of the wall. A German aeroplane was overhead. As he watched it Grace saw it drop a glistening signal. I was compelled to slow down, the road at that point being full of cavalry horses and ammunition waggons. The ditch was lined with resting troopers. *Rumph! Umph!* A Black Maria fell close on our left, its sinister pall of smoke drifting almost on to us. "Get on, old chap," said Grace. I "got." Down went my foot on the accelerator pedal. The car leaped forward. I narrowly missed a horse and swung away at full speed. *Crash!* went a shell where we had been a second or two before. It seemed as if fear lent the old car wings. Grace looked back and remarked, "If I'm not mistaken that one hit some of the fellows we came past a moment ago."

Not long after, having bumped over the pontoon bridge at Bourg and back again, we returned over the road past the *château*.

As we drew near, a wounded black mare, her side covered with mud, galloped madly past. A scared group of transport drivers were huddled behind a stone cairn by the roadside. We came to a pile of accoutrements, then a dead horse in the road. Reaching the wall we found the ditch piled full of dead horses and men. Two dismembered horses lay in the way, other dead horses were piled in the field, and stretcher bearers were picking up still forms in khaki from under the trees.

Fifteen horses and a dozen men was the toll taken by that shell. It burst just by the roadside two or three seconds after we had sped past.

I was kept busy, up the hill and down again time after time, till late in the evening. Cold bully beef was the *pièce de résistance* of our dinner that night, a dish of which I think I could never tire.

For the next two days we "hung on" in the trenches on the ridge. Most of the time we were under shell-fire. The weather was damp and cold, the rain making the trench-life miserable enough. The cavalry had seen the last of open mounted fighting. An officer of the 18th Hussars made an interesting reconnoissance with a squad of men, crawling close to the German trenches. Captain Kirkwood, of the 4th D.G.'s, did a "stalk" on the following night, returning with useful information as to the enemy's position. For the most part we could see the German lines in the daytime quite clearly, but the night adventures put us in close touch with the parts of their line that lay out of our sight.

One or two incipient German attacks were reported, causing headquarters to rush to the trench-line, but nothing serious materialized. Once an officer sent word that the enemy were advancing in force, and he could not hold his position unless reinforced. Upon the anticipated attack proving a false alarm this officer was interviewed by the chief. After this interview he heartily wished the Germans *had* come.

A battery commander was ordered to move his guns to another position and go into action at once. On the arrival of the gun horses the battery was heavily shelled. Back the horses were rushed under cover. Again they were ordered up and again the Germans commenced to shell them. After a wait of twenty minutes the horses were brought up for the third time, only to be shelled and driven back as before. This puzzled the gunner commanding the battery. Our troops held the ridge above him, and no enemy position was in sight from the spot occupied by the guns. A village lay on the hillside. Taking a couple of men he searched the houses, and in a cottage far up the rise found a strapping chap in peasant garb who proved to be a German guardsman. In a stack beside the hovel the spy had concealed himself for days, lying at the end of a telephone wire which led over the hill, past or under our front line and into the German trenches. The gun horses had been brought up in front of his very eyes. When he gave the word by telephone to his own guns they banged away until he told them the target was withdrawn.

To execute the spy and shift the battery was but a matter of moments. The guns were moved not a second too soon, for before they were far away a battery of German howitzers was turned on the field they had left, and in a short time had torn the surface with great rents into which one could put a gun-team.

The Germans did not always have such fine targets for their gunners. One morning a sudden burst of sun from behind a bank of cloud found a couple of officers on the ridge just back of a line of trenches, lying on the grass enjoying a respite from the usual sodden weather and overcast skies. Together they gazed on the panorama together. The Valley of the Aisne was an entrancing sight. Here lay this town and there that, some smashed by shells, some practically unharmed.

As they looked down the wooded hillsides into the lower land toward the river, one of them called out, "Look! a helio'."

From under a hedge back of Moussy came the flash, flash, flash, in regular intervals. A junior signals officers tried to read the message. Once, he said, he caught a word, but for the most part it was Greek to him. "Must be some fool sort of code," he confessed. "I never saw anything like it before."

As they watched it, the Germans saw it, too. Bang went a big black Jack Johnson not far from the spot. *Smash!* came another. Still the flashes twinkled from the surrounding green.

The first two shells were the forerunners of dozens that crashed through the hedge and into the turf all about the tiny centre of light.

Black shell-clouds showed all round that field and the next. Soon the sun crept behind a cloud, as if intent on protecting the object of the Huns' iron wrath.

Next morning a brief ten minutes of sun caused eyes on the ridge to wander valleywards again. Sure enough, a couple of flashes, intermittent and apparently quite without coherence, came from the spot at the hedgeside.

Soon the enemy howitzers played on the vicinity, fiercer than the day before.

After the sun had gone from sight, they kept up their bombardment of the unfortunate spot for half an hour. Dozen of shells fell thereabouts, then scores on scores.

A signals officer on the crest, watching the play murmured: "What idiots are our helio' lot are to choose a spot in plain sight of those Germans on the far ridge."

That afternoon a cavalry officer had a journey to make which took him to General Monro's headquarters near Moussy. His work done, he continued a few hundred yards, and sought the spot that had suffered the awful shelling.

It was not hard to find. The hedge was smashed in places. A tall tree was knocked down near by. Great black holes were torn in the green fields. On one side of the hedge law a dead cow. No sign could be seen of the helio' party. This was hardly surprising, as for over half an hour shells had fallen all about the flickering light until it seemed no man could live thereabouts.

The staff officer strolled over to a battery position not far distant, and asked for news of the signallers. The gunners had wondered at the heavy shelling not many hundred yards from their funk-holes, but had seen no human beings near the hedge, before or after the bitter bombardment.

Nonplussed, the officer walked back to the devastated area, and, just as he was leaving, discovered the cause of all the trouble.

There, caught on a twig of the hedge, swinging lazily in the wind, was a bright-bottomed empty sardine tin, thrown carelessly aside by some satiated luncher.

The sun, catching the bright bit of moving tin, had made of it a tiny reflector.

Surely, never had so insignificant an object or one so intrinsically worthless caused the Huns so great an expenditure of costly ammunition.

A detachment of 18th Hussars were bringing about 150 led horses from Bourg to Chavonne over a road that was within telescopic range of the Huns.

Two or three Black Marias in the midst of the column made a scatterment thereabouts, and for the rest of the afternoon the new mounts were careering all over the surrounding country. A few horses and two men were killed, and many of the horses slightly wounded. All but eight were recovered by nightfall.

The same day the German look-outs must have taken a herd of a couple of dozen cows for some of our horses. A battery of howitzers opened on the inoffensive cattle, driving them from one corner of a large field to another. For quite half an hour the enemy guns pounded away at the herd. It seemed odd that any of the poor beasts were left alive, but only five were killed—in spite of the tons of metal embedded in their pasture by the Boche gunners.

The effective strength of most of the commands on the Aisne was low. That of the 2nd Cavalry Brigade was but fifty *per cent*, of its full complement. The brigade had, since leaving England, lost twenty-five killed, 120 wounded, and 220 missing—some 365 casualties all told—over one-third of its original strength.

On the afternoon of Friday, the 18th, unable to catch forty winks owing to the banging of a dozen 18-pounders just below our house, de Lisle gave me permission to walk up to the trenches and watch the shelling. A short cut through the woods was the route advised. As I got well in among the trees the enemy began to shell them. No troops were in the wood, but every day the Germans seemed to deem it necessary to visit a certain amount of iron wrath upon it.

The crashing and splintering of the branches, and the ripping of bits of shell through the thick foliage overhead, were among the most thoroughly unpleasant sounds I have ever heard. A feeling that I might be wounded and lie helpless in the undergrowth, to die of starvation or thirst before being discovered, entered my mind. A quartet of particularly vociferous shells burst above, a splinter striking the good-sized tree trunk behind which I was endeavouring to compress myself into as small a space as possible.

That settled it. No route was too far round if it obviated the necessity of traversing that dreadful wood. I incontinently fled downhill, and after a long detour reached the crest by the main path up the slope. A natural tunnel ran through the rock at the summit. Twenty to thirty feet from its outer end were our trenches. The Coldstreams were in occupation, "well dug in," and quite happy. In front, the ground sloped away for a thousand yards, then dipped gently. A further slope was not so far distant, but that I could see German reserves coming over it toward the enemy trench-line that faced us.

At the time I arrived, the German gunners were shelling our trenches 100 to 300 yards to the right of the tunnel's mouth. One or two landed, now and again so close as seventy or eighty yards from me. Most of the shells hit the ground a few hundred feet short of our trenches. Many burst in the air at close range. Not a few went over and exploded close behind. The men in the part of the line in which I sat were utterly careless of the bombardment of the bit of trenches so close beside them. They had an air of absolute detachment, as if it had nothing to do with them. Comment and criticism followed each new arrival. A few Tommies had mounted the trench parapet, and sat coolly in the open as though ticket holders and entitled to good front seats.

"What if those devils start on this bit of trench?" I asked a captain, whose dugout I was sharing.

"Oh, the men would get down quickly enough if the shells start this way," was his reply.

The space between the lines had widened. At least 1,300 yards separated the entrenched armies on that immediate front. Now and then a German walked across the skyline, 1,400 to 1,500 yards away. Both sides were beginning to learn the value of deep, well-made trenches, and the comparative safety such shelter gave from shrapnel fire. Hundreds of shells burst over the crest and left hardly a single casualty to record.

That night I tried sleeping in the open; but, as usual, a nocturnal rainstorm came up and drove me to the shelter of the hood of the car. A bitterly cold night it proved to be. A bad night for the many gun crews that had to sleep on the ground beside their batteries. The men in the trenches had made nests of straw which were much warmer than might have been expected, though the persistent rain eventually soaked through such make-shift shelters. One gun crew near me were drowned out of their "funk-holes," and gathered round a somewhat discouraged fire till morning. At daybreak I met troopers from the front trench-line who for hours had been standing in a foot of water.

Saturday, the 19th, was a rest day in which our brigade retired to billets at Longueval, south of the Aisne, and thoroughly dried out. I ran to G.H.Q. at Fère-en-Tardenoise, where Ted Howard, an R.A.C. member driving the provost marshal, had boasted a comfortable lodging. He was out and his little billet empty, so I took possession and managed a bath under the water tap in his kitchen sink. A tedious process and fraught with some general saturation of the entire culinary domain, but it served.

CHAPTER 8

Diary Under Howitzer-Fire

The Sunday was an eventful one for me.

General de Lisle was up at three o'clock and away half an hour later. The brigade was ordered to Paissy. A couple of squadrons of the 18th Hussars were to go into the trenches close to the firing line while the remainder of the command was to act in reserve.

I crossed the river on the pontoon bridge at Villers, the water almost covering the boards.

Paissy was built half in and half out of the rock of the hill proper. Some houses were so constructed that part of the rooms were mere caves in the cliff. The farms all boasted a cave in the wall side, convenient for storage of such rude property as implements of toil and carts or the stabling of live-stock.

We arrived at five o'clock. The general left the car and went on mounted. On the left the cliff ran sheer to a point above the highest building in the town. To the right of the roadway the ground dropped away into a miniature crater, the bottom of which was mapped with tiny squares of growing crops of green pasture, low hedges marking their boundaries. The cliff side ran round the valley in the form of a horseshoe. At the far end a steep wide path led to the summit.

The Germans were firing regularly, the shrapnel bursting a couple of hundred yards from us. A Sussex supply column was busy harnessing its horses in the farmyard I chose for shelter, so I backed the car under the outside wall. The shrapnel began singing over my head. I sat on the step of the car and watched a robust French farmer try to drive three huge white oxen into the gate. Swinging their heads low as if feeling their way with their great branching horns, their mild eyes opened wide in astonishment at the noise of the bursting shells.

A Sussex Tommy begged a drop of petrol to fill an automatic cigarette lighter. Around the corner came a line of wounded Algerians, some supported by comrades and one swarthy fellow carried by his companions. They seemed to have suffered a bad mauling. The dazed look of mute questioning, a failure to understand, was on their faces. From red fez to blue putties, their uniforms were a riot of colour. Blue capes over light blue jackets trimmed in yellow and red, once white trousers, unusually baggy, with here and there a head dress of odd hue, they presented a variegated but woebegone appearance. They might have been part of a pageant which had started out gaily enough only to meet catastrophe. Some of them were almost white. Some were quite black. One was grinning. From another a sharp cry of pain caused his bearers to let him gently down for a moment in the roadway.

A loud explosion came so close at hand that it ripped the air apart. The shock struck me like a blow in the face. Bricks, stones, bits of debris, and shrapnel fell in every direction. A rush of fumes and smoke came through the gateway from a German shell which had burst inside. The farmer shot through the air, falling on his back in the roadway by me. After an effort to raise himself, he fell back with a shudder, and lay twitching convulsively. A couple of horses and two forms in khaki were piled together against the cliff side. One of the big white oxen lay a few feet away, his snowy side turning crimson. Debris of all sorts rained down, the heavier bits with a sharp *staccato* as they struck the *pavé* roadway.

The impulse to leave the spot where a shell has fallen is overpowering. I gained the shelter of a further wall, when a shell burst behind me in the pathway that led from the crest. It lit among the fleeing Algerians. Numbers of them were hurled aside. Loud cries told of pain and terror. A great black fellow came down the hill screaming shrilly, dashed round the corner and speed away, lurching and straining as he ran. Down the road came a flash and a milky shrapnel cloud over the roadway. A shell had toppled the Big Algerian over in full flight.

Under a wooden gate, torn from its hinges, I cuddled close under the wall of a house. Shell after shell burst over the roadway. Huddled groups of Algerians still came down the path. They had no idea of how to seek cover. The wounded lay thick on all sides.

A tiny man, his ebony face distorted into a ghastly grin, struggled under an enormous comrade limp as a sack of meal. Through that hell of shell-fire the little Algerian made his way slowly, stepping gingerly over the dead and skirting shell-holes with the greatest care. At last he reached one of the hillside caves, and deposited his load at the feet of one of our brigade doctors, who was busy dressing a most heterogeneous collection of wounded.

No sooner had the little man got clear of the roadway than a shell burst over it. Involuntarily ducking at the force of the explosion, I felt a sharp blow in the ribs. It literally "knocked the wind out of me." At the moment I was afraid to feel my side, apprehensive of a nasty wound. A glance showed me a large brick had struck me, hurled as though shied from a catapult. My ribs were sore for days afterwards.

I fled a few yards further, keeping close to the wall. I stopped by Captain Algy Court, of the 9th Lancers. Court was standing beside his horse in such shelter as the wall afforded, waiting orders to move his squadron up the hill. We tried to talk to each other, but bursting shells rendered conversation impossible. A piece of shell struck Court's charger in the chest. The blood spurted in a stream. The captain led him inside the gateway. I followed. As I came past, the poor animal fell backwards and all but pinned me against the cliff side.

An English soldier and an Algerian were brought into an adjacent cave. A couple of old peasants looked on sympathetically while our doctor dressed both wounds with equal care. The doctor asked me to accompany him to a larger cave, where several of our wounded were reported to be.

There we found forty or fifty cases, mostly Algerians. Standing in the doorway of the cave, the shell-fire seemed louder, but I was in comparative safety. A passing officer advised me to get my car away if it was still runnable. It was covered with debris, but no beams or large pieces of wreckage had fallen on it. It was by that time but six o'clock, though it seemed as if hours had passed. I crept along the wall towards the car, when the noise of a passing shell sent me back to the cave mouth. A pale little French soldier, with spare black beard, was brought in wounded—a splendid, plucky little chap.

A high explosive terror burst in the road in front of the gate of our adopted dressing station. Then for twenty minutes the din of exploding shells was without a break. Most of them burst just above the roadway. Now one would light on the crest above the cave mouth, and shower mud, stones, and pieces of shell over us.

The yard was full of harnessed teams. The effect of the shell-fire on the horses was interesting. Some were apathetic; others were nervous and jumpy; most of them took it quietly.

A woman came from a house, leading a four-year-old child. She was making for the safe retreat of the cave. The little girl was wonderingly interested, but not in the least afraid. She prattled incessant questions to her mother as they hurried to shelter.

Well up the steep path that led to the crest, I could see the wide, low mouth of a cave that faced the direction from which the enemy's shells were coming. A dozen Algerians with their horses were gathered there. I watched them as they stood near the opening. Then came a flash and a red smudge right over the cave mouth. Black smoke poured out in dense masses. A Black Maria had exploded inside the cave. Not a man nor a horse of the group escaped instant death.

An hour later a lull in the shelling induced me to walk forward and look at the car. It was intact, though covered with still more masonry and debris. A piece of shell hit the road in front of me, and threw the mud in a conical little spurt, whereupon I lost no time in regaining the mouth of the cave.

The general was in the firing line somewhere ahead.

A battery of 18-pounders on the crest had been "answering" at times during the morning, but had been unable to "find" the enemy's howitzers.

At last came a full five minutes' lull in the firing. Its effect on the artillery drivers and reserves standing near was electrical. The men walked across the yard and into the road quite as unconcernedly as though a truce had been declared. To judge from their demeanour the danger was over. A German aeroplane sailing high above slowly turned and circled over us. German aeroplanes spelt trouble. We had not long to wait for it to materialise.

Just as I had planned to remove the car the shellfire began again, to last for another half hour. In the lull which followed I dug the car from under the debris which covered it and moved it to a point of greater safety. Pieces of shrapnel had left their mark on its sides and made a hole through one of the mud guards. One of the panels was spattered with blood.

In a house selected for our headquarters, I found a kitchen fire, which was most welcome, as a chill rain was falling. All forenoon the shelling continued at intervals, until my head rang with it.

The line in front of us was held by the newly arrived 18th Brigade of the 6th Division. This brigade, under General Congreve, consisted of the 1st West Yorks, 1st East Yorks, 2nd Notts and Derby and 2nd Durham Light Infantry. The extreme right of the line was in the hands of the West Yorks, a green regiment so far as German tricks were concerned.

The Algerians had been driven from their position on the far left of the French line. Three trenches in echelon, facing north-east, we hoped they would hold, for their retirement from those trenches uncovered our right flank. As a precaution de Lisle ordered Colonel Burnett, of the 18th Hussars, to prepare and occupy a couple of trenches between the right of the West Yorks and the left of the Algerians to protect any possible gap.

Still the fire rained on Paissy. One shell in the roadway killed a lieutenant and four men of the 18th. The roof of our headquarters house was continually peppered with hot splinters. The Sussex Battalion (1st Division), were in Paissy. I saw a message from General Lomax to the Sussex, saying that the 2nd Cavalry Brigade were to support the right of the West Yorks during the day, and rest in Paissy that night, to be on hand in case the French on the east of us were compelled to fall back. The Sussex were "resting." I had a good laugh with their commanding officer at the idea of "resting" anywhere near Paissy that day.

The commanding officer of the West Yorks called. He was very nervous about his right, but de Lisle reassured him. Personally I thought there was altogether too much talk of the precariousness of the situation. Such a thing exists as unnecessary apprehension.

The general suggested a visit to divisional headquarters after the West Yorks colonel had departed. As I lowered the hood a shell burst across the road twenty feet distant, and dirt and stones showered over me. I felt myself well over to be sure I was not hit. A piece of another shell hit a tree on the opposite side, and a shrapnel burst over the yard behind. How delighted I was to clear out of the place, if only for a short time! At General Allenby's headquarters, by a haystack above Tour de Paissy, a heavy shower gave me a thorough drenching. When the rain ceased we had a fine view of the country round. The French trenches and those of our troops could be seen with the naked eye.

Standing at a safe distance, watching the enemy shrapnel over our trenches or seeing clusters of four or eight burst over Paissy, with a Black Maria in frequent interlude, was a very different matter from being under the bursting shells.

On the way back to our own headquarters we had to wait outside Moulins until the enemy gunfire, covering the road ahead of us, had died down. One of the recently-arrived 60-pounder batteries, cleverly concealed, was thundering as we sped by its hiding-place.

At headquarters I felt drowsy and tried to sleep, but found it impossible. The German 8-inch howitzer shells were coming at regular intervals, their explosions rattling the panes and jarring the very foundations. The patter of debris on the roof, the sharp slap of a bit of shell or a shrapnel bullet in the yard, and the screams and moans of passing missiles, put my nerves on edge.

The general and Phipps-Hornby rode out to keep an eye on the trench positions. The hammering, hammering, hammering was growing painfully monotonous. The hopelessness of escape from it was galling.

Like a bolt from the blue came a West Yorks officer with news that the Germans had once again attacked the *Zouaves* on our right and pushed them back, getting in on the West Yorks' right flank. The Huns had taken some of the West Yorks' trenches, and driven back the line. Two companies of the Yorks Battalion had been captured. No sooner had he told his tale than Phipps-Hornby galloped up. General de Lisle, he said, was trying to get a company of the Yorks together, and wished all available troops sent up at once to reinforce him. All was bustle. The 4th Dragoon Guards were off instanter, the 9th Lancers hard on their heels, with the Sussex not far behind.

A real breach in the line and Paissy lost meant serious business. The muddy roads and the narrow pontoon bridges over the Aisne would not allow a thought of retirement. Nothing remained but to regain the ground that had been lost.

I was ordered off post haste to 1st Division headquarters, and then to General Allenby to bear messages explaining what had transpired. Speeding over the greasy road I soon reached General Lomax, and a few moments later was at 1st Cavalry Division headquarters. The fight was in plain view. The Germans were, coming over the brow of the hill. A couple of hundred dismounted 4th Dragoon Guards, the first line of the counter-attack, under Major Tom Bridges, could be seen climbing the stubble-covered hillside, dotted with still forms in khaki, and crowned by the lost trench.

Batteries—French, British, and German—sent round after round as fast as the men could serve the guns.

Still up the stubble crept the thin line, Bridges' tall form in the lead. The support, eager to have a hand in the game, pressed on in haste, but could not overtake the invincible Dragoon Guards, who swept away the Germans in their vastly superior numbers as if endowed with some superhuman power.

They gave the Huns no rest. Pouring a deadly and accurate fire into the blue-grey ranks as they came on, Bridges and his 200 reached

A TEMPORARY HEADQUARTERS ON THE AISNE

the front trench at last under a very heavy canopy of whizzing bullets. With a wild cheer, they leapt at the Germans, and threw them back from the trenches. The fierceness of the onslaught could no more be withstood than one could stem a cyclone.

The lost position regained, the big major leaped ahead, and again his men poured on after him. The enemy was not only to lose what he had won, but more. Before the 4th Dragoon Guards stopped, they had taken the Chemin des Dames, three or four hundred yards ahead of our original position. There we stuck and held on against counter-attack on counter-attack—our line to be kept without losing an inch of it during assaults that for the next few weeks were to leave pile on pile of German dead as an earnest of their stubborn refusal to admit the ground for ever lost.

A splendid charge was that at Paissy. A triumph of individual leadership and splendid quality in a handful of men. To watch it made the blood run hot and fast. To have taken part in it was worth a lifetime of mere ordinary existence.

Running back through Pargnan, the roads and fields were full of the battered Algerians. Out of 6,000 of them only 2,000 were left after five days' hard fighting.

I was under shell-fire a number of times during the remainder of the day. At dusk the staff was in the road under the brow of the Paissy hill when shells fell closer than usual. Captain Hamilton-Grace suggested I should back the car further round a turn, under shelter of the height of ground. I was too tired to bother, but at his second suggestion I backed for some fifty feet to please him. The moment I brought the car to rest in its new position, a shell lit on the spot from which I had moved it. I voted Grace's foresight little short of uncanny.

To cap the climax, the French won back their original positions on the right, and night closed with the line in better position than dawn had found it.

We seemed firmly installed in our billets in Longueval. The men were very comfortable in the picturesque stone-built village nestling low between the steep hill sides. The village folk were exceptionally friendly. A little bakery did the trade of its lifetime. A dry, warm billet at night makes a vast difference to the efficiency of a command, and for a fortnight the 2nd Cavalry Brigade waxed fat in Longueval, in spite of sundry days spent in the ever-shelled Paissy.

On Monday, following the Sunday fight in front of the Chemin des Dames, the brigade was ordered to rest and refit. The line was comparatively quiet, save for the inevitable intermittent shell-fire. The weather was exasperating. A flash of real warm sunshine at times gave hope of a change, but the hope always vanished in cold, dispiriting rain. General de Lisle made a tour of divisional and corps headquarters that put us in accurate touch with the march of events. At Braisnes we found General Gough, in command of the newly formed 2nd Cavalry Division, consisting of the 3rd and 5th Cavalry Brigades. General Smith-Dorrien's headquarters were in a great medieval *château* at Muret, a picturesque spot.

The universal feeling was that the new form of warfare, the trench fighting, might prove a tedious business. In spite of the arrival from England of half a dozen batteries of 60-pounders, the Germans were able to fire thirty shells to our one. Their preponderance in machine-guns was also marked. But few days of the trench war had passed before the machine-gun had come into its own. Officers who had given but little thought to the intricate mechanism of the death-dealing quick-firers could be heard cursing administrations of all sorts because of the obvious shortage of rapid-fire guns in the British army.

A well-informed gunner gave the following twist to one such conversation:

> I know of reports impressing the necessity of an increase of machineguns and machine-gunners that for years went annually into the War Office. Why was nothing done? Because no money was forthcoming, that's why. The taxpayer wouldn't stand it. No unlimited amount for army expenditure has ever been available, and rapid-fire guns are costly things. Reduction of army appropriation, not increase of its ordnance, is what a politician preached if he wanted to court popularity. Machine-guns, indeed! It's a wonder we have *any* guns!

Point of view differs, does it not?

Hard on the heels of Monday's peace came Tuesday's disquiet. It was Paissy again for the day. A jaunt to the reserve trenches and over the ground of Sunday's battle was interesting until the German gunners commenced shelling that part of the field. At the first quartet of shrapnel I decamped. Rifles, coats, kits, and all manner of personal property were thrown about the trench where the fiercest part of the action had taken place. Bibles, notebooks, match-boxes, bits of clothing, knives—the jumble of oddments contained everything a soldier ever carried and many things one would never associate with Tommy or his German prototype. In a little rain-washed gully a miniature case lay half-covered in the mud. Inside it was the work of an artist of ability, a lovely face painted deftly on ivory, the sort of face possessing a sweetness of expression that makes one wonder where one has seen the original.

A transcription from my diary pictures life in Paissy.

11.30 a. m. Have been sitting on a rock under the lee wall of a house we are using as headquarters. The shelling of this town has gotten to be a German habit. As I sit I face a narrow path from the opposite edge of which the ground drops away to the valley below. Big shells and little shells are going over and around me. Now and again they explode behind my back with a concussion that is nerve racking. White clouds for shrapnel and big black clouds for Jack Johnsons follow the explosions in front after the shriek of the shells in passing. Those which strike near by frequently send a jagged piece of projectile hurtling through the air with a peculiar demoniacal wail of its own. The shells which land behind jar the whole hill. The house wall at my back trembles with the explosion.

When the big black melinite ones land in front, if they are anything less than seventy-five to a hundred yards distant, I feel the concussion. If they are closer, there is a real physical shock when they explode. Down the road, tree branches fallen, great holes torn in the side of the roadway, and a pile of dead horses are evidences that yesterday's shell-fire was effective. In front, and a bit to the right, half-a-dozen troopers are sorting out a pile of rifles and ammunition which have been brought back from the scene of the battle.

11.50 a.m. Four came close all at once. Could almost feel one of them. It seemed just overhead. Major Frazer has called, and with Captain Hamilton-Grace has climbed a winding path which leads to an old stone church on the top of the hill. The tower of this church is an artillery observation post, and the boys have gone up to have a look.

12.05. Fairclough asked if I would like to go up into the church tower and have a look. Quaint old place. I climbed the narrow winding stairway, the stone steps worn down six to eight inches, and then a rickety ladder to the bell loft. We had a fine view of our trenches, and high in the sky, on the right, was a German

LONDON SCOTTISH IN GUARD OF GERMAN PRISONERS AT FÉRE-EN-TARDENOIS

MOROCCANS AT TOUR DE PAISSY (AISNE)

war balloon—a 'sausage,' as the men call it. A lot of shells came near the tower while we were in it. They whirr past in a weird way when one is far up. When I came back down to this back-to-wall position, a Sussex officer and a sergeant were looking over my car. They told me they thought it must have been hit by a shell that came a moment ago, but they could find no new shell marks on it. It was well I put the car in the shelter of the wall. While I was in the church tower, I am told, a shell burst on the other side of the wall, wounded six troopers in the yard and one of the party who were sorting the ammunition under the big tree. His companions had left that job for the moment!

12.10. An orderly holding a couple of chargers is sharing my wall. One of the horses is very restless under this cannonade, and jumps nervously when a shell bursts near us. The other horse seems to be watching the lower levels where the green fields are cut with dozens of big black holes, close together, in even circles, which show where the big melinite chaps have burst. I wonder if he is deprecating the spoiling of that fine pasture-land?

12.15. A dozen shrapnel came over at the same time bursting in such close succession I could not count the separate explosions. All but one or two of them went off over and a little back of me. There is a nasty, singing, twanging sound to those that burst behind as the contents of the projectile and pieces of it whirr over. The nervous horse nearly walked on me. Shells cannot come any closer and not score a hit. The troopers have stopped running out and picking up hot pieces of shell. A while ago they thought that good fun. I can't understand it. For my part such keepsakes never interest me. I am far too likely to be taking away a piece of shell as an internal souvenir, without troubling to fill my pockets with similar keepsakes.

Our guns across the valley are replying now, and their shells sing over our heads on their way to the enemy trenches. Major Frazer came up and asked if I was writing home and telling how much I am enjoying myself! The nervous horse belongs to him. He and his orderly mounted and rode away during a lull in the shelling. I wish him luck getting down that road.

12.25.—Another bunch of shrapnel all in a heap. Six or eight bursting at once make a din. Now the great melinite fellows are coming again. A couple of enormous black clouds from the ravine tell where they struck. There go two just behind on the cliff. They left their cards in the form of scattered bits which fell on the pathway in front of me, not more than four or five feet distant. Close work. Too close for comfort. A piece of shell about four inches long and sharply pointed has stuck right into the gravel path about thirty inches from my foot.

12.30.—Five or six more, all high explosives. The air in the valley is black with smoke. Two of the last lot went through the trees a few feet away. If one of them hit the tree trunk and exploded it would be nasty here. Immediately afterwards a dozen or more shrapnel, again in a group, went through the same trees. Leaves and branches fell in showers. An absolute rain of shells now for five minutes. I dislike most the ones that burst behind me. The noise of the whirring pieces is trying.

1 p. m.—Still steady firing. Our batteries have taken a hand in the noise production at the rate of thirty to forty shots to the minute. There is nothing to do but sit here and hope I shall get a run out of it before long. It is better here than up on the crest, for I am, I suppose, quite safe under the cliff side behind the wall.

2 p. m.—The general is going now to pay a visit to another part of the line. I am not sorry, for three hours of this sort of thing are quite enough for one day."

By General Allenby's haystack at Tour-de-Paissy was a big telescope mounted on a tripod. It was in disgrace. It served the Divisional Staff soberly and well until the very moment of the German attack on the West Yorks' trenches. Seeing men coming over the ridge, Colonel Home, General Allenby's G.S.O. 1, declared his field-glasses made him think them Germans. To make sure, the big telescope was turned on the ridge. For the first time in its history a moist film formed over the inner lens. A line of grey smudges was all that could be made out through its formerly far-seeing eye. When later events proved that Home was right, and the men in sight were Germans, moments precious to the guns had been for ever lost. Had the telescope possessed a soul it would have shrivelled in the heat of some of the remarks caused by that unlucky atmospheric visitation.

Not far from the haystack beside a muddy lane rose a knoll. Under a small tree a couple of gunners were on observation post. By the tree stood a wayside shrine, on its pedestal the inscription, in French, *"Jesus is the way, the truth and the life."* Flanked by trenches, the guns of two Christian nations hurling death from so little a distance that the mound trembled with each discharge, the shell-fire of a third we once thought Christian searching every foot of ground about it in frenzy to kill, I was struck by the numbers of passers-by whose eyes were caught by the familiar words, their faces softened as by a memory of other days.

Fitting it should be so. The Englishmen who were shedding their blood on those hillsides were battling for the Cross as surely as those of their forebears who followed Richard and the Crusades. It is modern to be cynical and hard, but the old faith has deep root in most of us, after all. We Anglo-Saxons should be proud of such a heritage.

The 2nd Notts and Derby came in for an awful hammering during the afternoon. Battery after battery of the enemy's guns were turned on the trenches above Paissy, but our men stuck to their line in spite of the inferno the howitzers made of it. The men reported seeing many Germans in front of them in British caps and tunics. The Hun trenches were 400 yards from ours, and the desire of the German soldiers to show themselves in their newly captured khaki outfits was overpowering until the Notts and Derby sharpshooters convinced them of the foolhardiness of so doing.

A sight that attracted daily attention on the Aisne was the appearance of German aeroplanes, which dropped signals to their guns, and thereupon were shelled violently by our field batteries. Lines of tiny white shell clouds, in long arcs across the sky as the fire followed one of our airmen, told of enemy anti-aircraft guns, the criticism or praise of whose marksmanship aroused continual controversies among the Tommies.

At dusk General de Lisle suggested scouting a new route around the Paissy crater. An army map showed a road none of us had thus far found. To pass through Paissy was an unpleasant experience. At a corner, dead horses were piled high, and, in the vernacular, "stunk horrid." A hole, three feet deep and six wide, had been torn in the centre of the road since I had made an earlier run over the same route. In the dusk, I landed the car with a smash and a jar plump in the middle of it. With badly bent front axle we pushed on, wondering at being able to do so. Over piles of debris from shattered dwellings, and past felled trees we crawled, then circled another shell-hole in the road so wide that one side of the car dipped into it at a dangerous angle in passing. The road became a mere lane, then a grassy, slippery track along the edge of the precipice. A drop meant a fall of eighty feet. Struggling up sharp ascents with wheels skidding in the mud, at last we came to the end of the path. We kept on a few hundred yards over the long grass, negotiating one stretch with the car canted at an angle of forty-five degrees.

We mounted a short, stiff gradient, and before us lay a black abyss, trackless and sinister, obviously too steep to allow of safe descent.

Turning the car on the edge of that drop, the grass slippery from the early dew, no light permissible to aid us, was at last safely accomplished. We retraced our way, and took the usual route to Longueval, having thoroughly proved the unreliability of the map.

The bent axle necessitated a run to the G.H.Q. repair shops at Fère-en-Tardenois. "Rattle" Barrett and I borrowed a car there from Westminster, who had two, as we had an errand for de Lisle which took us to Sablonnières, where one of the General's horses had been wounded and left to convalesce.

At Fère-en-Tardenois I received my first letter from London since my departure, thirty-three days before.

French Divisions were moving to the north-west and had been doing so for days. Joffre had started de Castelnau's 7th Army and Maud'huy's 10th Army toward Maunoury's left. The flanking movement to turn Von Kluck's right had begun. De Castelnau was to reach from Roye northward to Chaulnes, and Maud'huy from north of the Somme near Albert to Arras and beyond.

On September 24th we were up at three o'clock, and once more made our way from Longueval to Paissy, where the brigade was to "stand by" in support. From Paissy I took the general to Troyon by way of Moulins and Vendresse.

German shrapnel were paying the customary attention to the road from Paissy. We waited by a farm for a moment watching the shells burst ahead. "Go slow," came the order. I crawled. De Lisle, who was seated beside me, turned and looked sharply at me. "Go! Go!" he cried. I had misunderstood him. "Now, go!" he had said; not "Go slow!" I pushed on as fast as the car could gather speed. But the momentary delay had upset the general's nicely turned calculations. Before we had crossed the open plain, *Bang!* came the first shell; and *Bang, bang, bang!*—three others, just above us.

The slivers rattled on the metal panels. A shrapnel bullet made a clean round bed in the top of the radiator, and a good-sized splinter cut a deep incision in a front wing. The door panel alongside de Lisle was scraped by a sharp bit that buried in the step. A piece the size of a pea struck the chief on the nose, and a similar one gave me a stinging blow on the shoulder. The floor of the car held half a dozen fragments as we pulled up and took stock beyond. Our luck had held, and we were none the worse.

A bright, pretty day for a change, made our visit to the "sugar mill trenches" above Troyon all the more enjoyable. The men of the 18th Brigade were burrowed in the high road bank. Tiny cave-like shelters, canopied with branches or straw, made snug quarters, safe, under the brow of the hill, from the everlasting shell-fire. A subaltern of the East Yorks said his lot had three killed and eighteen wounded by high explosives in the front line the day before. The same regiment, he said, lost eight officers and seventy-three men when the Germans attacked so strenuously on the previous Sunday. Two companies of the enemy had come straight on, that day, in close formation, and suffered such casualties from the East Yorks' fire that they had to retire in confusion.

A persistent rumour had spread that the Canadians were "out."

"They won't be worth much until they have had some of this sitting under Black Marias. The best troops on earth would have to take a day or so to break into it," sagely remarked a beardless junior subaltern. His Division had arrived on the scene but few days before, but he looked with the eyes of a veteran on all newcomers.

Real quiet rarely visited the Troyon ridge. Our shells howled over, and the German shells screamed back. Rifle-fire rose and fell in spasmodic waves of sound The evenly-punctuated barking of the machine-guns echoed across the gorge.

On our way back to Paissy two new shell-holes showed where eight-inch projectiles had dropped since we had passed over the road. Once a howitzer shell burst so near we ran through its smoke-cloud—an ill-smelling mess.

All wished to take advantage of the rare opportunity of a warm sun-bath. We lined the wall, all the staff lying sleeping or reading as the afternoon wore on. I slept soundly. An overwhelming crash awakened me. A wicked high-explosive chap had burst above the headquarters yard. My eyes and mouth were full of dust and evil-tasting smoke. I could not see a foot in front. As the smoke-cloud cleared I saw Barrett swaying, and thought him wounded. He had merely stumbled in rising. Not one of us had been hit, though pieces of shell had rained down.

We scampered through the gate and into the cave in the cliff. For an hour or more Paissy underwent a bombardment that eclipsed anything in that line with which it had been visited formerly. Venturing to sit on an overturned bucket at the cave's mouth, I was toppled back by a brick, which took me fair in the middle. Thereafter I was content to keep well inside the cave until the Hun-hate had been somewhat appeased, and the shelling died down.

CHAPTER 9

A German Attack

The Germans pounded our troops well during those first weeks on the Aisne. Their shell fire, scored until our positions were strengthened and the shelter from bombardment improved. Day by day this work went on, the continual shelling taking less toll of men as time passed.

We had our "days." A fresh division of the enemy, brought by train from St. Quentin to a point fifteen miles from our lines, were seen at daybreak one Saturday in front of Troyon. Our first sight of them was when they marched in column of fours over the brow of a hill not 400 yards from our advance trenches. At their head strode a tall Hun bearing a white flag tied to a long stick. The first rows of men behind him were dressed in khaki. An interesting procession. Over the crest of the hill they came, every second bringing more of them to their certain fate. To those who were watching it seemed the enemy could not know the position of our lines. The strain was too great for a sergeant behind one of our machine-guns, and he "let go." His officers nearly wept with rage. The forepart of the German column shrivelled under the stream of bullets from the quick-firers and rifles. Our whole line was ablaze in a moment. Many huddled forms lay in plain sight of our trenches as the light grew, but most of the Germans had safely reached the cover of their front; trench, from which they kept up an incessant and perfectly harmless fire for more than an hour.

"If that blessed sergeant had been a bit patient," said his company officer to me that morning, "we would have jolly well bagged the lot."

The same officer was gazing idly toward the front during the late afternoon. His glance rested on the still bundles of grey lying between the lines. Storms of bullets from both sides had swept over the dead

11TH HUSSARS ON THE MARCH FROM THE AISNE TO FLANDERS

A WAYSIDE LUNCH; GENERAL DE LISLE AND THE STAFF OF THE 2ND CAVALRY BRIGADE

all day long. A thought came to his mind. What a crowning horror it would be to find that some of the fallen were merely wounded. As he watched, little bits of earth were kicked up here and there by bullets that fell short and cut the soil of no-man's land. Shell fire had ploughed furrows in it at frequent intervals. Shrapnel bullets were sown broadcast over it.

Suddenly, as if in answer to his soliloquy, one of the inanimate bundles seemed to come to life. It rolled over. The man inside the grey coat leaped to his feet. Hands held high in air, he ran like mad for our trench line. Over the parapet he tumbled, crashing on his head in the soft earth. Gaining his knees, hands still held above him, a beatific grin spread over his decidedly Teutonic features.

He spoke English quite well. "I shall to England be sent, no?" he queried. "It was too long, the time I lay out there. At first, I would to stay till dark come. But my nervous, it was finished. I could no longer quiet keep, no?" And the cheerful Hun, happy as a clam, was marched off under guard, to be turned over to the London Scottish, who were guarding lines of communication, and entrained for the South.

General Allenby and his headquarters staff lived at Villers, south of the Aisne. A trooper was pulling bundles of grain from a stack near Villers when he found a man covered in the straw. Jerked from his hiding-place, a tall young German Guardsman in uniform stood before his captor. Examination led to the alarming discovery that the German had been lying at one end of a wire that tapped a telegraph line from divisional headquarters. For thirteen days, possibly, the messages over that wire had been heard by ears for which they were by no means intended.

General admiration for the German's pluck was heard on all sides. To have stayed so long hidden so far within his enemy's lines required coolness and bravery.

Many were the conjectures as to how the information which he gained was transmitted to his own army. No other wire leading from the stack could be found. Careful search of the vicinity resulted in no enlightenment. At points the Aisne was dragged with long rakes by energetic signallers, but all in vain. The news of the capture was made a secret, and night after night a vigil kept to intercept possible callers laden with food for the German or in search of messages from him. No result was forthcoming, save that the watchers caught one another one night, and the next night caught cold, and the solution of the puzzle remained a mystery.

Periodical visits to the trenches made me sure that one day a fat howitzer shell would land in the wrong place for me. The enemy made some roads impassable, but we always found another way round.

Colonel Steele of the Coldstreams showed us a souvenir one day in the form of a ruined poncho. His shelter above Vendresse was a short way back of the trenches on the crest. Lying on his back, his legs spread out, and his poncho so arranged that it served for bed and coverlet, he dropped off to sleep. He was awakened by one of our own 18-pounder shrapnel, fired from somewhere in the valley below, which fell short. The misguided shell went directly between Steele's knees, ripping two gaping holes in his poncho and burying itself, unexploded, in the bank on which he was lying.

Tom Bridges was promoted Colonel of the 4th Hussars, but four days after he had assumed command of the regiment a motor-car from G.H.Q. called for him and hurried him off to Antwerp, for service with King Albert and his Belgians.

Major Budworth and H Battery of the Royal Horse Artillery came from England and joined the 2nd Cavalry Brigade while we were in Longueval. At dinner on the night of Budworth's arrival General de Lisle said that he, the major, Captain Skinner of H Battery, and I would next morning take "a run around," visit our gun positions past and present, and "show the major what German shell fire was like." From experience I knew that meant we would more than likely go "looking for trouble."

Heavy cannonading continued throughout the night. "Promiscuous" one of the troopers called it. Seemed wasteful, but at the end of two weeks of it the British Army had suffered over 3,000 casualties from the shell fire alone.

Our men were learning to keep to cover, and our batteries had learned to disguise themselves well. Miniature groves would spring up over the guns in a night. The "heavies," what few we had of them, were made to look like sheds or haystacks when concealment of the battery was impossible. These tricks our gunners learnt from the enemy, who was a past master at such contrivances.

After doing the rounds of the guns our party visited the trenches above Troyon. Serrocold's Battalion of the 60th Rifles and Steele's Coldstreams were in front that day.

The Sugar-Mill Position, so called from the huge mill above Troyon, since destroyed, that had been taken and retaken a dozen times and had afforded the Lancashires a chance to gain fine laurels, was our nearest point of vantage in one sector of the line.

There our barricade was one hundred yards south of the summit of the ridge, and the German trenches but eighty yards to the north of it. The Sugar-Mill barricade had seen heavy fighting, but was comparatively quiet at the time of our visit, though sniper bullets occasionally sang overhead and shrapnel came past at intervals.

Tucked under the brow of the hill, not far from the front line, were Colonel Serrocold's headquarters. A mutual friend had a few days before sent by me a case of most welcome provender to Serrocold's mess, and in consequence I called to sample the goods.

"We will get out of this today, sure," said the colonel.

"I think not, sir," I replied. "I have heard nothing of a change so far this morning. Why do you think you are to move?"

"Because we have just finished the construction of the first good dry shelter we have had for some days," was the answer. "I'm sure this is so perfect a spot now that we are doomed to be sent elsewhere, and others will spend a comfortable night in our snug quarters."

I laughed at his mock pessimism, and had another laugh the next day when I learned that sure enough the 60th had been shifted late in the afternoon. Serrocold's prophecy had come true most unexpectedly, and his palatial quarters had to be turned over to his successors.

We visited General FitzClarence and his staff in a typical cave Brigade headquarters under the brow of the Aisne Heights. Well inside the cave the Brigade staff work could be done without fear of interruption.

These cave headquarters were quite "comfy." But any spot in those days might be a headquarters. I remember one that consisted of the body of a defunct W. and G. taxicab.

In Vendresse half an hour later we were treated to some fairly close shelling, the first projectile landing on the other side of a high stone wall as we passed. A run to Paissy and a view from the church tower concluded our tour of sightseeing. We returned to Longueval for luncheon. We had taken Budworth under rifle and shell fire and shown him heaps of German dead a few yards distant from our trenches. As we pulled up, one of the party made a comment on the quiet and security of quaint Longueval, far from scenes of violence which had become the daily round in such towns as we had visited that morning.

But Longueval had proved less safe, in spite of its distance from the firing line, than the trenches and the hill towns close behind. Half an hour before our return five great howitzer shells from long-range

A British gun on the Lys firing

guns had "crashed into the village. One struck the centre of the stone-paved yard of a farm where a squadron of 9th Lancers was billeted. Lieutenant Whitehead was directing the cleaning of an open space between the barns. He and eleven of his men were killed and thirteen wounded. Among the killed was the sergeant-major of the 9th and two sergeants. Five horses were killed, and others wounded so badly it was necessary to destroy them.

The general was of opinion that the few shells had come that way as a chance bit of itinerant bombardment, to which most of the Aisne towns within range of the German guns would be subjected at one time or another. At two o'clock five more Black Marias fell near Longueval, but did no more damage than to rip up the field in which they fell.

After luncheon I ran to Rheims with the general to see the ravaged cathedral. The stately Gothic pile was reported to be a heap of ruins. It was hardly that, but nevertheless had been cruelly knocked about. Streets near by were choked lanes between rows of desolate monuments to the German love of wanton destruction.

Back in Longueval late in the afternoon we found the brigade saddled and ready to move from the village. Less than an hour from the time of the general's departure a dozen high explosive shells had been hurled into the little town. One lit in a narrow street outside the door of our headquarters, killing a man who was standing in the doorway and four other troopers who were grouped near by, and wounding twelve who were passing. My bedroom had been used as an emergency dressing station, and my bed as an operating table. The place was soaked in blood. As in the morning, the 9th Lancers had been the regiment to suffer. Of the two dozen killed and nearly as many wounded that day in Longueval all but one or two were 9th Lancers.

An explanation of the shelling was at last forthcoming. A supply train had been halted by an injudicious Army Service Corps subaltern on the brow of the hill above the village and in plain sight of the enemy's observation posts on the heights across the Aisne. The lorries on the skyline had caught the attention of our gunners on slopes far in front. Word was sent at once that such advertisement of our billeting centres would bear sinister result, but the message came too late.

I spent the night on a bundle of straw in the open. My only warm blanket had disappeared in the *mêlée* attending the hurried dressing of the wounded and their prompt dispatch to the hospital at Villers. In consequence I woke on the morning of Wednesday, September 30th, with a decided chill. The brigade moved at daybreak to St. Thibaut, a village on the Vesle between Braisnes and Fismes. I had planned a joy ride to Rheims. With Major Solly Flood of the 4th Dragoon Guards, Osborn, the 4th Dragoon Guards' sawbones, and Fairclough, I paid a second visit to the cathedral.

The fields and roadways near Rheims were full of townsfolk driven from their homes by the German shells.

A high fever induced me to take a couple of hours' rest between clean sheets at the Lion d'Or, across from the great church. Not even the novelty of a cool white bed lowered my temperature, which had so mounted by afternoon that Osborn bade me spend the night in Rheims, while he and the others went back without me. From three to five o'clock, and again at seven in the evening, German shells were poured into the town, one striking the hotel. It was by no means the first that had done so. The sole remaining chambermaid apprised me at night that at one time during the afternoon I had been the only occupant of the hotel who had not taken refuge in the cellar. This was due largely to the fact that I was sound asleep during the hottest part of the show. Twice, she said, she had run upstairs to see if I was still whole and sound, to find me pouring forth scornful snores to the accompaniment of the frequent crashes of the howitzer shells.

The next day I sallied forth, very shaky on my pins, but comparatively free from fever. My old friend Frank Hedges Butler was in Rheims, braving the bombardment to procure the pick of the vintages. With him I visited the Pommery and Greno caves and those of G. H. Mumm. Crowds hung about the entrances waiting to rush inside the moment further shelling began. The Pommery *château* was demolished by the scores of Black Marias that had sought it out. The champagne had been but little disturbed, and most of it lay safe and snug in the miles of subterranean passages that honeycomb underground Rheims. Mumm, a German, was a prisoner in French hands. Robinet, his French partner, was delightfully cordial.

> The day the Germans came into Rheims a colonel stamped his way into my house, and told me abruptly I was to prepare immediately fifty beds for German wounded. I replied in his own tongue that fifty beds I could not possibly arrange, but would be glad to provide ten if he would give me sufficient time to do so. The colonel was very brutal. He left the house swearing he would return in an hour's time. If I failed to produce the fifty

beds demanded I would, he said, be shot forthwith.

An hour later a thin young German officer came in, a couple of bottles of champagne in one hand. Depositing the wine tenderly in a corner, he asked to see what accommodation I had provided for the wounded. I showed him the ten beds, which were being got ready as rapidly as possible. 'This one,' said the young German, 'I wish to have reserved for a member of my staff who has been severely wounded. See that it is kept for him, please.'

Something in his tone and manner made me look closer at this officer, and suddenly it flashed over me that it must be the crown prince. As he left the house, after carefully turning over the two bottles of champagne to one of his staff officers who had appeared on the scene, I asked if he was the prince, and found my conjecture was correct. He called several times thereafter, evincing the greatest interest in the welfare of the wounded member of his staff until the latter was sent back to Germany.

The colonel who had threatened me with death as a punishment for not acceding to his demand for fifty beds called the same night and very elaborately apologised. He told me he had been wounded, and for four days his wound had been undressed. For three days he had hardly tasted food. 'To go so long with no time for eating or sleeping,' he said, 'and with the irritation of constant pain, made me inexcusably uncivil. I wish to be pardoned.' He was so punctilious about it that the following day he asked me to step down to his headquarters, where he called in several officers, some of whom had witnessed his abusive conduct of the day before, and again apologised in their presence. He was decidedly thorough about it, once he took it into his head to make amends.

One of the crown prince's staff said to me, 'Why do your Parisian papers lie so? They say the British force is here or there, as if they do not know that French's army is either killed or captured to a man. I can assure you,' he continued most vehemently, 'on my word as a gentleman, the British Army no longer exists. It is finished absolutely.' He was equally dogmatic in his assertion that the German Army would enter Paris in three days' time.

Eight hundred wounded Germans were cared for in Rheims. Some were there still at the time of my visit.

An early start after a second night's rest at the Lion d'Or landed me at St. Thibaut for breakfast.

The day before, an officer from G.H.Q. whom I had met in Rheims had told me of the prospective change of area of operations of the British Force. Antwerp was like to fall, he said, and the Huns to press on towards the Channel with their eyes on Calais, Boulogne, and even Le Havre. Joffre's movement on the left to outflank Von Kluck's right was being met by a German offensive in the same area that had not proved altogether unsuccessful. To move the British force west and north would put it in direct touch with the seacoast and the British Fleet, and free it from the inconvenience of having its line of supply crossed by those of the French 6th, 7th, and 10th Armies to the westward. Besides, he argued, the trench warfare on our front had degenerated into a stalemate.

To hold the line along the Aisne much less seasoned troops could with advantage be employed, and French's men, already veterans, released for more important and exacting work in the northern theatre. West Flanders, he opined, would see some stiff fighting. All this was secret and much of it left to implication, to be pieced together as the next days passed. That but few had an inkling of the prospect of such change I am sure. It was not anticipated in our own command, or if it was, not a soul breathed a word of it.

On the morning of Friday, October 2nd, the 2nd Calvary Brigade left its billets at St. Thibaut and moved up to Chassemy, in front of the enemy's stubborn position at Condé. The next day Gough's 2nd Cavalry Division moved west *en route* for the Allied left flank. Allenby's 1st Cavalry Division, of which our brigade was a part, followed on the night of Sunday the 4th.

The Condé salient had proved a strong one. We flanked it on right and left, but the German batteries on the heights dominated the level ground to the south of the Aisne in and about Chassemy. Taking General de Lisle and our three regimental commanders, Colonel Mullins, Colonel Burnett, and Major Beale-Browne, to Chassemy from Braisnes, our route lay over a road where a crawl at intervals was enjoined, as the smallest dust cloud meant a rain of German shrapnel. Chassemy was battered and the road from that town to Condé a mass of shell holes. Leaving the car in the shelter of a house, a walk along the edge of the forest in front, the Bois Morin, gave a good view of the German position. One hundred yards beyond the Condé bridge a

German outpost was securely dug in on the hill side, ready to sweep the causeway with machine-gun fire. By the bridge lay the bodies of Captain Henderson of G.H.Q. and his chauffeur, alongside their riddled car. Henderson was thought to have lost his way about September 20th, and run into the Condé outpost by mistake.

Dodging in and out of the forest edge, keeping well out of sight of the enemy to avoid attracting his ever-ready shells, blazed trees told us the safe path. Now we passed a battery of guns, now a reserve of machine-guns protected from the searching shrapnel fire. Splintered trees and fallen branches showed that the German artillery had played frequently on the wood.

In Braisnes I chatted with a guard of London Scottish at the railway crossing. They had been "out" for a fortnight, they said, but, as a fine-looking sergeant disgustedly informed me, "had seen nothing as yet." The day was to come when he would have no complaint on that score, and, little as I imagined it then, I was to be with him.

Our forty-eight hours in that part of the line was uneventful, and on Sunday night, when the darkness had closed in sufficiently to veil our movements, the Brigade started off to the westward.

The Aisne we had reached with such sanguine hopes twenty-one days before was still the high-water mark of our advance. The three weeks-fighting had cost the British Army in France nearly 600 officers and 13,000 men. We had learned much of warfare, and were off to green fields and pastures new to further our education.

CHAPTER 10

Night Marches

The march of the 1st Cavalry Division from the Aisne to the zone of operations in West Flanders occupied a week.

Until clear of the Aisne country our marches were made at night. In the daytime the troops were kept under cover in order that enemy aircraft should be able to collect as little information as possible.

An airman told me the secreting of troops from air scouts was much more of an art than most folk might imagine.

The Germans are adapts at hiding their guns, but not so good at concealing moving troops. They were very much ahead of our people at covering traces of their ordnance, and are still so, though not to such degree as formerly. I have seen some of our batteries that were well protected from the front, but perfectly visible when viewed from the rear. The Germans cover the wheel tracks when they take their guns from the road and across the soft earth of the fields. I have noted the position of one of our batteries, splendidly hidden as far as the actual field pieces were concerned, which I could "spot" with the greatest ease from the marks left by the wheels as the guns were brought into position.

A French *Zouave* was taken prisoner and escaped, making his way back to Rheims. He reported a German battery at a certain point which neither we nor the French airmen could locate. Questioned, he described the enemy guns as being so hidden that only the muzzles protruded from elaborate shelters built around them in the form of low sheds. We were then able to find the exact spot, and not long after our howitzers blew those fake sheds to pieces, scoring at least one, if not two, direct hits on the enemy's guns.

On the night of Sunday, October 4th, we made Hartennes, south of Soissons, by bright moonlight, and there spent the following day. The change from the pestilential Braisnes district to the quiet country was delightful. The gently rolling hills, well-cultivated, seemed far indeed from scenes of war and pillage, though Soissons was less than ten miles from us.

My work for the week's trek was to push on ahead, reconnoitre the roads, and wait to guide detachments at points where errors in direction might be made. Taking the billeting officers from the column to the area of the next stop also fell to my lot. Last, but not least, I kept touch with the general, ready to carry messages for him or take him for a frequent journey.

The G.H.Q. printing office was productive of pages of extracts from diaries and letters found on the enemy. All the ills that flesh is heir to had been absorbed by the pessimistic writers whose quotations adorned those sheets. One read depression and despair in every line. The prevailing tone was in sharp contrast to the inevitable grousing good-nature of Thomas Atkins.

Information about Engagements with the Enemy was another cheery publication which told of doughty deeds of never varying success. The editor of these effusions at times waxed solemnly humorous, as the following paragraph bears witness:—

> It is reported on reliable authority that on one occasion when the opposing trenches were within seventy yards of each other, our men made frequent attempts to tempt the enemy to come out by gentle badinage. All efforts were unavailing until someone shouted in a peremptory tone, 'Waiter!' when no less than twenty-three heads appeared.

Our objectives on Monday night were three villages not far west of Villers-Cotteret. I landed Bernard Neame, of the 18th Hussars, and Algy Court, of the 9th Lancers, in the billeting area in good time, after passing battery on battery of French guns *en route* for the north-west. Largny, one of our villages, was found filled to overflowing, in possession of two battalions of the 13th Infantry Brigade. The colonel of the West Kents said he had received orders to move, but before he could do so the orders were countermanded. Two other brigades held Vez, our second village, and Haramont, our third, was providing standing room for the greater part of six or seven hundred French infantrymen.

The arrival of "Rattle" Barrett and Solly Flood, the other billeting officers, cast but little light on the situation. A bivouac for the brigade in the thick woods was planned, but about midnight further instructions reached us that three other adjacent villages had been assigned us. The wild hunt in the dark, past batteries of guns, troops of cavalry, hordes of French infantry, and all manner and condition of Allied supply trains, was temper-trying, but we won through at last.

The *château* at Coyelles, the second station of our journey, had been robbed by the Germans of every bottle of wine in its cellars. Big waggons were sent, the caretaker said, to cart away the loot. Yet the Germans had left the house otherwise unrifled. The cabinets were full of silver, rare ornaments littered the tables, and old tapestries hung on the walls. The many bedrooms each held a complement of French officers, so most of our staff reposed on the polished floor of the drawing-rooms. Beautiful rugs and embroidered draperies, carefully folded, were piled high on the centre tables. Without damage to them or inconvenience to their owners, we rearranged them in such wise that they made a softer couch than the hard boards, and slept the sleep of the justly weary.

In passing through Villers-Cotteret, I saw Langton, the secretary of the Paris Travellers' Club, who told me that for seventy-two hours a continual stream of troops had been pouring through the city day and night.

On Tuesday the brigade did not wait for nightfall to resume its pilgrimage, but were under way about noon. Short of petrol that morning, I begged some from an obliging French airman. Quite a collection of French monoplanes, covered in their nighties of canvas, cuddled around a quartet of stacks away from the road. At a short distance one could hardly distinguish them from innocent farm machinery, put aside, carefully swathed, till harvest time. No more friendly men live than the French airmen. I was never in want of anything they could supply for longer than it took to tell them my needs, in whatever part of the line I might be.

Reconnoitring routes on the edge of the Forest of Compiègne was fascinating work. At level crossings trainload after trainload of infantry and guns, mostly of Smith-Dorrien's 2nd Corps, sped by. We passed the town which had been occupied by General Smith-Dorrien himself the night before, and learned that he, too, had been hurried north by rail that morning. Huge pontoons across the Oise marked the change of our direction from westward to a more northerly course, rounding a corner close to Compiègne, and then heading for Montdidier. Remy was our night stop, a village missed by the Germans when Von Kluck pushed south towards Paris. The rich farm country gave us of its best. We revelled in incomparable produce, fresh as morning dew, and a great treat to our unaccustomed palates.

A still earlier start was made on Wednesday. I had suggested a quick dash in and out of Compiègne to purchase certain necessities. De Lisle said, "No, not this morning. Keep in touch with the Brigade. We are concentrating today, and may possibly go into action before night." By early afternoon we passed through Montdidier and turned towards the east.

Captain Baron Le Jeune, of the *cuirassiers*, a French liaison officer attached to the 2nd Cavalry Brigade, ran with me ahead of our column into Montdidier.

A French staff officer who knew Le Jeune told us of de Castelnau's push forward to Noyon in September, and the awful conflict that resulted in the Germans forcing the French line back from Noyon and Lassigny. Maud'huy, he said, had come into position north of de Castelnau, and hoped to envelop the enemy's right in the direction of Cambrai and Valenciennes. But Maud'huy had well-nigh been enveloped himself and thrust back to Arras and beyond it, News had come on that October 6th that Maud'huy had retired to the high ground west of Arras, though not giving up the town, while Lille, defended by a French Territorial Division only, was sore pressed.

A French medical officer on duty at the Montdidier railway station joined in the conversation. Over ten thousand French wounded, he told us, had been through his hands during the previous eight days.

The reason for the diversion of our 1st Cavalry Division to the support of the French forces fighting in front of Roye was a superhuman effort by the enemy the day before. Roye had been evacuated by the French, and the fiercest of the conflict was already a few miles to the west of it. Naturally, as the division was passing the very point of danger, the French asked that it should be held in the vicinity for twenty-four hours in case of need. We were taken up within sight of the shells and sound of the battle, but the French line held to the satisfaction of its commanders, so by nightfall we pushed on to the north. We slept at Aubvillers, *en route* to Amiens, and the next day passed through that thriving metropolis to Villers-Bocage, where we spent Thursday night.

At daybreak on Friday, the 9th, we were awakened by interminable lines of troop-laden motor lorries and convoys of armoured cars. French troops were being poured north at breakneck speed. The race for the sea was daily becoming more exciting. The collision of the hurrying armies was to make a bloody meeting-place of Flanders one day soon. By night we had passed Doullens and were to the west of Arras.

The following morning an early start found us proceeding eastward, the sound of the guns hourly growing louder and louder. Arras was being shelled by the Germans, and conflicting stories as to operations thereabouts were afoot. I was alone, with orders that allowed considerable latitude as to route. Reaching Aubigny, I turned towards Arras, and was soon on the outskirts of the city. Parks were full of French transport, villages and towns were crowded with French troops in reserve, and refugees were swarming along the broad highway. The entire population of Arras seemed tramping that road. Dozens toiling towards the town met scores hurrying away from it. Acquaintances bound in opposite directions met and argued the wisest procedure. Every hamlet within miles was full to overflowing. The merits of a roof over one's head in the path of the shells were weighed against a night spent in the open fields out of range of the guns.

I met two residents of Arras, apparently men of substance, both well along in years.

Two days ago the Germans demanded the surrender of Arras. The general in command sent back word that the city would never surrender, but would be defended to the last man. Every pick and shovel was in use day and night to entrench our soldiers. After a vicious bombardment the enemy attacked in mass. The Germans came on well within the suburbs to the southeast of the city, between our trenches, cleverly concealed, that commanded the line of their advance from two sides. When at last the waiting defenders opened fire the carnage was awful. Back the Germans were driven, and still back, to a point a good five kilometres to the south-east. Seven thousand dead and wounded Germans were picked up in Arras, and two thousand more behind the sugar factory outside the city, from the shelter of which the fleeing Germans were driven like sheep by the glorious '*soixante-quinze*.'

It was thrilling to hear the recital of it. The good man's tally of the casualties may have been high, but the pride of French achievement that vibrated through his story dwarfed detail.

His white-haired companion told me the whole of Arras was destroyed by German shells, but he who had recounted the tale of the fighting shook his head.

No, not all destroyed. Hurt, but not so greatly. My friend's house was hit by two shells and lies a mass of ruins. To him, indeed, little of Arras remains. It is natural, is it not?

He smiled sadly, but his eyes lit up as we parted, and he said:

They came on between the two lines, and when the fire leaped at them they were mown down like corn. Arras is not in German hands, nor will be.

He strode on with thin shoulders thrown boldly back, full of that wonderful fighting spirit that has fallen over France and enveloped the race—man, woman, and child of every age and calling.

That afternoon we learned of the evacuation of Lille by the French Territorials and the screen of German cavalry, reported to be seven divisions or more, thrown out to the westward. Villers-Brulin, a village west of Lens, was our halting-place on Friday night. We were within a day's march of where Smith-Dorrien's 2nd Corps was being hurried, some brigades on foot and some by columns of light French motor lorries. The 2nd Corps had detrained at Abbeville and the 3rd Corps at St. Omer. We were drawing near to the fighting zone. A French woman was brought to our headquarters that night who had seen French infantry and cavalry retiring in our direction during the afternoon through Bruay. Country folk there told her of German troops in Vermelles and Mazingarbe, not far south-east of Bethune, and less than a dozen miles from our billets.

So Sunday, October 11th, found us at the end of our peaceful trek from the Aisne. By night we were launched into the fight in an area that was to see the troops of the British Expeditionary Force for weeks that were to lengthen into months, and months that bid fair to lengthen into years in turn.

Our first objective was a village close to Bethune. During the early morning our way led through France's Black Country. Crowds of people poured from the big factory and mining towns to watch our passing. Chocques, Gonneheim, Robecq, and St. Venant were on our line of march. Names strange to us then, but to grow in time as familiar as names of Midland towns at home. At Chocques a long column of 2nd Corps infantry was trudging eastward, to be thrown into the battle line the next morning.

Firing had been heavy to the east of us as we had pushed on northward, the roll of the rifles sounding clear in the near distance. As we lunched word came that the enemy were hammering hard to force our infantry from Vielle Chapelle, and Conneau's French cavalry were prosecuting a vigorous attack in the direction of Laventie. Gough's 2nd Cavalry Division had been fighting in front of us.

By dusk the 2nd Cavalry Brigade had reached the outskirts of Merville. Our orders were to press on through the Forest of Nieppe, holding through the night a line on the eastern edge of the forest.

I covered many miles that day. I was rarely without a message to deliver to Divisional headquarters or one to take back to de Lisle. Colonel David Campbell, of the 9th Lancers, arrived from England with his wounds healed. I took him from Merville to General Allenby's headquarters at St.Venant. Returning, we sought to follow the road Hamilton-Grace had carefully marked on my map, as the Brigade had moved on into the forest.

The French soldiers lowered the drawbridge and we ran through Merville, the streets full of Briggs' 1st Brigade, troops of French cavalry and French Territorials. A barricade had been thrown across the road by which we sought to leave the town. Long argument preceded its removal to allow our passage. A few yards further a second obstruction had been placed at the edge of a canal and the drawbridge opened. No pleading could move the French non-commissioned officer in charge. His orders were to allow no one to pass. Besides, he said, the Germans were just beyond. Incidentally, he remarked that should be allow his barricade to be pulled down the bridge had been so wedged as to prevent its spanning the canal until some missing parts had been replaced. Nothing remained but to retrace our steps, again derange the first barricade to allow our return to Merville, and make a detour.

Next day we learned that had we crossed the canal we would have encountered German cavalry outposts and our own, an almost equally hazardous proceeding in the dark. One of the 9th Lancers was shot by a patrol of the 4th Dragoon Guards that night along the same road, and not far away Lieutenant Montefiore, leading the advance squadron of 9th Lancers, came upon a German outpost, whose discovery at eight to ten yards distance led to a sharp exchange of fire, in which a trooper was killed and Montefiore received two bullets through his arm. Withal I was quite pleased the road had been so well blocked.

The night in the wood was cold and damp. The headquarters staff was housed in a rude *estaminet*. We slept on bundles of straw spread about the floor.

Before the thick mist had risen from the long lanes through the forest I was off with the General to visit the outposts. A dead German charger nearly blocked the road beyond La Motte du Bois, and the villagers tried to stop us to present us with the saddle. On our return our appetites for a waiting breakfast were not augmented by the sight of peasants taking steaks from the dead horse. The fighting started early, and desultory actions took place all morning, the enemy gradually falling back before us.

The formation of a cavalry corps, with General Allenby in command, was announced. General de Lisle succeeded to the 1st Cavalry Division and assumed his new duties at once. He kindly asked me to accompany him to the divisional staff. I had become a genuine admirer of de Lisle as a soldier, and we had grown to be fast friends. Nevertheless, it was with not a little regret that I changed the blue brigade flags on my car for red divisional ones. Never had I met, nor shall I ever meet, a finer body of soldiers than were in the 2nd Cavalry Brigade.

General de Lisle's headquarters after being hit by a "Jack Johnson"

CHAPTER 11

Fall of Antwerp

The 1st Cavalry Division saw hard fighting soon after its arrival in Flanders. On October 12th, Smith-Dorrien started an action with his 2nd Corps which had for its objective the capture of La Bassée and the occupation of Lille. For five days the fight raged. A frontal attack on La Bassée was early found to be abortive. The Germans at that point, occupied the strongest natural defensive position in' the whole northern area. Consequently Smith-Dorrien attempted a swinging movement to the north of La Bassée, to get astride the road to Lille, and attack the La Bassée position from the rear. It so far succeeded, after strenuous work, that the Lille road was almost in sight. Then it stopped, hard against the main position of a heavily reinforced enemy.

While Smith-Dorrien's 2nd Corps was winning ground, step by step, between Laventie and La Bassée, and pushing as far eastwards as Aubers and Herlies, Pulteney's 3rd Corps was sweeping eastward to Armentières. Disentraining at St. Omer and hurriedly marching to Hazebrouck, a sharp engagement took place at Meteren. Bailleul and Armentières were occupied with but little effort, and by the night of October 17th Pulteney faced a strong German line to the east of the River Lys.

Allenby's Cavalry Corps, the 1st and 2nd Cavalry Divisions, was on the left front of Pulteney's advance, and Conneau's French Cavalry on his right, the latter coupling the 3rd Corps with the left of the 2nd Corps. To Allenby fell the forcing of the Lys from the left of the 3rd Corps near Armentières to Warneton, a task which was quickly proven to be beyond the powers of the small force at his command. The cavalry corps then became the connecting link between Rawlinson's 4th Corps in front of Ypres and Pulteney's 3rd Corps in front of Armentières. The thin line of troopers held on gallantly in the centre of the British line, though overwhelmingly outnumbered by the enemy, while the German attacks on Haig and Rawlinson at Ypres and on Smith-Dorrien at La Bassée surged forward and back in the bloodiest fighting of the war.

Our knowledge of the situation in Belgium was slight. We knew Antwerp had fallen on October 9th, and that Rawlinson's 4th Corps, consisting of Capper's 7th Division and Byng's 3rd Cavalry Division, having landed at Zeebrugge two or three days before, were covering the retirement of the shattered Belgian Army westward along the coast, but that was all.

The night of October 12th found us in possession of Vieux Berquin and Strazeele after an afternoon of desultory fighting. Gough's 2nd Cavalry Division on our left had pushed north through Caestre and Flêtre, and reported the Germans in Meteren.

In mid-afternoon the 9th Lancers moved from Strazeele towards Merris and came under the enemy's shrapnel fire. Budworth was sent post-haste to Strazeele with two guns of H Battery to draw the attention of the German gunners from the 9th. He had to guess at the position of the enemy's guns. The H Battery field pieces went into action at the edge of the town. No sooner had they done so than the Germans opened on them, and after the first few rounds got the range to perfection. Budworth directed operations from behind a tree close by. The shrapnel burst all about the guns. Of sixteen men serving them seven were hit. Still they replied, keeping hard at it until dusk. The 9th Lancers took Merris, though they retired in the evening to the line at Strazeele.

That night an ambulance arrived to remove the wounded H Battery gunners. Budworth went into a house, the only building in the vicinity that was not on fire, to say goodbye to five of his wounded men before they were taken back. The doctor said one of the five, though a piece of shell had torn away part of his head, would, he thought, pull through safely. Of the recovery of the other four he was very doubtful. Two of them he considered hopeless. One had lost both hands.

A lump in his throat, Budworth passed from one to another with such words of cheer as he could muster. Each of the four who could speak—the poor fellow whose hands had been shot away was half-unconscious—eagerly pressed upon their chief but one request. Every man was concerned with the paramount idea that he must get fit again as soon as possible and return to duty with his battery. "Promise, sir, that I can come back to H Battery when I am right," was the one thing they had to ask, the one desire of their hearts. Such is the morale of the men of the Royal Horse Artillery. In spite of the severity of their wounds, each one of the four pulled through, and every man of them lived to see the day when he was back in France and again serving with his beloved battery.

Early on the morning of Tuesday, the 13th, after a comfortable night in the ample La Motte *château* in the Bois de Nieppe, we ran to Strazeele, then on at noon to Flêtre. General Keir was at Strazeele, and his 6th Division, the 16th, 17th and 18th Brigades, was pushing the German rearguard to the east while the cavalry circled round the left flank of the advance. Gough's Brigades were on the extreme left and swept over the picturesque Mont des Cats, rising like an artificial mound from the level plain and crowned with its quaint monastery. Boeschepe and Berthen were in Gough's hands, and his troopers were feeling their way across the frontier line of Belgium.

Prince Max of Hesse was badly wounded, left behind in a village by his men, and soon died of his wounds.

The broad road, poplar-lined, that covered the two miles from Flêtre to Meteren ran straight as a die. From Flêtre, the Meteren church spire marked the exact centre of the end of the path between the tall trees. The infantry attack on Meteren, planned for one o'clock, was delayed until three. By that time a drizzle which had set in early in the afternoon had become a steady downpour. Our headquarters were in an inn bearing the imposing name of the Estaminet de Rouckelooshile.

The dame who dispensed such cheer as could therein be obtained was busy. Black coffee and cognac of sorts were not to be despised as the cold mist settled down on the damp countryside. Bustling about, she made no bones of disturbing a conference of general officers, pushing a map away to reach a cupboard as she sought a relay of tumblers wherewith to meet the exceptional demand. Her shrill voice rose high in an altercation over change of English coin, drowning the low-toned words in an ante-room that were outlining plans of battle. Unconscious of her, the stern group of officers merely raised their voices to carry above the din, thoroughly engrossed in the grim business of war, but no more so than the old virago in her pursuit of nimble coppers.

Keen to see an infantry charge at close quarters, I walked on towards Meteren. The rifle and machine-gun fire made one long roll ahead. Wounded men passing rearwards in search of a dressing-station told of a very hell of a hollow where the German quick-firers swept the ground clean. Our guns had been firing earlier in the day, but the mist closed in and stopped their further participation in the fight. The enemy in Meteren seemed to have no guns. At least no shrapnel came our way. I reached a reserve position as the troops were moving up, the bullets singing overhead in swarms. Rain and mist made it impossible to see far enough ahead to get a view of what was going on, so I ploughed back to headquarters through the mud.

The enemy had placed machine-guns in the roofs of houses, removing a few tiles to allow just sufficient aperture through which to fire. These quick-firers accounted for most of our casualties at Meteren, which totalled some two hundred odd. The town was taken at the point of the bayonet, and the Germans in the houses captured while still serving the machine-guns.

Nearing the *estaminet* I passed a horseman in the dim light whose face gave me a shock. I would have sworn him to be Captain "Rivy" Grenfell, of the 9th Lancers, killed at Vendresse on the Aisne. Involuntarily I gasped out "'Rivy' Grenfell!" A closer look confirmed the uncanny feeling that I was faced by a man I knew was in a soldier's grave far to the southward. The uniform was that of a captain, and the regimental insignia of the 9th was plain on the collar of his tunic.

"Not 'Rivy,' but Grenfell," said a grave but pleasant voice, which went on to explain that the officer I had taken for the gallant captain killed some weeks before was his twin brother, Captain Francis Grenfell, also of the 9th Lancers, who had recovered from the wounds he had received at Audregnies in August, at which time I had had a brief word with him. He had been awarded one of the first V.C.'s of the great war. The likeness between the two brothers was perfect. I became great friends with Francis Grenfell, whom I was afterwards to see carried back wounded from Messines, again to recover and return to France. Months after that I was to look on his face for the last time as he was prepared for burial after his third wound, a fatal one received while distinguishing himself by gallant work in the trenches of the Ypres salient.

Fine men of noble character, the Grenfells. Surely the monarch responsible for a war that mows down the flower of the world's manhood in the fullness of its youth must one day answer for his crime, in this world or the next.

In the farm where we spent the night food was given us which the day before had been ordered by the Germans. Hardly had the good woman of the house started to comply with the Huns' demands when the cry was raised that the British cavalry was approaching, and her enforced guests stood not on the order of their going.

General de Lisle's Divisional Mess was formed that night. It consisted of the General; Colonel "Sally" Home, of the 11th Hussars, G.S.O. 1; Major Percy Hambro, of the 15th Hussars, G.S.O. 2; Captain Cecil Howard, of the 16th Lancers, G. S.O. 3; Colonel Drake, of the Artillery; Captain "Mouse" Tomkinson, of the Royals, well known as a polo-player and gentleman rider, Assistant Provost Marshal of the Division; "Pat" Armstrong, of the 10th Hussars, the general's *aide-decamp*; and myself. Not long after, the mess was to be enriched by the addition of Captain Hardress Lloyd, of the 4th Dragoon Guards, as *aide-de-camp* to de Lisle.

My first job on Wednesday, the 14th, was to take the other divisional motorcars in tow and go by road to St. Jan Cappel, towards which the general and his staff rode across sodden fields. My road lay over the Mont des Cats and past the forbidding monastery at its top. I arrived in St. Jan Cappel ahead of the main body of our advance troops. The villagers gave the cars an enthusiastic reception. The German troops after five days' occupation, had been driven out an hour before by the Queen's Bays. The dead German horse in the main street was the only sign of the fray.

The advance squadrons kept the enemy on the move, headquarters following close behind, and by afternoon we had crossed into Belgium and occupied Dranoutre, out of which the 5th Dragoon Guards chased the Germans at midday. As we neared the town a trooper unearthed a handsome Bavarian boy, whose horse having been shot and his knee hurt in falling, had hidden in the cellar of a house near by. He blushed like a girl as he was hauled forth, devoured with disappointment and chagrin at such an unheroic end to his campaigning.

Headquarters were in a nunnery at Dranoutre, a dispiriting habitation, rendered no more cheerful by the cold, sullen rain.

News of Rawlinson's 4th Corps coming southwest and not far distant led to an evening journey. De Lisle, with "Mouse" Tomkinson, took a run towards Ypres. Past Locre a patrol, aware that he was the "furthest north" of his own command, impressed us that we were on a road "where no English had gone." La Clytte was mysteriously darkened, the inhabitants scurrying off at the slightest sound. Dickebusch was little better. Germans had been about all day, said one habitant.

Had he seen any English troops? Not he. In Voormezeele we found the first gleam of intelligible information, and I began to be reassured that the 4th Corps was not, after all, a phantom army. Deciding to draw Kemmel next, we ran as far as Groote Vierstraat, and at last heard British voices in the dark. Prince Alexander of Teck was the first officer we met, and he gave us warm welcome. We found General Rawlinson at Wytschaete.

I chatted with many old acquaintances who had been "chased around the biggest part of Belgium," as one of them put it, with the 7th Division. Evidently they could qualify in the severest of tests of pedestrianism. Vague news of heavy German forces heading west was rife. The German army that had faced Antwerp was on the move, and other German troops as well, it was said. The Belgians were badly smashed, as an army, was the general verdict. Thirty to forty thousand of them were between Ypres and the sea, stiffened by some French Territorials. Time, the best judges averred, must be given the Belgians before their recovery could be expected.

"Big German forces coming west," was the recurrent topic. Strange how Dame Rumour and Madame Coincidence take tea together at times. Von Beseler with two or three Corps from Antwerp was, we found later, marching on Ostend, and that very day passed Bruges. That day or the next four new corps had left Brussels for Courtrai, and were soon to be distributed on a front from Tourcoing through Menin to Roulers. Looking back, I can remember rumours afoot that night in Wytschaete which forecasted that movement with uncanny accuracy. But G.H.Q. had no information in corroboration of those tales, as was witnessed by Rawlinson's orders four days later to take Menin with his 4th Corps, unsupported. No support was available, for Allenby, Pulteney, and Smith-Dorrien had their hands full, and Haig with his 1st Corps did not disentrain at St. Omer until October 19th.

We returned at a late hour to Dranoutre, where I learned that the 18th Hussars were in Neuve Eglise, Captain Thackwell with C Squadron of that regiment having pushed on to Ploegsteert. The next morning I took de Lisle to Neuve Eglise, where the headquarters of the 18th and the 11th Hussars were located.

No word had come from Thackwell. Lieutenant Gore Langton, of the 18th Hussars, at the head of a patrol, passed Nieppe, on the main Bailleul-Armentières road, and reached Pont de Nieppe, a mile from Armentières, in the middle of the night. A small road came into the main highway from the north. Along it troops were marching, lighted here and there by flares. A barrier extended halfway across the street. The patrol halted beside it. A trooper dismounted and walked towards the files of soldiers tramping past. "Are you infantry?" he asked of a dark form standing by the barricade. Peering towards him in the drizzle the man he had addressed took a step forward and suddenly ejaculated, "*Mein Gott, Englisher!*"

It was a German officer! The passing troops were files of German soldiers bound for Armentières.

The trooper threw his rifle forward until the muzzle almost touched the German's body, and pulled the trigger. An uproar followed. Leaping into the saddle, the trooper and his fellows put spurs in deep and tore back along the roadway for dear life. *Ping!* went a bullet beside them. *Ping, ping, ping,* came others, closer still. One found its mark, and a riderless horse sped on with the patrol. The scattering shots merged into a fusillade, but the troopers were well away, and not another man received a scratch. The flashes of the rifles behind died down. Sparks along the *pavé* told of pursuit. On sped the little band, German cavalry hard on their trail. Through Nieppe they dashed at full speed, then settled down to a steady gallop for Neuve Eglise, where they arrived safely. The Germans kept on until a few miles from the town, at daybreak returning whence they had come. A villager told us that he saw eight hundred of them passing, which gave us the opinion that their numbers may have been at least one hundred, if not two.

Crowther, a 2nd Brigade motorcyclist, was dispatched towards Ploegsteert to find news of Thackwell's squadron. Crowther was a doctor about forty years old, who had been in charge of an asylum in Surrey before the war. A brave chap, very useful as a motorcyclist dispatch rider. He was instantly killed by a shell a few days later while carrying a message along a road in front of the Ploegsteert Wood.

In his quest for Thackwell that morning he rode to the village of Romarin, on the way to Nieppe. As he could see no one of whom to ask a question, he headed his motor-bicycle towards "home," placing it just behind a street barricade, and left its engine running while he started to pull down the barrier. He had worked at the pile of stone and earth but a short time when he descried a trio of German troopers ahead. They had not caught sight of Crowther. One hundred yards away they dismounted, and cautiously crept forward along the walls of the houses, apparently trying to locate the sound of the motor. Crowther jumped on the machine and made off.

When he returned without news of C Squadron of the 18th, some anxiety was felt for Thackwell, but later in the day news came that he and his squadron were safe. He had sent three messages to headquarters, each carried by a bicycle orderly. The next day we found all three dead along the road. Germans in ambush had shot each one through the head at close range as he passed, and piled man and wheels in the ditch by the roadside.

Care to stop when challenged by our own sentries at night was impressed upon us by news of a French interpreter attached to one of our brigades and his chauffeur, who had rushed a sentry and been fired upon the night before. Both Frenchmen were shot through each leg.

On Friday, the 16th, we ran to Ploegsteert, Messines, and Wytschaete, little dreaming that in scarcely more than a fortnight thousands of men were to be killed or wounded in the defence of the three towns, two of which were to be taken from us by the enemy. The morning was foggy, preventing military operations of much consequence, but in spite of the weather Pulteney's 3rd Corps occupied Armentières, meeting no serious resistance.

A Belgian said eight Germans had come to his house at dawn and changed their uniforms for peasant garb. Everyone was on the watch for the spies, as the eight uniforms had been discovered and the Belgian's tale corroborated. Howard had news of one of the Germans, tracked him from village to village, and finally caught him. After pretending for some time to be drunk, the spy admitted he was a German soldier, and ended his career against a wall.

A Belgian farmer came to an officer of the 4th Dragoon Guards and reported that a German soldier was hiding in his cottage. Surrounding the house, the officer and four of his men entered it. A thorough search was made, but no German was found. As they were about to leave, a trooper looked up the chimney of the kitchen fireplace and saw a heavy boot. Strong hands pulled until the boot came down and left a stockinged foot dangling above. Increased efforts were at last crowned with success, and crash came the hidden fugitive into the ashes. After a struggle on the floor, during which each member of the party received his mark of the prowess of the soot-covered captive, superior numbers triumphed. For a moment he lay with eyes closed, breathless, pinned hand and foot.

"Let old Jack Johnson up," said a trooper as he nursed a bruised eye, "and I'll hit him a crack with the butt if he tries any more of it."

At the words the prostrate man's eyes opened. He gave a start and yelled, "You bloomin' rotters, I thought you were dirty *Deutschers!* Why don't you sing out who you are before you pull a feller's leg off?" Then, catching sight of the officer, "Pawdon, sir, I come in here 'cause I saw some 'Uns comin' up the road. I was out alone and didn't 'ave no rifle, so I 'ooked it and 'id away. 'Ow was I to know, sir, that it wasn't 'Uns as got me?"

The officer sat down and laughed heartily, while his squad took stock of sundry bruises and a tear here and there in tunic or breeches. "At would have served you right, young feller," growled an old non-com., "if we'd a-knocked in your foolish nut for you, but you *did* fight like hell."

From Saturday, October 17th, until the following Wednesday we were hard at work in front of the Ploegsteert Wood, facing the German position on the Lys. The cavalry fought dismounted, and were not to see warfare of other sort for many and many a long month. First we attempted to force a crossing of the river. Unable to do that, we held the enemy's attention on the Lys front while the infantry pressed north from Armentières on the further bank. Houplines fell to the 3rd Corps, but Frelinghien, the next point to be taken, remained in German hands, in spite of repeated attacks. Once or twice our infantry penetrated the town, but were always compelled to retire to a position in front of it.

Our cavalry attacks on Saturday and Sunday and the attacks of our infantry on Sunday and Monday were productive of only partial results. Tuesday saw the inception of a German attack on our front, which had been stiffened by the 12th Infantry Brigade. Wednesday found the infantry east of the Lys still hammering in vain at Frelinghien, and the German attacks on the Ploegsteert line west of the Lys increasing in violence. On Wednesday morning the enemy had a decided success at Le Gheer, but the 12th Brigade snatched the fruits of victory from them before the day was over.

Running with the general and Colonel Home early on the morning of the 17th from Ploegsteert to Messines, de Lisle impressed it upon me that he was in a hurry. A sentry not far beyond the Ploegsteert *château* tried to stop us, and was waved aside. He persisted, standing in the centre of the road until the car was almost upon him. At Home's suggestion, the general told me to back to the insistent Tommy, and see if he had any particular reason for his action. When we reached him he said, "Sorry, sir, but I just saw a party of German cavalry in that village down there," pointing to St. Ives, a few hundred yards distant. "Some of them rode out that way, the way you were goin'. I thought you ought to know, sir." How I did bless the lad and his pertinacious common sense.

We backed the car around in the lee of a wayside inn, ran to the *château*, and reported the proximity of the enemy patrol to the colonel of the Essex Regiment, whose men were hard at work digging trenches.

Our divisional headquarters moved to Ploegsteert to watch the forcing of the Lys. Briggs's 1st Cavalry Brigade were to cross at Pont Rouge, by Deulemont and Mullins, who had succeeded de Lisle in the command of the 2nd Cavalry Brigade, had orders to take the bridge at Frelinghien. A patrol of 9th Lancers had visited the Frelinghien bridge the night before. I talked with one of their number, who said they had discovered the enemy well entrenched to the east of the Lys. "Those bridgeheads will want some taking," said he. A sound prophet.

On our left Gough was to capture Warneton and win across the river at the eastern edge of the town.

The panorama of the battle lay before us from the tall tower of the Ploegsteert chateau, high on its hill above the wood. Our field-guns and the few sixty-pounders at our disposal started the ball. Watching their white shell-clouds made me long for a couple of batteries of good big howitzers with plenty of nice fat high-explosive shells. That was the proper medicine for Huns entrenched and Huns behind the houses. Care had to be taken with the shrapnel. An unlimited supply was not at the disposal of the gunners. Allen, responsible for the transportation of the ammunition, spent his life in being cursed for the shortage, and cursing in turn his inability to get what he wanted at the base. He wore a haunted look and mumbled things in passing. Was it imagination, or did I hear him mutter, "God knows I don't *eat* the damn stuff. I give the ungrateful devils all I can get of it."

The sky was leaden, though the daily drizzle had ceased. The roads were awful. How motorcyclists stayed on them no one knew. Often enough they failed to do so, but the cheerful dispatch-riders always "showed up smiling" sooner or later, save now and again when one of them "ran into" a shell. Heroic work, that dispatch carrying over roads that never knew complete freedom from shell fire.

Four German prisoners marched past. An R.A.M.C. man and a bombardier, both unarmed, in some occult manner took the four Bavarians, though each bore a rifle. The two British soldiers came upon the Germans unawares. Beckoning madly as for assistance to imaginary companions behind them, they ran straight toward the badly-rattled quartet, who put hands in air with a will when they saw they had been discovered. Odd little episodes those "all-over-in-a-second" experiences. A quick brain and plenty of nerve worked wonders. Sometimes. The majority of us, however, would generally have "done it infinitely better" if we "had had a bit more time to think." Which, of course, accounted for the success of the flash-in-the-pan minority. Two unarmed men capturing four that were armed was by no means an unparalleled incident.

The village idiot busied our spy department for an hour or so. His antics were so identically those of the average Hun spy when fate placed him in British hands that the real was definitely established as counterfeit. The Ploegsteert *padre* rescued the unfortunate man from our "Sherlock Holmes contingent."

The net result of the day's fighting was that the Germans were pushed back to the railway that ran alongside the Lys on our side of it. We did not take the bridges. General de Lisle ran in the car to General Briggs's headquarters between Le Gheer and Pont Rouge. An hour before, the enemy had been there, and were but five hundred yards in front when we called. Rifle fire was constant. I was unaware of the proximity of the enemy until a horse beside me was struck in the shoulder by a bullet, when I at once assumed a humble attitude in a ditch until the general's departure. At Mullins's headquarters at Le Bizet we were treated to a shelling, so the day was quite sufficiently exciting to suit the most bored of onlookers.

Towards evening the 12th Infantry Brigade came up from the right and took over part of the line.

Sunday morning the weather took a slight turn for the better. From our headquarters in the Ploegsteert *château* we ran to Messines and called on General Gough. His troops had gained a foothold in Warneton. Operation orders directed Gough to watch the point of the advancing German column coming south-east from the Roulers-Coutrai region and give it a check. This advance was reported to have reached America, a village six or seven miles from Messines. Gough was also to operate against the Lys front.

Sydney Green, of the R.A.C. twenty-five, by that time depleted to half that number by sundry resignations, was attached to General Gough's staff. He told me of a visit on the 17th to the east of Ypres. Rawlinson's 4th Corps was in force on the Ypres-Roulers and

Ypres-Menin roads, and two divisions of French Territorials, the 87th and 89th, were between Rawlinson's force and the Belgians on the north.

While we were discussing the situation in Messines, General d'Urbal's 8th French Army was that day forming on the British left in front of Ypres, to take the responsibility of holding the line from Ypres to Nieuport and the sea. This was to prove no mean task before the German onslaughts on the northern road to Calais were to wear themselves out against the stubborn resistance of the Allied armies.

The 18th of October was the date for Rawlinson to commence his futile movement against Menin, on the second day of which his advance had to be transformed into a hurried retirement in front of the onward surge of the German flood that Haig was soon to check so gallantly and with such narrow margin of success in the bloody first Battle of Ypres. G.H.Q. was still unaware of the fresh German movement west from Brussels, or Rawlinson's attempt on Menin would never have been ordered.

Back in Ploegsteert *château* we had sufficient work to keep our minds off operations further eastward. About one o'clock the enemy sent half a dozen shells at the *château* tower. Those who were about the grounds had one or two close calls, though the only damage done save to the turf, was the killing of one of Hardress Lloyd's chargers.

During the morning the 9th Lancers had attacked in front of Ploegsteert Wood, with the Inniskillings on their right. A battalion or so of Germans behind the railway embankment waited patiently until the 9th line had come within 400 yards, then poured a deadly machinegun fire into the advancing troopers. Francis Grenfell's squadron was in closest proximity to the withering fusillade. He kept his men down, returning the enemy's fire until they ran out of ammunition, and then lying under cover of the rifles of the Inniskillings until our gunfire made retirement possible. Of Grenfell's squadron six were killed and ten wounded. Our total casualties only reached the modest figure of thirty-two, a wonderfully small number under the circumstances.

My work for the afternoon included bobbing back and forth from the *château* to 2nd Brigade headquarters in front of St. Ives, carrying artillery officers up to see the enemy positions and cavalry officers back to the *château* tower to show the gunners where to drop their shells. Enemy shrapnel splintered the roadway thirty to forty yards from us once, but we came through sound enough. When our observation officers spotted the exact location of the Germans our shells soon found them. The gun-work was exceptionally fine. From the tower I counted shrapnel after shrapnel that burst over the precise spot upon which the guns had been told to direct their fire.

At daybreak on Monday the guns commenced where they had left off at dusk the night before. German "coal-boxes" were thump-thumping in Le Touquet, a village to the west of the Lys, across from Frelinghien. Le Touquet had been taken by our infantry after a sharp fight on Sunday afternoon.

The din of the early morning battle came clearly over the low river-bed as the pressure of our 3rd Corps on Frelinghien increased. No effort was to be spared to take the town.

Rumours reached us of Rawlinson, fighting hard away to the east. The 2nd Life Guards had been badly knocked about, said someone.

Our line was never really quiet. Machine-guns rattled away frequently. The noise at Frelinghien overshadowed other operations near at hand, but as the afternoon wore away it died down and left a season of comparative quiet. At twilight Le Touquet was ablaze. The fire lit up the night for miles around.

Morning brought further entertainment from the gunners. Major Hutchinson, brigade major of the 1st Cavalry Brigade, called at the chateau at eight o'clock and pointed out three targets from the tower. A Belgian had told of a farm on our side of the Lys where an enemy howitzer was placed behind a stout stone wall. The exact location of the German trenches along the road from Deulemont to Frelinghien had been learned from another Belgian. An outpost had discovered that two enemy machineguns were "dug in" in a clump of bushes at the corner of a burned factory on the edge of Le Touquet. All three points were plainly visible from the tower, and soon the fun began.

A dozen rounds went hurtling towards that part of the sky where once the sun was wont to rise. Wrapped in the contemplation of our own efforts, we forgot for the moment the enemy gunners. At least, two of our officers acted as though they had forgotten. Not content with the view afforded from the lower tower, where watchers were screened from sight, the two climbed higher. On the small landing at the tower's top they stood, eagerly marking the splendid accuracy of our shells, and incidentally exciting the Bavarian gunners to try their skill at so unusually fine a target.

Crash! A hole in the lawn by the *château*. *Bang!* An officer's horse hit in the drive. *Crash!* A stifling black cloud drifted in the window. A man was brought round the corner of the building with a hole in

Mr Coleman's car hit by a shell outside Messines

his back. The headquarters horses scattered this way and that, one on three legs as a red stream poured from his fourth, badly torn by a piece of shell. *Bang! Bang!* Shrapnel. Then two more. Soon they were coming fast. *Crash!* Another high explosive that jarred the whole hillside.

Hurried preparations were made for the shifting of headquarters. A quartermaster's clerk jostled the mess waiters, who bumped into the hospital orderly in turn.

I sped down the path to the lodge gates where a woman had essayed that morning to laundry my linen. Our six divisional motor drivers were bunched by their cars. "What orders?" I queried.

"We are told to take the cars out at once," was the reply.

"Force the lower gate and go out that way," I advised, and walked towards it with one of the drivers to see if the gate could be opened. We had not taken thirty steps when a smash behind us threw us forwards. A shell had lit by the group we had left, killing three of the drivers and rendering one unconscious from the shock of the concussion.

As I gathered my damp clothing together and climbed the path to the *château*, a horse near by, hit by a shrapnel bursting overhead, screamed with pain. Five or six other chargers lay here and there on the turf. Stretcher parties hurriedly gathered the wounded and bore them swiftly down the hill.

At last the place was cleared of men, horses, and cars. Two of the latter were well marked. A jagged sliver shattered a head-light on my car, and splinters marked one or two of the panels.

General de Lisle was the last to leave. While waiting for him, Colonel Ludlow, the Divisional A.A.Q.M.G., told me of a visit to the kitchen when the first shell fell. Our mess boasted a chef, a French soldier, among whose experiences was a trip round the world with Madame Melba. The first few shells had come and preparations for departure were proceeding apace. The chef's assistant, Hawes, was hurrying matters, or, at least, advising haste.

The chef was seated on a chair, his head bent low in earnest preoccupation as he wrestled with a refractory puttee, always somewhat of a trial to his unfamiliar hands. From his lips came calm advice to the impatient Hawes. "*Reste tranquil, mon ami*" breathed the chef heavily as he began the maddening task for the third time. "*Reste tranquil.*" As he spoke the last word a big Black Maria went off just outside the kitchen window at his back.

With one dive he cleared the chair and landed on hands and knees under the kitchen table, ejaculating as he gathered himself together, half-dazed, "*Reste tranquil—reste tranquil!*" A combined examination by everyone in the vicinity was necessary before the chef could be convinced he was not a dead man, or, at least, well on the way towards becoming one. Fortunately for the mess, he had fully recovered by dinner-time, but to arouse his ire for days to come, the servants averred, it was only necessary to murmur, "*Reste tranquil—reste tranquil.*"

An old *château* further from the line and less exposed to the eye of the enemy became our headquarters. Beside it was a battery of sixty-pounders, the 31st Horse Battery of the Royal Garrison Artillery, which rattled the windows with loud volleys, deafening at such close quarters. A cheery grate fire was welcome, as the damp, lowering day grew quite cold.

At about three o'clock a heavy German attack developed all along the line. The air became charged with the continual crash of a modern battle. Enemy shells, our own guns, rapid-firers and rifles all merged into one *mêlée* of sound, utterly beyond the comprehension of one who has never heard it. The colonel in command of the 12th Brigade sent a message asking for support in front of Ploegsteert, and the 11th Hussars were sent to his aid. Ambulances streamed back. In one of them I saw Captain Thackwell and Lieutenant Holdsworth, of the 18th Hussars. The 18th had suffered heavily from a fierce onslaught on their left.

Travelling on the by-roads, deep with mud and as slippery as they could well be, was slow work. On one trip back to headquarters the Queen's Bays passed me at a trot, to dismount not far beyond and go into the line in support of the 2nd Cavalry Brigade, which was in front of St. Ives.

Grenfell galloped up to where I was stationed and shouted, "Do you know, President, who is on our left?"

"Tins," I answered, "or at least some of Goughie's lot." The Tins, as the Life Guards are called, was a composite regiment made up from the 1st and 2nd Life Guards.

Turning, Grenfell said, "Right! I thought so!" Then, anxiously, "You are sure, are you?"

"Not I. Don't take my word for it. I heard someone say they were there, but it may be wrong. Ask de Lisle. He is along the road a bit."

Grenfell started towards the general, but a trooper, riding hard, stopped him. With an exclamation the captain tore off at a gallop.

A moment later I was despatched with a message to the *château*.

As I arrived three horsemen pulled up at the door. One of them, a wounded officer, could not dismount without assistance. After he had been taken inside and turned over to the doctor, I said to the sergeant, "Who was that? His face was a strange one to me."

"Mr. Wallace, of the 2nd Life Guards," was the reply.

"Where is your regiment?" I asked.

"We were just over there a bit," he answered, "but we were driven out. The lot of us were in a proper death-trap."

When I again reached the general I learned that Grenfell and Colonel Campbell of the 9th had luckily got wind of the retirement of the left of the line in the very nick of time. Throwing a squadron across our left flank and bringing up another in support, they held off the enemy, who were coming straight for a battery under Major Wilfred Jelf, whose left had been completely exposed.

For an hour or so the fighting raged madly in that sector, but dark came on with the line very little changed. Our troops had fallen back from the more exposed low-lying ground to positions prepared for just such an attack.

At dark I took Generals de Lisle and Mullins and Colonel Home to the Ploegsteert *château*, out of which we had been shelled that morning. Its devastation, soon to be completed, was well begun. By candle-light the damaged walls took odd shapes, and shadows distorted twisted ironwork and ragged shell-holes grotesquely. General Mullens and his staff used the *château* as headquarters that night, but were shelled out of it at daybreak.

On the way home de Lisle stopped alongside McCarthy's batteries and told the tall Colonel-gunner his guns had enabled us to hold our line, which without them we would have lost. Once before, to my knowledge, McCarthy had been given a like message at the close of a hard day's work—at Tour de Paissy, on the Aisne.

At early light on Wednesday we were off to Messines to see Briggs, then back to Ploegsteert Wood to Mullins. A cold wet night had been followed by a strong attack at dawn on the Ploegsteert position. The Germans succeeded in thrusting a wedge in our front that gave them Le Gheer and a corner of the Ploegsteert Wood, but before the middle of the forenoon the Inniskilling Tommies, supported by the 2nd Cavalry Brigade troopers, had driven them back, and, in official parlance, had "straightened the line."

The sixty-pounders seemed to make more noise as days passed. The headquarters *château* rocked with the din. A great flash, a thin, sickly, brownish-yellow cloud that hung in the damp atmosphere, and a reverberating crash; then as the sound echoed, leaving ringing ears, the whistle of the big projectile, in pulsating waves, died in the distance as the shell seemed to limp along through the air.

Before noon word came that the Germans had moved four batteries across the Lys near Warneton and concentrated a large force in front of that town for an attack on Messines. Briggs, with his 1st Brigade, was ready. Mullins and his 2nd Brigade was to be relieved at once and hurried towards Messines as support. At once the guns were turned on the German attacking force and began hammering away with increased vim. It became apparent as the day wore on that they had arrested the threatened advance.

Fifty-five German prisoners, taken by the Inniskillings at Le Gheer, were marched to our chateau. With them a dozen of our own men were retaken, having been captured when the enemy took Le Gheer at daybreak. The Hun prisoners were *Landwehr* for the most part, and all Saxons. A few first-line men were among them. They were of all ages, and many wore glasses. A sober, serious group, drawn from a very good class of citizen. One told me in French he had been enlisted eleven weeks, and during the previous seventeen days had marched 250 kilometres. Their uniforms were faded and worn.

A man of forty, a pair of huge spectacles over sad, patient eyes, seemed so miserable I tried to cheer him with some fatuous remark to the effect that he was safer far in an English prison-camp than in the firing-line. Earnestly he shook his head. "No," he said with unmistakable pain in his voice, "war is hard. I enlisted to fight for the Fatherland, not to be taken by the enemy. Better I had been killed, if need be." His face was a picture of real suffering. He believed his cause was just.

1st Cavalry Division Headquarters slept that night in Neuve Eglise. We said goodbye to Ploegsteert, save for itinerant calls, and set our faces towards Messines, where grim days awaited us. Before I went early to bed, de Lisle said to me, "Some of the troops that came with the Indian contingent are to join us tomorrow, President. I will load the car with a few of the new officers and take them round where the Black Marias are bursting to acclimatise them." Whereupon I retired to dream of a weird run on some strange planet that seemed one mass of seething flame and smoke.

CHAPTER 12

A Visit to Ypres

While the fighting at Ploegsteert was growing daily fiercer, the Germans were pressing hard on our lines a few miles away at Messines.

On Thursday, October 22nd, the whole of the 1st Cavalry Division left Ploegsteert to the defence of Wilson's 4th Division. The cavalry, with the Ferozepore Brigade of the Lahore Division of the Indian Corps in support, was assigned the task of holding the corner of the line that swung round Messines, where every day for a week and a half was sanguinary battle, culminating in the capture by the enemy of the Messines-Wytschaete ridge, and the consequent evacuation of Messines on November 1st.

In ten days of continual fighting against great odds in men and guns, one third of the 1st Cavalry Division was to fall, and the magnificent qualities of the British cavalry were to be tried to the utmost. Tried in the fire they were with a vengeance, and never for a moment found wanting.

The closing days of October were well-nigh the bloodiest the world has ever seen. On the far right of Messines for six days Maud'huy at Arras held off an attack by Von Buelow in the hardest battle fought since the beginning of the war. Smith-Dorrien's 2nd Corps, facing La Bassée, was hurled back by the Bavarians in ten days of awful fighting, but held its new line in the face of hammering of a sort of which veterans of Mons and the Aisne had never dreamed. In front of Armentières and Ploegsteert the Germans threw battalion after battalion in overwhelming numbers against our line.

To the left of the Messines position Von Beseler and his Antwerp Army, on the coast, all but crumpled up the poor remnants of the Belgians, saved from utter destruction by the guns of British men-of-war, d'Urbal's 8th French Army, and by the flooding of the canalised Yser. To the south of the Belgians at Dixmude, Admiral Ronarc'h and his 8,000 French marines saw fighting that was almost superhuman in its intensity and persistence. The Ypres salient at its northern re-entrant was held by part of Dubois' 9th French Corps, the tale of whose casualties in the combat for Bixschoote ran high. But Ypres, in front and on its right to where de Lisle held Messines, was to see the greatest conflict of all. Haig's 1st Corps, the 7th Division, and the 3rd Cavalry Division were to suffer casualties unheard of in the history of wars.

Thus the battle of those last October days, over one hundred miles of front, raged with unparalleled violence. One million German troops, well towards half of them of the first line, strove to break the thin ribbon of less than a fifth of their number of the soldiers of France, England, and Belgium co-operating as if units of one army.

There was heavy fighting all along the line on the 22nd. Early that morning Briggs, in Messines, told us of an attack at dawn, vigorously pressed and beaten off with equal vigour. Our line ran well in front of Messines, and the 2nd Cavalry Division took it on north in front of Oosttaverne, past Hollebeke to Klein Zillebeke. News was brought from Armentières of an unsuccessful enemy assault on that front, beginning at eleven o'clock the night before, continuing for a couple of hours, to be renewed at dawn. Before night 1,000 dead and wounded Germans lay in front of our line between Le Touquet and St. Ives.

An *estaminet* on the road from Wulverghem to Messines, about a mile from the latter town, was chosen as divisional headquarters. The 1st Connaught Rangers, part of Egerton's Ferozepore Brigade, were set digging reserve trenches not far from the inn. One of their officers ran to Messines to see the shell-fire, which was fairly hot that morning in the ill-fated town. He saw it. While he was in the square a shell lit on one side of it, killing four troopers of the 1st Cavalry Brigade. I stayed under the lee of a house wall near the square while he explored the town. I had no curiosity.

Coming from Wytschaete I met the first Indian troops I had seen in France. They were Wild's Rifles, North-West Frontier men, fine-looking soldiers. Their arrival on our front added to a motor driver's trials.

In Messines in the afternoon shells burst all about. A man who stood boldly in the streets, when cover was conveniently available, was foolish. He was likely to find a shell splinter mixed up with some part of his anatomy as a reminder of the proximity of German howitzers in considerable numbers. Spies were in the town. General Briggs was shelled from three houses in succession, finally repairing to a cellar to obtain peace and quiet. The manner in which the German gunners followed brigade headquarters from one place to another could not have been due to coincidence.

Towards dusk I had another wait in Messines. I found the few troopers who were not in the trenches in front, or in reserve behind, were lying very close. A loose bull and an escaped canary were attracting marked attention. The bull was foraging and the canary apparently trying to find its home, perhaps also in search of food. M. Taurus was obviously ill-tempered, and was given a wide berth.

The general chose a spot at a corner near a barricade not far from the square, which we concurred was as good as any other in which to leave the car. Its good fortune during those days in Messines never wavered. Another headquarters' car went by, its occupants continuing to the square, where two minutes later it was put *hors de combat* by a big shell. The passengers and driver had stepped from it and into safety but a moment before.

Machine-guns blazed away in front of Messines all the evening. As dark closed in the howitzers scattered huge "coal-boxes" all along the trench front, our guns flashing fitfully in reply. The 2nd Brigade relieved the 1st that night. At Gough's headquarters on our way to Neuve Eglise and a night's rest, I heard that during the day the enemy had launched strenuous attacks on FitzClarence's 1st Brigade at the extreme left of the British line near Bixschoote, on the 2nd Cavalry Division at Hollebeke and on the 3rd Corps front at Frelinghien. Smith-Dorrien had been fighting hard further south. The German struggle for a road to Calais had begun in earnest.

The interesting situation in front of Ypres so overshadowed all else that I was glad to spend Friday, the 23rd, in touring the line. I ran to Ypres by way of Wytschaete and Voormezeele. The roads for the first part of the way were crowded with tall Indians, each group surrounded by its quota of admiring Belgians.

General Haig's and General Rawlinson's headquarters were in Ypres, and the square by the great Cloth Hall was full of the flotsam and jetsam of armies. The town presented a busy scene. Bulfin was attacking towards Pilkem with considerable success. Near Langemarck the 1st Division was repelling a furious push forward by the enemy, and the 7th Division, by that time beginning to feel the strain of continued fighting and heavy casualties, faced a strong assault near Becelaere. Proceeding past Klein Zillebeke to General Makin's 6th Cavalry Brigade headquarters and to General Byng's headquarters not far beyond, I found the German pressure on the Hollebeke front, which Byng's 3rd Cavalry Division had taken over from Gough, had been so staunchly met the day before that nothing had been heard of it since.

As I passed Ypres, long lines of French infantry were marching through the streets of the town to the eastward. Splendid troops, the 17th and 18th Divisions of the famous French 9th Corps, they ambled on leisurely to relieve the 2nd Division, so that the hard-pressed 7th Division could in turn be given aid and its front shortened.

Reports of the operations were so confused and varied that I obtained permission to return to Ypres on Saturday, the 24th. Passing Messines, Mullins said his brigade had repulsed two attempts by the enemy to break through to the town, one at seven the night before, and the other at two in the morning. At Haig's headquarters Bulfin's 2nd Brigade success of the day previous was declared to have been splendid. Six hundred German prisoners, a field strewn with 1,500 German dead, and the relief of the Cameronians from an isolated position were among the fruits of his victory. Little runs to points of vantage disclosed that the new French troops were advancing on the Roulers road and the 7th Division being pushed back, with severe losses, to the west of Becelaere and past the soon-to-be-famous Polygon Wood. Wounded poured along the salient roads in streams.

Ypres had not echoed to the crash of its first shell. The townsfolk were busy supplying the needs of their martial visitors, little dreaming of the devastation that was soon to visit every home.

Hardress Lloyd was beside me on our return homeward as we crept through Wytschaete, winding round chaotic Indian transport, then dashed on at a good pace towards Messines. Halfway, I heard a pop! behind. "Puncture," said Hardress. Pop! The second sound caused dismay. "Great Scott, another tyre," I groaned, as I released the clutch, and applied the brake. *Pop-ping-g-g. Popping-g-g.* Punctures, indeed! Punctures of a sinister sort. Someone was plugging away at us at close range. The last two bullets came alarmingly near. *Pop-ping-g-g!* One went between our heads, close enough to make us feel the swish of it in passing.

Ducking low we sped on. A dozen more bullets came over us, but in a few seconds we were out of range unharmed. Still speeding, we discussed the situation, which had its alarming features. The shots had undeniably come from our right. The Germans were on our left and a line of our trenches in between. Could the enemy have won the trenches and got over the road? If so, we were properly "done."

"Are you sure you are heading for Messines?" asked Lloyd. "You don't suppose you are on the Warneton road by mistake?"

"Road is right," I answered. "For that matter there is the Messines church tower ahead. Maybe the Huns have taken Messines."

"If so, we will know it soon enough," and Hardress grinned.

We were certain Messines could not have fallen and we not heard of it, but there was the disquieting fact that rifle-fire had come from the west of the road. Consequently, it was with some relief that we drew near the barricade in the edge of the town and saw a khaki-clad figure beside it.

"Fresh Indian patrol, probably," laughed an officer from whom we invited a solution of the puzzle. "Took Hardress for a German, perhaps, from the red band on his cap. Seems their marksmanship has gone off, though, since I knew the Punjabis. I don't quite see why they didn't get one of you."

We left this comforting person to his regrets at the deterioration of the Indian marksmanship, thankful to be whole of skin.

By Sunday, the 25th, Briggs was again in Messines and Mullins in support. Sullen days had been succeeded by a morning of bright sunshine. A pleasant breeze drove white clouds across a sky of pale turquoise. Before night the clerk of the weather had regretted this lapse. Rain was descending in torrents, promising an unpleasant night in the trenches, particularly for the Indians, who felt the chill damp of Flanders keenly. Casual fighting was the order of the day, no great change taking place for better or for worse.

On Monday Wytschaete was given its baptism of German shell-fire. We passed through not many minutes after. The roads near at hand were lined with fleeing inhabitants. Four or five shells had come into the town, killing a four-year old child and wounding Colonel Grey of the 57th Wild's Rifles.

I saw Captain Sadleir-Jackson of the 9th Lancers, signals officer of the cavalry corps, in Messines. He had endeavoured to utilise a quantity of fine German field telegraph wire. His men had run it through the square at Messines. Four times that morning zealous individuals had cut it, thinking it an enemy line. He had it put up for a last time, but had no better luck. In an hour a passing trooper had severed it at some point, and Jackson gave it up as a bad job.

That afternoon at three o'clock a big forward movement along the whole line was ordered. We were the pivot at Messines, and were to hold the trenches with Briggs' Brigade and the Inniskillings. Gough's 2nd Cavalry Division with the 129th Beloochis at his disposal, and the 57th Wild's Rifles and Connaught Rangers in support, were on our left. Houthem, two miles and a-half east of Oosttaverne, was Gough's first objective. Byng's 3rd Cavalry was to push south-east from Hollebeke and reach Kortewilde, just north of Houthem. The orders of the 7th Division, next to the left, directed their advance to the tenth kilometre stone on the Ypres-Menin road. Kruiseik, well in front of Gheluvelt, was the village they were asked to reach. Still further left, Haig's 1st Corps were to win Becelaere, after dislodging the enemy from the edge of the Polygon Wood.

Had that advance succeeded as planned, a great change would have been made in the line.

The atmosphere was charged with tense anxiety. Eagerly we awaited news of the progress of the work as the afternoon wore away. From the failure of the line to advance on our immediate left, we knew something had gone awry; but not until the following day did we learn that from daybreak until noon the enemy had struck blow on blow at the 7th Division front near Kruiseik. All that saved Zandvoorde and a bad hole in the line was a brilliant counter-attack by the 7th Cavalry Brigade.

Advance against such overwhelming odds was futile. The Hun was hammering for a pathway to the Channel forts, and for the next three days we had no thought, on our front, save that of holding the line against his threatened onslaughts. No day was free from fighting on some sector of the front, but not until the 29th did the full fury of the storm break on the Ypres salient.

On the 30th it was to spread to Messines. For seventy-two hours from the bursting of that tempest of mad fury, we lost all thought of operations on other battlefields. Each hour brought carnage and death; each minute was pregnant with action. All that could be done was hold the line intact, and that at times seemed well-nigh impossible, but never hopeless.

So the intervening days, viewed in the fierce light of that after-period of gigantic conflict, seemed tame indeed. Yet each bore its story.

Messines was becoming a death-trap. Sheels had fallen in every quarter of the town, which had been cleared of inhabitants. One resident told me the village had surfeit of wars in bygone days, and was razed to the ground once in the eleventh century and again in the seventeenth. Its demolition in the twentieth bid fair to eclipse its former woes.

While waiting in Messines for de Lisle, who visited the town many times each day, I became quite accustomed to hot pieces of projectile falling within reach, and black, pungent shell-clouds drifting over and around me from the nearby explosion of a Black Maria. Experiences one afterwards deems narrow escapes are ludicrously plentiful in a town continually under bombardment. I have ducked nimbly round a corner to a doorway grown familiar as a shelter, and left intact but half-an-hour before, to find it choked with debris from the chaotic mass of wood and plaster to which a howitzer shell had reduced the interior of the dwelling. A walk across the square was never a leisurely procedure after I had seen a couple of shells light in it. But in reality no surer road to fatalism exists than work in such surroundings. The futility of haste or loitering is demonstrated a hundred times each day. A power far more potent than mere human gunners and the engines of their ingenuity guides shells. 'Tis just as well to leave it to Him.

A deep approach trench in front of Messines enabled the change of troops in the front line to be effected with but very few casualties. The garret of a house at the outer edge of the town, close to the end of the approach trench, was used as an observation station for our gunners. I spent some time there, standing well back from the little gable window to escape the watchful eyes of the enemy. From the window I could see our own trenches, and the German ones not far beyond. Shells often came near, once setting the next house alight. One evening General Briggs was in the garret when a shrapnel came through it, passing both walls and entering the adjacent house before it exploded. He left the building, which was hit by eight shells in that many minutes, the first one coming as he walked out of the door.

On Monday afternoon German shells, which for days had battered the great square tower of Messines' eleventh century church, fired the ancient pile. The eastern sky grew ominously black. The red flames licking at the roof were pictured fantastically against the sombre background. White smoke poured upward as the conflagration grew, a study for an artist.

In the trenches in front of Wytschaete that night, a farm on fire near by, the great Messines church blazing hard in the darkness, bursting German howitzer shells lighting up the line, and the sudden flash of our batteries behind us made a pyrotechnic display of unequalled magnificence.

The ruins of the eleventh century church in Messines

A couple of days later I accompanied Generals de Lisle and Briggs to the ruins of the church and the adjoining convent.

Inside the doorway the bare, unroofed walls rose to a grey sky. The masonry and stone of the sturdy tower had withstood the storm of shell and the fiery ordeal it brought. At the far end, under the noble blackened arch, a heap of debris marked where the altar had been. The devastating conflagration had devoured all save the walls of stone, except one figure which the fingers of the fire had left strangely untouched.

On the facia of a column under the tower hung a life-size Christ on the Cross. But for a small hole in the side, made by a falling bit of masonry, it remained intact, unharmed. No single object in the ruins existed in its normal form save that figure.

A few townsfolk, allowed an hour in the town to collect belongings, stopped in the doorway. Their curious eyes were caught and held in awed homage. One group of garrulous women, chattering like magpies, stopped transfixed, on reaching the door, their voices hushed. Crossing themselves, they drew away whispering.

Major Hutchinson told us he stood as near the doorway as possible on the night of the fire. The interior was a seething mass. Shading his eyes with a bit of tin, he could see the figure of some saint of the church on the opposite facia, wrapped in smoke and flame, already almost indistinguishable. Across the floor, isolated on the bleak wall, the Christ on the Cross stood out in the clear light of the blazing fixtures that surrounded it, as if set aside by some hand that guided the tongues of flame away from it.

"Weird," the major characterised it.

As I was standing in the doorway, knots of troopers, having heard the story, gathered to the ruins of the ancient church.

Pausing on the threshold, peering under the high, blackened stone arch above, each eye was raised to that commanding figure.

For a brief moment in the midst of turmoil, death and battle, many a mind was focussed, all-devout, on one great thought.

I saw more than one soldier, his head bared in respectful silence before that fire-spared crucifix, who plainly felt the Mighty Presence of the King of Hosts and Lord of Battles, whose cause, the triumph of the Right, was that for which he fought.

A major of Connaught Rangers reported after his initial experience in the front line the night before that his men had taken three lines of German trenches. His report attracted immediate attention.

Questioned, he said:

> The enemy had gone back before we arrived. The first line we got to was only waist deep. The second we fairly walked into. I noticed a funny thing about that line. The beggars had dug the trench just in *front* of a barbed wire fence. We had to cut through it. Devil of a job, too. The next line we had a bother with. Lot of sniping, though they got out of it as we came in. I didn't hold on to it; but went back into the second line, as it was a better position.

I listened attentively, wondering. Walking into abandoned German trenches sounded too good to be true. De Lisle said little, but grunted once or twice. Later developments led me to characterise the sound as a snort. Days later, I heard the correct version of the incident. The Connaught Rangers, in "taking over" had found three trenches not long vacated by the Tins. In his occupation of them the inexperienced major had cut up a most carefully arranged reserve wire entanglement. Just sufficient sniping had come his way to make him think the enemy were in the fore trench—a not unnatural error in the dark. The yarn went the rounds, gathering detail, until it assumed unique proportions, but it served to raise many a laugh where there was little enough over which to make merry.

A major of the Queen's Bays, in the trenches before daylight one morning, heard a party of Germans approaching. "Come here!" called out a voice from in front. "Come over here!"

"Hands up," responded a trooper though little could be seen in the darkness.

"Send on one man," was the shouted suggestion of another Dragoon Guardsman.

Unintelligible words were mumbled in reply. Curious, the major raised his head and looked over the trench parapet. A volley at close range missed him, and our men pumped bullets into the adventurous Huns in quick time. When day broke half a dozen Germans lay dead a few yards in front in witness to the accuracy of our fire.

The 2nd Cavalry Brigade was sent south to Smith-Dorrien on the 26th. The next day I ran de Lisle to Smith-Dorrien's headquarters at Hinges, behind the La Bassée line. On the 28th the newly-arrived Indian contingent attempted the capture of Neuve Chapelle, which had been taken by the enemy the day before. The Indians faced German shells for the first time. The 2nd Cavalry Brigade was in support. The

47th Sikhs bore the brunt of the work. The 9th Bhopal Infantry was in the fight, and two companies of the Indian sappers and miners.

The Sikhs charged magnificently. They got into the town, and the houses were the scenes of many a hand-to-hand fight. One big Sikh brought back three prisoners. He had cornered eight Germans in a room, he said, and went for them with the cold steel. Five of the enemy he killed outright. Asked why he stopped, he naively explained that his arm had tired, so he spared the remaining three and brought them back as evidence of his prowess.

Close-quarter fighting and individual conflicts in the buildings of the town scattered the Sikhs. Soon the Germans brought a couple of machine-guns into play at the end of a street, mowing down the big black fellows in squads as they came within range. Their officers were down, save one or two. No cohesive body could be formed to take the quick-firers, so back the Sikhs came, straggling and demoralised, the effect of their splendid charge largely nullified by their inexperience of this kind of warfare. Howitzer shells fell by the hundred. The 2nd Cavalry Brigade were sent into the scrimmage and fought hard till nightfall. They were relieved at daybreak next morning Neuve Chapelle had been taken, lost, retaken and lost again. When night closed in the Germans were in possession of the greater part of the town. The cavalry suffered seventy casualties, a light list for that part of the world in those days.

Many of the 2nd Corps regiments on that front had lost all but a couple of hundred out of a full thousand. Men of that command had been fourteen days and fourteen nights in the trenches without respite, but the line had held, and the arrival of the Indians had greatly relieved the situation.

The enemy's plan of attack on the long front from Arras to the sea never varied. His guns shelled hard, preparing the way for his infantry, massed, often deeply, on a narrow front. Battalion came behind Battalion, regiment behind regiment. The foremost body repulsed, the reserve stepped into the breach and continued the attack. Should the first onslaught prove successful, and a foothold be gained, reserves were brought up without delay to hold, and, if possible, widen the breach in the line.

Hurling back the initial attack and pounding to atoms each front line that pressed on was of vital importance in those tense days. Every foothold had to be torn loose, no matter what the bloody cost. Easier far to expend at first that strength which lay beyond what man had learned to term the limit of human endurance. No limit bounded the endurance and effect of the British soldier save death itself. The impossible was achieved so often in front of Ypres that its performance ceased to cause wonder, and hardly attracted attention.

Fighting became mechanical. Men lost their identity as men. Rank assumed less importance. Each atom fought, and fought, and fought, until to fight became as natural to the savaged Tommy as breathing. No explanation will ever be forthcoming as to why the Germans did not win through to Ypres. Time after time they won a hole in the line, blocked by no reserves, because there were none. Companies faced Brigades of the advancing enemy, and somehow held them off. Never had so much killing been done. The dead seemed to outnumber the living at times. Yet the line held, in some way. It was beyond comprehension.

The Menin road and Gheluvelt, on the 29th, was the scene of an all-day battle, to be renewed at daybreak on the 30th. The storm centre drifted our way. Gough was driven out of Hollebeke. De Lisle sent the 4th Dragoon Guards and 18th Hussars to Wytschaete to aid Gough, if he found help necessary to hold the new position in front of St. Eloi, to which he had fallen back. The day was big with action all along the line. Reports came of stubborn resistance by the 7th Division at Gheluvelt, costly to us and trebly so to the enemy. New German units had been brought up, and the Kaiser was with them, we heard.

I noted a score of wounded Wild's Rifles, almost to a man shot in the left hand or arm. One of their officers told me this was due to the peculiar way the Indians shield their head with the left arm when firing. The Beloochis got home with the bayonet one morning, inflicting frightful execution and repelling a determined attack.

A message came from the 11th Brigade at St. Ives that the enemy was advancing in great numbers. The 11th line was broken that day, to be made good by the Somersets. With Gough on our left in need of reinforcements and Wilson's 4th Division on our right barely able to hold its own, the 1st Cavalry Division was faced with a grave situation at Messines, where showers of howitzer shells were followed by massed attacks hourly increasing in intensity.

Saturday, October 31st, was not two hours old when the German bugles were heard in a dozen places in front of the Messines line. Lanterns could be seen darting back and forth like glow-worms in the black night. Shouted orders were borne on the wind to the British trenches. The rhythmical cadence of German soldiers' voices in loud marching chorus told of singing columns moving forward to the attack.

The 9th Lancers were in the front trench. On their left were two short trenches facing the left front and left flank, occupied by the 5th Dragoon Guards. On the right of the 9th the trench line continued in a gradual curve to the southward, the 57th Wild's Rifles holding that section of the line.

The enemy reached the Indians before daybreak, pouring over their front like a flood, and driving the 57th back into the town in some confusion. Messines had been shelled all night long. Driven from their position by overwhelming hordes of singing Huns, whose ranks, mowed down, filled up with numberless others from the blackness beyond, the poor Indians found the path of their retirement led straight into an inferno of scattering earthquakes that spread death over the whole district like a mantle. The blinding flash and nerve-shattering roar of the big howitzer shells, ever punctuated by the dozens of wicked whirring shrapnel that searched every quarter of the town, might well have demoralised troops of much more experience of the new gun-cult of modern warfare.

In support of that part of the line was a reserve company of the 57th and a squadron of the 5th Dragoon Guards. These two contingents went into the Germans with the bayonet most gallantly, but were hurled back by overpowering numbers.

Every European officer of the Wild's Rifles was killed, making a rally of that regiment impossible.

Also before dawn a column overran the 5th Dragoon Guards' position on the left. There pile on pile of German dead blocked the way of those who followed after, never wavering until the trenches were won and the gallant regiment forced back inch by inch, dealing death at every step.

The 9th Lancers beat off the first attack on its front. As the night began to pale the German bugles were sounding and their lanterns flashing behind the 9th and towards the town on both right and left. With the first streaks of dull light began a fight on three sides of a square that was to cost the Germans dear. On came the enemy, steady as if on parade, a maxim at each end of the advancing grey line belching forth a stream of fire at every few yards. Every man in the 9th—cool as a cucumber and full of that glorious pride of regiment that makes the super-soldier—fired shot after shot into the oncoming mass, every bullet bringing down its mark. Once the pressure on a flank uncovered the end of the trench, but the enemy's brief advantage was won back by a hand-to-hand struggle.

Then the shells came. The air was one mass of rending flashes. Shock succeeded shock, and deadly missiles fell like hail—so fast and thick no living thing could remain long untouched beneath the torrent of metal that sprayed over the trenches.

Back came the 9th, firing as they retreated. Shrapnel followed them every inch of the way. The enemy's gunners never showed better marksmanship. At the edge of Messines, Francis Grenfell turned, and with some of his squadron started back down the approach trench. One trooper who went with him said to me an hour later, "I didn't know where the captain was going, but he said, 'Come on.' It looked to me as if he was starting off to take the bally trenches back with a blommin' pistol." Grenfell had noticed the enemy were not advancing, and had heard a storm of fire from the trench ahead. He knew someone had been left behind and was still fighting hard, so back he went to get into the fight.

He found the lost trench momentarily re-won A corporal in charge of one of the 9th machine-guns had placed a low bush above it to hide its position. When the regiment was ordered to retire by Colonel Campbell, the corporal had stayed in the trench by his gun. Waiting until the Germans were almost upon him—until some, indeed, were climbing the parapet not far on his left and piling into the trench—he loosed off his deadly quick-firer. He poured a thousand rounds into the enemy at such close range the execution was beyond realisation. Men were mowed down like grass. The surprise of the manoeuvre added to its effectiveness. Leaping back out of the death trap the Germans rushed rearward in a close crowd for cover, the machine-gun in the corporal's deft hands playing on them as they ran.

By the time Grenfell reached the trench the Germans had peppered the corporal and his bit of ordnance until the gun was pierced with a dozen Mauser bullets, six or eight of which had punctured its water jacket and rendered it useless. Not long afterwards the corporal passed me outside Messines. He was carrying the tripod of his abandoned gun and almost wept as he spoke of having to leave it, useless, behind him and in the hands of the adjectived Germans, who had again come on in force to the trench, not to be denied by the few of the 9th who were left to face them. The corporal was subsequently awarded a well-deserved V.C.

De Lisle was worried. He left headquarters for Messines that morning at an early hour. On the way he called on General Hunter Weston, of the 11th Brigade, at Ploegsteert. Weston ordered two companies of Inniskilling Fusiliers to be so placed at once that his line would extend its left to near Messines. This gave de Lisle his own division and four battalions of 2nd Corps troops that arrived in Neuve Eglise during the night for the defence of the town and that part of the Messines-Wytschaete ridge which our line covered.

Reinforcements, without which the line could not be held much longer, were coming. Second Corps troops from the south and the French 16th Corps from the north, with Conneau's French cavalry as well, were on the way. The need was sore, and their prompt arrival a matter of more than life or death.

As we sped on from Ploegsteert, we tarried a moment by McCarthy and his guns. He nodded his grizzled head when asked to help. McCarthys were rare in any army. Oh for a dozen of him in that war of guns!

As we came in sight of Messines, smoke-clouds rose from every quarter of the town. A dozen houses were ablaze, the flames leaping high in the light breeze.

Swinging up to our reserve trenches, narrow, deep, and so placed as to be well concealed, turbaned heads peeped above the level of the unharvested beet-field, for all the world like khaki cabbages in a row.

Straggling Indians were all along the road, many of them wounded. At one point a procession of the poor fellows were rapidly filling a convoy of horse ambulances gathered at the roadside. A big Punjabi, covered in blood, came up, pale and tottering, supported by a comrade. Most of the wounds were in head or arm, allowing the men to navigate rearwards under their own power. One passed, insensible, borne on a door by four of his fellows. The next was in a motor-car, half lying on the front seat, huddled with pain, a blanket between his set teeth: a brave chap, horribly wounded, but holding on with sublime courage and never a groan to tell of his awful agony. Many a hero tramped by among those black soldiers of the king so far from their own land. Their stretcher-bearers, with their incessant gabble, gabble, gabble, sounding like a flock of excited turkeys, did yeoman work in their own Oriental way.

As we entered the town, a German war balloon loomed high in the near distance, a line of gaily coloured flag-signals suspended from it.

The black cross showed clear from the under wing of a German aeroplane droning above.

I saw Basil Blackwood, attached to the 9th Lancers, taken past, shot through the shoulder. Francis Grenfell, an ugly bullet-hole in his thigh, was also sent back. The 9th had suffered heavily. Seventy-five *per cent*, of their officers and a third of their men had been hit that morning.

A moment in the edge of Messines, where the fighting had reached the barricades at the eastern edge of the town, and we were speeding back to our own headquarters inn a mile behind.

A squadron of the Oxfordshire Yeomanry arrived that morning, and went up towards the front, a splendid looking lot. They were to take their places in action with the finest cavalry in the world, and to make a record of which the oldest veterans would be proud.

Coal-boxes began to search the country round more persistently. A dozen dropped on a ridge not far on the right of our *estaminet*. They were feeling for McCarthy's guns, and coming close to him at times. As I was watching the ridge I saw a wagon, loaded full of men, women, and children, leave a spacious farm and start for the rear. A sharp flash, a great black column rising, rising, and the double *rumph-rumph* of the howitzer shell, told of a hit in the road in front of the fleeing farm folk. Two seconds later another flash, again the mounting, twisting column of black, right over the wagon. Out from the shell-cloud galloped a horse. One or two scurrying forms dashed from the lane, and scattered like frightened rabbits over the fields. I turned from the sight with a shudder.

Clatter, clatter over the cobbles, the remainder of the Oxfordshire Hussars went up at a trot.

A dirty, cheery, devil-may-care motorcyclist pulled up with a message from Briggs's headquarters in the burning town.

"How is it up there?"

"Absolutely bloody."

But the Germans had not won the town. They were in an edge of it, but there they stuck, every sally thrown back at heavy cost. Every minute the firing grew heavier. More shells rained on the blazing buildings. The rattle of small arms rose to a high continuous note and hung, piercing the booming din of the howitzers and the racking fury of their bursting shells. At times the "coal-boxes" burst so fast, it seemed a fierce thunder-clap had spread itself over minutes which imagination lengthened into miniature ages of nerve-tension.

"Looks up there as though most everyone is hit or scratched," said the cyclist as he started back. "Absolutely bloody, that damned Messines. So long!" A grin, a nod, and off he dashed, straight into the thick of it.

Ambulances full of wounded wheeled slowly back to Wulverghem, dumped their shattered freight at the dressing-station, and returned at a trot into the zone of shell-fire.

A couple of wounded troopers bumped and jolted about on a bundle of straw in the narrow box of an empty limber that rattled rearwards for a fresh supply of ammunition. An officer came slowly down the road, supported by his subaltern. He was shot through the shoulder. "Only a scratch," he said, with an attempt at a smile as he staggered on.

News reached us from Weston's headquarters of Germans massing in front of Frelinghien and Le Touquet for an attack in force. Too much was going on in Messines to allow even a passing thought of what might transpire elsewhere.

Two armoured cars, attached to the Oxfordshires, moved up, to retire discreetly shortly afterwards. Messines was no place for an armoured car. A healthy, full-grown Black Maria would scatter one to the four winds.

By ten o'clock the six-inch howitzers went slowly back, their attendant transport wagons following soberly. A couple of days before those howitzers had come up fresh from the base, the gunners eager to "get into it." The change in their position to the region of the Kemmel road meant that the enemy had come too close for the sixes to be used effectively.

The 9th Lancers filled the trenches of the reserve line not many yards in front of headquarters. If we fell back from Messines those trenches would mark the new line.

A hurried dash to Messines and back in the car was found to be unwise, and a stop was ordered at the bottom of the hill leading into the town. Bullets were singing overhead. The struggle for each street was a battle in itself.

Colonel Ludlow drove up. Two battalions of Worcesters were in Neuve Eglise, he said, and the Scots Fusiliers, Northumberland Fusiliers and Lincolns had pushed on half an hour before for Kemmel. Good news that. Seventh Brigade and 9th Brigade troops of the well-tried 3rd Division. Reinforcements from Smith-Dorrien's hardened lot, well worth having, every man of them.

I chatted with Colonel Campbell and Major Beale-Browne of the

9th for a few minutes, then strolled back towards the headquarters *estaminet*. By dint of great persuasion we had induced the proprietress to send away her four-year-old daughter in charge of an elder sister that morning. The woman herself, her husband, and a girl of sixteen remained, though repeatedly advised to take up safer quarters.

I passed Pat Armstrong in the road. "Yhere away," he queried.

"Only to the car to sit and scribble," I replied.

The car stood by the inn.

"*Bang!*" went a Black Maria sixty yards from us. General de Lisle was in the roadway. "How far from us was that one?" he asked. Pat and I turned to him to reply, both laughing as each paused, waiting to criticise the other's estimate.

Before the answer, a crash that beggars description came without warning, sudden as a thunderbolt. A howitzer shell had struck the house fifteen to eighteen feet from where we were standing.

I distinctly felt the shock of the concussion. Others by me did so and others, even closer, said they felt no shock.

My head was driven violently downwards.

I jumped the roadside ditch as I recovered my balance and ran for the shelter of a haystack a few yards away. I think my idea was to avoid a possible second shell. I hardly knew what had happened. My chin was bleeding, grazed by some flying bit. The air was choked with dust and debris. A black, stinking pall hung over the *estaminet*, a farm across the road, and all between.

Yomen's screams came shrill and high from the thick bank of smoke. I could not, at first, see the outline of the inn or what, if anything, remained of it. No voices could be heard for a second or two, save the heartbreaking shrieks from the women.

Leaping back to the road I saw the General standing on the bank. As I joined him the smoke drifted. The house showed dim, then clearer. Its eastern end was torn away. A skeleton-like frame of rafters remained where the roof had been. The interior was a confused heap of debris.

Major Davidson, of the R.A.M.C., who stood in the road a few yards beyond the inn, said it opened up like a stage house blown asunder by an explosion in melodrama, tumbling inwards and collapsing as a house of cards falls.

The screaming women were extricated. Though badly hurt they could both walk and were led off toward the dressing station. The aged owner of the estaminet was severely wounded.

Corporal Smallman, one of the 2nd Cavalry Brigade motorcyclists, was in the kitchen. Both his legs were blown away, and he died in terrible pain on the way to the field hospital. His grim pluck never failed, though when he knew that both limbs were gone and no chance of life remained, he asked through set teeth for a release from the warping, frantic agony in the shape of a kind bullet to hasten the inevitable end.

Smallman was one of the very best of our motorcyclists. No finer epitaph could be given him.

We lost another motorcyclist by that shell, killed in the road close to where I was standing.

When the shell came the largest of the two rooms in the front of the house was empty, for the first time any member of the staff could recollect. An occupant of that room would have met instant death. Colonel Home and Percy Hambro were in the smaller, further room. Both were buried in the falling debris, but clambered from the window unhurt after digging themselves from under a pile of bricks and mortar.

A chair Hambro had adopted as his own stood in the larger room. The explosion hurled it high in the air. Alighting on the ruined roof it hung there on a splintered rafter, mute evidence of the fate that would have met one who had been its occupant a few minutes before.

Captain MacFarlane, of the Queen's Bays, was the Divisional signals officer. As the black cloud over the scene lifted, MacFarlane came from the farm gates, black from head to foot. I thought some new form of Hun explosive had dyed him. "What's happened to you?" I asked in amaze.

"I jumped out of the signals office in the barn to see what was up," said Mac. "I couldn't see a foot ahead of me in the muck, and stepped plump into the centre of that stinking stagnant pond in the farmyard. However, I'm none the worse, bar looks."

I turned to my car. The raised hood was smashed under a load of brick and splintered beams, about which were wound a woman's bodice and odd bits of feminine headgear. Jagged holes in the panels showed where pieces of shell had torn their way through the sides. Pulling my muffler and Burberry from under debris that covered the front seat, I found each had been pierced in more than one place by shell-splinters.

The car was equipped with a self-starter, a mysterious device that sometimes started, sometimes not. Eager to get away, still fearful of another shell, a movement of the starting lever proved that it was to be a case of sometimes not. I went to the starting handle and gave it a swing. As I did so I heard a shout of warning, and involuntarily ducked my head. Close under the mud-guard I crouched. Swish, swish, swish came the shell. I strained forward, bracing myself for the crash. But swish, swish, swish was all that came. In a twinkling I realised that the half-hearted efforts of the self-starter were turning the engine slowly and jerkily. No shell was near. Guiltily I peeped under an arm and saw Ludlow, across the road, bent double in laughter. "That look of anticipation on your face, President," said he, "was certainly the real thing."

I moved my load of brick to Wulverghem, where I took stock of damage and cleaned the car. I scrapped the broken hood, but otherwise the car's usefulness was unimpaired. A mud-guard was splintered and its general appearance marred, but it would run.

From Wulverghem I could hear the incessant din of the never-flagging battle.

A couple of German prisoners were brought back. Their uniforms were dirty and faded, but the men looked sound and fit. One captive said he had had no food for three days, but his appearance went ill with the story. Another German taken during the day told of orders received direct from the *Kaiser* that Ypres must be taken by Sunday, November 1st. A prisoner stated that his contingent had come from Verdun, *via* Lille. He told of eighteen German howitzers that he had seen in front of Messines operating in lots of three.

What a difference eighteen howitzers at our disposal would have made!

By early afternoon Briggs reported the Germans holding the eastern part of Messines, while he held the west side with his 1st Cavalry Brigade. The Inniskillings had regained their trenches on the right, and were within half a mile of Messines, firm as a rock. On the left, toward Wytschaete, the 4th Dragoon Guards and the King's Own Yorkshire Light Infantry held the southern part of the ridge, with the London Scottish, lately arrived, in the fields behind in reserve.

The heaviest of the street fighting fell to the lot of the Queen's Bays and 11th Hussars.

The wounded poured through Wulverghem in a never-ending stream. One complete convoy of ambulances was filled with troopers of the Bays and a couple of their officers.

I asked one of them if he had seen any Germans.

"Loads of 'em," was the reply. "Brave beggars, that lot. Three of us

THE FIRE-SPARED CRUCIFIX IN THE BURNED CHURCH AT
MESSINES

were in a house facing the square. Close behind us, a few yards down the street, was our barricade. We saw the Germans start another charge from clear across the open. We pumped a few rounds into 'em, and as they came on we hooked it for the barricade. When those chaps came round the corner where we could get a pot at 'em, how many do you think they was? Just eight! It seemed a pity to kill the plucky mugs. Eight of 'em! Just think of it! Charging like as if they was a whole damn army. I wouldn't minded takin' 'em, but we couldn't. It wouldn't 'a done. Besides, maybe they wouldn't. So we wiped 'em off."

"But"—he shook his head sagely as he climbed aboard the ambulance—"they was plucky beggars, if they was Germans. *I* don't want to see no pluckier. They've been killed off like pigs up there, in that town, and they keep on comin'. They fight stiff, that lot—they fight damn stiff!"

Weeks afterwards I read a letter, written by a German officer to a friend in Zurich, which paid a counter-tribute to that trooper and his comrades. It read as follows:—

> On November 1st, Messines was stormed by our troops, with great losses on our side, for the English had erected wonderful barricades, which defied all attempts to break down. As we went to the attack we were told to spare the village as much as possible, but this order proved easier to give than to obey, for the English had so ingeniously hidden themselves on all flanks that they were able to shoot down our men as they approached without our being able to locate their whereabouts. On finding that it was impossible to oust the enemy in this manner, we brought our heavy artillery to bear on the village, thus clearing the path somewhat and enabling us to move forward with less molestation from the enemy's deadly snipers. Still, even after two hours' bombardment, every house had to be stormed singly, and it was well into the evening before the place could be deemed anything like safe.
>
> If we Germans were given to understand formerly that the English soldiers were not to be feared, then that idea may now be banished from our minds, for the general opinion of those who have fought against them in these districts is that one Englishman is more dangerous than any two of the Allies.
>
> After a luncheon of bread and black coffee, the best fare procurable in the Wulverghem inn to which headquarters had been shifted,

de Lisle took the car to General Briggs's headquarters in the hollow behind Messines. As we reached the cover of the little valley a company of the King's Own Scottish Borderers trudged past and started up the hill toward the inferno above. The short distance to the scene of the conflict was emphasized by the frequent "*Sing-g-g*" of a Mauser bullet.

At dusk de Lisle had a talk with Mullins, whose 2nd Brigade was to relieve Briggs's 1st Brigade at dark. With the depleted 9th Lancers, 18th Hussars, and 4th Dragoon Guards, Mullins was to have the King's Own Scottish Borderers and the King's Own Yorkshire Light Infantry. General Allenby wanted the position held at all costs, even if it became necessary to give up the town. "De Lisle could evacuate Messines, for that matter," said Allenby, "if he held the ridge from Messines north to Wytschaete." But to lose Messines, said de Lisle, would be to lose the ridge with it, so the town must needs be held.

The situation was bad. The Germans had a strong position on the eastern side of the town. A night attack was planned, the King's Own Yorkshire Light Infantry on the right, the cavalry in the centre and the King's Own Scottish Borderers on the left. Pulling up a field-gun to within a few yards range of a German barricade was discussed, and the idea abandoned. Curiously enough the Germans adopted that very procedure during the night, blowing away an old barricade behind which, luckily, only a couple of men were posted. Neither of them was hurt.

To the north of Messines the London Scottish carried the line along the ridge from the left of the 4th Dragoon Guards to the right of the 4th Cavalry Brigade, a part of Gough's 2nd Cavalry Division. The 4th Brigade consisted of the 3rd Dragoon Guards, the "Tins" (Composite Regiment of Household Cavalry) and the 6th Dragoon Guards (the Carabineers). The last-named regiment was on the extreme right, next to the London Scottish. The keeping of the centre of the precious ridge was chiefly in the hands of these two regiments.

On our return to Wulverghem we heard that the 1st and 2nd Division headquarters had been shelled near Hooge that day, Generals Lomax and Monro being wounded, and half a dozen Staff officers killed. Three divisional headquarters struck by enemy shells in one day was certainly a record. During the morning I had overheard a staff officer joking about staff school teaching, that divisional headquarters should be well out of range of interruption and distraction of thoughts from the work in hand. A grim joke in the light of the day's events.

The line in front of Gheluvelt had been lost by the 1st Division, and regained by the 2nd, said the news from the Ypres salient. The 7th Division was holding on by the skin of its teeth. The French in front of Zillebeke were in like case.

Twice that night I ran to General Allenby's headquarters at Groote Vierstraat, and was greatly cheered by the sight of long lines of Conneau's Cavalry on the road. Reinforcements were close at hand. A French officer of cuirassiers told me of thirteen Battalions of the 16th French Corps well on the way to join hands with us on the morrow. Nevertheless, I went to sleep on a bundle of straw in a house in Dranoutre that night with anything but a light heart.

Could we hold the line?

What price could Germany pay to break it?

I was not the only one to ponder those questions that night in Flanders.

We rose at daybreak on Sunday, November 1st.

General de Lisle was at breakfast when General Allenby and Colonel Barrow came in.

"I hear things are much the same in Messines this morning as they were last night," said the corps commander.

"The night attack was only partially successful," de Lisle admitted. "We gained part of the convent, but could make no headway on the left. We have bettered our position in the town, though we were unable to drive the enemy from it."

"Well," I said to myself, "things might be worse."

The French were attacking in two places that morning between St. Eloi and Wytschaete to relieve the pressure. The 32nd Division of the 16th Corps, containing some of the finest soldiers of France, were pressing forward to the attack. The sacrifice of the past days had not been in vain. The line had held, and help was in sight—at least, so it seemed.

By six o'clock I had started for Wulverghem, de Lisle alongside and Colonel Home in the tonneau.

As we pulled into the town a grey-haired colonel, without a cap, ran into the road ahead.

"Is this General de Lisle?" he asked. "To whom do I report? I am Colonel Malcolm, of the London Scottish. The Germans are through," he went on, speaking with some excitement. "They are through the 4th Brigade. They came across the Messines-Wytschaete road, and broke through. My lot out there have stood an awful shelling—Black

Marias, shrapnel, every kind and sort of shell we had—all outside any trenches, for we had no trenches to get into. We drove them back twice, and got into them with the bayonet; but they came on the third time in such numbers we could not stop them again. I lost my two majors and I don't know how many of my poor men."

"Where have the Germans got to?" de Lisle broke in.

"They are right out there a little way," said Malcolm, pointing beyond the church to the northeast.

From the din of small-arm fire I thought he was right, and that they were "out there," but a very little way.

The general ordered me to push on sharply. He chose a lane by the church too narrow to allow the passage of the car. Leaping to the ground he seized a near-by-horse and galloped across the field, sending Colonel Home post-haste to Neuve Eglise to bring up the good old reliable 1st Cavalry Brigade. No matter how battered Briggs' lot might be, ft was a host in itself. In a short time we had finished that job, and had come back hot-foot to Wulverghem.

De Lisle returned. He had ound a fair-sized contingent of the London Scottish, who had been driven well back by the heavy shell-fire, but were eager to take a further hand in the fray. They had seen severe fighting. While they inflicted heavy losses on the Germans at close quarters, accounting for many of the enemy when they "got in "with the bayonet, the rush of overwhelming numbers, their unfamiliarity with the position, the darkness and the awful storm of shell to which they were subjected at dawn, had pressed them back some distance from the line.

They rallied like veterans when de Lisle called on them. One of their number told me afterwards a wave of quiet laughter went over those of his comrades who heard their major say: "The men have had no breakfast, sir." De Lisle replied: "They will find plenty of breakfast over that ridge in front. They look the sort that would thrive on that kind of food."

As they started off with two squadrons of the Oxfordshire Yeomanry, dismounted, to give the enemy a further taste of their mettle, the major said to de Lisle, "The colonel and the other major are dead, sir, I'm afraid."

"No, no," answered the general; "they will show up all right."

"But," insisted the major, "the colonel is gone. I have *reported* him dead."

"Now, major," laughed de Lisle, "you\ will find it will take a lot more than that to kill him. I have just left him in Wulverghem, sound as a drum."

The London Scottish and the Oxfordshires were in support of the Lincolns and Northumberland Fusiliers for most of the day, and both acquitted themselves nobly.

At 7.30 the General decided to go towards Messines and find General Mullines. We lost no time on the journey. I bumped at good speed past the ruined inn that had been our headquarters. Just beyond we flashed past the 9th Lancers, grim and determined, in the reserve trench which was soon to be the front of the battle line.

When we reached the brow of the hill which stood across the dip in the ground on the western edge of Messines, the road was so swept by bullets that de Lisle ordered me to back quickly behind a heavily foliaged tree. Dismounting, he walked down the slope to Mullins' headquarters, where we had visited Briggs the day before.

That was a warm corner. Turning the car in the narrow road with bullets singing over me in dozens, was a nervous business. I could see the Germans coming over the ridge not far away on the left. The enemy held the north part of the town. Having broken our line on the ridge further to the north, they were starting to come westward past Messines, while our troops were still fighting hard in the south-west corner of the town.

The Mauser bullets came so fast and furious, it was not difficult for me to imagine I was the target, though more than likely I was merely sitting in the line of fire, unnoticed by an enemy busy with far more important game.

The whizzing pellets came lower. I took to the ditch, and from it watched couples and trios of wounded and stragglers trickling rearward along the ditch across the road from me, *Sing-g-g! singg-g!* went the little devils. *Zip-p-p—zipp*; as one cut its way through the leaves. *Pawk!* One hit the tree trunk. A sharp slap from across the road and a quick "Hi!" from a passing Tommy told of a bullet that had found a billet. The boy who was hit was helping a wounded comrade. He fell when hit, but rose and hurried on. He would not stop and let me bind his wound.

Still lower the fire came. One or two hit the cobbled road-bed. I lay on my back in the damp ditch. Twigs and leaves cut off above me floated down lazily. Of all that stream of fire only two bullets hit the car.

It was only 7.35 when the general walked up the hill to the car. It seemed as if he had been gone three times as long. I jumped into the seat in a hurry.

"No rush," said de Lisle. "Wait for the colonel." A tall figure in khaki was coming easily up the rise, unaware of our delay on his account. I longed to shout an invitation to him to quicken his pace.

At last we were off, and soon back safely in Wulverghem. Divisional headquarters was moved at eight o'clock to the Station Inn, on the Kemmel-Neuve Eglise road, beside which, in a field, a battery of 6-in. howitzers was making a deafening row.

I stayed in Wulverghem with Colonel Home until nearly nine o'clock. The wounded poured through the village. Many fine London Scottish lads were among them. An 18th Hussar officer went by, his jaw tied with a reddening bandage. He made as if to speak, spat out a mouthful of blood, then shook his head and waved his hand as he rode on. Two old Belgians made useful trips to the edge of the town, to return supporting tottering soldiers to the ambulances.

Indians appeared in twos and threes at intervals. Unable to speak English the poor fellows knew not where to go. One lay dead on a bank outside the town, a worn-out comrade crouching huddled beside him.

Crean, V.C., the R.A.M.C. officer with the 1st Cavalry Brigade, one of the bravest men who ever won the cross, was doing the work of a dozen.

Thinking Wulverghem would soon become unhealthy he started moving the wounded from a temporary hospital in an *estaminet* which faced the end of Wulverghem's main street. Inspired by some intuition, he hurried the ambulances up and filled them in unusual haste. The last wounded man was out of the house and the last ambulance fifty yards down the road toward Neuve Eglise when crash came a howitzer shell, crushing the *estaminet* like an egg-shell.

Major Wilfred Jelf, who had succeeded Colonel Drake as our Divisional C.R.A., did a good piece of work that morning stopping the fire of a battery of our guns that were hurling lyddite into a part of Messines occupied by the King's Own Scottish Borderers.

At 9.15 the general went up to the line again. McCarthy's batteries had been hard at it all the morning and the German gunners were searching madly for them. The enemy were within rifle-range of the left of our reserve line. Between the shells and the spent bullets no place held much security.

The ridge was gone. The enemy's success in breaking our line between the London Scottish and the 2nd Cavalry Division could not be gainsaid. Holding on to Messines meant a useless sacrifice of men's lives, for the town had been held only to make the ridge secure, so at 9.30 de Lisle ordered our troops back from the edge of the town.

We had to content ourselves thenceforth with holding our strong reserve line.

Wytschaete had been captured by the Germans when the ridge was taken. The Beloochis on the left suffered heavily and fought like demons. A barn along the line became a point of vantage. The enemy drove the Indians from it. They rallied, charged, and retook the building, killing or wounding every German in it.

The 3rd Cavalry Brigade relieved the 4th Brigade, in turn to be relieved by the French troops.

Wytschaete that day saw a charge of the 12th Lancers, supported by the 3rd Hussars, in which scores of Germans were put to the bayonet.

There, too, the Lincolns and Northumberlands were caught by a tornado of German shell, which cost them many casualties.

The French attack, after one abortive effort, won the town at midday, and cleared it of the enemy. The place was rendered untenable by howitzer fire, and once more it was evacuated and a line taken to the west of the town.

Our new line of defence, since the incessant bombardment of Messines, Wytschaete, and the ridge between had won the ground to the enemy, ran from the west of Wyschaete, past a hill known as Hill 75 (from its designation on our maps), to our carefully prepared position to the east of Wulverghem. From there it circled round St. Ives and the Ploegsteert Wood to Le Gheer, and thence beyond to the trenches in front of Frelinghien.

At eleven the general took another spin to the line. *En route* we met General Allenby's car, and behind it General Wilson of the 4th Division. The three commanders held a roadside conference. When we arrived at the ruined *estaminet*, the enemy's shrapnel was bursting in dozens over the 9th Lancers in the trench line.

Germans could be seen digging in the open near a windmill on the Messines ridge. Major Hambro jumped into the car and told me to hurry him over to McCarthy, whose guns were provided a splendid target by the busily-entrenching enemy.

I dropped down the hill outside Wulverghem like a shot, and piled through the town at a rate of knots.

I did not expect to meet another vehicle in Wulverghem, but as I swept toward the corner a big car came toward me at good speed.

I tried to swerve to the right, but the slippery cobbles threw me round. The space between the houses on the left and the approaching car seemed small indeed, but no alternative existed save a smash. I dived left and through, winning the passage by a hair's breadth. As I escaped I caught a horror-stricken look on the face of the driver of the other car, whom I recognised as Jimmy Rothschild, driving one of General Pulteney's staff.

At noon, returning to headquarters, we passed long lines of London's motor buses debouching infantry near Neuve Eglise. Reinforcements in plenty had arrived. Though they came too late to save Messines and Wytschaete, they were in time to nullify the German gain and hold the enemy to the ground so dearly won.

Early in the afternoon airmen reported the enemy forming for attack at Gapaard, a village east of Messines. French guns and English guns hammered at them for an hour or so, and the threatened attack fizzled out.

Visits to the ruined inn on the Wulverghem-Messines road became more and more exciting. Wulverghem was shelled at frequent intervals. Coalboxes dropped everywhere. No field was free from a miniature cellar or two excavated by the howitzer shells.

"If they begin shelling you, move out," was de Lisle's usual caution. Move out, indeed! Little would be left to move if a Black Maria came too near. Fifty yards from where I stood two great black fellows ploughed the turf. Yet not a splinter came my way.

A run to La Clytte late in the day, to General Allenby's headquarters, took me past innumerable French foot soldiers. They bred confidence in their sturdy appearance, crowding along swiftly in undulating lines. They looked eminently business-like.

Passing through Kemmel at dusk de Lisle saw a detachment resting in the ditch at the side of the road. Pulling up, he said:

"What troops are these?"

"London Scottish," came the answer.

"Is one of your officers with you?"

"Yes, sir," and Colonel Malcolm rose and came to the side of the car.

"Ah, colonel," said the general, "you are on the right road. La Clytte, where your regiment is to reform and get some rest, is only a couple of miles ahead."

"On again?" said Malcolm. "My men have had no sleep for three nights, and we have had no rations today."

But before he had finished, word had passed from mouth to mouth along the line of sturdy youngsters that food, rest, and, best of all, the gathering of their comrades scattered in the charge, were but two miles away. Cheerily prodding sleeping forms, stretching weary limbs, they jumped into the road and were off in a jiffy. Their temper, when so completely worn and tired, was good evidence of the fine stuff of which they were made.

One day they were to be brigaded with the 1st Division, Haig's lot of seasoned heroes. In that collection of regiments, whose fame was one with Britain's greatness, I was, months later, to hear a veteran officer of the line say with feeling, "No better battalion of soldiers exists in the whole army than the London Scottish"—high praise indeed, and well earned before it was won.

So the Battle of Messines ended. Our losses were great, and those of the enemy far greater. The 1st Cavalry Division had nearly forty *per cent,* of its numbers killed or wounded, and the battalions brigaded with it suffered almost as heavily.

Chapter 13

A French Attack

The Germans attacked the line of the Ploegsteert Wood and Le Gheer violently on the morning of Monday, November 2nd. The detonation of the heavy firing came dully through the rain to us. Early in the forenoon the noise of battle lessened, the rain ceased, and the sky brightened.

One who had been talking with Sir John French told of the conversation. "The war surely cannot last *much* longer," he reported the field-marshal to have said. "The butchery is too frightful. The losses in themselves will stop it sooner or later. The enemy cannot stand it long."

So it must have seemed to one who knew what price the enemy had paid to win the few miles of ground he had so far won on our front in Flanders.

The Germans were pressing hard on our line in front of Wulverghem to Hill 75, west of Wytschaete, and north to our positions before St. Eloi. The sound of the guns was incessant.

A cyclist from the 11th Hussars passed our headquarters on the Neuve Eglise-Kemmel road and told me of his regiment, which had been shelled out of its trenches. A First Brigade motorcyclist supplemented this information. A gap between our strong line of trenches in front of Wulverghem and Hill 75 led across soft ground that presented great difficulties. To prepare it for defence in the sodden state of the low levels was well-night impossible. The 11th had been told to hold that part of the line, and had dug themselves in as best they could during the night. The German howitzers had torn the soft fields to bits in the morning, utterly destroying the trenches. Half of the 11th were hit or buried, and the remainder of the regiment was withdrawn to save it from total annihilation.

The enemy tried to follow up the advantage thus gained, and grey lines could be seen pushing west from Wytschaete. The French seventy-fives were in action, however, and our own guns were reinforced by batteries from the 2nd Corps. Shells rained on the front towards which the German attack was directed, and it soon fizzled out in front of the wail of fire and smoke that barred the way.

A Belgian staff officer drove past, pausing to tell us of the flooded Yser. From the sea southwards almost to Dixmude, he said, the land was inundated. Germans were drowned in hundreds, their guns were sinking in the all-enveloping mud, and the coast route to Calais was closed to the Huns.

A run to General Conneau's headquarters near Kemmel showed that the road would not long be passable for cars. Great cellars in the *pavé* road had been dug by the Black Marias, which were falling at frequent intervals all about the district.

The *Kaiser* had been in Hollebeke the day before, we were told. Incidentally came the news that our airmen had dropped one hundred and ten bombs on that village during the day in honour of His Imperial Majesty's presence. Who could hear such rumours without hope that one of the aerial missiles had found its mark and ended the mad career of the man responsible for the carnage, he had come to engineer?

Tuesday morning I spent behind the ruined wall of the *estaminet* that had been our headquarters on the Wulverghem-Messines road. A house on the eastern edge of Neuve Eglise had been dynamited out of existence to clear the line of fire for one of our batteries thereabouts. As we passed the pile of debris that marked where it had stood an officer was trying to get a snapshot in the dull light. Later I saw the result of his efforts in the form of a picture in a London paper. Under it was the inscription, "The work of a German shell." A large amount was advertised to have been paid for the photograph.

Shells came so close to the ruined inn during my sojourn behind it that I took to the ditch, snuggling down behind the dead body of a red cow that had been thrown from the field to the ditch the evening before.

The 1st Cavalry Division held the Wulverghem line, the 3rd Corps on the right and Conneau's Cavalry on the left. Sir John French had sent a commendatory dispatch to de Lisle's command, asking us to "hold on." It might be a matter of days or only hours before support came; we were to keep the position at all costs until its arrival. The 2nd

Cavalry Division was in billets, to be called upon by the 1st Division if its assistance became necessary.

While the day was young the enemy forced back the French line on our left. De Lisle ran to the headquarters of a French general, whose troops were bearing the brunt of the attack, and sent the 1st Cavalry Brigade up on his flank. French wounded littered the highway. The seventy-fives were firing with wonderful rapidity from a dozen positions near by. Kemmel came in for a rain of howitzer shells that made the vicinity a most unhealthy spot.

Foch attacked on Conneau's left, hoping to drive the enemy from Wytschaete, and then press on to retake Messines. Excitement reigned. A wave of optimism engulfed everyone. Our 2nd Cavalry Brigade could see the French attack from their trenches. De Lisle moved up to the ill-fated *estaminet*. All eyes were on the French. When they could be seen approaching Messines de Lisle was to let the 2nd Brigade loose. The 1st Cavalry Brigade would also attack Messines from the south-west and the 3rd Army troops close in from the west.

The ceaseless roar of guns intensified in fury. Stray shells began dropping in threes and fours close to our headquarters. Pieces from one of them spattered the walls and rattled on the tiles of the roof.

At General Mullens's headquarters back of Wulverghem shells were falling in even closer proximity. One splinter came through a window of the cottage occupied by Mullins and his staff and found the slim form of Jeff Hornby, but fortunately damaged him so slightly as to wound his feelings more than his attenuated anatomy. The irrepressible spirits of the 2nd Brigade staff bubbled forth in unquenchable hilarity at this incident, and messages of mock condolence were showered on Hornby, as though the very war itself were one huge joke.

In the midst of the fun the laughter subsided abruptly on the arrival of Lieutenant Chance of the 4th Dragoon Guards. The boy was covered from head to foot with dirt, as though he had rolled in a mud bath. His hand had been painfully smashed by a shrapnel bullet He came in to report that he had been compelled to pull his squadron back from the line to a position not far behind it.

Chance was one of the many junior officers who were in senior positions in those days of heavy casualties. His squadron had been on the right of our line, adjoining Conneau's Frenchmen on his left. His task was the holding of the soft sandy ground that had been so shell-swept the day before. Digging a deep trench line, his lot "sat tight" under a bombardment that had been terrific. A senior officer on the

IN THE FRONT TRENCHES FACING WYTSCHAETE

FRENCH 16TH DRAGOONS IN THE TRENCHES AT LINDENHOEK

left of that position told me later in the day that for thirty-five minutes the bursting shells over Chance's squadron formed a curtain of fire that hid from sight the windmill just beyond.

Eight, sixteen, twenty-four, and then again eight, sixteen, twenty-four came the Black Marias in line. The ground in front of the trench was thrown up as by a series of mines. Then close behind the trench line, eight, sixteen, twenty-four, until the soft ground caved in in all directions and no trenches were left. Men were buried alive in squads.

Digging out those who had not been buried so deeply as to be hopelessly immured, Chance led his men back, through a hell of shrapnel fire, to the protection of a road-bank a little to the rear. Not a rifle was unchoked, and some time had to be spent in cleaning them. Wiping the sand and dirt from their mouths and eyes, they cheerfully followed the young officer up to the ruins of their trenches and began digging themselves in again.

Once more the German howitzers were turned on them, and once more they were buried in their obliterated trenches. Again Chance took the remnants of his squadron back to the road-bank. Realising the futility of further effort to hold the line where the trenches had been, he adopted the new position and improved it as best he could for defence. The wound in his hand, received during the early part of the morning, became so painful he came back to get it dressed, but before seeking the doctor he called on Mullins to acquaint the general of what had taken place, and to apologise for having to give up the part of the line that had been assigned to him.

Chance was only one of many youngsters who showed such mettle. Truly an army containing a multitude of youths of that mould may be well termed invincible. The lads among the officers were given full opportunity in the Messines fighting to show their worth. The few days on that front cost the 1st Cavalry Division seventeen officers killed and sixty wounded. The total divisional casualties were not far from seven hundred.

It was evening before we gave up all hope of the success of the French "push," but it could not get on. Guns, guns, guns, all day. Aeroplanes sailed over friends and foes. The latter dropped streamers in the sunshine, and at dusk fire-balls, over us. Shells, shells, shells, till one wondered if the supply was inexhaustible. One of our airmen reported that our guns hit a German battery twice sure, and possibly three times. Our gunners said the Huns did our batteries no harm, in spite of the incessant shelling.

A G.H.Q. summary recorded that "the absence of men in the active list from amongst the prisoners captured during the last month is remarkable, and seems to point to the exhaustion of that class. Between the 14th and 20th of October 7,683 German prisoners have been interned in France, excluding wounded. News from Russia continues to be good."

That was the news from the outside world to us. Our news in return was no more or less than that we had "held on," and darkness had come on another day of continual struggle.

In the night the dismounted French cavalry filed past us in two long lines. On one side of the lane little fellows trotted along in red trousers, light blue tunics, and high-peaked blue caps to match, armed with short carbines and big sabres strapped to their backs, with a great blanket roll atop. On the other side marched the orthodox cuirassiers, tall forms in dark blue coats and capes, their helmets cased in cloth covers.

With every hour the enemy was to find our thin line growing stronger and his last chance of breaking through on that front fading away. The day cost the 4th Dragoon Guards two officers killed and two wounded and over thirty casualties among the men. Only seven officers in the 4th Dragoon Guards were left. The 9th Lancers, too, lost a couple of officers and several men from the everlasting shellfire.

Conneau's attack brought his line 500 yards nearer the enemy.

Late at night the 2nd Cavalry Division took over our trenches, and we stood in support of them, the men gaining a momentary respite from five days of incessant battle, during which hardly a man, from general officers to troopers, had his boots off.

A sad incident marked the next day. Lieutenant George Marshall, of the 11th Hussars, an aide on General Allenby's staff, and a universal favourite, went to Ypres with a fellow staff officer, as Cavalry Corps headquarters was resting. General Haig's headquarters were in a hotel in the square at Ypres. A big shell lit just outside, killing Colonel Marker of Haig's staff, and also instantly killing Marshall. Our headquarters had been moved to a comfortable *château*—just in time, it proved. During the morning the Germans shelled Neuve Eglise, our former home, killing seven and wounding more, immediately in front of the house which had been our domicile for some nights past.

After a second day in support, our troopers again took over the trenches, which meant a night of hard work in the rain and mud. A night attack on the French position on Hill 75 had resulted in some success to the enemy, which made the connecting of our left with the French right a troublous matter in the wet darkness.

The morning of Friday, the 6th, was quiet; at; least, judged by the standard of its predecessors. British optimism was at once forthcoming, as always, when given a ghost of a chance. A glimpse of the sun made all forget the mud underfoot. A G.H.Q. officer was authority for the rumour that the Germans were evidently preparing to "get out," and moving their howitzers back with that idea in view. All were willing to accept any cheerful interpretation that might be offered.

At noon the French gallantly attacked Hill 75 and won it nobly. With a trio of staff officers I tailed along across the fields ankle-deep in mud, watching the advance of the lines in blue. We could see little enough, but quick rushes up slopes not far ahead were now and then visible, and the rattle and roll of small-arm fire so clove in front was inspiring. French troops charge over almost impassable ground with unbelievable rapidity.

Our first big 9.2 guns arrived, whereat there was unlimited rejoicing. For days after the arrival of the first one or two to be apportioned to our part of the front, marvellous tales of direct hits far inside the German lines were current.

Visits to the trenches near our old headquarters inn in front of Wulverghem were daily increasing in interest, as that locality was never free from danger. A dozen howitzer shells fell round the ruined *estaminet* that day as we approached it, but luckily no more followed. The road beside the dead red cow, that I had adopted as shelter in the ditch, was torn by a great shell hole, and paving blocks had been scattered broadcast. Rifle-fire became an added distraction while I was waiting on the hillside, stray bullets cutting leaves from the tall poplars that lined the roadway.

Heavy fire away to the north told of battle towards Ypres. We ran to General Allenby's headquarters on Mont Noir that evening and heard of fierce fighting in front of Klein Zillebeke. The French infantry had been violently attacked and driven out. The 7th Cavalry Brigade had been sent in to make good the line, as the retirement of the French uncovered the right of Lord Cavan's Guards Brigade. The 1st and 2nd Life Guards and the Blues had won back the lost ground, but it had cost them dear. Colonel Wilson, of the Blues, and Hugh Dawnay, who had left French's staff to command the 2nd Life Guards, had been killed. Seventeen of the officers of the two regiments had been killed or wounded, and many of their men. To Lawford's 22nd Brigade also

1st Corps (Haig's); Men coming out of Ypres trenches during the first great Battle of Ypres

A hidden British Howitzer

was due a good share of the glory of snatching victory from defeat.

Thus swung the tide of battle. One day, in one part of the line, it seemed the rush of onslaught had been stemmed, only to break forth with increased fury in another sector.

What would be the end? We crawled home to our *château* through a heavy fog. The mud, the deep ruts in the broken *pavé*, the great shell holes in the road, French troops and English along the way, horse and motor transport, an odd battery or two of guns changing position under cover of the night, motorcars and motorcycles, all without lights, made such a run a trial of temper and of skill.

Colonel Seely called and provided some amusement to offset the strain.

Saturday, the 7th, came, wrapped in cold fog. All night the rifles had spat into the darkness, each side firing at the flashes when they showed dim through the mist.

Once more we poked our way to the ruined *estaminet* that was our daily port of call. Just before nine o'clock Hardress Lloyd came back from the trenches, where he had gone with de Lisle. He said the General had walked down the line, and we were to make a detour through Wulverghem and meet him on the road to Wytschaete.

In the outer edge of Wulverghem we found a barricade across the street, which had been so solidly constructed that there was no question of pulling it down and getting the car through. Consequently Lloyd suggested that I should put the car under such shelter as I could find, while he walked down the road and explained to the general why we did not come further. I left the car in the lee wall while I went on a tour of inspection. I found no one in the village; at least, no one alive. There were four dead soldiers in the tartan of a Scottish contingent down one street, and three dead soldiers who had been laid out, with a sheet put over them. I discovered I was the only live person in the town, which was by no means consoling. A sharp burst of rifle fire started not far on the left, and I returned to the car. Our field-guns had been hard at it since daybreak, and so had those of the enemy, and the small-arm fire had also been heavy at intervals. The French were attacking, and the heavy high explosive German shells were going off with their double *rrrumph-r-rrumph* not far away.

I sat on the step of the car, took out my notebook, and scribbled. My notes recorded the events of the next few minutes in detail that tells of effort to forget my nervousness.

9 a. m.—Across the road from me is the convent building which was used as General Allenby's headquarters for some days recently. It is a sight. Every pane of glass in the first story windows is shattered, and many of those in the windows of the ground floor. A great gaping hole in the roof is surrounded by scores of smaller holes in the tiles. The roof as a roof is not of much further use.

Bang! A shell has fallen in the town. *Whizz! Bang!* Another one just over me. To go on with my description of General Allenby's house (*Bang!* another), a big hole has been torn in the wall of the upper story (*Bang!* one has fallen closer still), and a sister to it appears in the side of the lower storey.

The four shells that last came this way appear to be shrapnel. The French guns are replying, and so are ours. *Whizz!* There went one that did not burst. Now for the other three to make up the quartet, as the German batteries are apparently firing in fours.

9.5 a. m. Bang! That is number two. Close and just on my left. It exploded. Quite a shower of bits of debris and pieces of shell fell over me. Nasty sound. *Bang!* Number three. That was a good shell as well, also a bit to the left of me and a little further beyond. A couple of bullets from that one hit the convent. *Whizz!* and a crash just at my side. That was No. 4. Well over and in a fine position. Fortunately that it did not explode, as it could not have been more than eight or ten feet from where I sit, and just across, the thin wall which is the best protection that I can find at this point. If it hadn't been a 'dud' they would have more than likely had to cart me out of this rotten town.

9.8 a. m. Sometimes the German gunners stop after firing a series of eight, and sometimes after a series of twelve. Rarely with this itinerant shelling do they send more than two lots of four, or at the outside three lots of four. There are occasions when they keep it up for a long time. I wonder what will be their policy this morning as regards Wulverghem? One more right where the last one lit would do the business so far as I am concerned.

9.11 a. m. Beginning to feel better, for it looks as though the eight finished the salvo.

9.13 a. m. The German shells are searching the vicinicty of the town on both sides and in the front and all behind it, but the eight did finish that lot. What luck! They are looking for the French batteries which are firing steadily from quite a number of positions hereabouts. A French artillery officer has come up the road and greeted me with great cordiality. He asked me if I had seen another French officer in the uniform of his battery hereabouts. I have not, and told him so. We passed a joke about the fact. Wulverghem is a nice healthy spot at the moment, and I told him I thought the shell-fire had for the moment ceased. I was constrained to knock on a piece of wood beside me as I made the remark, which brought a curious glance from the Frenchman. Superstition apparently has no nationality.

9.15 a. m. I dislike being the only occupant of a town that is being shelled. If I could have held the French officer for company I should have done so, but he has returned to his battery, after wishing me good luck.

9.17 a. m. Here, at last, is the general, and I can get out of this place, and back to our headquarters, which I shall not be loath to do.

The general told me, as we returned, that he had been interested in watching the shelling. He, too, had been wondering whether the Germans had commenced a consistent bombardment of the town which would last for some time, or whether they were only dropping a couple of rounds of shrapnel thereabouts. He said, "When I saw they were shelling the town I knew that you would be having an engrossing few minutes, so I remained in the trenches a little while. It was quite as interesting to watch the shelling from that position as it would have been to observe it from Wulverghem, and I did not want to steal any of the enjoyment from you."

The K.O.S.B. and K.O.Y.L.I. went past us during the forenoon on their way to the line. The former regiment suffered heavily during the last hours of the fighting in Messines. A captain told me all but two of his fellow officers were hit and the strength of the battalion reduced by nearly 150 men.

French infantry moved to the right of our Wulverghem front and planned an attack on Messiness for the afternoon. General de Lisle rode up to watch the progress of the French, and said I could come as far as our familiar ruined inn, see what I could, and bring him home when the show was over. At the French general's headquarters I learned that the attack on the slopes of Hill 75, where the line was swaying back and forth each day, was successful. A good length of trench was taken, the Germans leaving scores of their dead in it.

At the smashed *estaminet* howitzer shells were falling in sufficient numbers to dispel any illusions as to the withdrawal of the enemy's big guns from the Messines area. Odd rifle bullets hit a tree or a broken wall with a nasty smack, and the wicked *zipp-zipp* of the little fellows came every few seconds. Once a German machine-gun spattered that part of the hill, but the damaged house wall was good cover from any such missiles. The sound of Black Marias shrieking not far above and crashing into the pasture beyond was disconcerting, but they were doing no real damage.

By chance I discovered that a deep trench had been dug in the lee of a haystack that stood at the corner of the ruins of the farm across the road from the inn. There was safety. The field about the stack was littered with dead cows, and monster shell holes were thickly spattered in front of it.

I could see the French and German lines on the sides of Hill 75, not far across a ravine at the foot of the steep slope surmounted by my haystack.

The noise of the bursting German shells and the sharp barking of a number of batteries of seventy-fives behind me was painful. Black Marias fell near in search of the French guns. The noise really hurt me.

When under shell-fire, I have more than once tried to sense the pain of the constant banging as on might define physical suffering. My brain was sometimes numbed, sometimes made acutely sensitive to it. When the howitzer shells came in dozens and scores the sound waves have caused me positive agony of a mental sort. The sensation was indescribable. A tearing at my nerve-centres seemed like to wrench apart some imaginary fabric of feeling and sensibility. It grew unbearable, but generally subsided with a lull in the shelling, leaving me tired, as if having suffered physical pain.

The Oxfordshire Yeomanry were in our front trenches not far away, and one of their officers was on observation duty behind the stack. He saw a company of Germans file down a cross trench a couple of hundred yards in front of the French line on Hill 75, and at once told the French gunner who was observing in the trenches. Back ran the Frenchman to his battery, to point out the exact spot. In a moment the seventy-fives were sweeping the ridge in front of the French trenches. Back and forth and back again went the devastating shower of shrapnel. "Some observation," remarked the Yeomanry officer with a grin.

As de Lisle had suggested my going into the trenches and "talking to the boys "if I became lonesome, I crept along the roadside ditch that served as an approach trench. "Keep down," came the sharp order as I drew near. I stooped lower. In a tiny dugout I chatted with a couple of Oxfordshire officers.

One of them, Lieutenant Gill, I had heard mentioned as having handled his men with great coolness on the morning we lost Messines, the first day the Oxfordshires were under fire. Shelled while lying in a beet-field, Gill had quietly moved his men a hundred yards from the path of the howitzer shells, which followed him to his newly-chosen position. Thereupon he as quietly moved the men back whence they had come, losing but few of them. Repeating this manoeuvre at intervals saved his squadron heavy casualties, and taught them that disregard of Black Marias on soft ground which is so hard to learn, but so comforting when once one has thoroughly absorbed the idea.

The French attack on Messines "made some progress," but was stopped a long way from its objective.

News came at breakfast on Sunday the 8th of the heavy Ypres fighting of the day before. Byng's 3rd Cavalry Division and Lawford's 22nd Brigade were specially commended. Owing to them we regained practically all our lost line at Klein Zillebeke. The French on Haig's right had a terrific struggle and gained a mile.

On our immediate left Conneau reported that the enemy had evacuated some of the Wytschaete trenches, leaving their dead in considerable numbers. The attack on Messines was again to be pressed.

Taking advantage of the cool bright day, General de Lisle ran to the headquarters of the Indian Corps at Hinges. Twenty-three thousand of Willcocks' men were in the line, I was told. General gossip told of Seaforths, whose trenches had been invaded by Germans, only to be bayoneted to a man, and of Ghurkas who hated shell fire, and could not understand why they should sit still under it without retaliation of a personal sort.

The Germans pushed our 3rd Army troops back to the edge of the Ploegstreet Wood during the morning.

The French were confident night would find them in Messines, but were doomed to disappointment.

Waiting outside General Allenby's headquarters at Westoutre the next morning, a 3rd Cavalry Division officer told of a captain in his regiment, killed in front of Ypres, whose body had been found the next day robbed of coat, cap, and boots. A listener retailed a story of a visit paid to a French battery by an officer in an English staff uniform. He spoke good French, and showed no less intelligence than interest in the position and the battery's work. Two other British officers came past. Noting the khaki, they called out a query as to the route to a nearby town, and were answered in French. Neither of them had any proficiency in the Latin tongue, and said so feelingly.

"What swank!" said one to the other; "the beggar must want to show off in front of the French chaps."

"Please direct us in English," he concluded to the staff officer. "Sorry to have bothered you."

But not a word of English could they obtain in reply. About to depart in mystification and somewhat ruffled in temper, one became suspicious.

A moment sufficed to prove the pseudo staff officer a sham. He was no other than a German spy in British uniform.

A subaltern of the Warwickshires rode up asking the way to Bailleul. The 2nd Royal Warwicks, the 2nd Queen's (West Surreys), the 1st Royal Welsh Fusiliers, and the 1st South Staffords composed Lawford's 22nd Brigade, which had loomed large in despatches. We piled question on question. The Brigade was retiring from the line for rest, said the Warwick lad. Of its original 124 officers only fourteen were left, and its men were reduced to less than half the strength in which they had left England. When the enemy broke through between Cavan and the French the 22nd Brigade and the 3rd Cavalry Division were hurled into the breach. Out of the fourteen officers left in the 22nd eleven were killed or wounded, leaving only three, including Lawford himself, who led one bayonet charge in person. The young officer said:

> The general plugged on ahead of all of us, waving a big white stick over his head and shouting like a banshee.
> There was no stopping him. He fairly walked into Germans, and we after him on the run. We took the German trench in front of us and held it, but they mowed us down getting up there. How Lawford escaped being hit is more than anyone can tell. I can see him now, his big stick waving in the air, and he shouting and yelling away like mad, though you couldn't hear

AT THE CORNER OF THE CLOTH HALL, YPRES,
IN NOVEMBER, 1914

A SHELL HOLE IN FRONT OF THE CATHEDRAL IN YPRES

a word of what he said above the sinful noise. My Sam, he did yell at us! Wonder what he said?

The boy rode off down the road in a brown study. It had just struck him he hadn't heard a word his chief had been shouting. He had come through that awful charge alive—one of few to do so. Yet he forgot all that. His own part in the fight never entered his head. "Wonder what he said?" And he rode away thinking.

Oh, such men! Could the whole world beat them?

That afternoon I met General Lawford himself in Bailleul, looking fit as a fiddle. After great efforts I persuaded him to dine with us that night at our *château*, on condition that I should convey him there and back, and "not keep him more than an hour," as he was busy.

Someone from St. Omer told me the "Terriers" were coming out in increasing numbers. The 10th Liverpool, 5th Black Watch, and Leicestershire Yeomanry were across the Channel, soon to be followed by other Territorial Battalions.

General de Lisle had watched with increasing interest the splendid observation of the French gunners and the terrible execution of their seventy-fives. Taking Major Wilfred Jelf, our divisional gunner, he ran to the ruined *estaminet* in front of Wulverghem to spend an hour or so watching French gun practice.

As I pulled up at the familiar spot I saw ample evidence that the Germans had been paying marked attention to our former headquarters since my last visit. Six or eight new and good-sized shell holes showed black in the soft earth of a nearby field.

The rickety old chair I had rescued from the debris a few days before and placed in the less of the wall was smashed and tossed aside. A stretcher which had stood against the wall for some days was broken in pieces. The *pavé* road was badly battered, the grey stones of the surface being spattered with holes of varying sizes and ground to white powder. Odd-looking little holes those, and sinister in appearance, telling of flying splinters of stone, not less deadly than pieces of shell.

As we crossed the road and entered what had once been the gateway of a farm, one of the buildings, a mass of ruins well burned out, was blazing fitfully.

Two partially burned rifles were mute evidence that some soldiers had been about when the building had been struck.

Of the two buildings that still bore some semblance of their original form, one had been as completely demolished by high explosive shell as had its fellow consumed by the flames. It had not caught fire, but shell after shell had passed through it till the mere skeleton of a building was left.

A signal corps man in a trench behind a haystack at the corner of the farm reported that his wire had been cut half a dozen times by shells that afternoon. While cut off from all possibility of communicating with his fellows, he busied himself by counting the German shells. During the first thirty minutes he had counted fifty that had fallen within a short radius.

The German gunners were evidently of the opinion that the French batteries were closer to the *estaminet*.

In order to reach the French observation officer we walked down the road in the direction of the front trench. The enemy trenches at this point were about four hundred yards from our line. It was growing dusk. We covered a quarter of the distance, when a shrapnel, followed closely by three more, burst almost over our heads. Had we been in the field on the other side of the hedge beside which we were walking we should have been in the direct path of the shrapnel bullets. All three of us stepped down into the ditch that ran by the roadway. I ducked as low as possible as we quickened our pace to the trench in front of us. Four more shells, closer it seemed than the first four, burst over just as we reached the shelter of the trenches. The general and Jelf went into a tiny dug-out with two officers of the 2nd Life Guards, and I crawled on my hands and knees into the mouth of the main trench. This trench was fairly deep, and at the bottom the men had hollowed out a snug shelter underneath the front wall. The men, lying head to feet at the bottom of the trench, well under the cave roof, were quite secure.

The French batteries behind us began a fast and furious reply. The enemy's fire quickened in turn until shells were bursting with nerve-racking regularity over the roadway immediately behind us.

I could find no room in the bottom, so lay in the approach part of the trench. How I did wish for a foot or two more depth to the end of the trench that was left to me!

The French batteries continued to fire steadily. They were shelling a farm in the near distance in which the enemy had placed a group of machine guns. As dusk approached apace, the Germans were afforded an increasingly better target by the flash of the seventy-fives close behind us. After fifteen or twenty minutes of nerve exercise the general decided that he must return to the car. So many successive quantities of shrapnel were bursting over the road that to return by the way we had come seemed suicidal. The Germans now and again turned their guns on to the ruined inn and the farm. I told Jelf I was sure they knew we had to go back there for the car. But jokes fell a bit flat in that atmosphere.

Finally the general tried a detour. Walking down the road a few yards, we turned across it, when we reached our trench line on the further side. I glanced down in the trenches as we went behind them. The men were lying tight and close at the bottom. A French observer who was in the hedge by our side warned us to keep low on account of the French shells that were screaming over our heads.

As we turned back towards the car the French guns seemed to throw more vigour into their firing. The swift rush of the shells and the sharp bark from the muzzles of the seventy-fives so little distant made one think uncomfortably of prematures. Once in a while shells will burst before their time and scatter from the very mouth of the field-piece death and disaster to him who chances to be in the near foreground.

A bough from a low tree under which I was standing was cut by one of the French shells. I ducked and involuntarily jumped for a nearby trench. I was at once called back by the general, who was off across the open space before I could catch up. As I stepped through the hedge a rain of German shrapnel, from twelve to sixteen coming at once, burst over the part of the field just ahead of de Lisle.

We could not veer further towards the French batteries, as to cross their line of fire at any closer proximity would have been madness. It was equally unwise to stay where we were. To return to the trench which we had been occupying might very well have landed us in difficulties, and, at all events, would find us no nearer our objective—the car and "home."

The general walked steadily across the field, unmindful of the shrapnel. I was never more sure of being hit. I hardly know whether I was paying more attention to the French guns roaring away and their shells whizzing over our heads or to the enemy's shrapnel bursting in front of us, on our right, over us, seemingly everywhere about us. I kept my eyes strained in the dusk for shell holes which were deep enough to offer some shelter. Had I been alone I would have run, I think, rabbit-wise from burrow to burrow rather than walk so steadily and with such maddening slowness across that awful beet-field.

In the centre of the field we suddenly stumbled across an empty trench. Much to my delight the general suggested that we should retire into it for a moment. As I lay prone in the bottom of it the shells continued to come over, bursting not far above. We were quite secure unless a shell actually came into the trench and burst, in which circumstance we would have been, as Jelf said, "finished up properly and consequently beyond all worry." Turning their attention from the field for a moment, the Germans began to burst shrapnel over the ruined *estaminet*. Time and again the major, after a particularly violent burst of shell, remarked, "That lot finished the car thoroughly, I think." De Lisle was of like opinion. I said that I hoped that the Germans would keep on firing at the car. It was much better than to burst big and little ones all around us.

"But," said the general, "I certainly don't want to walk home."

"I do," said I. "I would be quite willing to walk home and walk back again to get out of this."

Once or twice we started to leave the trench, but each time the French batteries seemed to quicken their fire and the enemy shelled back violently in return. When it was almost dark we cut across to a line of trees, then up towards the road, leaving the tree line for the temporary shelter of a low haystack in an open field not far from the motor. I sallied forth to the car, losing no time. I started the engine, jumped quickly into the seat, and dashed away from the *estaminet*. Pausing a moment to pick up the general and Jelf by the haystack, I sped down the hill towards safety.

Inspection of the car on the following morning showed a couple of jagged holes in the sides of the body. A large piece of shell had gone through an empty petrol tin and ruined a rug in the tonneau. So but little damage was done after all, save to my nerves.

We were gaining the belief that German high-explosive shrapnel defeated its own object. The propulsive power necessary to scatter the bullets was often counteracted by too powerful a bursting charge.

Lawford dined with us as promised, and told us something of the hard times that had fallen to the lot of the 7th Division, which had but forty-four of its officers left and only 2,336 of its 12,000 men.

The 1st Cavalry Division was once more in the trenches on the morning of Tuesday the 10th. General de Lisle started early for the front. We passed Neuve Eglise, running to the Brewery Inn on the Kemmel road. Marks of shell-fire showed this spot an enemy target, so it was voted unhealthy for headquarters. A point near Wulverghem was reconnoitred, but dead horses were near-by in such numbers and

The Cloth Hall and St. Martin's Cathedral, Ypres, November, 1914

state that we returned to Neuve Eglise and settled in our old home. German shells came daily to Neuve Eglise, a fact that caused some thought to more than one member of the staff.

The location of headquarters for the day having been settled, we visited General Briggs on the Kemmel road, then ran to Wulverghem.

De Lisle rode in front, beside me. Hardress Lloyd was in the tonneau.

At the entrance of the town I glanced at the General questioningly. "Surely," I thought, "he is not going up to that unmentionable ruined inn again. The place is a death-trap."

"Straight on," said de Lisle. Yes, he was going to the *estaminet* after all.

I set my teeth and "let the car out."

Three seconds later, "*Crash!*" a shell exploded in our faces. The sound of splintered glass and of the shell striking the car mingled with the deafening blast of the explosion. Bullets whizzed past, striking on all sides. A French soldier close to whom we were passing dropped with a groan.

I felt a sharp blow in the chest and a twinge of pain as I caught my breath.

I reached for the brake. "The general," I thought, "*must* be hit. Lucky *I* appear to be all right. Now to back round and clear out before number two shell comes."

"Back out of it," came from de Lisle, with sufficient emphasis to show *he* was alive, right enough.

I tried to put in the reverse, a maddening process on my car at the best of times. Force! Force! the gear would not go in. Any moment number two and numbers three and four, for that matter, might arrive. At last the reverse grated home and I started back.

Turning, I saw de Lisle was sound and unhurt. But Hardress! His face was in his hands, his head bent. Hit! And in the head! I was sure of it. But no, a moment later he assured us he was all right bar bits of glass from the splintered screen that had got into his eyes.

Backing as fast as I could, I narrowly missed a French soldier who had fallen behind us, sorely wounded. Swinging the car round, I headed for Neuve Eglise. No need to stop for the French boy, whose comrades were close at hand. Away we dashed. "*Crash!*" came another shell as we tore out of the town. I never learned where it struck; all I know was that we were clear of it.

A good-sized piece of shell had hit the heavy plate-glass screen, shattered it to bits, and luckily glanced past the general and struck me in the chest. Had I known of its coming the night before I could hardly have been better prepared. Feeling the cold weather intensely, I had worn an unusual amount of clothing.

A heavy flannel vest, a thick winter khaki shirt, a weird sweater, double-breasted, annexed in Rheims, and my tunic were covered by a double-breasted Irish frieze coat. This last had been sent out to me by mistake as it was dark grey in colour. So unorthodox a garment could not be worn along the lines without a plentiful display of khaki. Consequently I had wrapped round my neck a huge khaki muffler of thickly-knitted wool, tying its ample folds at the chin, and letting its double ends provide me with a wide front of the prevailing shade.

The piece of shell tore its way through the double folds of muffler and played havoc with the great coat. None of the remainder of my voluminous wardrobe suffered, but my breast-bone felt the shock. It was some time before I could believe that it or various ribs attached to it had not been broken. Time proved that a bad bone bruise was the extent of my injuries after all. As the general hadn't a scratch and Lloyd's eyes were none the worse, all ended merrily, save for the car.

A halt at French headquarters along the road showed that a shrapnel bullet had penetrated the radiator, passing through it, and leaving a clean hole, from which the water was spouting.

"No water of any sort at this farm," said a French staff officer. I hurried on to Neuve Eglise, and from there took the damaged vehicle back to the base for repair.

A halting, limping run found me in St. Omer by afternoon, *hors de combat,* but hoping soon to be ready to return to duty.

CHAPTER 14

The Battle in the Salient

Wednesday, November 11th, marked the onset of the great attack on Ypres by the Prussian Guard.

The *Kaiser* had spurred his Bavarians, *Landwehr* and *Landsturm* to superhuman efforts. No troops could have fought with greater bravery, but they fought in vain. Their failure to hammer a hole in the thin British line left William the War Lord but one arrow in his quiver— the Guard.

The onslaught of Germany's most seasoned veterans was in keeping with their proud name.

The enemy hurled itself simultaneously against the line held by Haig's depleted 1st Corps, the 32nd and 9th French Corps on his left and the 16th French Corps on his right. Heroic charges were repulsed with enormous loss to the oncoming Battalions, which dashed themselves in solid masses against men to whom fighting had become a natural as drawing breath.

Haig's troops met the brunt of the fight along the Menin road, in the vicinity of Gheluvelt. One division of the German Guard Corps, a portion of the 15th German Corps and a portion of the 27th Reserve Corps surged forward indomitably, and drove our 1st Division from its first line of trenches, only to have the most of the ground gained torn from them by such counter attacks as warfare had never seen before.

The story was told simply and effectively by Haig's general order of the 12th. This read as follows:

The commander-in-chief has asked me to convey to the troops under my command his congratulations and thanks for their splendid resistance to the German attack yesterday. This attack was delivered by some fifteen fresh battalions of the German

Guard Corps, which had been specially brought up to carry out the task in which so many other corps had failed, *viz*: to crush the British and force a way through to Ypres.

Since our arrival in this neighbourhood the 1st Corps, assisted by the 3rd Cavalry Division, 7th Division, and troops from the 2nd Corps, have met and defeated the 23rd, 26th and 27th German Reserve Corps, the 15th Active Corps, and finally a strong force from the Guards Corps. It is doubtful whether the annals of the British Army contain any finer record than this.

De Lisle's 1st Cavalry Division came out of the line in front of Messines on the evening of the 11th for a well-earned seventy-two hours' rest. For ten days little or no opportunity had been given to take stock of heavy casualties and refit.

The men left the trenches on Wednesday afternoon, and at dinner on Wednesday night orders came to headquarters that the division must move to Ypres at once in support of Haig's men, to whom, after three weeks of constant battle, had fallen the task of repulsing the fiercest attack of the whole war.

The 1st Cavalry Brigade was on the road to the north by 11 p. m. and the 2nd Cavalry Brigade an hour later, all thought of the seventy-two hours' rest forgotten, eager to press on to the succour of their gallant comrades, with such strength as in them lay. That strength was not to be gauged by their attenuated numbers, for the troopers, who had held on to Messines till the ridge was lost and their withdrawal ordered in consequence, were equal to a force of the enemy outnumbering them six to one.

The 12th they spent in the salient in reserve, and on the 13th, Friday, they took their places in the line and showed their temper to the Prussian guardsmen.

My shell-smashed radiator temporarily repaired, and my chest better for a few days' doctoring, I rejoined the division on Friday evening, as it was going into action.

The days required for the repair I had spent in St. Omer, at G.H.Q. Rain fell unceasingly. The work on the car was carried on in the open, regardless of the storm, the mechanics standing ankle deep in a quagmire of ooze and mud. Efficient repair seemed well-night impossible under such circumstances, though the men worked like Trojans. Oftentimes they toiled far into the night, for no matter how diligently they strove, broken down cars surrounded them in droves, their impatient drivers clamouring ceaselessly. Poor Scott, the A.S.C. captain in charge of the repair park, was vainly trying to do the work of ten men.

Hieing to the cosy Café Vincent I delivered myself to the tender ministrations of a pretty auburn-haired waitress, who had become the pet of junior officers at General Headquarters. The soup was excellent, and then came sardines. Heavens, was I never to escape them! Sardines, alternated with their more lowly blood-brethren *maquereaux*, had dogged our footsteps for months. Even in the most opulent hostelry in St. Omer they followed me relentlessly.

After a careful search of the town I found a yard stick marked with inches, the property of a local draper. From it I made a tape measure. With a friend's assistance careful figures were compiled and despatched to my London tailor. A winter uniform was a necessity. Aghast at such a falling off in my ample proportions, the man of scissors and thread in London town obeyed my behests. A month later the new clothes arrived. To my horror they were so small I could not get into them. Research showed the St. Omer yardstick to have been a delusion and a snare. Its inches were marked for profit, not for accuracy.

An evening in the Hotel du Commerce at St. Omer was great fun. Harry Dalmeny, Shea, Baker-Carr, Hindlip, and kindred spirits gathered at dinner. Marlborough was sometimes present. Jack Seely discoursed at length on subjects concerning all and sundry, Dalmeny ever joking him unmercifully. A stranger whose ears caught the conversation would have been shocked to hear Seely told that all ills of the army were due to rottenness of the administration of his office on the part of that Minister for War who held the portfolio the year preceding the outbreak of hostilities. But Seely was imperturbable. Nothing ruffled him. Not even Dalmeny's oft-told tale of Seely—"I am Colonel Seely. I have been directed by the commander-in-chief to receive and impart information."

This, according to Dalmeny, was the invariable formula hurled at staff officers dashing past in the heat of battle or in the stress of frantic hurry at some critical moment of the retreat. It was all good fun. Every man present knew Seely as a very gallant officer. F. E. Smith's languid sarcasm glanced off the hardened front of this gay gathering like feathered shafts from a coat of mail. Freddie Guest and Guy Brooke were neither of them strangers to the party.

An unusually severe downpour made my departure from St. Omer for Ypres a wet business on Friday, the 13th. I missed the comfort of a hood. A new hood for my car had been ordered from England, but was to lie, mislaid, at Woolwich Arsenal for many a long week.

Past Cassel on its hill-top, the road lined with camions awaiting French reinforcements, soon to disentrain from the south, I sped to Steenvoorde and Poperinghe. A veritable nightmare, that run. Of all the maddening road obstructions the Algerian horse and cart column easily took first prize.

At Poperinghe application to Headquarters of Echelon B of Haig's Corps produced the information that the 1st Cavalry Division was "somewhere on the Menin road, east of Ypres." I was recommended to "proceed through Ypres and push on east a few miles, then enquire again." Cheerful!

A newly-fledged fleet of Red Cross ambulances worked its way autocratically on toward my goal, and I fell into its perturbed wake. At last, a block—impassable. West of Ypres, at the railway-crossing, traffic was banked up like a log-jam. French horse-transport, side by side with ubiquitous British lorry drivers in considerable force, tried to forge eastward over, around, or between a column of French cavalry and a brigade of British field-guns, which were persistently disputing the right of way to the west. French officers shouted orders to English gunners, who swore softly, while a British officer ploughed through the sticky mud and drenching rain, urging reason on French *cuirassiers*, who politely wondered what in the world he wanted. A tired Jehu behind the wheel of a lorry laughed loudly as a flare showed a mud-plastered sergeant who had lost the road, his footing, and his temper. At the roar of merriment his woebegone appearance produced, he let loose a searing blast of reproof that was in itself a liberal education in expletive. The driver's laugh subsided to a chuckle, then died in wonder at the storm it had unwittingly raised.

Entranced, I watched the scene till I caught sight of Major Macalpine-Leny, of the 1st Cavalry Division Staff. Hailing him, I learned de Lisle's whereabouts, and pushed on, when the block cleared, to Division Headquarters on the outskirts of Ypres.

From Ypres the flash of guns showed through the pitch dark of the rainy night in front, to left and to right. German shells were falling in most unexpected quarters. No rule or reason seemed connected with their arrival, save to make night hideous with their din and chance a hit at bodies of troops r transport moving in the night.

Howitzer shells exploding near at hand, momentarily flashing from the blackness ahead, produce a picturesque effect for all their terrifying detonations.

The 1st Corps units our division relieved were sadly cut to bits. One battalion consisted of but two officers and sixty men. Another had only one officer left, and numbered less than two score all told. We found a brigade headquarters with a major in command, whose brigade-major was a subaltern.

On all sides stories could be heard of terrible slaughter inflicted on the enemy. The Guard had come as if on parade, men said. Whole regiments had withered away under a stream of fire, and others relentlessly advanced over their dead bodies as if unmindful of their own certain fate. A gunner told me one Battalion of the Prussians had broken through our line and marched straight towards our guns. Coming within one hundred yards of his battery, they had literally been blown back from the very cannon's mouth, leaving 500 of their dead in ghastly heaps to mark the limit of their bold advance.

I saw half a hundred prisoners, huddled in the rain, examined by lantern-light. Fine, big men, broad-shouldered and tall. They looked defiance on their captors, as if to remind the hated English they were German Guardsmen still, though their teeth were drawn and their comrades littered the slopes they had thought to win.

Haig's heroes were generous in their tales of German bravery. Death held no terrors for the Guard, they said. I was often reminded of this as, the days wore on. The German line would surge up to our trenches only to be swept away, the remnants staggering back from the withering fire. Recovering from the shock of the recoil, small detachments, twos and threes, dozens, or perhaps a score, would come trudging back where death was being dealt out with lavish hand. Some marched boldly, more came doggedly. Many were seen advancing with an arm across their eyes. These futile manoeuvres, always ending in the total annihilation of such a group, were inexplicable until a captured German officer gave the key. Men of some battalions, he said, ever remembered that their regiments had never known and never could know retreat. Death, yes, but not retirement. There was no place at the rear for them, so they went on to join their fellow comrades in a glorious death.

It was better so, from our standpoint. Every dead German meant one less with whom to deal. It may have been magnificent, though none but Prussians would have called it war.

Haig's troops held men who never thought they would have an active role in the Ypres fighting. Cooks, orderlies, officers' servants, and transport men were called into the line to reinforce the thin battalions.

I saw soldiers who had spent eighteen continuous days and nights in the actual firing line without respite or reprieve. No billets for them, save the water and mud in the bottom of the trenches, to which they were hanging by tooth and nail. Bearded, unwashed, sometimes plagued with vermin, the few who remained in that front line were a terrible crew.

One of their officers, unshaven, unkempt and unbelievably dirty, told me the remnants of his command might be divided into three classes. One or two had succumbed to the frightful physical strain and were broken past all probable recovery. The rest were sullen or fierce, according to temperament, equally to be dreaded as fighting units. Whether they killed with a lustful joy, half-wildly, or with the deadly matter-of-fact calm of desperate determination, killing had become the one paramount business of the hour, and never ceased for long.

Such was the handful of bull-dog breed against which five to one and even heavier odds of the flower of the greatest Army in the world's history threw itself in vain.

No more glorious achievement rests to the credit of the British Army than that of Haig's sorely tried 1st Corps in the first Battle of Ypres.

The fight was by no means over by the 13th. For four days more the struggle was waged with unvarying effort, on the part of the Germans, to break through.

The early morning of Saturday, the 14th, gave me my first sight of the destruction wrought in the ancient Flemish city. Great cavities in the streets and piles of debris, ever increasing in number, made Ypres barely passable for motor traffic. The Menin road was under constant shell fire, which made me thankful that our headquarters were on the Zonnebeke road, between Potijze and Verlorenhoek. A room in a modest dwelling served as headquarters. A stream of wounded soldiers, French and British, rolled back towards Ypres. Ambulances passed and repassed, crowded with shattered forms. They had little room for a wounded man able to walk back to a dressing station.

The British line crossed the Menin road about a mile west of Gheluvelt. The irregular front followed the eastern edge of the woods on both sides of the road. The position was well "dug in," and tunnels and underground rooms were scattered here and there.

South of the highway, the opposing lines, a few yards apart, ran through the grounds of the Herenthage Château. The *château* was held by the enemy. Our troops were in possession of the barn. By a fierce attack during the morning the Germans captured this barn, and we heard of the organization of a night attack to regain it.

The salient was alive with French and English batteries. The noise of their firing was ever with us, augmented by a continual shower of enemy shells.

Sharp intermittent bursts of rain hourly spread a thicker covering of slimly mud over the road surfaces. The temperature fell rapidly, and night closed in cold and dreary.

The Northumberland Fusiliers made the attack on the Herenthage Barn. It failed, and the officer who led the assault was killed. A gunner officer volunteered to wheel a field piece to within a couple of hundred yards of the barn and smash it at close range. Five shrapnel were hurled into the stronghold, and a sergeant led the Northumberlands a second time to the attack. This time the charge was successful, and the position was won. The shattered building was a shambles. In addition to its defenders, it had contained a number of wounded when the five shells came crashing through it. Not a soul within its walls was left alive.

An effort to reach Ypres after dusk landed us in a hopeless tangle on the Zonnebeke road. A column of Yeomanry transport, badly handled and very badly driven, was the initial cause of the trouble. The mud in the roadway was ankle to knee deep, and the ditch alongside full of black slime. An R. E. lot from one direction and a long column of French cavalry from the other added to the confusion. One *cuirassier* became mired—his horse fell, and he disappeared beneath the mud in the ditch. The driver of a mess cart, who constantly reiterated that he was of the "'Erts," tipped his vehicle over in the midst of the *mêlée*. Hours passed before the tangled skein was unwound. A dozen shells had fallen along that road a few hours before. A dozen more would have caused trouble awful to contemplate had the German gunners known of the jam.

We dined to the accompaniment of bursting Black Marias, though none fell nearer than a couple of hundred yards from us.

Sunday brought a driving sleet. A run down the Menin road and back found it so torn and smashed as to be practically impassable for a car. All day shells traced its length from the trenches back to Ypres. No man who traversed it in those days finished his journey without wondering he had not been hit. Hourly I "strafed "the respective shells that had smashed my hood and screen. The sleet made the work of driving bitterly cold.

Still the troops held back the German attacks, and piled up their dead in front of our trench line.

Our own part of the line saw less fighting than other sections that day. An attack by a party of sixty or seventy of the enemy was pushed on as if forced from the rear. One of our staff officers suggested that the German commanders might find it necessary to promulgate some sort of an attack each day, no matter how small its area or how remote its chances of success, "to provide the daily notes for their official diaries."

Numbers of German dead lay close to our trenches. An officer of the 4th D. G.'s was asked why he didn't clear away one corpse that could be reached by a bayonet from the trench. "Oh, sir," the officer replied naively, "he is quite inoffensive."

Lord Cavan was almost a *demi-*god in the eyes of his devoted men, whose position adjoined ours. What was left of the West Kents, Munsters, Grenadiers, Coldstreams, Irish Guards and London Scottish were in Cavan's force. His personality had figured largely in the stubborn defence of the line. No words could paint his services in too glowing colours.

The German snipers merited and soon gained our full respect. From thirty to one hundred yards from our line in their own trenches, or concealed individually in the wood, woe to the man who unduly exposed himself in front of them. Some of them had notorious records. One at a point in front of Cavan's force had hit nine West Kents, two grenadiers and a Munster. None of our men could locate him.

Sniping at the Germans was most diverting work. An officer of the 9th Lancers took out a trio of sharpshooters, and in an hour was offered a target at one hundred yards, which enabled his men to "get" four of the enemy.

Monday one of our brigades was in reserve. The men busied themselves in more or less futile efforts to dry out. The rain never ceased for long.

French troops arrived hourly, and the ferocity of the German attacks seemed to wane somewhat. That night the 1st Cavalry Brigade was relieved, and sent back to billets in the Flemish farms north of Caestre and Flêtre. The next night, Wednesday the 18th, the 2nd Brigade followed to billets in the Mont des Cats-Berthen area.

The ground was white with snow. Incessant rains had turned to freezing blizzards. The Prussian Guard had failed, and the line had held. The first Battle of Ypres was finished.

The French troops took over the whole of the Ypres salient. To the British Expeditionary Force was assigned twenty miles of front, to be held by four Infantry Corps. The 1st Cavalry Division was promised four days' rest before a few days in the trenches in front of Kemmel.

CHAPTER 15

The Christmas Truce

A simple, impressive ceremony took place at the *mairie* in St. Omer on November 16th. Lord Roberts's death touched a very tender chord in all hearts in France and Flanders. French and British, Englishmen and men of India did heartfelt homage that cold, dull, dispiriting day when, the short service over, the veteran general's body started on its last journey homeward.

The sun burst through the lowering clouds as the cortege was starting, and a brilliantly-hued rainbow appeared for a few moments, its bright arch standing forth in sharp contrast against the black sky.

Its sudden coming and its almost as sudden disappearance, as the funeral party filed out of the bleak square, seemed timed supernaturally for the occasion.

As the 1st Cavalry Division was in billets, I had come down to G.H.Q. for a new radiator, brought out from England by Oscar Morrison, of the R.A.C. Corps. I was glad to get it, for the repair of the shell-smashed one had been a sad business.

Heavy snow set it. Sir John French was ill in bed with cold, unofficially. On the 20th I paid a visit to Hazebrouck to see the splendid Du Cros ambulance convoy sent out by Arthur du Cros, M. P., and officered by two of his brothers.

The small light vehicles with canvas tops were just what we required at the front. My call was made interesting by the enemy airmen, who dropped eight bombs on the town. Their total bag was one poor civilian, an old man whose legs were blown off. The following day I rejoined General de Lisle at a *château* near St. Jan Cappel.

A crash when passing the hospital in Bailleul caused a halt. Entering, I found an aeroplane bomb had been dropped right in the hospital. A hall built against the side of a church wall was filled with thirty odd wounded, at eleven o'clock. A fleet of ambulances came for them, and before 11.30 all had been removed but two. Then the bomb came. The room was frightfully smashed. Each of the two wounded men was badly hurt, one being hit by eight shrapnel bullets. Two hospital orderlies were in the room, and though both were hit by splinters neither was seriously injured. The airman who dropped the bomb was pursued and captured by one of our flyers. When told that one of his bombs had smashed into a hospital he expressed great regret, declaring he was aiming at the railway station.

On the night of Sunday, the 22nd, the troopers of the 1st Cavalry Division went into the trenches in front of Kemmel for a couple of days, after which they were promised a long rest. General de Lisle, with four of his staff, took temporary headquarters in a little dwelling in La Clytte, where he could be close to the division.

We were fortunate in being allotted a part of the line where the Germans were using a very poor lot of shells. At certain points not one shell in ten was really effective. Quite fifty *per cent*, of them failed to explode.

The weather was bitterly cold, with hard frost each night. Our headquarters house showed a deep religious fervour on the part of its owner. A crucifix stood over the mantel of the main room, religious images of some size flanked it, and deep coloured prints of sacred subjects adorned the walls.

The 2nd Cavalry Brigade, numbering 600 rifles, went into the trenches at dark, joining the 1st Cavalry Brigade and relieving the 6th Cavalry Brigade. Approaching Kemmel by the light of the thin crescent moon, the snow-covered fields showed black patches on either side where rows of horses waited for their riders to come from the trenches. I bumped into a huge shell hole in the darkness. By great good fortune I had fallen into its edge and not its deep centre. Gun flashes from all sides, and in front a blazing farm, gave a touch of colour to the picture. In the distance the sky was alight where the old Cloth Hall in Ypres was burning.

For a couple of hours the "taking over" proceeded steadily and without the least excitement. Some few wounded, hit by itinerant snipers, were helped back, but for the most part the change was made with clock-work regularity and in a deep silence born of long experience.

As the 3rd Hussars,, coming out, passed the 9th Lancers, going up, low-voiced greetings were exchanged.

Using a periscope at 45 yards from the German trenches at Ypres

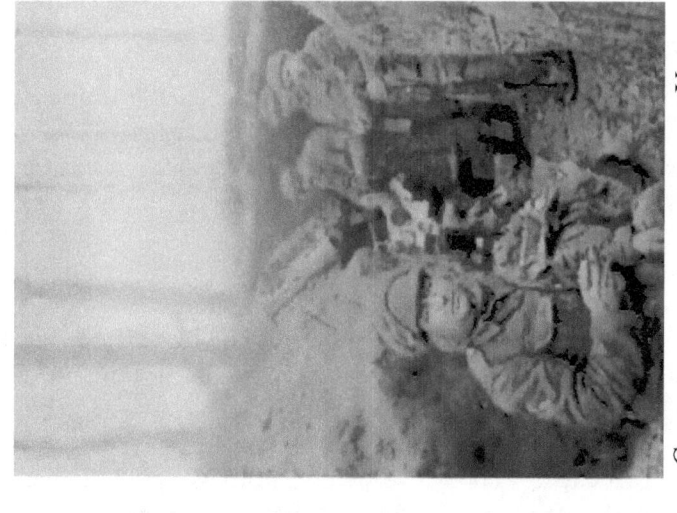

Cleaning a machine-gun in the Ypres front line trenches

"Nothing much going on up front," said a big trooper, "bar snipers."

"How's Nobby?" queried an acquaintance.

"Nobby?" came the low reply. "Oh, Nobby. 'E stopped one. But not proper—only with his 'and." And he trudged on into the snow-rimmed blackness.

Everybody was cheery.

Cold, dark, but dry, the night wore on.

"It's warmer in the trenches," said the departing ones. "Plenty hay; not half bad."

Food went up and ammunition. All as orderly as such events can be when every man knows his job and sets about it silently and seriously.

The general strolled up, walking first here, then there, seeing that the detail of the work was being carried out efficiently.

All the while the sniping went on merrily. The bark of the rifles nearby was given an added sharpness by the cold, tingling atmosphere. Our field guns not far away fired at regular intervals.

At last we were "in" and our predecessors "out."

I slept in La Clytte. I chose a very soiled mattress close to the diminutive but energetic stove. Cecil Howard was condemned to a bed much too short for him, to which he attributed a powerful and persistent nightmare. The quarters were far from luxurious, but we soon dropped to sleep to the sound of the everlasting sniping, which kept up all the night through.

The world was hidden in a mantle of hoard frost in the morning. A bottle of Vichy in a suitcase in the tonneau of my car was frozen solid.

We ran to Kemmel, and walked from there towards the trench line. General Briggs was indignantly bemoaning the stupidity of his chauffeur, who had covered the engine of his car with straw and in some way set it afire when starting in the morning. Result, car burned! Most drivers kept their cars in going order by a liberal mixture of methylated spirit with the water in the radiator—an excellent wheeze.

Tramping the white fields was inviting trouble with snipers. I returned to Brigade Headquarters, and gossiped about the new rifle grenades. Our hand grenades were very effective—much more so, we thought, than those of the enemy. The latest German device was a big valise-like thing, thrown by some means unknown, that came hurtling end over end and lay before exploding for two or three seconds after its arrival. The noise it made "beat a Black Maria hollow," a trooper said. The smoke from one of these projectiles lay and drifted low in great clouds. Its energy seemed wasted, however, for while it tore a great hole in the earth it apparently scattered no pieces of projectile about. At least that was the verdict of those who had close acquaintance of it.

A German prisoner had a rare fairytale for us. He reported eight cases of self-mutilation in his company, the strength of which had been reduced to fifty-six. After hearing his talk one might imagine that all Germans would soon be on strike against further warfare. His efforts to retail welcome information were unfortunately a bit overdone, particularly when one knew of a fierce German attack on Hollebeke the day before. But he meant well.

At mid-forenoon the quiet of La Clytte was shattered by eight German howitzer shells. One fell thirty yards short of our house, showering pieces of shell in the front yard. Another lit across the road. Not far from us a woman was beheaded and an old man killed.

A few minutes before the shelling, Major Steele, our Divisional R.A.M.C. officer, and Baron Le Jeune, our French liaison officer had called. Le Jeune came to obtain the General's signature to a permit for a few days' leave. News spread that seventy-two hours in London was forthcoming for all of us in turn, whereat was great rejoicing. Le Jeune told me his little boy had been brought by his mother to Paris, where the baron was to join them on the morrow. Everyone was happy in anticipation of soon seeing the loved ones at home. Gay quips and cheery laughter were on every lip.

Shortly after the brief shelling, Major Davidson, of the R.A.M.C, came in and told us that one of the shells had lit a few yards down the street, at the crossroads, where General Short, of the Artillery, has his headquarters. One of his staff looked out of the door to see where the shell had struck. Lying in the roadway were the still bodies of Major Steele and Le Jeune, who had been passing at the moment the shell came. Poor Steele's left arm and shoulder were shattered, and he was badly wounded in the side and leg. Le Jeune was suffering horribly from a piece of shell that had torn its way through his body. Another bit of the shell had made a hole in his head. Both of them died— Steele on his way to the hospital, and Le Jeune soon after his arrival there.

Colonel Home, Hardress Lloyd and "Mouse" Tomkinson were starting for England, on leave, the day following. We had all been "bucking" about our "last day under shell-fire for a bit." Such hard luck for Steele, a greatly beloved and very gallant chap, and poor Le Jeune made everybody quiet.

More shells came in the afternoon. Towards evening we started for "home" at St. Jan Cappel. As we stepped into the car a shell screamed through the air and landed with a loud bang just in front of us. One last Black Maria had "come over" only a few yards above our heads, and sent up a high column of dirt and smoke from the corner of a field fifty yards distant. It was in perfect line.

The seconds dragged by with leaden feet until the general's order came to "let her go." Our way led down the street to the crossroads, where our two friends had been killed a few hours before, then left to Reninghelst. Number two was overdue, I thought, as I gathered speed. I took the corner on two wheels, and Home sung out from the back seat as we left La Clytte behind: "Those are my sentiments, too, President."

That evening in Bailleul a Flying Corps officer told me a story of one of his airmen, named Blount. Blount was sent on a prosaic daily air reconnaissance. He duly returned, entered the office of his chief, and reported so many trains here, so many there, a column on this road, that road clear, and so on, as usual. Nothing seemed out of the ordinary in his story, or his manner of telling it.

As he turned to leave the room he said, "Coming back, I had a bit of a brush with a Boche flyer."

"Hold on," called out the officer to whom he was reporting, "don't run off. What happened?"

"He was killed, sir," was the laconic reply, and the airman opened the door.

"Wait," said the officer. Then, as he noticed blood dripping from one of Blount's hands, "What's the mater with your hand?"

"Oh, nothing much," Blount answered modestly. "The German chap got me with one shot and took off the end of a finger." The two upper joints were gone; "I am going to have it wrapped up." And with that he departed, as if glad to escape from the necessity of giving further details.

The encounter had taken place over Bailleul, in good view of the aero sheds not far from the town. It caused immense excitement and enthusiasm, and the officer found no difficulty in gathering a much more complete story from Blount's fellows.

Blount discovered the enemy airman when returning from the re-

ONE OF THE TRENCHES IN FRONT OF ZILLEBEKE

THE BATTLE OF YPRES ENDED IN A BLIZZARD;
COLD WEATHER IN THE TRENCH LINE

connaissance, and at once gave him battle. A very pretty fight ensued. Gradually Blount mounted higher and higher, until he was above his antagonist. Then circling round and round the German, both firing all the time, Blount forced him lower and lower. At last, just before the German came to earth, one of Blount's bullets found its mark, and the enemy airman fell over and crashed to the ground with the ruins of his machine.

The coveted seventy-two hours' came at last. Three days at home at the end of November soon passed, and on our return we took up headquarters at a *château* between St. Omer and Cassel, some miles from the groups of farms and one or two villages in which the Division was billeted for the winter.

On December 3rd the division was visited by His Majesty the King. The mounted troopers, swinging swords in high circles and cheering strenuously, made a fine sight as the king walked down the road between the lines of horsemen.

The next day I encountered a friend in sombre mood. "What's wrong with you?" I queried.

"I am just back from a jaunt with a batch of newly-arrived subalterns, who were turned over to me for map instruction," he said gloomily. "I daresay they are all right, but some of them are wonders. One of the cheerful idiots couldn't find a stream I pointed out to him, and after muddling along a bit, burbled out: 'Why, I thought all the rivers on a map ran north and south.'"

The days passed quickly. Shooting parties were formed and a steeplechase organised. Evenings found us frequently battling over chess or draughts.

The casualties for the division to December 1st had been 1,544. The Queen's Bays, 5th Dragoon Guards, and 18th Hussars had lost over 200 each, the 11th Hussars nearly 250, the 9th Lancers 288, and the 4th Dragoon Guards 323. New drafts were daily arriving, and the regiments busying themselves getting the fresh men into shape. Continual exercise kept horses and men fit, everyone spending much time in the saddle—from the General himself to the troopers.

Every man in the trenches means three to five men behind the line. An army "resting" finds itself well occupied if the enemy still faces it. The actual "business "of an army teems with detail. A divisional headquarters receives 700 letters and communications per day at times. Every other day de Lisle "did the rounds" of the brigades. Many days I was left to my own devices. Permission to visit friends of other units was sometimes granted.

On a trip to Armentières, I heard the following story:—The town was lighted by electricity generated in Lille. For three weeks after the occupation of Armentières by our troops they found their use of the electric light uninterrupted. At last the Germans in Lille discovered that "their" town's supply plant was supplying the "juice" for lighting "our" town, and they forthwith put a stop to it. Some of our officers in Armentières, who chortled over the unique situation, suggested that a message should be sent to the Huns, asking for the bill for electric current.

Young Von Tirpitz, son of his notorious father, was taken prisoner, said a gossip in Armentières. The youthful Von T. tried to escape. Discovered and baulked, he found that his guard became increasingly attentive. Baffled and angry, minor restrictions goaded him to frenzy. Forgetting himself, he spat in the sentry's face.

The guard was a Jock of considerable proportions. He stared a moment, then quietly laid his rifle by his side, unbuckled and took off his accoutrements and gear, and spat on his hands. For a few minutes thereafter, the fur flew, or, at least, von Tirpitz's fur would have flown, if he had been a furbearing animal. The Jock was intent on giving the scion of the noble house of T. a severe lesson. Young Germany was inclined to show fight, but was promptly thrashed soundly, and finished off with a belting—his own belt being used for the purpose. As a fellow-Jock, a spectator, said, "Man, it was a noble beating."

Well castigated, but by no means injured, young Von Tirpitz was sufficiently an ass to report the occurrence and demand reprisals. The sentry was, of course, court-martialled. The full facts were laid bare. The sentence was given sonorously. "Twenty-four hours' imprisonment for laying aside your arms while on sentry go," was the penalty.

Such yarns were typical, and, if not always true, were entertaining.

A jaunt in the Ploegstreet Wood was a muddy experience. I was told to leave my car behind a house in the village and walk to the point where the corduroy pathway led away through the trees. Winding in and out of the southern edge of the wood were the trenches. All about were broken and splintered branches and tree trunks—a weird place. Various paths were placarded with such names as Regent Street, Oxford Street, Piccadilly Circus, Hunter Lane, etc. The Tommies in the trench line were knee-deep in water. Men passed rearward plastered in mud. An officer told me a Tommy's overcoat, weighed in the village, had tipped the scale at forty-five pounds on his return to billets after forty-eight hours' trench duty! Withal, every man was cheerful. As an observing friend remarked to me, "You can't *beat* these soldiers. No amount of hammering, casualty, or hardship seems to affect their splendid spirit in the least."

I asked this friend what impressed him as of greatest interest in the trench-warfare. He replied, "The wonderful *assortment* of shells and projectiles one sees."

At tea time one day I found the regimental censor hard at work over the letters of a yeomanry squadron.

"Hear this," he said. He read at length from an interesting letter written under shell fire, in the trenches:

> Mother, you could not imagine the noise. *Bang!* There came one only a matter of feet from me. Shells are bursting every second, and pieces are flying all about.

After a page or so of detailed excitement, the writer drew a line, then added an explanatory note to say that at the point indicated he had been bowled over by a huge Black Maria, but had miraculously escaped a wound.

"Very good," was my comment. "Writes jolly well for a trooper, doesn't he?"

"Yes," agreed the officer who was acting as censor, "but he's a farrier who hasn't been within three miles of the line. If he has heard a shell, it's been a long way off. He was mad all through because he couldn't go up with the regiment, which is in the trenches now. So he has taken it out in epistolary zeal. It's pure imagination. What am I to do with it?"

"Pass it," cried the mess in chorus. "It will do no harm."

So pass it he did.

A couple of months later he showed me a soiled clipping from a Midland newspaper. A glance at the well-fingered excerpt showed it to be a *verbatim* reproduction of the farrier's letter. "The best joke is that he keeps the good work up," said the yeoman. "Not a week passes he doesn't curdle the blood of the old folks at home with some yarn. We quite look forward to 'em. The paper fairly eats 'em."

An epidemic of stories of distress in Germany ran through the army: English interned who scribbled: "Food scarce; panic here," and hid the message with a postage stamp; veiled hints of food shortage in letters from German residents; tales from neutrals of hard conditions; reports that placards were put up in the streets of Berlin at night bearing such legends as: "Stop the War," and so on *ad infinitum.*

Anything in the way of cherry news or a hopeful report spread like wild fire. A pessimist seldom got a hearing.

Water in the trenches and the cold spell made for bad feet. I saw whole detachments whose feet were so swollen after their turn in the front line that a couple of days without boots was an absolute necessity.

The general health, bar feet, of the whole army was exceptionally good, in spite of the conditions. This was due to the inoculation of enteric, wisely made compulsory. No sensible man who spent that winter in Flanders and who kept his eyes open would declaim against inoculation.

On December 14th the division stood by in reserve while an infantry attack was launched on the German position in front of Wytschaete. The 8th Infantry Brigade and some French troops on its left made the sally. We paid about 500 casualties for an advance of about 500 yards in one little wood. The ground would not allow of a really successful offensive. After the men had gone a hundred yards across a field each foot was so caked with mud progress was impossible.

As December passed the "nibbling" continued. The Lahore Division at Givenchy, the Warwickshires at Bas Maisnil, the 11th Brigade at Ploegstreet, the French at Notre Dame de Lorette on the south, and Pilkem on the north of us, all reported minor gains. The official summaries recounted slow progress, thick fog and hard frost from day to day.

Gun-fire was held down by limiting the rounds allowed each gun for each day, and units in the trenches made a report of the rounds of small arm ammunition used.

On December 19th the Indian corps at Givenchy had a nasty time. The Indian line from north to south was composed of the Garhwal Brigade, Dehradun Brigade, Sirhind Brigade and Ferozepore Brigade.

The trouble started on the morning of the 19th, when the Garhwal Brigade made an attack. It captured about 360 yards of the German first-line trenches, but was promptly bombed out and forced to evacuate what it had won. The Dehradun Brigade left its trenches, and, though the Sirhind and Ferozepore Brigades had advanced in the general forward movement, they were compelled almost at once to retire. A portion of the Dehradun front, the whole of the Sirhind front, and most of the Ferozepore front, together with the village of

Givenchy, were soon in the hands of the enemy.

On the 20th heavy shell fire began at daybreak. The Sirhind Brigade fell back to Festubert, and it seemed that Givenchy was hopelessly lost. Finally Givenchy was recaptured by the Manchesters and the Suffolks. The remainder of the corps reserve was moved up, and counter-attacks organised feverishly. In spite of all efforts the front of the Meerut Division was broken, and the Black Watch and the 58th Rifles were sent to its aid.

The next day the whole the 1st Division was hard at it retaking Festubert and Givenchy, a task which they eventually accomplished.

So much for the bare outline of a story that was told in almost as many ways as there were men engaged in the fighting.

I visited the Festubert area to gain some first hand knowledge of what had transpired. I learned that the Indians had fought much better than the bare accounts would indicate.

The trenches in that sector were full of mud and water. One officer I met had discovered in the thick of the fighting that of a hundred rifles in his trench but three were sufficiently free from mud to be usable.

Another officer told me his men had exhausted their ammunition. A box of ammunition arrived. The men carrying it were jarred by a howitzer shell that fell a few yards away just as they reached the trench. They dropped the heavy box into the trench with a splash and straightway it sunk many feet into the soft ooze and mud, all efforts at its recovery seemingly only serving to immerse it more deeply.

The awful conditions of the ground and of the trenches out of which the Indian troops were driven were largely responsible for their initial repulse. They counter-attacked well, and in most instances gained their objective. Unaccustomed to the all-important work of immediate consolidation of art enemy position, they were much harder to withstand when charging than to dislodge by bombing after the completion of the actual attack.

From close questioning in various quarters and quite a general survey of the locality, I became convinced that the Indians worked at great disadvantage when so scattered, and particularly when the Brigade Staffs were so far from the front line.

If one point could be selected for criticism it would, to my mind, be the faulty staff work, owing in great measure to the much too great distance of the commands from the various Staff Headquarters.

The loss of their line was a sore disappointment to the poor Indians, who had been rendered unbelievably miserable previously by the awful weather and unusual climatic conditions. No criticism could possibly be launched at their valour. That they required more and closer supervision in such a kind of warfare was as undeniable as it was to be expected on the first place.

Christmastide found the British Army becoming accustomed to the stagnation of a winter campaign in sodden Flanders.

On Christmas Eve, at midnight, the Germans in the trenches in front of the Ploegstreet Wood began to sing Christmas songs in chorus. The Somersets faced them. Some of the Somersets were old acquaintances of mine. Theirs was the first infantry command, with the Inniskillings and the Rifle Brigade, to arrive at the Ploegstreet Wood in the autumn, when the 1st Cavalry Division was fighting hard to hold the position.

A couple of Somerset bandsmen, who had left their instruments in England and were assigned to stretcher-bearing, told me a day or so after Christmas what occurred at Ploegstreet on Christmas Day.

The Saxon Christmas songs of the night before had odd results. One of my informants declared:

The songs was fine. They sang a lot. But the best was to come. A German bloke had a cornet, and he could play it grand. He just made it talk. The songs and the tunes the cornet feller played seemed more and more like ones we knew. Some of the songs I could have sung myself. At last out came that cornet with 'Home, Sweet Home,' and nobody could keep still. We all sang—Huns, English and all.

The night spent in song produced a general peacefulness of spirit all round. As day broke the Somersets saw the Saxons on top of their trenches. Soon they called out, 'Come over and visit us, we are Saxons.' No shots were fired.

None of our chaps started for the German trenches. We had heard all about the white flags the Boches had fired from under and all that. But our medical officer is a funny cove, and he got an idea in his head that started the whole thing, he said he saw a chance to give a burial to some of our dead that had been lyin' between trenches no end of a while.

So he told me and my pal here to follow him, and afore we knew where he was goin', up he pops on the trench parapet. The Boche trenches was only fifty to seventy yards in front,

A DUGOUT NEAR THE MENIN ROAD
(YPRES SALIENT)

and up we had to get and over after the doctor. The Saxons was right there, in plain sight. I never sweat so, nor never did my pal here. We was sure there was a game on, and we would get it good as soon as we was well out of cover. Some of our dead had laid out there for eight or ten weeks, and was in a awful state. We picked up a Inniskillin officer, a captain, and got him on a stretcher—a big job—and got him back all right. No one fired a single shot.

So out that doctor sends us again. We got over near the Boche trench and up jumps a stocky little heavy-set German officer with a bushy black beard.

He steps forward and says rough-like, with a scowl like he was goin' to eat us, 'Get back to your trenches, we have had quite enough of you. Get back there at once.'

He spoke English all right, *he* did. We didn't need no interpreter for *him*. His looks went with what he said, too. We went all right. And I won't forget goin', not in this 'ere life, you can bet. That few yards seemed a sinful long way. Every step I thought 'Now I'll get it, right in the back,' but I didn't.

We got into our trench right by our major in command, and told him what old whiskers had said and how he said it. All the major said was, 'I didn't think they would really let us get our dead. I'm not surprised.'

But that little trip of the doctor's had fair started it. Half an hour later I could see some of our lads on our right going right over to the Boches in the open. The major saw 'em too. When he got 'em in his eye he said, 'You can go on now, you men, and get some more of those dead in.'

We went. We never saw the black-bearded chap any more, either. One of the Saxon fellers who spoke pretty good English sung out and said we could go right on with what we were doin'. He said all of us could bury dead till four o'clock, and they would, too. And sure enough they did get at it pretty soon afterward.

Of course with us all kicking round each other out there in the open, lots of chaps got to talkin'. The Saxons was friendly enough.

One chap said to me, 'You Anglo-Saxons, we Saxons. We not want to fight you.'

I thought I'd land him one, so I said 'What about the *Kayser*, then, old lad? What do you think of Mr. *Kayser*, eh?"

'Bring him here, and we'll shoot him for you,' said the Saxon feller, and we all laughed.

But I didn't take no stock of that. I knew he was only trying to be pleasant.

Some of our chaps changed cigars and cigarettes with them Huns, and had talks about all sorts of things. At four o'clock we all took cover on both sides, but there was no firing on our front that night. The next morning we kept up the callin' business. We didn't stop it for a matter of eight days.

Then the Saxons was relieved by the Bavarians. The Saxons warned us agin them Bavarians.

One of the Saxon blokes said to one of our sergeants, 'Saxons do not like Bavarians. Shoot them like hell.'

There was one Saxon chap, off a bit to our left, I heard one of our lot tell about that wouldn't have no truce. He was in front of the Rifle Brigade. He kept hammerin' away all through the piece, no matter what the Saxon chaps in front of us did.

An exchange of rations was a frequent occurrence during that remarkable period. Both sides agreed that tinned "bully" had no serious rival.

"Would the men who made friends with the Saxons fight them as hard afterwards?" I asked.

The reply was:

Sure. If our chaps got a chance to put the bayonet home in one of those fellers, there wouldn't be no difference in the way they would do the job. All the first moves come from them, not from us. They even said they would fire high if they got orders to fire on us. We didn't make no such foolish promise.

Our lot wanted to see the German trenches bad. They wouldn't let us right in, but we saw a lot and learned a lot. We could get right up to their wire, which was no end better than ours. But it ain't now. Wait till they try goin' against our wire, and they will find we learned a thing or two.

And the little group chuckled in anticipation.

The most amusing conclusion to this Christmas truce in its various phases here and there along the facing lines of trenches, was the trio of severe orders promulgated from three high headquarters.

Sir John French's order was short and sharp, but very much to the point. It expressed great displeasure at such carryings-on.

General Joffre issued an order not a whit less severe in condemnation of such tendencies.

But fiercest of all, and threatening direst penalties, was the order issued by the *Kaiser*.

That all three orders were necessary might give food for thought to psychologists.

That they were issued should, in kindness, have been told to Henry Ford.

Appendix

Lieutenant A. Gallagher, of the 4th Dragoon Guards, affectionately dubbed Golliwog by his messmates, had a mad Irish experience at Audregnies.

More than once he told me details of it, the last time while he was convalescing from a second shell wound in the head received in front of Ypres long after the retreat.

> We were watering in Audregnies when the order came to mount and charge. I was at the head of the second squadron. It was quiet enough before that. We were dismounted in the village street, watering from buckets wherever we could find one. We jumped into our saddles and tore off down a narrow lane without in the least knowing where we were going or what was up. The dust was thick, so thick one could hardly see the man in front.
>
> We went off in a rush all right, and rode down that choking lane with no other thought than keeping going. We had no order to draw sabres, and just galloped in a bunch. Before we had reached the end of the lane men began to fall. The bullets were coming from in front and seemingly from one flank as well. More men fell, but we couldn't do anything save gallop. At the end the lane curved round a cottage to the right. I remember seeing Colonel Mullins, and Major Solly Flood beside him, at the turn. Mullins cried, 'Not there—not there!' but it conveyed no meaning to me. We dashed on after the leading squadron round the corner and into a very inferno of shell and small-arm fire. It was hot. No time to wonder what was doing. Shrapnel was bursting right in amongst us and men falling every inch of the way, it seemed. Not far beyond the corner I saw a flash which seemed right in front of my eyes, and my horse went

down.

When I came round I was lying on my right side, with one leg under my dead horse. My head was bad. Alongside me was a French officer who had been attached to us—a Count, someone said. He was dead A bullet had hit him right in the centre of the forehead.

All was quiet for a moment. Dead and wounded lay all around, and everything seemed strangely still. Down the lane I saw Major Tom Bridges ride out into view. He stopped, shaded his eyes with one hand, and gazed about oddly. The Germans saw him and opened fire on him, the bullets singing by him as he turned and galloped away to safety. Months afterwards I learned that he had been hit in the head during the charge, stunned, and taken into a cottage. The Germans came in the front door as he regained consciousness. They were a bit too late, for he jumped out of the window as they came in the door of the room in which he had been lying. He found a horse, mounted hastily, and after finding which way the enemy bullets were coming, made off in the opposite direction and escaped without a further scratch.

I struggled out from under my horse and tried to run towards the point where Bridges had disappeared, but my leg was so numbed and sore I fell. Another attempt resulted in another fall, so I crawled on my hands and knees to the nearest shelter, a cowshed by the lane. Creeping inside, I found a wounded French interpreter and two wounded troopers. The shell fire began again and rifle bullets whizzed all about. One of the cows in the shed was hit in the back by a bullet, and with a startled effort broke the chain by which it was tied and rushed out.

A moment later a German officer and two German soldiers with bayonets on rifles came through the doorway. In the officer's hand was a tiny popgun of a pistol, which he kept pointed at each of the four of us as he went from one to the other. Reaching my corner, he stooped and relieved me of my revolver and my map case, the latter containing a notebook in which were an entry or two that I knew would hold his big round blue eyes. Running through my pockets, he came to a sovereign purse with seven sovereigns in it. This he tucked back in the pocket of my tunic, then stepped out the door to examine my notebook in the fading light. The moment his attention was well engaged, one of the German soldiers lost no time in extracting the sovereign-case and its contents from my pocket in a manner that left no suspicion in my mind that he intended replacing it.

A squad of fifteen or sixteen wounded prisoners—mostly cavalry troopers or Cheshire Tommies—were marched up from an adjacent house, hands in air. As they reached the door one man fell, a bullet through his arm—maybe a chance shot. I saw Sergeant Hynes of my regiment in this lot. He told me that in the house where he had been lying with a broken rib or two, injuries received when his horse fell sorely wounded in the lane, a Belgian woman had become incurably hysterical that the wounded men had put a sack over her head to keep her quiet. They hoped against hope to escape discovery. The Germans found them in due course and liberated the frantic woman, who ran screaming down the lane, only to fall from a German bullet before she had gone far.

A cook-wagon came up. After methodically milking the cow standing near, the Germans killed her, cut her up, and consigned her to the pot, foragers contributing turnips in profusion from the field hard by. Two great stacks of hay across the lane from us were lit at dark. The Germans threw British rifles and saddles on the blazing piles, with the result that a merry popping of small-arm ammunition commenced, bullets whizzing in all directions. At first our captors scattered, leaving us lying well in the line of fire, but soon they returned and shortly produced plentiful supplies of red and white wine. As the wine passed round they danced about the burning stacks to the music of a couple of accordions, a weird slight in the fitful light.

On the arrival of an officer the hilarity subsided. The slightly injured British soldiers were marched off to collect the dead and wounded, friend and foe. The more serious cases were taken to the convent in the village. The sergeant and myself were the last two to be moved. I was carried on the shed door. Before I was taken away, the German officer, who spoke no English, came over to where I lay and gave me first a drink of water, then a drink of milk. Stiffly and awkwardly, he reached down and shook me by the hand as he departed. I never saw him again. Not a bad sort, I suppose. Meant well probably.

Sergeant Hynes had fared worse. One of his arms was black and blue from the blow of a rifle-butt, delivered by a Hun for no better reason than that Hynes was the only one of a handful of wounded who had sufficient strength to sit up.

Audregnies boasted two convents. To one some 190 British wounded were taken, while an almost equal number of wounded German soldiers were placed in the other. The Audregnies fight was on Monday. On Tuesday and Wednesday I lay in the convent hospital occupied by the Germans. There was no doctor for a day or so. The sisters worked like Trojans and the Catholic father was never idle. Both convents gave their morning toll to the cemetery.

The priest exhumed the body of Lieutenant Garstin, of the 9th Lancers, and brought it for identification outside the window near which I lay. The villagers had given the poor chap a slight and hasty burial; the father transferred the body to the proper burying-ground, as well as those of two Cheshire officers. These, too, he brought to me for identification before interment. He carefully wrote down the names as I took them from the marks on the clothing, and the places of burial bear them, no doubt, today. A kindly soul, that priest. He would bring me an egg and a crust of bread at night under his robe. I was fortunate in having a request for transfer granted, and by Thursday was taken to the convent over the way which housed the British wounded. Two Belgian doctors came from Brussels. One was taken ill at once and incapacitated, but his fellow was a splendid chap and an indefatigable worker. He had hardly any bandages or anaesthetics. Four other officers, all of them Cheshires, were in the hospital, badly wounded.

My damage was not serious. A shell had torn up my scalp a bit, but I felt sound enough, although my leg was very painful. I put it down to a sprained ankle, and bound it tightly with a couple of puttees. The doctor had too much work to do for me to bother him with it. Not for some days did I discover that one of the bones in the lower part of my leg was broken, though the pain at times brought me to the conclusion that a sprained ankle was a most unpleasant injury.

Only a handful of German guards were about. The sisters tended us, and I suppose they had the feeding of us as well. By the end of the week I had planned to escape, and to take Sergeant Hynes with me. Monday, a week after the day of the fight, was chosen for the attempt. The four Cheshire officers were our only confidants. They suggested saving their food on the final day, so that we might take some provender with us.

During the morning a convoy of ambulances, due on Tuesday, pulled up. That they had come a couple of day before we had been told they would arrive seemed likely to upset my plans. All was bustle. Those best able to be moved were placed in the ambulances at once. My heart sank. The doctor came to me, and as he examined me I felt sure he would send me away then and there. By luck, my eyes were terribly bloodshot from the explosion of the shell that hit me, making me look much worse than I really felt. After a moment's consideration the doctor passed me over, saying I was to go with the second convoy, which would come at daybreak the next morning.

Sure enough it came. As a forlorn hope, I asked if I could hobble down to an orchard not far away and pick some apples before leaving. Permission granted, I limped through the trees, Hynes close behind. Under the fruit-laden branches we passed, with no eyes for the red cheeks of the fine apples within reach. Step by step we drew near to the hedge at the far side. No one was in sight. A last glance behind, a final effort to pull ourselves together, and we ducked through the leafy barrier, wriggled over a low wall, and rolled into a deep ditch beside it. Crawling as fast as we could, we followed this ditch for some hundreds of yards, lying flat and worming along wherever the varying depth made us nervous of possible discovery. We were convinced we would be shot if found by the Germans, The few guards at the hospital, the many dead each morning, and the confusion of evacuating the wounded might, we hoped, result in our escaped passing unnoticed.

All day long we lay in the moist, muddy ditch-bottom. I had begged a map from a sister on the plea of locating some guns within earshot. She had torn a map of sorts out of the back of a railway guide, and it proved of inestimable value to us. We planned to strike north, cross the Mons-Condé Canal, and then make for some of the large Belgian towns to the northwest.

It was stiff, tiresome work lying quiet in the ditch that day, but with brambles pulled together over us we were in comparatively little danger of discovery. At dusk we crawled painfully out of our hiding-place and slowly headed northward. Every sound meant Germans to us, and our first mile was a succession of limping and halting sallies forward, interspersed with sudden dives underneath the hedge by the roadside. At last we approached the point where our road crossed the main highway from Mons to Valenciennes. The moon was shining. From our hedge shelter we could see long lines of dusty shapes moving slowly towards Mons. Clank or harness and the gear of guns and wagons sounded regularly along the way.

Now and then a rough guttural voice rasped out an order or an oath. We waited for hours before a gap in the long, ghostly line gave us courage to cross. We passed safely enough after all, and skirting a couple of villages, reached a haystack near the Mons-Condé Canal before daybreak. We were not far west of the town of St. Ghislain. Before us lay the broad canal, spanned a few hundred yards distant by a ruined railway bridge, and a little further on by another bridge, over which we could see Germans passing in the growing light. At our backs was the home of the owner of the stack. He made his appearance at an early hour, and we hailed him. First he bolted back into his house. After a bit he gingerly approached the stack, and finally we induced him to mount the slight ladder against it.

A little man he was, with a thin black beard, great rings in his ears, and piercing shifty eyes. Only a few moments passed before we found our host was like to cause us trouble. He was all for giving us up to the Germans, and said so frankly. To be discovered harbouring us meant his house burned and death for himself, he said. For a time no argument could shake him. I told him the British were advancing behind us and would soon be in Mons again. If he gave us up, or allowed harm to come our way, woe to him when our troops arrived. It was a silly argument, but it won. He agreed reluctantly to let us stay unmolested until night, when I promised we would swim the canal and make our way northward. We lay close together as he piled bundle after bundle upon us, until the sergeant felt certain the little Belgian was trying to ensure our being smothered.

That was a tiring day, a hungry, thirsty day, but we lay as still as mice. From out the straw we could see German transports on the road, and what appeared to be guards on the bridges, which hourly reminded us of the necessity of keeping close cover.

That night, about nine o'clock, we climbed down from our

hiding-place, went to the edge of the canal, undressed, and waded out neck-deep. At the very moment I was about to start across Sergeant Hynes had to confess his injured side would not allow him to swim twenty feet. It was a bitter disappointment To return to the stack held little hope. To try to go on might mean the death of one or both of us from drowning. Choosing the less sure road to disaster, we dressed and regained our nest at the top of the stack, where we lay all night cursing our bad luck and improvising futile plans of escape.

On Wednesday morning the stack shook with the weight of someone ascending the ladder. 'Germans,' whispered Hynes. 'That light little Belgian never made such a commotion.' The perspiration broke out on my forehead. An age passed before the head of our visitor came into view. With inconceivable relief we saw the smiling face of a Belgian lady of most ample proportions. Blackbeard had told her of his unwelcome guests. The widow of a Belgian officer, she was as brave as an army. Rating the little man for his idea of surrendering us, and prevailing upon him to give up all thought of so doing, she had hastened to us with a bottle of red wine and a plate of beans. The Germans had taken everything eatable or drinkable from her house save these, she said. As to crossing the canal, she took n that contract with alacrity. Having a bit of money in her house, she told us she would arrange for a skiff to be ready for us at nine o'clock that night.

The day seemed brighter after her visit, and we rested much more easily. Nine o'clock came at last. With it the ample form of *Madame*, who, alas! could find no one who for any sum would venture to take us across the canal. But her resources were by no means exhausted. An urchin on a bicycle reconnoitred the bridges, and brought back word that no guard could be seen on the railway bridge. Though it had been blown up and rendered useless for trains, it afforded means for a crossing if we could climb over one or two obstructions and escape being seen by the guard on the road bridge beside it. We started without delay or demur, after I had thanked our brave benefactress in my best and most effusive French.

We found the bridge sadly damaged. Twisted metals were coiled over the way, and many of the timbers were torn bodily from the trestle work. A barricade presented difficulties which were soon overcome, and within a few minutes our feet trod the north bank of the canal. We had crossed safely and, apparently, undiscovered. Working northward, we struck the road from Mons to Tournai. At midnight we found we had made good time. Just how, I don't know. We went round all the villages and learned to anathematise all dogs in so doing. My leg was growing more painful, but a great stick helped me to hobble along at a fair pace. At first we were unduly nervous.

Faint moonlight played strange games with our fancies. Once a tree trunk held us at bay for some minutes before we discovered it was not a German with a rifle. A restless cow, changing her pasturage, sent us flying to cover. A startled rabbit dashed across the road, and I found myself face down in a gully before I knew it. The night made odd sounds, each one of sinister import to us. The wind sprang up, and in the exercise of its privileges caused our hearts to jump into our throats half a dozen times.

By midnight we had reached and circled round the village of Basècles, halfway from Mons to Tournai. We were sadly in need of food and drink. Approaching the house on the far side of the little cluster of dark dwellings, we lay by the door and under one of the windows listening for the heavy breathing that might betoken German occupants. All seemed quiet and propitious, so I gave a gentle knock and explained in a low tone that we were English and wished to enter. Sounds of commotion came from the cottage. A light flashed from the windows, an a woman's shrill voice advertised our presence.

A moment later, as we still waited for the door to open, a light appeared in the next house, then the next. More feminine voices passed the words, "*Anglais! Anglais!*" We had no desire for such a reception, so hurried off towards Tournai as fast as our disabilities would allow. Well, it was we did so, for no sooner had we reached a point some two or three hundred yards up the road than several shots were fired, and a few sinister bullets sang over our heads. We strained every nerve to hurry. Fortunately there was no pursuit. Nearly exhausted, and in rather bad case, we slowed down after a time, only to become a prey to all our former fears of night noises. A good-sized bird flew else to my head and gave me a shock that lasted many long minutes. Plodding along the highway, the clatter of hoof-beats coming towards us sent us to the roadside, where a ditch offered welcome refuge.

We jumped in, close together. At the bottom we hit something soft, which turned beneath us and gave a whistling grunt as our combined weight came down upon it. We had jumped full on top of a man. Who he was or what he was doing there were of no moment to us. A sound from him might mean recapture. The sergeant grappled him and crushed out what breath remained in him. I lent a hand. As a troop of German cavalry drew nearer we were well on the way to choking our chance acquaintance. At that very moment the *Uhlans* slowed from a trot to a walk. We held our breath. At least I held mine, while Hynes held his own and that of the third member of our party. Gradually the horsemen drew abreast, then past, then away. We waited until they were well in the distance, and then examined the man underneath. If we had been scared to have jumped on him, he was more than scared to have had us do so.

The relief when we found him to be a Belgian farmer, frightened out of his few wits, was truly comic. The Germans had imposed severe penalties on inhabitants who moved about between 8 p.m. and 6 a.m., he said. His quest remained unexplained, except in so far as a sack of something we did not examine might explain it. We advised him to remain where he was until daybreak, and pressed on. Before dawn we took refuge in a shed behind a house not far from Tournai. The distance we had covered must have totalled from fifteen to eighteen miles, evidence of what strength fear and desperation lend to tired and broken feet. The owner of the premises which we had chosen as sanctuary was a fine man, courageous and full of resource. Learning who we were, he took up from the outbuilding to his garret, where he fed and tended us with a will.

The Germans, he said, were not in force in Tournai, being chiefly interested in obtaining provisions therefrom. One train went each day to Bruges, leaving just before eight in the evening. Belgian guards were at the station, and the Germans were unlikely to trouble their heads about who left by the train during those days. Our host obtained a cart, in which he secreted us, driving to the station in such time that he arrived at the very moment of the train's departure. The engine whistled as we jumped through the station door and made for a carriage. But we were not to get away so easily after all. We were capless.

Our clothing was torn to rags by thorns and brambles. Truly we presented a sorry sight. We careered into a couple of Belgian guards with fixed bayonets, who seemed thereupon about to use them. Up went our hands, and we panted incoherent protestations that we were English. A look of utter incredulity came over the faces of the stolid civic guards. Someone yelled out that the Germans had come. Pandemonium reigned. Two Irishmen jumped from the train and recognised that we were really what we said we were. They were getting through as refugees, but they managed to put us right with the two with the bayonets.

The commotion that had been started, however, was not to be easily subdued. Passengers piled on the platform in a hopeless panic crying aloud their fear of the Huns. The crowd made for the door of the station and there jammed. More cries came from the outside that the Germans were coming. It was most unpleasant. A resourceful chap dashed up to the engine-driver and explained who we were. We were hustled aboard the train, and without more ado it pulled out, leaving most of its intending passengers behind. We threw ourselves back on the soft cushions and heaved sighs of relief. We were safe. At least it looked so.

A wire sent to Bruges brought the mayor and two soldiers with the inevitable bayoneted rifles to the station to meet us. Only one train per day ran into Bruges from the edge of the war zone. Thousands of anxious Belgians awaited it in a great square, eager for news of relatives and friends.

Our appearance in a carriage with the mayor and what appeared to the assembled multitude to be two guards gave rise to the belief that we were German prisoners. Booing grew from a deep murmur to an angry roar. The crowd surged forward. Things looked bad. The mayor leapt to his feet. The crowd stopped the carriage. Mounting a cushion the mayor, by dint of great exertion, gained a moment of comparative quiet and told the people we were escaped and wounded English soldiers. All was changed in a twinkling. The crowd made its onward rush—but to embrace us, not to tear us asunder. Before we were through we became afraid there was little to choose between the two. Our troubles were over once we won through the square, however, and next day we were sent to Ostend and from there home, to good old London town.

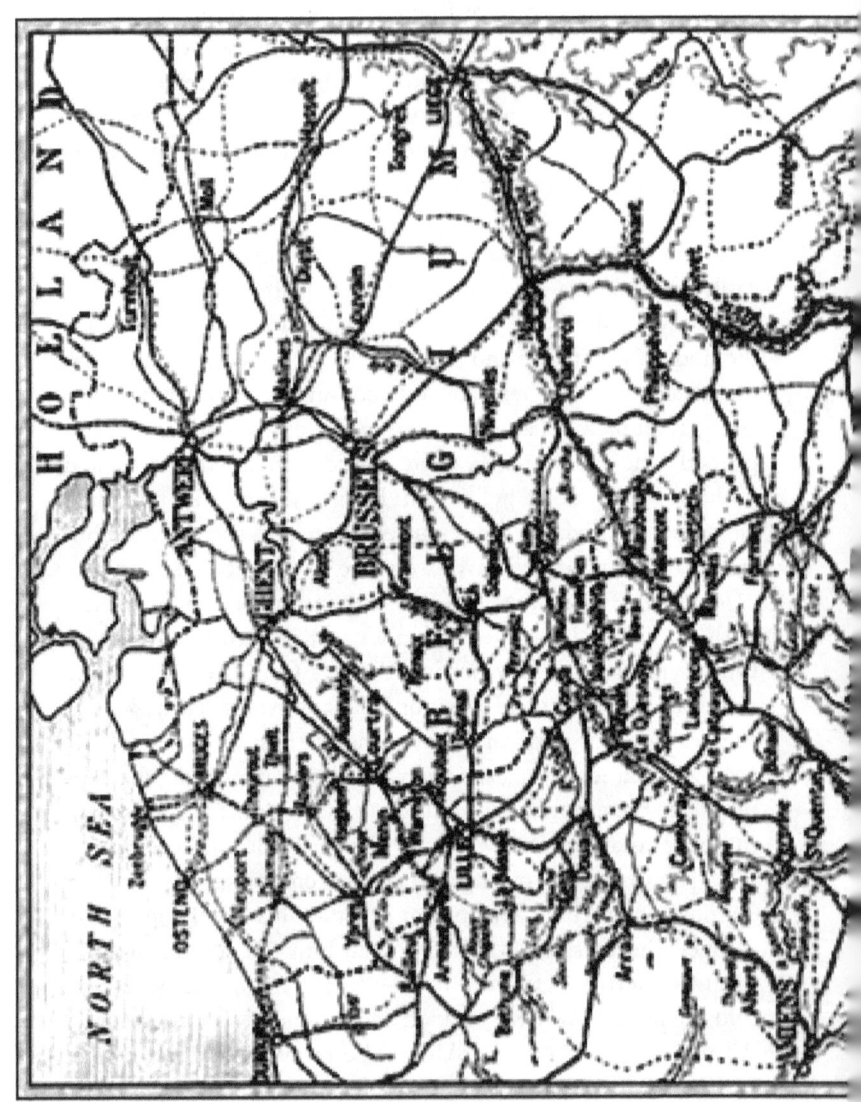

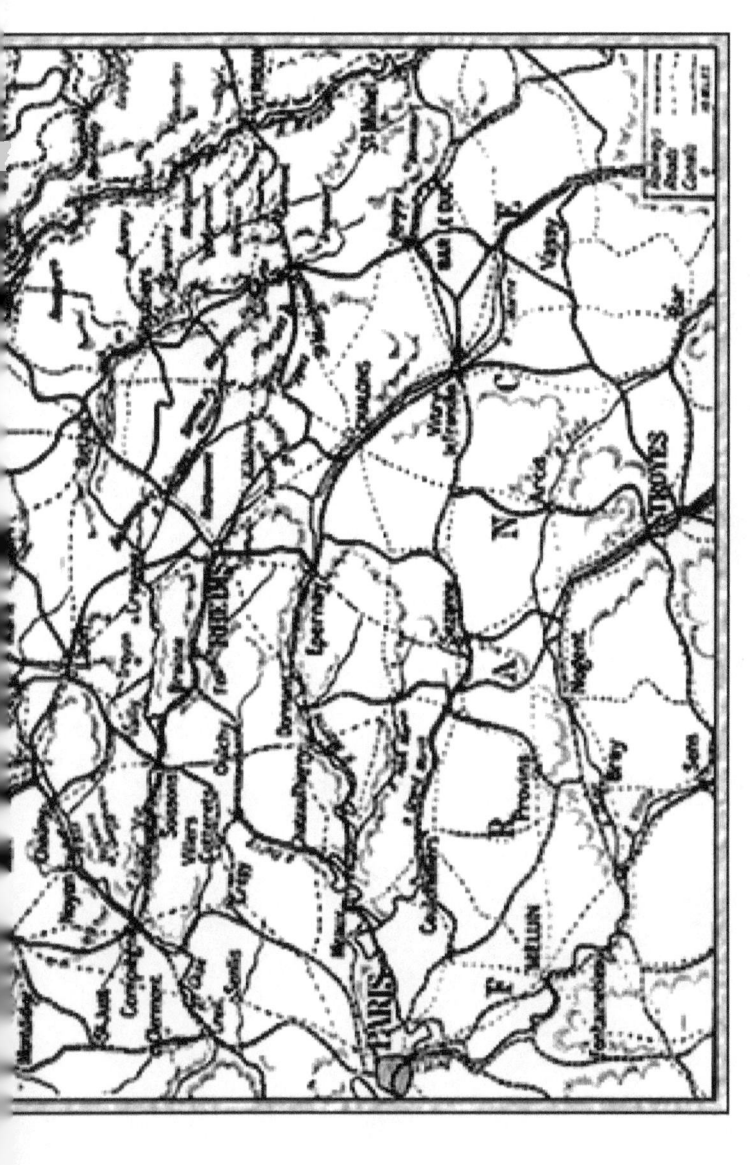

With Cavalry in 1915

THE AUTHOR

Contents

Author's Preface	303
Echoes of the Christmas Truce	305
A Run to Ypres	328
Mixed Plans	351
Lord Kitchener's Visit	376
More Hun Gas	408
The Great German Attack on May 13th	433

To My Wife
Whose bravery and self-sacrifice in the face of trying
circumstances made it possible for me so long
to continue to do the little that lay
in my power to help the
Cause we both
thought
Just and Right.

Author's Preface

The more than kind reception that Press and Public accorded my first book on the war, *From Mons to Ypres with French*, has encouraged me to put together a chronicle of further events.

With Cavalry in 1915 takes up the thread of its narrative where its predecessor left it—with the closing days of 1914.

If some notes of frank criticism have been included in this volume, it has been with no unkindly feeling, or with any other object than to try to give a fair picture of things at the Front as I saw them.

My unbounded admiration for the splendid soldiers of the British Army, gained in the darker days of the Great Retreat from Mons, has never wavered in its allegiance to them.

Never have I had occasion to change my opinion, formed in the first few weeks of the War, that the British Tommy is worth five or six of any German soldiers with whom he has yet come into contact.

In the machinery and organisation of war, the small British Army was at a disadvantage, particularly when faced with the necessity of great and rapid expansion. That mistakes should have been made was more than natural—it was inevitable.

I would not be so presumptuous as to criticise so freely, but that "*the old order changeth*:" to write of the past is, I hope, permissible, and likely to lead to no misconstruction. I mean no more than that which the plain interpretation of my simple phraseology will convey. I have no axes to grind.

The right men are in the British Army, and the right men are at the head of it.

For its work to be crowned with complete and lasting victory, it has but to have the undivided Empire behind it, and that, thank God, it has.

The man who cannot see that the Allies will win this war, and win it conclusively, is indeed blind to what the future holds for civilisation.

Frederic Coleman.

Melbourne, Australia,
June, 1916.

CHAPTER 1

Echoes of the Christmas Truce

January 1st, 1915, found me in damp, sodden Flanders. I was one of the dozen remaining members of the original Royal Automobile Club Corps, which had joined the British Expeditionary Force in France before Mons and the great retreat on Paris.

I was attached, with my car, to the Headquarters Staff of the 1st Cavalry Division, Major-General H. de B. de Lisle, C.B., D.S.O., commanding. The Echelon A Divisional Staff Mess consisted of General de Lisle; Colonel "Sally" Home, 11th Hussars, G.S.O.1 Major Percy Hambro, 15th Hussars, G.S.O. 2 Captain Cecil Howard, 16th Lancers, G.S.O. 3 Major Wilfred Jelf, R.H. A., Divisional Artillery Commander; Captain "Mouse"Tomkinson, "Royals," A. P.M.; Captain Hardress Lloyd, 4th Dragoon Guards, A.D.C.; Lieutenant "Pat"Armstrong, 10th Hussars, A.D.C, and myself.

We were housed in a *château* between Cassel and St. Omer. In the latter town General French and General Headquarters (G.H.Q.) were located.

The 1st Cavalry Division contained the 1st and 2nd Cavalry Brigades. The 1st Brigade, under Major-General Briggs, was composed of the 2nd Dragoons (Queen's Bays), 5th Dragoon Guards and 11th Hussars. Brigadier-General Mullens commanded the 2nd Cavalry Brigade, in which were the 4th Dragoon Guards, 9th Lancers and 18th Hussars.

These troops were billeted in Flemish farms and villages north of the road that led from Cassel to Bailleul.

Sir John French's army in the field at that time was composed of the 1st Army under General Sir Douglas Haig, and the 2nd Army under General Sir Horace Smith-Dorrien. The corps units were as follows:—1st Corps, General C. C. Monro; 2nd Corps, General Sir

Charles Fergusson; 3rd Corps, General Pulteney; 4th Corps, General Sir Henry Rawlinson; Cavalry Corps, General Allenby; Indian Corps, General Sir James Willcocks; Indian Cavalry Corps, General Rimington; and the Flying Corps under General Henderson. Of the new 5th Corps, which was to be under the command of General Sir Herbert Plumer, only the 27th Division was as yet "out," though the 28th Division was ready to embark.

Most of the news parcelled out to those who were "resting" in billets back of the line came from the London newspapers.

Typed sheets, dubbed "summaries of information," and issued by G.H.Q., were distributed daily, but were never valuable and rarely really informative.

The G.H.Q. information sheet of January 1st, 1915, read:

"The Germans made an attack on the right of our line, south of Givenchy, yesterday evening, and captured an observation post. This post was retaken by a counter attack early this morning, but later on was again captured by the enemy. The line has now been reorganised."

A friend in the 1st Army, which was covering the part of the line thus attacked, showed me the 1st Army summary of 7 p.m., January 1st, which added the following to the news on the situation:

> All is quiet in front. Fighting on right of 1st Corps last night was not as serious as at first reported. Casualties in Scots Guards believed to be about five officers and fifty other ranks. Most of these casualties occurred owing to the regiment pushing on beyond the original trench, and attacking the enemy's position. This wet weather is entailing great hardship on the men, who are fully engaged repairing trenches, some of which have had to be abandoned owing to water. The Germans are reported to be no better off.

Such brief, dry, official summaries applied to most of the wet days of January, 1915. Trench warfare in winter has a very stoggy sameness about it.

A 3rd Corps advance in front of the Ploegsteert Wood resulted in several of our men being drowned while attacking, so deep was the water in the submerged shell-holes in the flooded area.

Discipline, the capacity to go forward in pursuance of an order, in spite of the fact that doing so seems utterly futile, is possessed by the British troops to a remarkable degree. Small operations, comparatively unimportant in scope and result, served to demonstrate daily the splendid spirit of the men under inconceivably trying conditions.

One trench at Givenchy was taken and retaken time after time, and the men ordered to capture the trench were ever found ready to "go up" in the same dashing way, though they knew to a man that the assault meant inevitable loss, and would more than likely be followed by a further enforced evacuation, by their own comrades, of the untenable position.

The Huns were well supplied with trench-mortars, bombs and hand-grenades, and used them with great effect. Our men had practically none of these indispensable attributes to trench warfare, or at least had so few of them that their use produced comparatively negligible results.

The Christmas truce between British and German units confronting each other in the trenches produced echoes for weeks. The order from General French stating clearly that "the commander-in-chief views with the greatest displeasure" such fraternising with the enemy had produced a partial effect, but instances still occurred where the Huns took the initiative in the matter of peace overtures for short periods.

A visit to one part of our front line unearthed the following story: The opposing trenches were separated by a highway, across which, one morning, a German soldier shouted:

"Let's have a truce for today. We don't want to kill you fellows. Why should we kill each other? We are to be relieved by the Prussians tomorrow night. You can kill them if you like. We don't care. We are Saxons."

The extraordinary proposal was taken in good part, and the truce kept for thirty-six hours. No men of either army left their trenches, but not a shot was fired from German or English trench at that point.

A few miles from the scene of this incident the men of the opposing armies became quite accustomed to calling across the intervening ground to their enemies. Each side, one day, boasted of the excellence of its food supply. A British Tommy declared his lunch ration included an incomparable tin of sardines. A German soldier shouted his disbelief that Tommy possessed any such delicacy. There upon an empty sardine tin on the point of a bayonet was raised above the British trench parapet in proof of Tommy's statement

"That's a sardine *tin*" yelled a Hun derisively, "but there is no sardine in it, *mein* friend."

Members of the Staff outside the headquarters of the 1st Cavalry Division

A few minutes passed, then a tin of sardines, unopened and temptingly whole and sound was thrown from the English trench towards the trench of the enemy. It fell short. Over his parapet vaulted a big German, who dashed at the tin with outstretched hand. As his fingers were closing over it, it jumped from his grasp. Again he stooped and reached for it. Again it leaped away. Tommy had attached a thin but stout line to his sardine tin, willing to prove his assertion, but with no idea of losing his luncheon.

Two or three times the big Hun grabbed wildly at the elusive prize, amid the shouts and laughter of the men of both armies, who cheered in unison as Hans was at last convinced of the futility of further effort and retired in confusion to his trench.

In the early hours of the New Year a trench full of Westplialians and a party from a section of our line held by the 4th Corps, fraternised to such an extent that visits were paid by each contingent to the "no-man's land" between the trenches. When the British soldiers returned to their trench, they found a man curled up in the bottom of it. Investigation showed him to be a German soldier.

"'Ere, git out o' this," said Tommy indignantly. "You're bloomin' well in the wrong 'ouse."

"No," said the Hun decidedly, "me prisoner, prisoner!"

"Not you," was the indignant reply. "Play the gime, you silly old 'Un, an' 'ook it."

But such was not the intention of the Saxon lad. With hands in air to indicate his abject surrender, he insisted he was a prisoner and refused to budge.

Nonplussed, the Tommies shouted over to the Germans: "'Ere's one o' your chaps 'ere as won't go 'ome, the silly beggar. 'E's lorst 'is way, poor chap, an' don't know where 'e are."

"Send him back to us, please," was the prompt request from the *Deutschers*.

But not a move would the Hun make, until at last half a dozen stout Tommies hoisted him over the parapet with the butts of their rifles. Still he tarried. With an oath a burly British corporal called two of his comrades. They leaped out of the trench, grabbed the hesitating Hun, and marched him at quick time to his own lines. There they turned him over to his officer, presented arms in salute, wheeled and marched gravely back to their own trench.

"What did the German bloke say when you chucked the chap to him?" was asked the corporal.

BETWEEN PHILOSOPHE AND VERMELLES: ON THE LEFT THE CHÂTEAU WALL

"Thanks," laconically replied that worthy, "an' no more, except to sye, 'We'll fix the rotter.' An' so they bloomin' well should—desertin' durin' a bally troose that wye—the dirty dog."

As the 1st Cavalry Division was "resting," visits to points of interest were the order of the day. On Monday, January 4th, General de Lisle, Captain Hardress Lloyd, and I ran, *via* quaint old Bergues and Dunkirk, to Furnes, where King Albert of the Belgians had his headquarters.

Belgian sentries were plentiful after Dunkirk. They frequently stopped us, but generally the word "*Anglais*" was a sufficient passport. Now and again Lloyd produced a British pass, at which the Belgians would invariably look blandly, if uncomprehendingly, then salute and urbanely wave us on our way. Any sort of pass would have served with ninety-nine out of a hundred such sentries.

The coast district in Belgium was not interesting in itself. Roadways ran between sluggish, morbid looking canals and flat, dispirited fields—a sad, soggy, flabby land, in very truth.

Furnes was a picturesque relief. The architectural beauties of the Hotel de Ville and one or two other buildings in its fine old square were undeniable. Not long after our visit Furnes was viciously shelled by the Huns. Later it was practically devastated by big howitzer shells. Three or four days before our visit to the town a Black Maria had landed in a busy spot near the square one noontide, killing ten people and wounding a dozen others.

Nieuport, not far away, was under a heavy bombardment when we arrived in Furnes. Three days before sixty French soldiers had been killed in one day in Nieuport, which had proved so great a death-trap that all troops had been moved to dug-outs outside the town.

I had a chat with one of King Albert's Staff whom I had previously met in London. He was a very outspoken critic of the Belgian officers, and of the policy that had resulted in the Belgian evacuation of Antwerp before such a *débâcle* was absolutely necessary.

We had lunch in Furnes with Colonel Tom Bridges. I had seen much of Bridges during the first months of the War, when he was attached to the 4th Dragoon Guards as a major. He led a charge at Tour de Paissy, on the Aisne, which saved the British line. Promoted to the rank of colonel, he was given command of the 4th Hussars. A very few days afterwards, while on a night march, he was sent for by General Sir John French. Arriving at G.H.Q., Bridges, who had been the British Military *Attaché* in Belgium prior to the war and knew the Belgian

Army well, was given certain instructions, placed in a Rolls-Royce car, and at once started for Antwerp. He arrived late at night, after a continuous run of over 600 kilometres, and saw King Albert, who at once convened a Council of War. Bridges then jumped into the work at hand without a moment's delay.

Tom Bridges arrived in Antwerp on November 3rd. The city was evacuated by the Belgians on November 8th.

Having heard so much of the prominent part Bridges had played in the affairs of the Belgians, I looked forward with all the more anticipation to again meeting him.

Major Prince Alexander of Teck, attached to Colonel Bridges' mission, and Mrs. Bridges, who had recently been at work in the Duchess of Sutherland's hospital at Dunkirk, were at luncheon.

Colonel Bridges talked of King Albert:

> The king gives to a stranger the impression that he comes to a decision slowly. I have heard men, who have met him, say they thought him extremely deliberate, but all recognise his solid foundation of determination. But for that rock on which the king's stern determination is set, there would be but little Belgian Army left today. To King Albert personally much more is due than is likely ever to be known.

The more I saw of the Belgian Army along the Yser, the more I appreciated what Bridges had said of the king.

After luncheon, I drove General de Lisle, Colonel Bridges and Hardress Lloyd to Nieuport-les-Bains, once a sea-coast summer resort at the mouth of the Yser. The Allied trench line was roughly the line of the canal. On the coast in the sandy dunes, the Allies' trenches had been pushed a bit to the Ostend side, but Dixmude was still in German hands.

Not a single inhabitant of Nieuport-les-Bains was in the town— not a man, woman or child. The French *Tirailleurs d'Afrique*, part of a splendid division of French Colonials that had been sent by Foch to "stiffen" that part of the line, occupied the ruins of the summer resort that was. The typical French summer hotels in Nieuport-les-Bains were, for the most part, shapeless piles of debris.

The Huns never succeeded in actually penetrating the town, though Von Beseler's troops tried hard to take it. The Germans reached the river bank which formed the town's boundary on the north.

The main thoroughfare was blocked at frequent intervals by great barricades made from bathing machines, hauled in a row and filled with sand and paving stones. Asphalt tennis courts were scarred with shell-holes. No open space had been spared during the weeks of itinerant bombardment.

As we approached the town French batteries of "75's" were firing hard from positions in the dunes by the roadway.

The French general officer commanding arrived as we alighted from our car. But one house was standing in the northern edge of the town. Into it we filed on the heels of the French general, up its stair to the garret, and still up a rickety ladder to a point of vantage under the very eaves. Through shell-holes in the tile roofing, French observers directed the fire of the batteries below. Across the Yser, in front of us, we would see the French and German trenches among the low sand hills. For long spaces they ran but fifteen to twenty yards apart and in one sector a German sap was but five yards from the French escarpment.

For a time we watched the shells from the "75's" bursting over the German trenches. Descending, we crossed the Yser practically at its mouth. A pontoon bridge, vaunting a placard showing it had been christened the "Pont Gal Joffre," led between twin piers. The bridge swayed and tossed like the deck of a channel steamer as we picked our way gingerly across it. Some months later a Jack Johnson, luckily placed by the enemy, entirely smashed that pontoon bridge.

Gaining the northern bank we zigzagged through deep trenches in the sand, reinforced here and there with timbers and stone. An open crater and a pile of debris marked what had once been a lighthouse. Dugouts, shelters in miniature, lined the sides of the crater nearest the Huns. The open bowl of sand was about forty feet in diameter. Near its centre gaped a shell-hole in the soft sand made by an unwelcome visitor which had come less than a half hour previously. Digging for a few moments, I unearthed the still warm timing-fuse of the 105-millimetre shell that had made the hole.

The lighthouse position was, the sergeant of *tirailleurs* said, a *mauvais place*. From morning until night of the day before the Huns had shelled it. Many shells had fallen in the hours just preceding our arrival. General de Lisle and Colonel Bridges left Hardress Lloyd and me there, "for safety," while they walked through the front line positions, which were from a hundred to a hundred and sixty yards further forward.

I investigated the interiors of the tiny dugouts during the general's absence. No shell fell near, however, and soon we were all retracing our steps to Nieuport-les-Bains. Once a sniper spied one of the party, and a bullet from his rifle kicked up a spurt of sand a few feet from my head. We acknowledged the attention by an additional foot or so of "stoop" thenceforth.

Over a cup of tea at Colonel Bridges' headquarters, I met an old acquaintance in Lady Ross, who had that day handed to the Queen of the Belgians a cheque for £1,000 for Belgian sufferers. Lady Ross told me of an interesting conversation with King Albert at luncheon. After discussing at length the general subject of the difficulty of realisation of war's hardships and atrocities by those whose homes have been far from the actual scenes of war, the conversation drifted to the refugee question. King Albert agreed that all able-bodied Belgians of military age should be with the army, and declared emphatically his intention to press for steps that would lead to such a consummation.

The result of my visit to Furnes and Nieuport-les-Bains was to confirm my impression that the Germans had fortified their positions along the coast, and so entrenched themselves that to take Ostend by direct land attack was impossible, except at very great cost indeed.

The assistance that could be given by the Admiralty to such a project was greatly discounted by the fact that the ships available were out of range when outside the sandbanks that lay near the coast, and outclassed by the enemy's land batteries when inside the banks.

Many folk visited the Belgian Army in the trenches during those January days. Less than a week after we had visited Furnes, a couple of us ran to Dunkirk on Sunday to buy some fresh fish, a delicacy as rare as it was wholesome. While in Dunkirk I saw Lord Northcliffe and my old friend Max Pemberton, who had come over for a "weekend at the Front" with the Belgians. The next day eighteen German aeroplanes flew over Dunkirk and dropped several bombs, doing some material damage and killing one civilian.

On Tuesday, January 12th, General de Lisle ran to Boeschoeppe, south-west of the St. Eloi area, to see General T. O'D. Snow and his 27th Division. While waiting for the General I had good opportunity to see and talk to some of the newly arrived men. They had been marched about fourteen miles before being put into the trench-line, then marched back to billets when relieved. Some had come back from eight to eleven miles on foot. As they were not supplied with changes of socks or any sort of patent solution for their feet, and as the trenches were at places knee-deep in water, a general epidemic of frost-bitten feet could but be expected.

Limping along the frozen road, with socks wound about their poor feet, I felt great sympathy for the Tommies. Before three days had passed I heard that the 27th Division sick-list had been augmented by over two thousand cases of "bad feet." One brigade major in the division told of over one thousand cases in his brigade alone. A bad business, entailing great suffering and more permanent disablement than a little, all for want of proper foresight.

Small engagements with the enemy all along the line were constantly taking place. Official reports teemed with briefly and baldly told stories such as the following:—

> The following are details of the capture of a German trench to the north of La Bassée on the night of the 3rd-4th January. Time—8 p.m. January 3rd, 1915.
>
> Artillery—Nil.
>
> Strength of attack—One officer, twenty-five men.
>
> Distance between opposing trenches—150 to 200 yards.
>
> Enemy's trench consisted of a short length of trench which had been dug outwards from a saphead, and which was occupied by one officer and twenty-five to thirty men. (Two sentries.)
>
> Attack—The attack crept forward noiselessly to the trench A A, two German sentries were awake and were bayoneted, the occupants were asleep and were all bayoneted; the officer's head was broken in with the butt end of a rifle—not a shot was fired—some men set to work at once and cut the ground A B, thus flooding the trench A A.

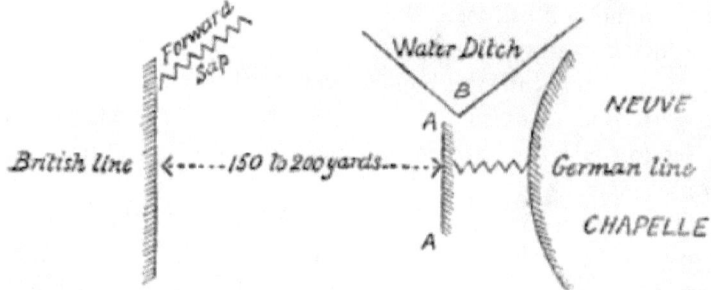

> The attackers were only fifteen minutes in the German trench and left the bayoneted Germans in the water, which was then running in from the water ditch. A A was only a short length of

trench without wire.

British casualties—One wounded and two missing. The latter may have since returned.

Quiet days found many a British soldier hard at work over a French-English "conversation-book." Some of these were hurriedly prepared and of a character truly extraordinary. One such book, made up for the benefit of an industrious young man, contained a question that, translated, ran thus:—

Q. Where is the cat of my mother's aunt?

A. No, but the kittens are drowned.

In Vermelles, on January 15th, I took a dozen photographs showing the devastation that can be worked by French high explosive shells.

Vermelles was an object lesson. Held by the Germans as strongly as any town was held in front of the French position south of the La Bassée canal, trenched and barricaded with wonderful skill, and well supported by a mass of guns, its capture was only effected after weeks of sapping and an artillery bombardment that had up to that time been without parallel. Its ruins held texts for innumerable sermons on the newer strategy of present-day warfare.

A French officer of standing had told me that he considered the taking of Vermelles from the Germans a most hopeful sign that the French could take any and all German positions in like manner, if they cared to pay the price in men and ammunition.

Geographically, Vermelles was in what was bound to prove a "warm corner." The German thrust westward from La Bassée, with Bethune as an objective, had cost the British Expeditionary Force some of the hardest fighting it had seen.

In that area our Second Corps, then the Indian Corps, and lastly our First Corps, with the French troops at times in action with us, had withstood a battering that no other point in the long line from the sea to the Vosges, save possibly the Ypres Salient, had been called upon to stand.

The German advance to the westward had reached Vermelles, and there been held. Their farthermost line was in front of the western edge of the town, and close to the main road that led through it. The enemy was in possession of Vermelles for a couple of months.

As no English troops had participated in the taking of Vermelles from the Huns, except for the assistance rendered by some of our heavier batteries, we knew little of what had happened in that theatre save that six weeks of sapping, a mad rush after an unprecedented bombardment, and terrific hand-to-hand bayonet fighting in the streets, had resulted in the French occupation of the town on December 7th.

Our visit had been arranged for us by Captain Fresson, the French liaison officer attached to 1st Cavalry Division Headquarters. General de Lisle, Colonel Home, Major Hambro, Fresson and I were in the party.

Coming out of Bethune, on the Lens road, we passed through Beuvry, then through Shilly-Labourse.

In the fields by the roadside were trenches, increasing in frequency along the road from Sailly to Noyelles-lez-Vermelles.

When Noyelles was passed, and we could glance across the slightly rolling fields that led eastwards to Vermelles, a mile distant, a little world of trenches met the eye. Some giant, prehistoric mole, crazed with pain and bent on expending his agony on the surface of Mother Earth, might have so ripped the fields.

Not rows of trenches, but curved and twisting galleries upon galleries of them. For the first time I began to get an inkling of what real trench warfare—the battles of the pick and shovel—meant.

At the headquarters of the French general who was in command of that section of the line a most elaborate *déjeuner* had been prepared for the party, with the result that it was well into the afternoon before we left the hospitable Frenchman and, in tow of a member of his staff, commenced our tour of sight-seeing.

Most buildings thereabouts were shell-scarred; some were burned. No inhabitants were to be seen. The boom of distant shells was ever present, and now and then one burst in sight of us. Detachments of French infantry marched past frequently.

We ran to Noyelles, which was full of hard-as-nails-looking French soldiers.

There the party alighted, and guided by a young French infantry officer, who had seen the fighting over that ground, walked across the trench-scarred battle-field eastward to Vermelles.

I followed sufficiently far to gain an idea of the lie of the land, then returned to Noyelles and took my car to Vermelles by road, arriving in advance of the others. This allowed me a long stroll of inspection, to be augmented later by a second tour in the company of the general, with a French Staff officer as escort.

The German first line trenches to the west of the town were well constructed. Though they had been considerably damaged by the rain of shells that had been poured on them, they were not as badly demolished as one might expect. Back of this first line of defence was a second line, weaving in and out—here in front, now behind, now through, the string of houses on the west of Vermelles' main street.

In the southern portion of the town were the ruins of the Château Watteble. The grounds of the once imposing *château* allowed a sufficiently clear space for still another formidable trench-line. Behind that the enemy had placed other lines, burrowing here and there at points of vantage through the town. Adjacent to the chateau were piles of bricks that once had been a fine farm, the Ferme Brion, and in front of it, completely demolished, and bearing no semblance of shape or form that would indicate its original outlines, was a chapel, where a German gun had been placed. This gun, a French officer told me, had been served gallantly until the French were but fifty yards distant, when a battery of the famous "75's" found the range and totally annihilated the gun, the chapel, and any of the enemy who were so unfortunate as to be in its vicinity.

The church, its square tower battered out of shape, was still the most conspicuous landmark of the country round. Another sample of devastation was the brewery, and attached to it an elaborate dwelling, one portion of which was built over a metal frame. All the covering had been torn from the iron girders, leaving the mere skeleton of the framework practically intact, a weird sight.

The German trenches and communications burrowed so consistently everywhere from the western edge of the town, and on through to the eastward, that every foot of ground afforded opportunity for study. These lines of defence, all connected and fed by approach trenches, cleverly constructed, with their traverses and reserve offshoots, led away for hundreds of yards to the rear of the front line.

That, then, was the town the French had to face, defended by machine-guns in splendid emplacements, every position well manned. The first line commanded an open front of slightly rising ground, clear of all obstacles and capable of being swept for 800 to 1,000 yards. Military science in trench construction had been aided by ingenuity of a high order, and hours of wandering over and through the rabbit warrens made for men, as cleverly as ever rodent designed his burrow, found one discovering new wonders at every step.

The trenches proper were for the most part deep and narrow, stout

A BIRD'S-EYE VIEW OF SHATTERED VERMELLES, JANUARY, 1915

of wall, reinforced with every manner of material likely to strengthen the defensive ramparts and bastions. Here the thickness of a piece of house wall had been doubled by sandbags. There the face of a trench had been reinforced by huge stones, interspersed with all sorts of receptacles, such as water-buckets, cooking utensils, wheel-barrows, and all manner of tins, filled with brick, small stones or cement.

A woman's bodice neatly tied about a few pounds of stone, the wooden cover of a household sewing-machine, loaded with brick, and even a stout brown-paper cardboard box full of mortar, caught my eye as I searched the stoutly-built wall curved round and back and round again through what had once been a house-yard. Traverses that demanded admiration from the most apathetic student of engineering, loops of trenches that commanded every front, approach trenches that wriggled like some great yellow-brown snake off toward the rear, were perfect each one in its own way.

Practically every point in the town could be reached by a German on tour of inspection of its defences, without the necessity of his leaving cover, save to cross the roadway of the main thoroughfare. Beside all this under-the-surface protection, the shelter of the buildings, all constructed of brick or stone and strongly built, was by no means to be despised.

Truly, when the French officer said no place could be made more secure, there was some reason for his words. But strong as it was, and in spite of its splendid artillery support, the position was one that the French had to take, whether or no. Six long weeks of constant work was represented by those torn and wounded fields that stretched away westward to Noyelles. Sapping their way, entrenching and consolidating every forward step, the little men in red and blue crept up to a line varying by from one to two hundred yards, and even nearer at one point, to the German front.

But sapping and mining, and entrenching and consolidating, so valuable in themselves, responsible for the finely fortified position of the Germans in Vermelles, and the splendid mole-advance against them by the French, was not the chief factor that was to play the decisive part in the war-game that culminated in the capture of the town on December 7th.

Gun-fire was the decisive element. To the beloved *"soixante-quinze"* was to go the chief honour. Only a careful personal inspection of the town could tell one the real story of Vermelles as I saw it on January 15th. The camera might assist, and, in spite of the dull weather, I ob-

Major Desmond Fitzgerald of the Lancers and a gas-pipe trench-mortar

tained a few pictures with that end in view, but the camera could give one the story only haltingly and in part.

Not one building in all the town was unwrecked. The French "75's," with some aid from the British howitzers, reduced Vermelles to ruins in the most literal and complete sense. Every edifice, from the piles of brick around the few tottering walls that was once a proud *château* to the humblest barn or outbuilding, was in itself a study. The evidence left by such shell-fire of its power for evil is of fascinating interest owing to its infinite variety. One wall had withstood half-a-dozen punctures of varying diameter, holes four or five feet in width, some of them, while its fellow beside it had crumbled into a formless mass of debris. Side by side were two houses, one with front practically intact, its roof gone and its interior and back portion blown to bits, the other minus front wall, but still standing, its roof at a crazy angle, resting insecurely on the remainder of the building, which, save for a scar here and there, escaped comparatively untouched.

It is this caprice of shell-fire that makes such a veritable hell of it.

Trenches with sides blown in; here a hole like a good-sized cellar; there a traverse filled to the level of the ground around it; a gap in the defence wall in front; iron-work twisted into grotesque shapes; stone-work pulverised; debris in piles; with clothing, bedding, household implements, farm machinery and gear, child's toys, religious emblems, personal effects, and bundles of every description, all jumbled together in such an odd, unnatural way, that a laugh and a catch in the throat often came together.

Vermelles on that sodden day in January was full of French soldiers in reserve—men of the 131st and 262nd Infantry Brigades, some from 16th and some from 18th Corps units. The firing line proper was from three to four kilometres to the eastward. On the west side of the town a French battery was firing regularly, the shells singing over our heads. The German shells were falling frequently half a mile in front of us.

It was my good fortune to discover a French soldier who had seen the actual final bayonet attack which won the position. His story was graphic, but told in few words. The creeping up to the forward French trenches, the fierce bombardment, the wild charge, the discovery that in spite of the fact that the place had been literally blown to bits, and German dead strewn everywhere, some defenders still held on and manned the murderous machine-guns, until they felt the cold steel—it all seemed so matter-of-fact, and such a matter-of-course sort of story in such surroundings.

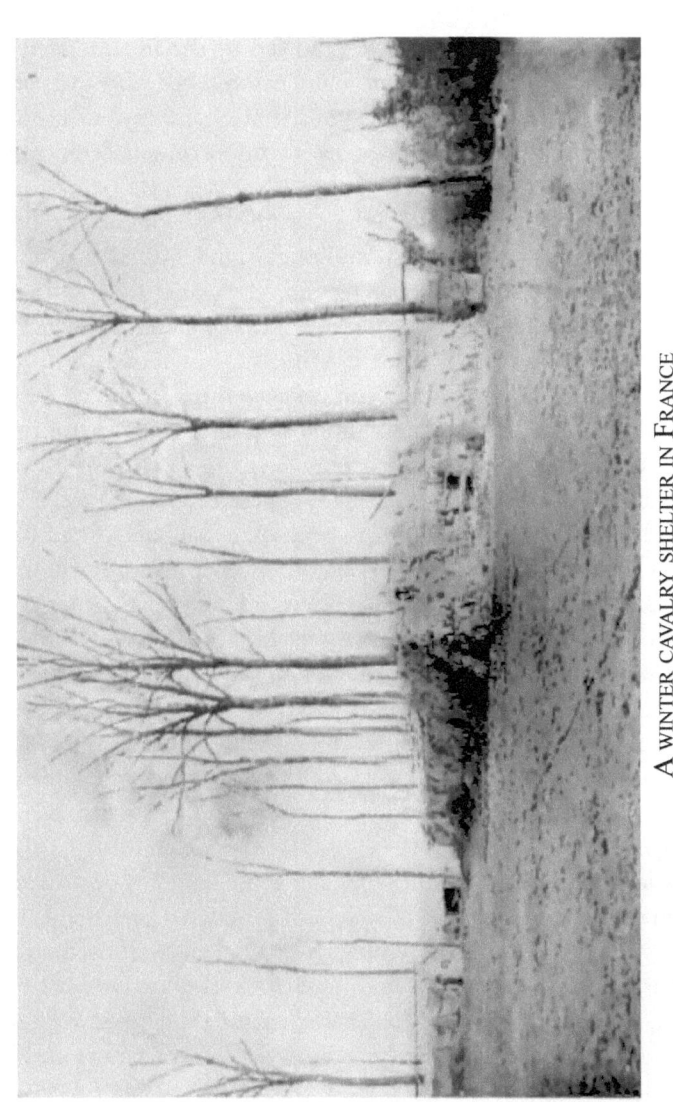

A WINTER CAVALRY SHELTER IN FRANCE

In each of the yards of the better-class dwellings and farms, including the grounds of the *château* and brewery, were graves of German soldiers. Many of these were marked with rude crosses bearing touching inscriptions. One such epitaph that caught my eye described the dead soldier as a good comrade; another as a brave man who had died for the Fatherland. Many of them bore a simple religious touch. One grave covered a German officer, buried by the French after the capture of the town. The French soldiers had marked his name and a respectful word or two on the rude cross above it, in obvious keeping with the inscriptions the Germans had written on adjacent crosses raised while they were in occupation.

In an effort to tell me how full the redoubts were of German dead, when Vermelles was at last taken, my soldier guide found that words failed him. They were everywhere, he said.

Many of the graves, particularly those of the French soldiers buried thereabouts, were headed by black or white metal wreaths.

"It cost dear," said my soldier, "and we paid. But a Boche who lived through the last few days of the fighting here, and escaped from that last charge, will be able to tell a story."

The deep cellar of a ruined house—a mere brick arched cell of a place without a ray of daylight—had been quite habitably fitted up as a cave-dwelling by the Germans, who had saved a piano from one of the wrecked rooms above and cosily stowed it away in a corner.

One or two underground caves just back of the German front line of trenches, bomb-proofs for the officers apparently, were ingeniously secure.

Though Vermelles at the time of our visit had been in French hands for more than a month, one could find many such souvenirs as shell-heads and timing-fuses without troubling to stir the piles of wreckage.

I could, I thought, sit in Vermelles and write reams of detail in description of the terrible havoc of war, but I found that mere generality as to the scenes of desolation wrought in the town soon used up my vocabulary. The place was no less a graveyard of brave men than of strenuous human effort, none the less to be admired because it proved abortive. Over all brooded the horror of war and the more specific and tangible horror of gun-fire. "Low trajectory and high explosive are twin demons, and this is their devil's work," the shattered town seemed to say.

Knots of French soldiers or visiting British officers walked about

Construction of cavalry shelter in France

sombrely and spoke in low tones, as if in the actual presence of the dead, in spite of the weeks that had flown by since Vermelles had echoed to the crash of a bursting shell.

The French soldiers were a tough-looking lot of customers. A bit nondescript as to uniform, and universally campaign worn, unshaven, and mud-plastered, they looked stout and fit for anything. A friendly class of men, respectful to British officers to a degree, a fact that spoke not only of good discipline, but of fine French traditions of politeness. They impressed me as splendid war material, and more, as men of fine character and indomitable determination.

Sport behind the lines began to assume quite a healthy state in January. Packs of beagles and hounds and pairs of greyhounds were brought "out" by enthusiasts, and cross-country courses with rare jumps were carefully mapped out.

Alas! for "*Le Sport.*" An order came along one day from G. H.Q. which stated that:

"The commander-in-chief regrets that it is necessary to prohibit any more hunting, coursing, shooting, or paper-chasing. This order comes into effect at once."

The 2nd Cavalry Brigade drew up a splendid steeplechase programme, which the state of the ground would not have allowed, had no order from G.H.O. been promulgated.

A card of "beagle-meets" was issued, and formed the following somewhat pretentious propaganda:—

The 2nd Cavalry Brigade Beagles Will Meet:—

Sunday Jan. 3rd, C Squadron 4th Dragoon Guards.

Tuesday Jan. 5th, St-Jans-Cappel, Berthen, Cross Roads.

Thursday Jan. 7th, Headquarters 9th Lancers.

Saturday Jan. 9th, Berthen.

Monday Jan. 11th, H Battery.

Wednesday Jan. 13th, Headquarters 18th Hussars.

Fri Jan. 15th, St-Jans-Chappel Church.

Sunday Jan. 17th, Headquarters 4th Dragoon Guards.

Each day at One o'clock.

The Prince of Wales ran more than once with that pack of beagles, and ran well.

Football matches were allowed, and were daily fought out between the various regimental teams.

General Robertson succeeded General Murray as Chief of the Staff at G.H.Q., a change generally welcomed, as Robertson was held in very high esteem throughout the army. Many of us considered him the greatest man the British Army had produced throughout the campaign. That is certainly how I should describe him.

CHAPTER 2

A Run to Ypres

Broken car springs on February 1st took me to Poperinghe, where a Belgian carriage-maker made a villainous repair for a considerable charge.

Motor car repairs were fearfully and wonderfully executed at the front in the earlier stages of the war. The G.H.Q. shops were not bad, and once in awhile I found clever, conscientious young chaps in charge of a roadside repair shop attached to a division, an ammunition supply column, or some such unit, who had managed to organise a very creditable "first-aid and emergency hospital" for the ills a car was heir to.

All too often some A.S.C. officer in charge, however, knew as little of the mechanism of an automobile and how to put it in order as one could well imagine. I remember one youth, possessed of a wonderful opinion of his own efficiency, whose mechanical experience had been gained in a railway workshop. He ordered repairs to be done in weird fashion at times. As soon as he had delivered his *dictum* and departed, his chief non-commissioned officer would put the men right, generally by a complete reversal of the youngster's orders, and all would go happily until he might again put in an appearance, when the work would suffer proportionately to the time he spent in its vicinity.

Stories of the excellence of the performance of individual cars were often marvellous. One big limousine, which had been "out since the first of the show," was ever the boast of the major to whom it was assigned and of his faithful chauffeur. At tea one day it transpired that the car, which the major was always ready to declare had run *sans repaire et sans reproche* during the whole campaign, was in the repair park for its "initial derangement." Calling at the repair lorry early next morning, I was astounded to hear the A.S.C. sergeant-major in charge say to the major's chauffeur:

> So you have done in the old girl again, have you? Let's see, that's the third time this month, ain't it? Why the major hasn't sent the bally old wreck in months ago to get her put in decent shape, I don't know. Not a bit of use tinkering at her all the time. She's given us more bother than any car in the division.

How we did chip the major! Motorists' yarns bear some odd relationship to fishermen's stories, so I have heard.

Taken generally, the British cars at the Front ran most creditably. The conditions could not have been more trying, and the Daimlers and Rolls-Royces lived up to their reputations in fine style. Cars of half a score of makes were attached to the 1st Cavalry Division while I was with it, and I studied their performances with close attention. For reliability and lack of trouble a large Daimler easily bore away the honours.

Cold forges and a disinclination on the part of the smith to light them on an afternoon necessitated my spending a night in Poperinghe. The town was crowded with Belgian inhabitants and refugees, and with French troops of the 16th Corps, which was at that time being relieved from the trench work by British soldiers, and was mobilising in Poperinghe to be sent south and east, detachment after detachment, to its own dear France.

A winter in Flanders, particularly in Flemish trenches, is not a happy experience. The French were therefore openly delighted at the prospect of departure to more pleasant and congenial climes.

I should have had to sleep in my car but for the kindly offices of a French Staff officer, who procured for me a clean, soft bed in the Hotel La Bourse.

An evening among French soldiers, though they might be tired, trench-stained and campaign worn, was sure to be a pleasurable one. Songs from *chansons d'amour* to grand opera, from poor Harry Fragson's "Marguerita," to swinging marching airs of older wars, were sung with a vim.

The French troopers possessed a suspicion of the grand air when drinking a toast, carolling a love-ditty, or roaring out a rousing chorus. One or two veterans I met in Poperinghe might have stepped from a volume of Dumas. An elder one was a bachelor of arts and science, a man of studious and thoughtful mien. His comrade was a true Gascon, and a third of the group was blessed with powers of mimicry that made us laugh long and loud before the night was over.

Every man of them was proud and fond of his British allies.

French soldiers did not pay the same attention to cleanliness of uniform and kit that was given to such details by the British Tommy. An English battalion, relieved from muddy trenches, at once smartened its external appearance to a degree that had to be seen to be believed. Tommy worked wonders in a day.

The long-tailed blue coats of the French infantry were difficult to clean, once they became mud-caked.

The amount of equipment, and its variety, that the average French foot-soldier strapped upon his back, was wonderful. I saw one black-bearded *poilu*, with a typical load, start off with his company for a long, long march, with literally as much as he could pack about him, fastened securely by ingenious means. Over either shoulder was a strap supporting two good-sized canvas haversacks, one on each hip, both bulging with food. To his belt were attached two ample cartridge-pouches, one in front and one behind. A water-bottle dangled against a haversack. His principal pack, hung at the shoulder, was, he told me, full of spare clothing.

A blanket, rolled in a sheepskin jacket, surmounted this and towered above his cap. A cooking-pot adorned the back of his pack, while to one side of it was strapped a tin cup of ample dimensions, and to the other a loaf of bread, already become soggy in the steady drizzle. A bundle of firewood at his side, and a roll of clothing, holding an extra shirt or two, at the other, flanked him.

My examination of his equipment concluded, he said he must be off, and picked up his rifle with a cheery smile. A comrade rushed up and handed him a sort of leather portmanteau. He grabbed it without a word, threw the strap over his head, settled his various pieces of baggage into place with a strenuous shake, and stamped away sturdily, with a firm step and head held high.

He left me wondering that this sort of soldier should make marching records of which any army in the world might be proud, yet such was undeniably the case.

In billets, the British cavalry were having a thorough course of instruction in the work of the foot soldier. Dismounted attack, trench digging, musketry instruction, bomb-throwing classes, and all manner of miscellaneous tutelage progressed steadily.

I had a look at Ypres one morning. It was again peopled with a sufficient number of civilians to give me a sense of forgetfulness as to its proximity to the German gun positions.

Of all the attributes of the Belgian people, their persistence in making back to their homes in a shelled area, as soon as the shells ceased falling, was the most prominent.

Many of the peasants pursued their daily round of labour under shell-fire. Many others left the bombarded fields or villages, albeit reluctantly, only to return as soon as the shell splinters had ceased to spatter about.

What feeling actuated them was a psychological study. They were phlegmatic as a people. I have seen Russian soldiers perform feats that were described by different observers of the same episode as bravery or stupidity, according to the reading of the onlooker. Was the Belgian who drifted back to his own or some other man's home in shell-ruined Ypres brave or thick-headed? I left one opinion for another, only to abandon it in turn. A study of various types in Flanders helped me but little.

Hard-worked toilers, whose lives have been one continual round of labour, are, more often than not, fatalists. Such lives produce men and women who accept conditions blindly and uncomplainingly. A peculiar love of the soil which they have tilled, and from which they have sprung, seemed to take the place in many Flemish peasants of the more definite and definable Anglo-Saxon or Gallic spirit of intense patriotism. Many poor folk seemed possessed of a blind instinct that "home" was safest, and once "home" was lost, nothing worthy of preservation remained. Their attitude toward death bordered on indifference.

Motor-buses were bringing the 28th Division to the Ypres Salient as I passed on my homeward journey.

Rumours of an attack on the German line flew from lip to lip. That night I read from an eminent French military authority that "to attack, unless with a definite object in view, with a very reasonable chance of success, and with the surety that you can hold what you gain if the attack succeeds, is a crime."

In the second week in February, at a dinner in St. Omer, a member of the French Mission at British Headquarters told me that eighty-seven French general officers had been "relieved of their command" since the commencement of the war. These generals were "sent down" for incompetency, evidenced in various ways, to command the troops under them. The extremely small number of British generals who had been "replaced" stood out in very sharp contrast to this total, with which fact should be remembered the complete difference as to policy with reference to such replacements between the French and British War Office methods.

Early in February, the 1st Cavalry Division staff was blessed with the arrival of Major Desmond Fitzgerald (11th Hussars), who took Major Hambro's place as G.S.O. 2.

The total tally of British casualties was announced during the first week in the month as 104,000, having exceeded, in less than six months of warfare, the numerical strength of the original British Expeditionary Force.

A day "in front," with the engineers, mapping out new trenches and reserve positions, showed to how great an extent modern gun-fire had changed military theory.

Before the war, a trench line was sought in a position that commanded a good "field of fire," *i.e.*, that had in front of it as much open ground as possible.

This war had taught that the most important item in the selection of a trench position was the extent to which the line could be hidden from the enemy gunners. The space commanded by the occupants of the trench and the nature of the terrain were secondary to the cardinal point of keeping the trenches well out of sight of enemy observers.

Thus engineers might, years ago, select a hilltop as a trench position, the line commanding the receding slope to the valley below. After the experience of the greatest of all wars, they would preferably place it fifty yards behind the summit. More than fifty yards of "field of fire" was desirable, but not absolutely necessary. A fifty-yard space could be so covered with wire entanglements as sufficiently to delay an attacking enemy. Deep, narrow trenches with traverses to restrict the area of damage from shells bursting in the actual trench, and to protect from enfilade fire, were demanded by the newer conditions, but great care had to be taken that they should not be constructed in ground of so soft a nature that howitzer fire could too easily cave in the trench sides.

We found it possible to select a trench line that could be well concealed, which, if taken by the enemy, would be under perfect observation from our own gunners and by them easily rendered untenable for the Huns.

That the British were clever in this work of placing trenches in invisible positions was proven by the following report of an interview in Courtrai with a wounded German officer, whose regiment had been badly handled when attacking an English position in the Ypres Salient:—

> Our artillery cannonaded incessantly the enemy trench which our company was to storm—we could see it in the distance. Towards evening we were ordered to advance. We marched forward without taking cover, confident enough, because not a shot came from the British trench. We thought it had been abandoned after the terrible bombardment to which it had been subjected all day long. To make things quite safe, when we were 200 metres from the trench our *mitrailleuses* were brought into action and we gave the silent enemy another good peppering. Still there is no reply. The place must certainly be empty.
>
> Shouting 'Hurrah,' we rush forward to seize it, but we have not gone more than 100 metres before our whole front rank is stricken down by a volley from a point much nearer than the trench we had been shelling, and in addition to this terrible infantry fire the British quick-firing guns are brought into play, and simply mow our men down. Six times we reform to continue our assault; six times we are knocked to pieces before we can get going. At last such officers as are left realise that there is nothing to be done, and we retreat to our original position.
>
> This is how the English work it. The entrenchment, visible from afar, which we had bombarded, was not the spot where their troops were to be found. They were stationed in small subsidiary trenches in front of the principal trench, with which they were connected by means of narrow passages. The little advance trenches were concealed to perfection, and the troops sheltered beneath sheets of metal on which our German bullets ricocheted. So we had been shelling an unoccupied trench and had done no damage to the place where the enemy actually was hidden. Hence it is not surprising that our 'assault' should have proved to be—for us—a veritable massacre.

Careful study of German methods of counterattack were productive of many an idea.

The Hun counter-attacks were delivered immediately after the loss of a position—as successful counter-attacks must be.

A trench which was thought a good defensive one by its occupants was sometimes attacked by the Germans, taken, and immediately transformed into a good defensive trench from the other point of view. The way in which the German first line of attack was followed by a second line, bearing shovels, barbed wire, bombs, and grenades, and the manner in which this second line was put to work, showed that the brain conducting operations was close at hand, if not actually on the spot.

The planning and carrying out of some of these small attacks were worthy of great praise. Our troops soon caught the idea and put it into practice with increasingly beneficial results.

On Sunday, February 21st, the 2nd Cavalry Division were in the trenches in the Ypres Salient. The Huns exploded a mine in front of Zillebeke and took sixty yards of trenches that were occupied by the 16th Lancers. A counter attack, delayed a bit, was launched unsuccessfully, and cost the cavalry four officers killed, one died of wounds, one missing (thought sure to be killed), and four wounded—ten officers in all, and about fifty *per cent*, of the men engaged.

The Canadian Division arrived in France in mid-February—a splendid lot of men.

Trench-mortars and bombs of various sorts put in an appearance and classes were held daily to accustom the men to the new types of trench weapons. A 3.7 affair of gas-pipe, throwing a 4½-pound projectile, was the most prevalent mortar. Prematures and accidents of all kinds accompanied its introduction, and more than one good man was killed before the troops learned the intricacies of the bombs.

General Foch was at Cassel with his headquarters. Dinner in Cassel was always productive of a talk on instructive and entertaining subjects. The average French Staff officer was wonderfully "keen on his job."

The French system of espionage was by no means to be despised. The reports from their "agents" were astonishingly accurate.

That staff work should be the subject of many an after-dinner chat was but natural. The French view of the difference between French and British Staff work, compiled from many a conversation with officers of all ranks, I understood to be generally as follows:—

British Staff work could not fairly be compared to French Staff work, because of the lack of opportunity accorded the British Army, before the War, to handle large bodies of troops. Furthermore, the English Army contained many officers who entered the Army as something in the nature of a pastime rather than a serious profession. Some of these officers even went through the Staff School, though lacking that devoted concentration on their profession as a life-work, which characterised their French prototypes. Very few officers entered the French Army and qualified for staff positions who did not look upon a military career in a very serious light. French Staff officers gained their steps by force of sheer merit and close application to their work.

Nothing else counted, they said. Not a big staff, but one that was efficient beyond all question, was the French aim.

The British soldier, I found, was in most instances frankly conceded to be the best war material in the field—friend or foe. That the British leaders often bungled was openly alleged, but by no means always proven in argument, at least, to my satisfaction.

A failure to arrange support, a badly planned attack, bad staff work here and there, were quoted in more than one instance.

One of the most brilliant Frenchmen with whom I met said:

It is the soldier who suffers. He suffers in silence. Perhaps he what you call 'grouses,' but he stands it. The French soldier would *not* do so in anything like the same spirit. The waste of men and the bad handling of them that once or twice I have seen on the British front, would ruin a French commander for ever.

Universally the French officers praised General Sir Douglas Haig. He had completely won their admiration at Ypres.

Another French officer said:

But the best of the British Staff work is that it is improving. The English are not afraid to admit they don't know, and are quick to absorb new ideas. Give them time.

I have quoted the more trenchant criticisms that came to my ears, for they fell from the lips of the keenest and most brilliant French Staff officers, invariably those who held the British Tommy in the highest possible esteem.

These officers were from the class of man one would choose to put in charge of a dry dock, a line of railway, a huge business or a gigantic manufactory. They impressed me as good "business men." More than a few British Staff officers I met, particularly in the cavalry arm of the service, were equally clever, and every whit as keen on their work, but no one who wished to be impartial could fail to note the inclusion now and then, on the staff, of men to whom one would never dream of entrusting the management of a large commercial organisation or

The Rue de Menin in March, 1915, looking west over the Menin Bridge across the canal moat

the conduct of an important factory plant.

The 3rd and 2nd Cavalry Divisions having each done ten days of trench occupation in the Ypres Salient, on February 23rd, the 1st Cavalry Division moved to Ypres to take its ten days of duty in the firing line.

The run to Ypres, *via* Steenvoorde and Poperinghe, was a trying one. The road surface was inconceivably damaged and very slippery. All manner of French and British transport and general traffic filled the highway.

In the western edge of Ypres, in front of the first cluster of houses—buildings shell-marked and war-scarred from long bombardment—three grimy mites were playing in the dirt at the street-side. Further on, a trio of little girls in soiled black frocklets were enjoying a game of tag. Across the street they darted, under the wheels of cars and lorries, missing the hoofs of the passing horses by inches. One bright-eyed little girl, out of breath from dodging a fast-drawn artillery limber, took momentary refuge in a ragged gap in a shell-shattered dwelling. As we approached the Grand Place more children were to be seen, then a number of adult townsfolk. Round the gaping ruins of the once beautiful Cloth Hall, in the main square, the number of people in evidence might well have led one to believe that the bombardment of Ypres was past and done with.

Ruins, the work of shells and conflagrations, were on all sides, but no one noticed them. French and English soldiers and their officers, with a liberal smattering of civilian Belgians, filled the pavements. Down the Rue de Menin, at the approach of the Menin Bridge, we found the headquarters of General Hubert Gough, of the 2nd Cavalry Division, located in a brewery standing in the shadow of the high moat wall. The trenches lay, roughly, three miles beyond the city walls to the eastward. The junction of the British left with the French right was south of the Menin Road, in front of Zillebeke. The trenches we were to occupy ran east and west and faced south.

Detachments of sturdy French infantry marched past, their uniforms faded to a pale blue. With swinging step, each individual marched to his own time. I admired their fit and willing appearance. They were campaign-worn as to kit and clothing, but campaign-hardened, rather than worn, as to themselves.

A constant stream of people came and went. How long would the civilian population of Ypres remain to pay its toll of dead whenever the Germans decided further to shell the town?

Officers under the stone lion on the Menin Bridge at Ypres

Three women passed, two of them bearing month-old babies in their arms. Noting my interested glance they smiled and waved as they trudged on. What a place for a baby!

An old bent crone, crowned with a richly beaded bonnet of ancient type, in odd incongruity to the ragged condition and mean original state of the remainder of her apparel, hobbled along, pausing now and again to pick up and store safely in her apron small pieces of coal that had been dropped from a passing wagon.

More French soldiers passed. Then a couple of British officers rode by in the picturesque uniform of some Scotch regiment of the line. A transport wagon rumbled by, and behind it came a young girl, with a bucket of water on her head, smilingly exchanging banter with a soldier of the British military police, at the corner of the street.

It was a quiet Spring afternoon, a bit overcast. Hardly to be called lowering, and yet of a stillness that seemed ominous. A day to fit all the mixture of folk going stolidly, carelessly, gaily, or how they would, about their daily tasks.

No one seemed to realise that they were in Ypres—the Ypres which had so often been shattered by shell that the poor old town could hardly be surprised by any sort of new shell-caprice. No one saw the rent walls and gaping holes in every other building. I wondered if they could hear the guns! I could do so. They were hard at it every moment, all the time, from two to three miles distant. It was the old story of familiarity breeding contempt; or perhaps they were true philosophers, these Ypres folk.

General de Lisle ran to Potijze, to the headquarters of General Lefebvre, who commanded the French 18th Division. It seemed ages since I had been in Potijze. Our headquarters were not far beyond it in November, 1914, during the great first battle of Ypres.

On the way from Ypres along the Zonnebeke road we passed bunches of odd little French horse transport wagons. The road was very bad. We progressed in crawfish fashion, most of the way. The *pavé* was torn terribly by shell-fire, and there was sufficient mud and slime on it to make it extremely slippery. French soldiers were billeted in the dwellings along the road. At the edge of Potijze a dozen young boys and girls stood outside a house.

Returning to General Gough's headquarters we "took them over," as that night we were to relieve the 2nd Cavalry Division troopers in the trench line.

General de Lisle and Colonel Home ran up the Menin Road a

kilometre or so, and, leaving the car, walked across the fields past the ruins that will always bear the name of "Cavan's House."

The general told me to put the car in the shelter of a house on the south side of the road, as shell-fire and the Menin Road were never strangers for long. I settled down to wait until the general had concluded his rounds of the prospective positions.

The Ypres Menin Road will be remembered oh! so long, and oh! so well. It saw rough times.

Field guns near by started to work, and now and then German shells dropped in a field beyond.

The house behind which I was sheltered, in case of a stray shell, was a one-storey affair of modest mien.

Those of its windows which were not shattered were shuttered. Half of the roof had been shorn of its tiles. A shell had wrecked the interior of one end of the building. A glance out of a rear door-way showed a whole collection of shell-holes in the yard a few feet distant.

A door that still remained in position bore four lines of legend:

Vin a vingt
Sous la Bouteille.
Confiture, allumettes.
Bougies, chocolate.

Glancing through one of the remaining panes of a window by the door, I saw a glass jar containing a couple of sticks of chocolate, beside it three jars of jelly, a box of French matches, a blue paper packet of half a dozen candles, a score of small oranges in one box, and in another, alongside it, seven or eight very dry-looking kippers. Peering through the partly-obscured glass one could see a stolid-looking, red-faced, albino-haired woman.

"Business as usual," with a vengeance! Such an odd curiosity shop as this was not to be passed without examination, so I entered and talked to the woman.

Her whole stock-in-trade was what I had seen through the window. She was cheerful enough, though she huddled for warmth over a fire by which sat a despondent-looking brother. She chatted laconically about the situation, and told me she had been there continuously throughout the fighting. The shell that hit the building was a shrapnel and came a month before. Shells still came near, now and again, but that fact seemed to be accepted by her as inevitable and not to be worried about. These people had no means of existence except the sale of their pitiable bits of provisions. They were in daily danger of their lives. Yet they stayed on—odd folk. Typical Belgians.

The gun-fire dropped, then began again spasmodically. I could hear the snipers at work. In the gathering twilight the rattle of rifle fire and the storm of the rapid-fire guns sounded clearly on the left. A fusillade on the right reminded me that the Ypres position was a salient. Directly in front, down that Menin Road, which had seen the taking of so many tens of thousands of lives during the past months, a roll of rifle fire made waves of sound.

Night fell cold and damp. The making of a light was not permitted; so I waited in the dark, watching the night lights rise and fall over the trenches, until the General and Colonel Home returned, when we ran back to Ypres for dinner.

My first four days in Ypres were uneventful. On the fifth, I went up into the trenches, and saw more of actual trench conditions than I had seen for some time.

Our daily round led me out on the Menin Road, well towards Hooge, or to Potijze on the Zonnebeke Road, several times each day. Shells went over us now and again. Rarely did a day pass when the Huns did not bombard the railway station in Ypres. As we were quartered in the eastern edge of the town the shells aimed at the station bothered us but little. Sometimes a Black Maria lit on the moat wall, where we walked at times, but we timed our exercise so that our promenade and the arrival of the big shells never coincided. Once or twice bits of shell fell over the Headquarters buildings, or rattled down on our paved courtyard, but rarely.

Every morning saw Ypres wrapped in a snow mantle, which was turned before noontide, to a coverlet of black mud. No fires were allowed, except small wood blazes in the open, as smoke from a chimney would have invited a shell.

One day I was searching for a shop where bolts could, once upon a time, be purchased. As I was going down the Rue de Lille, half a dozen shells fell near. One demolished a house but fifty yards ahead. I took shelter in a doorway, and as I did so a Belgian of woebegone appearance, his most characteristic feature a pair of sad, drooping, yellow *moustachios*, ambled past me down the roadway, pushing a wheelbarrow. On it were three tiny tots, all under four years old. They cuddled together for warmth. One, round-eyed, at the crash of the howitzer shells, was hard at work with a nursing bottle. I warned the Belgian of impending danger, but he stolidly trudged on. Luckily, no more shells came for a time.

The Menin Road proper was never healthy. I spent as little time on it as consistent with the proper performance of my work. I never sat for an hour in its vicinity, waiting for the general, that some shell did not fall near it.

One afternoon shrapnel fell for an hour near a fork on the Menin Road, which all sensible men crave a wide berth to when convenient. Fifteen minutes after the bombardment died down, a procession filed by the fork, headed for a graveyard in the direction of Hooge. A white-robed boy, with red-tasselled black cap, led the way, bearing a cross. Behind him came a robed priest, then an ancient, dilapidated, one-horse hearse containing a rude, black coffin. A score of mourners, one or two of them men, the rest women and children, dressed in their poor best, brought up the rear.

I wondered that they ventured down that shell-swept highway. Yet many such pathetic little processions passed along that road in those days.

I saw one *cortège* wait for a cessation of the shelling, then proceed slowly over the ground that had but a few minutes before been peppered with bits of shell. It was an odd sight. A tiny lad trotted in front under a large wooden cross painted purple. A quartet of little boys behind him bore a rude unpainted sort of stretcher, apparently improvised from the nearest bits of shattered timber to hand. The coffin, resting upon this frame, was covered with a dingy white sheet. A mother, bowed and feeble, followed the coffin. A few youths and a handful of little girls formed the straggling *cortège*, tramping over the snow-covered cobbles, their eyes downcast and red.

Death was no stranger in Ypres in those days, but still the Belgians stayed on.

The wall of a ruined building, across the road from the Cloth Hall, fell one morning with a loud crash. A column of dust arose. That many were not injured was surprising. One woman was killed and a couple of passing French soldiers hurt, but postcard vendors were exhibiting their wares under an adjacent wall, equally dangerous, an hour later.

General de Lisle went personally over the whole of the line held by his division. The 1st Cavalry Brigade was in the front trenches for the first five days, the 2nd Brigade in reserve. Then the 2nd Brigade took over the trenches and the 1st Brigade came back, for the second five days, to the dug-outs.

The Grande Place at Ypres and the Cloth Hall, March, 1915

At points in the line the trenches were knee-deep and sometimes even waist-deep with cold mud and water. The amount of manual labour required to get them into better shape was enormous. New trenches had to be dug, the old parapets strengthened, the trenches drained, and all the while certain mining work must be pushed on at a rapid rate. In some parts of the line the parapets of sandbags had become so thin that a Mauser bullet could plough through them easily. The German snipers were at one place only thirty yards distant.

The drainage of the worst bits of trench, and the laying of a sort of corduroy road from point to point, soon made the trenches much more habitable.

De Lisle was most thorough. Only a couple of casualties occurred when the 1st Brigade "took over," in spite of the constant sniping. Careful preparations of foot baths and relays of dry socks saved the division from the epidemic of "foot-casualties," from which some other divisions had suffered heavily. A dozen casualties per day were inevitable from shells and snipers. Those who had to "go up" with food and ammunition had to cross a dangerous zone, a certain toll being taken day and night, in some localities.

Inspecting the trench-line, when the division had occupied it but the night before, was a precarious business. De Lisle and General Briggs were going over the ground when a German sniper but fifteen to twenty yards distant opened fire. Lieutenant Bell-Irving, General Briggs' A.D.C., received a nasty wound in the hip. He fell in the deep mud. Colonel "Tommy" Pitman, of the 11th Hussars, jumped out into the centre of the trench, and strove to lift Bell-Irving clear, and get him behind the protection of a transept. The bullets flew about the colonel, two cutting clean through his clothing, one on either side of his body, but he escaped unhurt, and pulled Bell-Irving into safety.

But the trouble was by no means over. A sharp fire was kept up by the Hun snipers, which prevented the removal of Bell-Irving to the dressing station. Captain Moriarty of the R.A.M.C. came up at considerable risk, and advised that the wounded officer be brought back at the earliest possible moment.

There were no means of doing this save to construct a traverse of sandbags, behind which Bell-Irving could be carried. The work must be done under the heavy sniping fire. The troopers of the 11th Hussars at once set about the work with a will, and soon accomplished it, but not before a private had been killed and a sergeant wounded by the German marksmen.

The choir of the ruined Ypres Cathedral

That night a bombing party "cleared out" the district near that transept, and made the snipers' point of vantage untenable.

Each night a splendid pyrotechnic display showed the curved outlines of the Salient. The German trench lights were far superior to ours. Each night, too, Ypres was full of French or British lines of soldiers marching on in the dark to relieve some of their fellows in the trenches outside the town.

The ruins of the Cloth Hall, and of the St. Martin Cathedral by it, formed interesting studies for my camera. The line mural paintings mi the walls of the roofless Grand Gallery in the Cloth Hall were crumbling to bits. My photographs were the last records made of them, for they fell piece by piece not long afterward.

I watched operations at a French Divisional Headquarters one evening. It was not more than a mile back of the line. Wagons were loading, preparatory to being taken trenchwards at dusk. Timber, thousands on thousands of empty bags, rolls of barbed wire, odd shaped completed wire entanglements, metal shields varying from curved sheet-steel bastions a dozen feet in length to small V-shaped iron castings, all manner of wooden troughs, boxes, stands, supports, periscopes, braziers, rolls of fine wire, boxes of trench bombs and grenades, shovels, picks, and many peculiar tools were among the collection of material that was to find its way to the firing line. I learnt much of the business side of trench warfare that night.

The supply of ammunition and food and its distribution are most methodically managed by the French.

Taking up giant powder for mining operation was an item of the day's work. A story was told by one of our sappers, of a couple of Irish troopers who had started across the fields in front of Zillebeke as night was falling, with a good sized load of powder in a box. Shortly after they left Cavan's House shells fell in profusion over the route that they had chosen. Another group started trenchward, carrying various types of grenades. Howitzer shells were falling, front and rear, and shrapnel bursting a few hundred yards away.

A flash and a crash came from in front. "Them fellers with the joynt powder was like to be in that shindy," said a member of the second party. "Close to 'em, it was, sure."

A moment later they came upon a strange sight. There in the field, just visible in the gathering darkness, sat the box. Behind it reclined the two troopers, snuggling close for cover.

"What are you doin' in this 'ere peaceful spot, Dan?" questioned

Scenes of battle of olden time in colours on the shattered walls of Ypres Cloth Hall

one of the second party as they reached the box.

"Takin' cover the whiles we do a bit of a rest-like," was the reply. "The divils sent wan so clost, it shure jarred the wind out av us, it did."

And they snuggled closer to the giant powder as he spoke.

Hour by hour I watched the "75's." Their marksmanship was wonderful. The rapidity with which the guns were served was an eye-opener. The French gunners burst shrapnel practically over the heads of our men in the front trenches, to cover the area twenty-five yards beyond them. One trooper swore a French shell, aimed to worry sapping operations by the Huns a short distance in front of our trenches, came so close that it knocked the top sandbag off our parapet. Certain it was that the word was frequently passed to "lie low while the '75's' fire just above us."

My day to go up to the trenches came at last. My guide was Captain Bretherton, the Staff captain of the 1st Cavalry Brigade.

Leaving my car at the "*Halte*," a point where the railway crosses the Menin Road, and the Zillebeke Road branches off to the south, we were soon slipping, sliding and ploughing along through the muddy fields. We followed no particular pathway, avoiding where possible fields where enemy shells were falling. The rotting mangel-wurzels dotted the ground all about us. Shell-holes in thousands, positions where French or British batteries had made a stand, trenches in lines and circles, and barbed wire entanglements, caught my attention at every step. Sprinkled everywhere were all manner of pieces of projectile—from complete 6-inch German shells, unexploded, to blue shrapnel cartridges, bright-nosed timing fuses, and jagged bits of all shapes and sizes.

Cavan's House was but a wall, a pile of shapeless bricks and mortar beside it. Cavan's Dugout, a series of holes in the road bank, roofed with sandbags, held a signal party. Every day a storm of shell visited the spot, and Hun snipers made one wary thereabouts.

We walked on, up the roadway, our objective the Sanctuary Wood. The bullets sang over us, and shells burst in front with a continuous din. A path led through the scrub. Entering the wood, we passed innumerable little individual funk holes. The trees were in splinters and tatters. Here I saw an abandoned shirt, there a khaki cap. My foot hit against a regulation mess tin, and as it turned I saw a rifle-hole drilled in its bottom. Now we were ankle, now knee, deep in sticky mud. Bullets became more plentiful overhead.

A COMMUNICATION TRENCH LEADING TO THE FRONT-LINE
POSITION IN THE SANCTUARY WOOD

A turn down a muddy path led us through a last piece of woods, across sloughs of slime, over a creek, up a slight slope, and there we were at General Briggs's Brigade Headquarters. These were a line of dugouts in the hillside, a corduroy road winding from entrance to entrance. A deep approach trench, looking like a drain, led one hundred and fifty yards further to the front trenches.

Shells fell all the afternoon on our right and behind us, and the song of the Mauser bullets never ceased. At dusk, I was "safe" back in Ypres.

On my way back through the woods, shell-smashed, that covered the gentle hills through which the front line trenches ran, I saw a burial party.

I stopped a moment, and watched the laying to rest of all that was mortal of three troopers who had paid the great price.

Their comrades placed them reverently in the shallow graves in the soft earth of the hillside, marking each grave with a white wooden cross bearing each hero's name, his rank, and regiment.

Oh, those rows of rude wooden crosses! What thoughts their memory brings to mind! Gone now, many of them, ploughed under by long months of shell-fire, or trampled under foot by the ebb and flow of battle, as the lines have swept back and forth with the tide of war. Gone, perhaps, from the scarred and mangled hill-sides of Flanders; but never to go altogether from the hearts of those who knew them, and who realised their worth.

CHAPTER 3

Mixed Plans

On March 1st Captain "Babe" Nicholson, of the 15th Hussars, who had joined General de Lisle's staff in place of Captain Cecil Howard, 16th Lancers, promoted to General Allenby's staff at Cavalry Corps Headquarters, had to make a careful map of our trench position.

Captain Bennie Wheeler, 15th Hussars, in temporary charge of Divisional Signals, also had duties that took him to the trench line.

As neither Captain Nicholson nor Captain Wheeler had made the two-mile tramp across the fields and through the woods, I was instructed to act as guide. To skirt one edge of a field was safety of a comparative sort. To walk along its opposite edge meant dodging snipers' bullets in plenty. To turn from the road to a path through the scrub kept one out of sight of the Huns, while to proceed a dozen yards beyond the turning would expose one to a fair chance of being shot, at good range, by crack German marksmen.

Leaving our car at the *Halte* on the Menin Road, we essayed the route past Cavan's House that I had travelled a couple of days before with Bretherton.

Bang! bang! bang! bang! went a quartet of shrapnel just ahead.

"I don't think much of your route," said Nicholson.

"I'll change it with alacrity," said I. "Which way shall we go?"

"I know an old route that we followed in the days of the fighting last autumn," Wheeler volunteered. "If we push down the Menin Road to a point near Hooge, and then turn off, we can't get *far* wrong."

"Lot of French were hit in Hooge yesterday," I reminded him. "The Huns shell it two or three times every day, so best not go too close to it."

We tramped down to the foot of the hill that led up to the ruins of what was once Hooge, then passed through a demolished farm. For a hundred yards, at every step, we sank knee-deep in the foul, slimy mud.

Then we wound over trenches which were nearly inundated, and through barbed wire entanglements that seemed to become more impassable as they lost their original form, until at last, covered in perspiration, we reached a dense wood.

A tiny creek ran deep through a sharp cutting, in the sheer banks of which the French gunners had burrowed like rabbits. Battery on battery of "75's" were hidden in the forest. Each gun was surrounded by a little hut of mud and leaves, an aperture left for each slim, blue-grey muzzle. We passed the first of these batteries without seeing it. Close behind us it opened fire, causing me to jump as if I had been shot. Before we left the wood, three other batteries went into action about us. The din was terrific, but the sound of the shells racing overhead was most fascinating. Each gun crew had cleared a neat line of fire in the tree-tops in front of its position.

Over further fields and through another wood we came upon a most picturesque cantonment. A French infantry brigade in reserve had built hundreds of mud huts and dug-outs with charming ingenuity. Dozens of veteran architects, past masters of rude shelter construction, vied with each other in improving on previous designs. As I took a snapshot in the dull light under the trees, the French soldiers crowded forward in twos and threes, and smilingly invited me to photograph their *maisons de luxe*.

Cavan's House, our landmark, we left well on our right, edging from it the more as we saw it a very storm centre of fours and eights of shrapnel that morning.

Snipers' bullets sang merrily above as we reached the reserve line and Brigade Headquarters. My work as guide finished, I started back with General de Lisle, who, having come up early in the morning, had left his horse in the wood which sheltered the French reserves.

Mounting, the general pointed out a new route for my return, shorter than the one by which I had come.

"Keep that rise of ground between you and the line of high ground beyond," said de Lisle. "If you don't, the Germans will see you and pot at you."

Crossing my first field, I seemed to be well in the line of spent bullets, as several kicked up the dirt in the front of me sufficiently close to make me imagine myself the target.

I lost little time for the first few hundred yards.

A maze of reserve trenches and wire pulled me up short. The only path through was a quagmire. Safe beyond at last, I started collecting German timing fuses, which lay thick on the surface of the muddy field.

Not far on my left was a ruined farm. The sun came out amid the swiftly-moving clouds. "A splendid example of what shells can do to a group of buildings," I thought. "I must get a picture of the piles of debris!"

I circled the smashed houses, took my picture, replaced my camera in its case, and turned to look sunward, as the clouds had cast a dull shadow all about me. An open bit of blue was racing toward the spot where the sun was hidden. Should I wait for it and essay a further snapshot?

As my eyes sought the sun, a bright flash in front of me, in my very line of sight, almost blinded me. A deafening explosion and the whirr of scores of shrapnel bullets was followed by another flash. *Crash!* The second shell seemed nearer than the first.

The *pluck! pluck! pluck! flop!* of bits of projectile striking in the soft mud all about me came from every side. Little spurts of mud and water were thrown up close around me. I imagined I could feel the breath of passing shrapnel bullets. A bit of stick hit me in the face, and a gob of black mud landed squarely over my mouth.

So many mud-spurts threw up in front of me, on my right, and on my left, it seemed to me impossible I had escaped being hit.

I must have been in the very vortex of the shell's storm-centre.

Turning, thanking God I had so miraculously escaped when death had seemed so near, I dashed off as fast as I could run, heading: blindly for the general direction of the Menin Road.

Fear lent wings to my feet as I realised I had, in my interest in my photography, advanced into plain sight of the line of heights of which General de Lisle had warned me.

I had not run a dozen steps when I thought of my heavy load, in pockets and hands, of shell heads. I tossed them away as I leaped on, tempted for a moment to hurl my camera after them.

Bang! Crash! Behind me came a second pair of shells, whose coming I had dreaded every second. To my delight, but one or two bullets came my way.

"I am gaining," I thought.

Bang! bang! another two burst overhead, throwing their deadly contents beyond me in the direction in which I was running.

I ducked to the right and ran diagonally to the Hun line of fire. Panting, I struck a deep bog. In I went before I realised it lay in my path. In a twinkling I was in a pretty mess. My feet sank deep in the slime and ooze. It took great effort to raise them. Well over my knees in mud, I felt trapped, but struggled on.

At last I trod on firmer bottom, and soon was racing away at much better speed.

Crash! Bang! I could see over my shoulder that the last two arrivals had burst over the muck through which I had just floundered, throwing spurts of liquid mud high in the air.

The Hun gunners were gradually increasing their range, though I was well out of sight of them.

My breath came in great sobs, but I dared not slacken.

Bang! Bang! Two fell behind me again, but not so near. That encouraged my flagging footsteps, and I jog-trotted on, until at last the Menin Road was before me. Reaching it, I laid down, utterly exhausted. The shells continued to burst nearer and nearer the road, and came in fours after the first half-dozen couples, twenty-four shrapnel having been fired in all.

Two British gunners, attached to a siege battery near by, hurried past me as I lay recuperating.

"Bad place to be, this," said one of them. "They shell this bit of road every day about this time. Those two holes were made yesterday"—pointing to two cavities not ten feet from me.

So I pulled myself to my feet and pushed on for "home," arriving safely enough, though completely tired out and literally plastered with mud.

As I was resting at headquarters, one of the staff told me I had "missed some fun" while "out front." Six Black Marias had landed on the earthen wall of the moat, not many yards from our brewery quarters, "shaking things up a bit," but fortunately hitting no one.

Examining my camera, I discovered, to my great chagrin, that the shutter had been inadvertently set at "time" when I took the snapshot of the ruined farm, away from which I retired in such a hurry. So I missed getting the picture which cost me such a strenuous race against the shells. As a solace, my photographs of the French reserves in the wood, and of our Brigade Headquarters, came out quite satisfactorily.

Shells fell not far from our Divisional Headquarters next day. More than once the signalmen brought in pieces of shrapnel, quite hot, that fell in the courtyard, which from that time began to lose its popularity as a lounging-place for waiting orderlies.

A run to Hooge, and a wait there in a dugout while the Huns threw a dozen shells about it, was made memorable to me by Nicholson's reconstruction of a bit of the fighting over that ground in November, 1914.

Nicholson had been with the 1st Infantry Division—a division that had Haig for a leader. At the beginning of the war it had come out 14,000 odd strong. In six months its total list of casualties had reached 34,000.

In the first Battle of Ypres its battalions had suffered cruelly. The 1st Coldstrcams had been annihilated. The Queen's (West Surreys) came out of the line with but fifteen men and no officers, the Black Watch with but sixty men and one officer, and the Loyal North Lancashires with but 150 men and two officers. When the division came back to billets, it was commanded by a brigadier-general. Every colonel in the division had been killed or wounded, and the brigades were commanded by officers of all ranks. A captain was in command of one brigade.

It was in front of Hooge, between that town and Gheluvelt, that most of the heaviest losses of the 1st Division were suffered.

Nicholson had seen some of it. One night the Prussian Guard broke through the line on the Menin Road. Nicholson's squadron of the 15th Hussars, acting as divisional cavalry, were sent to stop the gap. Forty troopers and forty cyclists, eighty rifles all told, went up. They had no trenches, as the Prussians held our original position. So they lay in a sunken road near the Herenthage Château. The Germans occupied a wood sixty yards away, though neither force knew of the whereabouts of the other until dawn.

Nicholson sought out General Fitzclarence, commanding the 1st Brigade, in the dark. Most of Fitzclarence's Brigade had been killed. Efforts to clear up the situation had borne little result. Every messenger he had sent out for information had been killed. Fitzclarence said five brigades were to be sent to him, with which he was to counter-attack. The five brigades came, and were found to total 1,000 men all told. Yet with the remnants of his force Fitzclarence counter-attacked at dawn. Though he himself was killed, his wonderful men won through. The position was recaptured, and Ypres saved.

A glorious page in the annals of the British Army, though it cost England men who were indeed hard to replace.

Our 1st Cavalry Division had come into the line that night, and supplied the reinforcements without which the exhausted troops could not have held on much longer.

Consequently the ground over which those heroic battles had been fought was of fascinating interest to those of us who had seen the most strenuous struggle of the war.

"As to the losses of the enemy," Nicholson told me, "I once scouted the wood in front of us. It was a terrible sight. In many places among the trees I could not set my foot without stepping on a dead German."

But the work of Haig and his super-men had been crowned with success. We had held the Ypres Salient, and were still holding it—a glorious record.

On the morning of March 3rd Nicholson found it necessary to go once more over the line of our front trenches to verify his map. I was to go with him.

Rain fell all morning, and we splashed over the cross-country route to Brigade Headquarters and the reserve line without incident, bar snipers and itinerant shells, most of which sang over our heads on their way toward Ypres.

One portion of the approach trench leading to the firing-line was so narrow that Jeff Hornby, of the 9th Lancers, A.D.C. to General Mullens, waded through it at my heels, "to see the President (my *sobriquet*) get stuck fast."

In spite of the rain, I procured a sufficient number of photographs to show trench life as no written description could picture it.

The top of the hill was cut and seamed with trenches at all angles, some narrow, some wide. The trench walls had been in a few places reinforced with tree trunks, though, for the most part, from two to half a dozen rows of sandbags served as protection. The line was rarely straight for more than a few yards.

The troopers in the front trenches were either standing about, near machine-gun or rifle, engaged in cleaning kit or accoutrement, or sleeping in one of the tiny shelters that lined the trench sides at the rear.

The fact that there was no uniformity to the trenches as to height, width, or direction made caution necessary as we wound along them. Expediency was the law that governed their original construction, and experience the guide as to their alteration and development.

Loop-holes covered with bits of sacking were marked by pieces

OFFICERS OF LANCERS IN THEIR DUGOUTS IN THE FRONT-LINE TRENCHES

of paper pinned above, warning occupants not to tarry in the line of German fire.

By periscope we could see the Hun trenches, not many yards distant, and dozens of dead Germans lying between the two lines. The smoke from the enemy's cooking fires rose slowly in the damp atmosphere. At corners, cautions to "keep down" were posted. Snipers' bullets, heralded by a sharp bark and twanging musically, kept me down without much warning. A German sniper's position was pointed out to me, and I had some good rifle practice endeavouring to dislodge him, but with questionable success. The Hun riflemen had learned to lie very low in front of our troopers.

We passed one of the 4th Dragoon Guards' marksmen, his eye along the barrel of his rifle as it lay in a loop-hole. As we came up he fired.

"Got him?" asked Nicholson.

"No," laconically answered the sharpshooter. "Got one this morning, though, sir. And I hope we are not shifted out of this for a day or so, as there are a couple more of the beggars I'll get if I'm given a bit of time."

Seeing a trooper of the 9th Lancers whom I had known since the Great Retreat, I asked him how much longer his squadron was booked to be in the front trench.

"Only twenty-four hours or so," was the reply. "But we could stick this sort of thing for a week and not kick. They're behavin' themselves much better as they go on," and he grinned as he nodded his head at the German trench. "They're learnin'."

Now and then an enemy marksman sent a bullet through a loop-hole in front of us or behind us as we proceeded down the line, until we learned to pass these danger spots without loitering.

Once we found it necessary to double back along a shallow trench a few yards behind the main parapet. The ditch we traversed was deep with cold water, which ran over the tops of my high boots.

The damage to the trees was so extensive that shells might be said to have literally cleared away the forest in some localities.

In spite of water in the trenches, the men were cheerily comfortable, many of them gathering around glowing braziers or cuddling close to the wall of a cosy dugout.

An enforced detour nearly landed us in an *impasse*. We had taken the wrong turning. The trench parapet became lower, the trench narrower, and the cold water deeper. Pressed for time, we pushed on. At

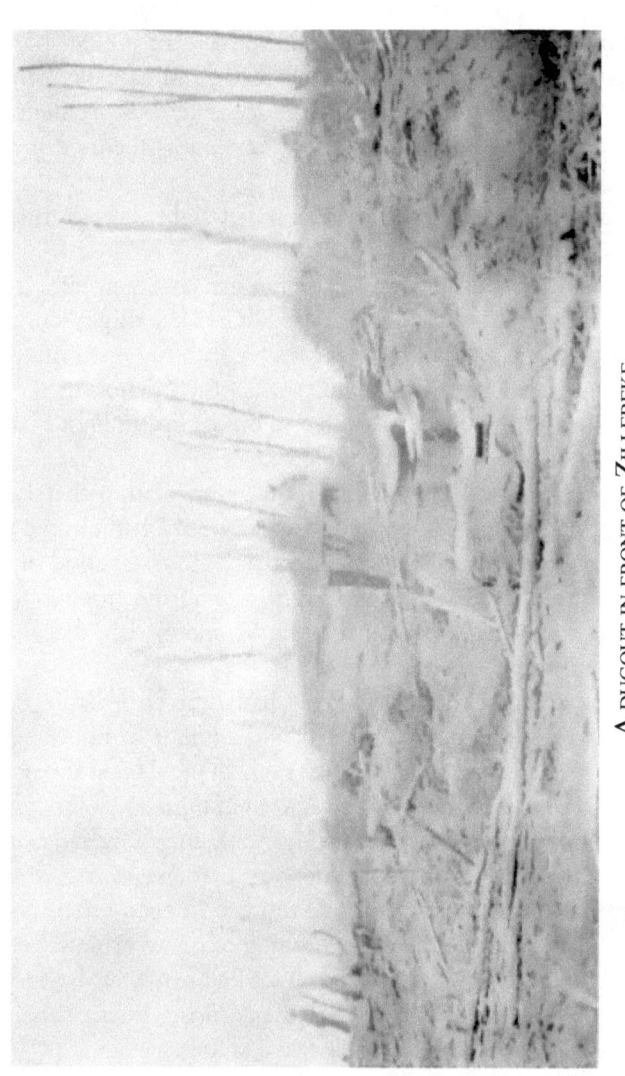

A DUGOUT IN FRONT OF ZILLEBEKE

last Nicholson, who was leading, saw an angle of front line trench ahead, and ran for it. I followed. Bullets sang overhead as the Huns got a glimpse of us, but we ducked low and splashed through for dear life in record time.

Nicholson became so interested in a view through a periscope that I took a picture of him while thus engaged. A genial acquaintance in the line offered to get a similar photograph of me. So I took the periscope, waving it slightly back and forth, and carefully inspecting the German trench forty yards distant. I detected a movement on the enemy side of the line. Steadying my periscope, I focussed my attention on the moving object.

As I did so, "*Ping! smash!*" came a bullet right through the top of my periscope.

"A clean bull," said Nicholson, beside me. "Are you hit?"

I had been about to call his attention, when the sniper scored, with the result that a shower of broken glass fell into my open mouth.

I was in great fear of swallowing some of it. Nicholson, seeing me dance about and spying a fleck of blood on my lip, thought I had been hit in the mouth by a glancing bullet.

He proffered help, I prancing about, gesticulating that I was all right, spitting out glass, but afraid to speak until I had cleared the last piece of broken mirror. The captain entirely misunderstood my dumb show, and we caused some merriment among the troopers near by until I managed to eject the final bit and could explain that I was not in the least hurt.

When I learned that one officer had suffered a badly cut eyeball, threatening the loss of his sight, and another had been seriously wounded in the jaw and neck by just such an incident as the one I had experienced, I was thankful to have escaped injury.

The "trench stoop" was astonishingly fatiguing. Covered from head to foot with yellow sticky mud, and very tired, we started to walk to the Menin Road. The snipers were more alert than usual, and more than one close call kept me from thinking of my weariness. Before we reached our car the German batteries shelled madly at the very point we were to pass, but considerately stopped firing by the time we approached the spot where the shells were falling.

One morning "Mouse" Tomkinson and Hardress Lloyd had walked down to Zillebeke, where folk rarely went in the daytime, to inspect some of the graves in the Zillebeke churchyard. Hardress Lloyd's brother-in-law, Colonel Wilson, of the Blues, was buried there.

The Zillebeke Church, March, 1915

I promised Captain Lloyd that if I could get off to do so, I would go down to Zillebeke and take a photograph of Colonel Wilson's grave.

Hearing of my projected trip, Lord Loch, who was at that time G.S.O. 1, on the staff of General Bulfin, commanding 28th Division, asked "Babe "Nicholson to obtain for him, if possible, a picture of the grave of Lieutenant Gordon-Lennox, which is also in Zillebeke.

Hardress Lloyd and Tomkinson told us they had been seen in the churchyard by the German artillery observers, who had commenced shelling. I was warned, therefore, that any photography I wished to do in that locality must needs be done quickly.

On March 4th Nicholson and I set out to obtain the desired pictures. I stopped on the way, at a cemetery on the Menin Road, and took a photograph of the graves of three officers of the 10th Hussars—Captain Annesley, Lieutenant Drake, and Captain Peto—who had fallen in the first Battle of Ypres.

Zillebeke was lonely. On one edge of it a couple of signal corps men were laying a wire. Otherwise the town, which was in ruins, was deserted.

We kept under cover of the houses as much as possible. I obtained a good snapshot of the damaged church, and then took some pictures in the graveyard, which was torn with great shell-holes.

"Remember what Hardress said about the Huns being able to see us here," I said to Nicholson. "Let's get out of it."

We started. No sooner were we under cover of the first cluster of smashed houses than four shrapnel shells burst right over the *pavé* roadway, not fifty yards ahead of us.

I dodged into a house, the walls of which, minus roof, were still standing at drunken angles. Doorless and windowless, the house seemed to offer little protection.

"I don't like going up that road over the hill," said I. "We will be in sight of the Huns for some distance. I wonder if this house boasts a cellar?"

Examination showed a cellar existed, but it was nearly full of water.

"I guess the cellar steps provide the best roosting-place," was my conclusion. "Me for the lowest one for a bit. Won't you share it with me? "

"I don't like it," replied Nicholson. "We will be much better out of it. Let's go."

German prisoners in Ypres, captured after the explosion of a British mine near Hooge

We argued the various possibilities, but Nicholson was so strongly in favour of departure that I acquiesced, and we started away.

We had gone about one hundred feet when a series of crashes close behind us quickened my pace. Nicholson turned and looked. I called to him, and he again came on.

As he came up he said: "Did you see where that lot landed?"

"No," I answered. "Too close to suit me, but just where I didn't notice."

"It interested me," said he, as we pushed on, "because all four of those shells exploded in that rickety old house in which you were so keen on taking cover. But little would be left of us by now had we stayed, for the poor building collapsed like a house of cards."

The Germans shelled the road vigorously as we kept on, but luckily the shrapnel fell behind us, and we were soon back in Ypres.

That day saw the German gunners increase their shelling all along the Ypres front. The trenches occupied by our division were vigorously bombarded, and several casualties reported. Ypres itself came in for a heavy share of the Hun "hate." The windows rattled and our house shivered as the howitzer shells smashed into all quarters of the town.

De Lisle visited the trench line, and both there and on his way back across the fields the shells fell very close to him. As he entered the headquarters house on his return, he said: "From what I can see, most of the big ones are falling at least four or five hundred yards from us thus far, but they may shell us out of this at any time."

The general suggested I should take a stroll with him along the moat wall and watch the trend of the bombardment. As we walked along the ramparts, the projectiles screamed overhead in dozens, seemingly coming continually closer. The *rumph! r-r-r-rumph!* as they exploded shook the high wall and made the whole city rock with the concussion. The Rue de Lille was rendered impassable that day.

General Plumer called, and after his departure I again started for a stroll on the ramparts. The shells searching for our batteries just across the moat were a fascinating sight. As I ran up the steep path, however, a crash came just ahead, and bits of metal showered about, striking sharply against the trees beside the path. My curiosity evaporated instantly, and I came down faster than I had gone up.

As dusk came, I took Major Fitzgerald to Hooge, from whence he went through a wood to the trenches to make the final arrangements fur the explosion of a mine—the construction of which had been worked upon feverishly for some days—that all might be completed and the mine fired on that night, our last one in the trenches. The French, who were to relieve us, had also constructed a mine on our left, and the two were to be discharged at an interval of five minutes.

First the French mine was to be fired at 7.45 p.m., and 7.50 to the tick of the watch was to be the time for the explosion of our mine, less than a hundred yards away from the French one.

I was seldom in Hooge when it was not shelled, and that evening was no exception. The French had built safe dug-outs under the buildings still left standing. The chateau was completely ruined, as were most of the houses in the village.

As I was being entertained by a French officer, who produced a glass of splendid red wine, some thirty shells burst over us, most of them of the 210-millimetre type. One of them knocked off a corner of the building behind which I had sheltered my car.

Never was a locality more offensive to one's olfactory nerves than Hooge. It fairly reeked with all manner of various noxious smells. The English language contains words of too mild a character to allow a description of that feature of Hooge.

The front line was less than a kilometre distant. Rifle fire swelled and died away in long, rattling breaths. I became so accustomed to the punctuation of my conversation with shell-smashes and periods of heightened din from small arms and machine-guns that, when all would die down suddenly for an instant, the stillness felt ominously oppressive. The next spasm of sound came as a relief to the uncanny moments of twilight silence.

A French engineer officer joined us. He told us General Lefebvre, the French general in command of that section of the Salient, had issued most elaborate written instructions for the joint explosion of the two mines. The French mine, he said, had been ready for two or three days, its charge lying at the end of a tunnel but two metres from the German trench.

The hour for the discharge of the French mine came, but no sound or shock of explosion came with it. The hands of the Allied watches, carefully synchronised, crept round to 7.50, then to 7.55.

Just before eight o'clock a huge bang was heard by the British sapper who was waiting in his tunnel, ready to fire his mine.

"At last," he murmured. "Now I must count off the five minutes to the second."

A squadron of the Queen's Bays was ready to rush into the enemy's trench. Ten of them, the forward storming party, were waiting in a saphead.

One, two, three, four, and at last, five.

Boom!

The whole earth seemed thrown skyward. The shock was terrific. Nearly one thousand pounds of blasting powder had tossed fifty yards of German trench, not two hundred feet in front of our line, high in air.

The great smash came as a complete surprise to the Huns, but, alas! an equal surprise to French and British.

The explosion which the British sapper, in his tunnel dugout, had mistaken for the discharge of the French mine, had been a huge German *minenwerfer*, or trench-bomb, thrown by a trench-howitzer.

The French mine, inexplicably delayed, had not been fired.

For a moment confusion reigned. Three men of the half-score Queen's Bays in the storming party were hurt. One suffered a broken arm, and the others, hurled aside by the unexpected explosion of our own mine, were badly bruised and strained.

In an instant, however, every man in the line realised what had occurred, and the Bays went forward with a yell, occupying about fifty yards of German first-line trench and the gaping crater left by the mine.

Fortifying the captured position and installing therein a couple of machine-guns, they met the enemy's counter-attacks staunchly.

For three hours and a half they kept the ground won, but at last were bombed out. The Huns threw hundreds of grenades among them, while our poor supply of trench-bombs ran out in but a few minutes.

I chatted with the remnants of the storming party when they came back. Many gruesome tales they told. One German soldier was blown high in the air, over a fringe of trees, and found some distance back of our front line, quite 150 yards from his own trench.

A trooper noticed a movement near a pile of timber, earth, and sandbags. Peering through the dim light, he saw a hand waving about aimlessly. Grasping it, he pulled with a will. A comrade assisted, and soon they unearthed a buried German.

The prisoner was a funny little fellow—a stocky Wurtemburger in green corduroys and a knitted helmet. When rescued, he lapsed into unconsciousness for an hour. He had been through the first battle of Ypres, he said later, in which he was the only one of his regiment to escape death or a wound. Blown high in air, very, very high, it seemed to him, he felt a great mass of debris fall upon him.

He told us, in a spirit of resignation to his fate, that to have lived through the October and November fighting on the Menin Road, and be thrown skyward by a mine, then buried, and still live, entitled him, he thought, to spend the rest of the War, without disgrace, in an enemy prison.

The French exploded their mine at one o'clock in the morning, and by daybreak the 1st Cavalry Division had "turned over" to them, and was on its way back from Ypres to billets in a more quiet locality.

Motor 'buses moved the men back, as they had brought the dismounted troopers up. The long lines of London 'buses, with khaki-painted windows, rendering their interior lighting barely visible, looked odd in the black Ypres streets. No outside lights were permitted.

To hear one bell, see the dark shape of the clumsy vehicle slow down, then hear the two bells that signalled departure, next the grinding crunch of gears, and finally, to see the ghostly 'bus slide forward in the night, brought strange parodies of London memories.

General de Lisle had planned to leave Ypres at twelve noon on March 5th. We left half an hour earlier, by chance. Next day we learned that ten minutes after our departure a Black Maria struck the very building we had occupied during our ten days' stay in Ypres, blowing the back of it through its front, and generally demolishing the premises.

One day, subsequently, I visited the house to learn if so strange a coincidence of timely evacuation was true, and found that the story was correct in every detail. The interior of the place was one mass of smashed walls and partitions, the debris bulging from the doors and windows of the front of the building, which still remained practically intact.

The handling of the division during its occupation of the Ypres trenches reflected great credit on General de Lisle.

We left our trenches in much better shape than that in which we had found them. Some casualties were inevitable, but the total number of men killed was only eleven during the ten days, a low percentage when the strength of the division, not far short of 2,500 rifles in the line, was considered.

At daybreak on the morning of March 10th the British attack was launched which was to become known to history as the Battle of Neuve Chapelle.

For several days the weather had been cold, raw and damp. On some days it rained and blustered, while at night snow fell, and the wind howled unceasingly. The morning of the 9th dawned clear and cold, the stormy weather having been driven away by a hard frost. The Tommies in the trench line were treated to every vagary of the treacherous climate of Flanders in March.

My car indulged in periodical attacks of the dumps and finally became a nuisance. Accordingly I ran to Sailly, where the Canadian Divisional Headquarters were located, and sought the Divisional Repair Park, which proved to be at Merville. On the 8th I left the car in the hands of the Canadian boys for a few days' repair. On the Canadian front I learned from an acquaintance of a projected attack of considerable magnitude, spurring me on toward getting my car in runnable shape at the earliest possible moment.

On March 9th, in Merville, I saw Sir Douglas Haig's Special Order to the First Army, issued that day, which read as follows:—

> We are about to engage the enemy under very favourable conditions. Until now in the present campaign, the British Army has, by its pluck and determination, gained victories against an enemy greatly superior both in men and guns. Reinforcements have made us stronger than the enemy in our front. Our guns are now both more numerous than the enemy's are and also larger than any hitherto used by any army in the field. Our Flying Corps has driven the Germans from the air.
>
> On the Eastern Front, and to the South of us, our Allies have made marked progress and caused enormous losses to the Germans, who are, moreover, harassed by internal troubles and shortage of supplies, so that there is little prospect at present of big reinforcements being sent against us here.
>
> In front of us we have only one German Corps, spread out on a front as large as that occupied by the whole of our Army (the First).
>
> We are now about to attack with about forty-eight battalions a locality in that front which is held by some three German battalions. It seems probable, also, that for the first day of the operations the Germans will not have more than four battalions available as reinforcements for the counter-attack. Quickness of movement is therefore of first importance to enable us to forestall the enemy and thereby gain success without severe loss.

At no time in this war has there been a more favourable moment for us, and I feel confident of success. The extent of that success must depend on the rapidity and determination with which we advance.

Although fighting in France, let us remember that we are fighting to preserve the British Empire and to protect our homes against the organised savagery of the Germany Army. To ensure success, each one of us must play his part, and fight like men for the honour of Old England.

In the evening when I returned to 1st Cavalry Division Headquarters I found the servants packing. My servant said on my arrival, "Your kit is ready, sir. We are to shift out of this at six o'clock in the morning. A big push is on."

The cavalry was to "stand by," in case the infantry attack succeeded and a hole was made in the German line.

The guns began before daylight, and hundreds of them, with an amplitude of ammunition, made a pandemonium.

I begged a ride in a G.H.Q. car and found myself during the forenoon near the headquarters of General Davies of the 8th Division.

Not many days before, General de Lisle had called at Estaires, and we had been hospitably given lunch by General Davies, when we had learned something of the general topography of the line on the 8th Division front. The ground in that sector was so water-logged and soft that it did not admit of the construction of a trench line such as we had held in the Ypres Salient. Each small point of vantage to the east of Laventie—a house here, or a rise of ground there—had been made into miniature forts by the British or the Germans. A trench line proper existed, but consisted, from the nature of the terrain, of trench-works and parapets of sandbags, all above ground. These were less impregnable than a trench line in solid ground, and could much more easily be demolished by shellfire.

The road from Estaires to La Bassée, on the morning of March 10th, was full of advancing troops and returning wounded. General Davies' headquarters were said to be at Rouge Croix, not far west of the town of Neuve Chapelle.

I did not go as far as the crossroads at Rouge Croix, as that point was under heavy German shell-fire.

Little could I see except the enemy's shells, and still less could I learn. That the 8th Division had taken the front line German trenches was common rumour.

Finally a wounded subaltern, a mere boy, came back, hysterically cheerful in spite of a nasty wound in his arm. He belonged to the 25th Brigade—Lincolns, Dorsets, Rifle Brigade and Wiltshires.

"We took Neuve Chapelle," he said.

"Many casualties?"

"Yes, plenty. You see, we had orders to take the bally town at all costs, and we did it!"

He was sure his fellows had the ridge that commanded Aubers, and had heard that our men on the right had reached a point a couple of miles beyond La Bassée. Cheerful lad, that. Neither the Auber Ridge nor La Bassée was to be ours, but it was not for lack of his sort. He and his kind, with the men behind them that fought that day at Neuve Chapelle, could have taken Aubers and Lille beyond it had someone not blundered that 10th of March.

Weeks passed before the occurrences of that fateful day were made clear to me. Every sort of rumour was afloat. On the 10th and the 11th I was between Merville (where General Haig had his headquarters), Estaires and Laventie, but no one seemed to know in those days as to just why things had gone so badly when the promise of success had been so great.

Later I knew.

General Haig had been quite reasonably correct in his estimate of the enemy's strength. Our chance to break through the German line was the finest opportunity of the whole war.

That, with such odds in our favour, with a preponderance of guns and shells as well, we should have so signally failed, and lost over 18,000 men into the bargain, required some explanation.

The tragedy of Neuve Chapelle was a failure to take advantage of an initial success. The 25th Brigade, with the 23rd Brigade on its left, nobly did the work assigned to it. It took Neuve Chapelle itself, and reached the position it had hoped to reach. The 24th Brigade was to come up, through the 23rd and 25th Brigades, and as it advanced, the 20th Brigade, on its left, was to move forward. Still to the left of the 20th Brigade the 21st Brigade was in readiness, and on its left the Northamptonshire Yeomanry, which had been put into the trenches previously occupied by the 20th Brigade, to free that command for the attack.

Thus, once the preliminary ground-clearing was done by the 23rd and 25th Brigades on the right, and the town of Neuve Chapelle was taken, the 24th Brigade was to come on and form the right of a line composed of itself, the 20th and 21st Brigades, which were to pivot on the Northamptonshire Yeomanry and sweep over the Auber Ridge.

On the left of the Yeomanry waited the 22nd Brigade, ready to jump forward the moment this swinging movement had developed.

The initial success won, the whole line waited, eyes on the right, for the signal to go on. Before nine o'clock in the morning all was ready, and the road cleared.

All day the watchers waited in vain.

It was after four o'clock in the afternoon before the word came.

It was then too late.

The great opportunity had been lost, and lost for ever.

The Germans had rallied, filled farms with machine-guns, and mowed down the gallant 23rd and 25th Brigades men who had so dearly won such splendidly advanced positions.

The 24th Brigade had come on part way, then concentrated, and was sadly cut up. That the line on the right had "dug-in," instead of moving forward, had resulted in a defeat when a great victory was within grasp.

And who was to blame?

A brigade commander and the general in command of the artillery of a certain division were promptly "*Stellenbosched.*" A divisional commander was reported sent home; his case reopened when he declared the fault was not his, as could be proven by certain hitherto unproduced papers from corps headquarters. A further inquiry resulted in his being reinstated. His corps commander went to England. "Sent home," said many. Shortly afterwards, back he came, to the discomfiture of the prophets, and took up his old command.

Who was to blame?

It is too early to tell. Let the writers of the future dig the story out of the tangled orders of the day, as between corps and division, division and brigade.

No battle of such magnitude could be won without fine Staff work, and the work of more than one staff on that 10th of March left much to be desired.

One thing cannot be gainsaid. The men in the ranks fought like heroes. Nothing that men could do was left undone by them.

One officer who saw as much of Neuve Chapelle, and knew as much of the tragedy as any one man said to me:

"The word 'concentrate' caused all the trouble. The troops that might so easily have come on had orders to concentrate along a certain road. That was the root of the mix-up. They concentrated, dug-in, and waited for orders, in accordance with their instructions. Those instructions did not come until half past four in the afternoon. The whole day had been wasted. The time had flown, and the great opportunity with it."

The cavalry would have had a fine part to play had all gone well.

The 2nd Cavalry Division was drawn up back of Estaires, the 3rd Cavalry Division in the Forest of Nieppe, and the 1st Cavalry Division was ready at its billets. A hole in the German line meant a strong push through by the three cavalry divisions.

On the right of the 7th and 8th Divisions the Indian Corps had hard fighting, the day of the Battle of Neuve Chapelle. The Gurkhas, one of their officers told me, took a wood, lost it, took it a second time, lost it again, and a third time took it, only to be driven out at last owing to the fact that no support was available.

On a visit to Bethune one day I heard dozens of stories of the fierce fighting on March 10th, on the 2nd Division front, where one brigade lost twenty-five officers and seven hundred men in an abortive attack.

But the interest centred around the 8th Division fighting, that began so well, then hung fire until the Germans recovered from the demoralisation of the smashing blow.

How utter was that demoralisation we learned later from "agents" near Lille and Tournai. The Germans were actually "on the run" that morning, and pressing forward would have indubitably borne results that would have loomed large in the trend of events.

On March 15th, the 1st Cavalry Division was called out at dawn, and placed in support of the 27th Division at St. Eloi. Just before six o'clock on the evening of the 14th, the Huns had fired a mine at St. Eloi, and then poured a rain of high explosive shells over our trenches for half an hour. The howitzer shells exploded so rapidly, that one continuous roar ensued, the separate detonations being with difficulty distinguished.

The moment the German guns stopped their fusilade, the German infantry rushed forward, the attack developing all along the 5th Corps front. St. Eloi itself, the southern re-entrant of the Ypres Salient, was soon in enemy hands.

By two o'clock on the morning of the 15th, a British counter-attack was launched. By daybreak each force held some part of St. Eloi, and the fighting grew fierce and fiercer. By night all the town was in British hands save one point, a mound which had been transformed into a kind of fort by the enemy.

During that fighting, the 4th Battalion Rifle Brigade was sent up to take a section of trench out of which one of the other 27th Division Battalions had been shelled. Once before, within the hour, another battalion had essayed to recapture the lost position, and had "retired" in considerable confusion.

The Rifle Brigade set its teeth and started for the hottest part of the fray.

"You must cross that road," its commander was told, "though Heaven only knows how anyone can get across it alive."

Sixteen Hun machine-guns were playing on the open space over which the battalion must pass.

Over it they went. In less than sixty seconds eleven officers and two hundred and fifty men were down, but the rest pushed on.

They reached the trench, some of them, cleared out the Huns with the cold steel, and consolidated the position—a splendid performance.

The 5th Corps made good the ground the Germans had won without calling on the 1st Cavalry Division troops for assistance, and thus ended the last chance of our division for active fighting during the month of March.

Inspections in the Flemish mud, bright sunshine and spring zephyrs one day, and snow the next, and more than once snow and sunshine alternating throughout the span of a day, marked the passing of the month.

Paris, Calais, St. Omer, Estaires, Lillers, Merville and Hazebrouck were visited by enemy airmen as the days went by, and bombs dropped, but without much damage to lives or property.

"The Huns don't care whether or not they hit anything," said one sage "sub." "They only want to show Sir Douglas Haig they have a copy of that March 10th Order of his wherein he said ' Our Flying Corps has driven the Germans from the air.'"

On March 25th I spent the morning in Bailleul at 2nd Corps and 3rd Corps Headquarters.

The Staffordshire Brigade of the North Midland Territorial Division marched past to the music of their fine brass band, drawn up in the square—the first band I had seen or heard since leaving England seven months before. Crowds of soldiers and officers flocked to hear it and see the sturdy Terriers march by with swinging step. They created a splendid impression.

The next day my work was to take General Lowe and General Lumley over the path of the early fighting in Flanders—from Meteren through Bailleul to Armentières, thence to the line on the Ploegsteert Hill and through the Ploegsteert Wood.

We stopped in the town of Ploegsteert, where, in the churchyard, General Lumley's son, a gallant young officer in the 11th Hussars, was buried.

The boy had been killed on October 17th, when our division was trying to force a way across the River Lys. At Le Touquet Lieutenant Lumley was reconnoitring a position preparatory to an advance when a German sniper's bullet struck him.

As the general visited his son's grave I learned from townsfolk how things had fared with them.

Months before the 1st Cavalry Division had been the first British contingent to enter Ploegsteert. The people told me of the severe shelling the town had suffered, though the shattered church and a black hole where the principal *estaminet* once stood were surrounded by many other evidences of the damage of the Hun gun-fire.

"We have been here through it all," said an old lady whose French had a heavy Flemish accent. "We go into the cellars when the bombardment begins, and when it ends we come out and go about our work. What else could we do?"

Some townsfolk had been hit, but none killed, they said. The merry baker, whose brown bread had been so greatly enjoyed by our mess, had been hit by shrapnel bullet a few weeks before and killed. His wife was running the bakery still, though in but a small way, she said, sadly.

The Bois de Ploegsteert and the line in its vicinity was much the same as when our division had left it months before. The wood was perhaps a little more smashed, the *château* a bit more flattened.

Our batteries fired regularly as we walked about, their shells whirring over our heads without eliciting a single reply shot from the Huns.

Down the corduroy roads through the Ploegsteert Wood and to its trench-line, where the men were far from uncomfortable, the path seemed sufficiently familiar to have been there for years instead of months.

Next day, the 27th, my work took me still further afield. General de Lisle, with General Briggs and General Mullens and one or two members of their staffs, were to walk over the reserve line of trenches from in front of Kemmel to Dickebusch. One of General Smith-Dorrien's Staff officers was to accompany them.

Dismounting from the cars at the Station Inn, on the Neuve Eglise-Kemmel Road, the party headed for the reserve trenches. I was instructed to convoy the other cars in the party to a spot on the Ypres side of Dickebusch.

"Don't stop at the cross-roads," said Captain Walker of the 2nd Army Staff. "The Germans shell the cross-roads two or three times every day. It's best to run up the Vlamertinghe Road a couple of hundred yards and wait there. You are not so likely to be hit."

Past Dranoutre and Locre, and thence through La Clytte and Dickebusch my route led. Familiar ground of months past, every inch of it. Here and there fields had been ploughed well by shell-fire, and many once familiar buildings along the way had been shattered or destroyed. It was uncanny to find that more than one spot which I had in former days selected as a daily stand for the car had become a great gaping hole dug by a huge howitzer shell.

Huts beside the road teemed with Tommies.

As I entered La Clytte I well remembered my last day there, in November, 1914. Major Steele, of the R.A.M.C., and Captain Baron Le Jeune, a French liaison officer, both of them popular members of the 1st Cavalry Division Headquarters Staff, had been killed in La Clytte by the same shell. Another shell had that day gone close over General de Lisle and me as we were leaving the town.

Picking my way past a clumsy farm wagon, I thought of those days of "close calls." I was thankful no shells had fallen near me *that* morning.

As I drew past the crossroad in La Clytte, however, a scream sounded over my head, and a shell burst in the field not one hundred feet beyond me.

I was off like a flash, abandoning all thought of saving my car from the rough bumping over the broken *pavé*. It seemed weird, that lone shell, so close to me in La Clytte. No more came, or at least, if they did so, I did not hear them, and I soon passed Dickebusch.

A two hours' wait in snow and sun and snow again saw the arrival of General de Lisle, and we were promptly off for "home."

Such days were fair samples of my work until March winds had ceased to blow, and April, with its promise of an early spring, had come.

Chapter 4

Lord Kitchener's Visit

On April 1st, I heard at G.H.Q. that within a few days the French 9th and 16th Corps, which were in the Ypres area, were to be moved south. The British were to take over the line from the Belgian left near Bixschoote, and make a continuous British line from that point to the left of the main French front near the La Bassée Canal. Events were to happen which prevented the completion of this plan—events due to a German initiative.

The days grew warmer, though rain fell with sufficient frequency to keep the fields deep with mud.

Rumours of a "push" could be heard everywhere. It was timed by most prophets for April 24th or 25th, though some declared it would develop by the 20th.

Many there were who scoffed at the idea of an advance. One story current at G. H.Q. told of a subaltern of an infantry battalion, which had long occupied the Ploegsteert trenches, who paid a visit to a brother officer in another division, which had been marooned in the Kemmel trenches for what had seemed an interminable period.

"You will notice," said the Kemmel man, "my men are planting daffodils on the parapets to hide 'em. We hope to have the line quite invisible in the course of time."

"Humph," replied he of Ploegsteert, "you *are* a lot of blooming optimists. *My* men have planted acorns in front of *our* ditch."

On April 3rd, Lord Kitchener came to Boulogne by torpedo-boat. On the next morning, Sunday, he landed, came through St. Omer, where he was joined by General French, and proceeded to Chantilly, where a conference with General Joffre was held. On the following day, Lord Kitchener and General French met General Foch at Amiens.

A dash to St. Omer, where Sir John remained, then a rush to Boulogne, and England's War Minister was again aboard his torpedo-boat and speeding back toward Whitehall.

As news of this visit spread over the army, rumour piled on rumour of the new "push" that was to accomplish such great results.

True, sinister minds attributed Kitchener's visits to the large loss in men and the small gain in ground of Neuve Chapelle, but they were greatly in the minority.

We obtained a copy of the *Lille War Gazette*, a newspaper published by the German Army in Lille, which contained many items of interest. Chief among them was an article by a Hun named Kaden, a lieutenant-colonel of a line regiment. The following is a translation of this article, which caused much comment:—

Fire.
By Lieutenant-Colonel Kaden.

As children, many of us have played with it; some of us have seen an outbreak of fire. First a small tongue-like flame appears; it grows into a devastating fury of heat. We out here in the field have seen more than enough of it.

But there is also the fire of joy—of red enthusiasm. It arose from sacrificial altars, from mountain heights of Germany, and lit up the heavens at the tune of solstice and whenever the home countries were in danger. This year fires of joy shall flare from the Bismarck columns throughout the length and breadth of Germany, for on April 1st, just one hundred years ago, our country's greatest son was born. Let us celebrate this event in a manner deep, far-reaching, and mighty!

Blood and Iron!

Let every German, man or woman, young or old, find in his heart a Bismarck column, a pillar of fire, now in these days of storm and stress. Let this fire, enkindled in every German breast, be a fire of joy, of holiest enthusiasm. But let it be terrible, unfettered; let it carry horror and destruction! Call it hate! Let no one come to you with "Love thine enemy" We all have but one enemy—ENGLAND!

How long have we wooed her almost to the point of our own self-abasement? She would none of us, so leave to her the apostles of peace, the "No War" disciples. The time has passed when we would do homage to everything English—our cousins that were!

"God punish England!"—"May He punish her!" This is the greeting that now passes when Germans meet. The fire of this righteous hate is all aglow!

You men of Germany from East and West, forced to shed your blood in the defence of your homeland, through England's infamous envy and hatred of Germany's progress, feed the flame that burns in your souls. We have but one War Cry: "*God punish England!*" Hiss this one to another in the trenches, in the charge; hiss as it were the sound of licking flames. Behold in every dead comrade a sacrifice forced from you by this accursed people. Take tenfold vengeance for each hero's death!

You German people at home, feed this fire of hate!

You mothers, engrave this in the heart the babe at your breast! You thousands of teachers to whom millions of German children look up with eyes and hearts, teach. Hate, unquenchable Hate! You homes of German learning, pile up the fuel on this fire.

Tell the nation that this hate is not unGerman, that it is not poison for our people. Write in letters of fire the name of our bitterest enemy. You guardians of the truth, feed this sacred hate!

You German fathers, lead your children up to the high hills of our homeland, at the feet of our dear country bathed in sunshine. Your women and children shall starve: bestial, devilish conception. England wills it! Surely all that is in you rises against such infamy!

Listen to the ceaseless song of the German forest, behold the fruitful fields like rolling seas, then will your love for this wondrous land find the right words, "Hate, unquenchable Hate! Germany, Germany above all!"

Let it be inculcated in your children, and it will grow like a landslide, irresistible, from generation to generation.

You fathers, proclaim it aloud over the billowing fields, that the toiling peasant below may hear you, that the birds of the forest may fly away with the message: into the land that echoes from German cliffs send it reverberating like the clanging of bells from tower to tower throughout the countryside:

"Hate, Hate, the accursed English, Hate!"

You masters, carry the flame to your workshops. Axe and hammer will fall the heavier when arms are nerved by this Hate.

You peasants, guard this flame, fan it anew in the hearts of your toilers that the hand may rest heavy on the plough that throws up the soil of our homeland.

What Carthage was to Rome, England is to Germany.

For Rome as for us it is a question of "*to be or not to be.*"

May our people find a faithful mentor like Cato.

His *ceterum censeo, Carthaginem esse delendam* for us means
"God Punish England."

Some people laud the "thoroughness" of the German Army.

I wonder if they laud the "thoroughness" of its hate.

The army under Sir John French was assuming considerable proportions early in April. In addition to the 1st, 2nd, 3rd, 4th, 5th, 6th, 7th, and 8th Divisions, the 27th and 28th, the Canadian Division and the divisions of the Indian Corps, as well as the 1st, 2nd and 3rd Cavalry Divisions and the Indian Cavalry Division, were well seasoned. The North Midland, 2nd London and South Midland Territorial Divisions were "out," and fast gaining experience and a good reputation with it, while the Northumberland Territorial Division was on the way.

G. H. O. information summaries in the early days of April said laconically, "Nothing to report on the British front," and were generally fairly correct.

On the 8th and 9th the roads leading from the Ypres district were filled with French troops moving southward. The veterans of the 9th Corps limped past, frost-bite having visited most of them during their long sojourn in the trenches of the Salient.

Lines of French guns ambled by, "75's," with their graceful light grey lines, were eminently business-like, their gunners clad in dark blue cape-overcoats that looked warm and comfortable.

The 1st Cavalry Division was given a new brigade, the 9th, which consisted of the 15th Hussars, 19th Lancers and the Warwickshire Territorial Battery.

Bumping over the bad roads at good speed meant frequent car trouble. I was fortunate to find Harold Smith, the Royal Automobile Club Engineer, one day at Boulogne, where he was superintending the installation of a first-class motor repair plant for the Red Cross Ambulances. Mieville, of the Red Cross, in whose hands were all matters pertaining to Red Cross motor vehicles, proved a good Samaritan. Between Mieville and Smith my decrepit car was given a new lease of life.

The Army Service Corps would have done well to have "co-opted" Smith and one or two more like him. His repair shop at Boulogne, when completed, was so far ahead of any repair park possessed by the army in France that comparison made the Army shops look very bad indeed. Yet Smith's work was done in three weeks or less and a building of quite a temporary character utilised.

While I was in Boulogne an Army Service Corps captain came to Harold Smith and said: "I have been told to lay down a foundry, and unfortunately know nothing whatever about the bally thing. Do you happen to know anything about a foundry?"

"Well," replied Smith, "I have a fairly good idea of what you will need. Suppose I draw up a specification of a foundry installation tonight and let you have it tomorrow?"

"Delighted," said the captain. "It would be good of you."

So Smith set to work, duly completed the specification, and turned it over to the A.S.C. man, who went away, quite happy, at once to put in the specification as it was handed to him. He admittedly had no knowledge as to its correctness and was quite satisfied to seek none.

I met Moore-Brabazon, of the Flying-Corps, on the quay. With a few days' leave in his pocket, he was as happy as a sandboy.

"Brab" said:

> We had a chap rejoin us a day or so ago who had a remarkable story to tell. His name is Mapplebeck. He is an officer in the Liverpool Regiment, attached to the R.F.C.
>
> Not long ago, Mapplebeck was up alone on a scout near Lille, when his engine went wrong, and he had to make a descent. He knew he was well inside the German lines, but was shocked to see a couple of Huns, apparently doing sentry duty, not far from where he had planned to land.
>
> The two Germans ran toward the machine as it came down, each grabbing hold of the left wing. The biplane tossed and rolled and pitched about as it came to rest. Mapplebeck tumbled out on the right side, dived head first through a thick hedge a few feet distant, and ran hot-foot down a deep ditch that led to a cross-hedge not far away.
>
> He lost no time in dodging through the further hedge, and was off like a hare down another ditch. The Huns must have taken the wrong turning when pursuing him, as he got clear away and hid in a dwelling till night.

Obtaining some peasant clothing, Mapplebeck made his way into Lille. Though the is full of Germans, his disguise was so is not bothered in any way. Finding a loyal French business man, Mapplebeck cashed a London cheque, for which he received French notes bearing a German stamp. With these he bought a suit of clothing, and started to tramp the road to Belgium.

He reached Belgium safely, kept on, and eventually crossed the Dutch border. Obtaining passage to London, he at once went to Farnborough and reported. There he was given a new machine which was ready to come to France. He lost no time in bringing it across the channel and reporting for duty, just as though nothing unusual had happened.

One by one we obtained from him the details of his experiences. He was mightily modest about it all, and laughed at the idea that he had done anything that was the least bit out of the ordinary.

On April 17th the 2nd Cavalry Division held a horse show at Vieux Berquin. The horses and the riding were worthy of the best that Dublin or Olympia could produce.

Sunday, the 18th, I had set aside for a joyride. Running to St. Omer, I picked up Major St. Leger, of the Irish Guards, assistant camp commandant, and then called at a farm near Meteren, where the 9th Lancers' Headquarters were billeted.

Beale-Browne, "Bimbo" Reynolds, Rex Benson and Alex Graham, were out enjoying the perfect morning, but we luckily found Captain "Algy" Court, of the 9th, who had been in the hospital when the Brigade was at Ypres, and thus missed seeing the Salient. This made him the more keen to have a look at the famous Menin Road. Calling at General Mullens's headquarters at Godawaersvelde, in the hope of annexing "Rattle" Barrett, "Jeff" Hornby or Romer Williams, but finding the brigade staff absent to a man, we pushed on to Poperinghe, where we procured a very passable luncheon in a crowded hotel.

Finally we reached Ypres, ran through it, and out on the Menin Road toward Hooge. Court was very anxious to run on to Hooge, but I had been told a car could be seen by the Huns as it approached that delectable spot, and I therefore counselled discretion. "Algy" pressed hard for a visit to Hooge itself, saying he was most eager to inspect the "trenches to the south of the road." St. Leger wavered, but finally agreed with me that to "run into one" when joy-riding would look bad, so we satisfied ourselves with watching the bursting shells from a safe distance.

Only a few weeks later, "Algy" Court was killed in those very trenches to the south of the Menin Road at Hooge, when the 9th Lancers, badly gassed and heavily attacked on front and left flank—all but outflanked, in fact—held on gallantly during a day of the fiercest of fighting, and saved the line.

While we were on Menin Road little groups of wounded Tommies came past. A Canadian Staff officer told us the K.O.S.B.'s, and the West Kents had rushed a German position on a hill in front of Zillebeke, after our engineers had exploded a mine under it. About 200 yards of enemy trench had been taken, and fifteen prisoners, including two officers, captured. From them it was learned that at least 150 Huns, most of whom must have been killed, were in the destroyed trench.

"The K.O.S.B.'s and the West Kents," said the Canadian, "are hanging on to the captured area, in spite of continual heavy counter-attacks by the Germans. We had just had a message from our chaps asking for help to hold on."

As he spoke a roar burst forth on the line not far away, seeming to me to come from a point just south of Cavan's House. For fifteen minutes Hun howitzer shells fell in scores on the luckless area of the successful advance. The air reverberated with the crashes of the huge shells, which fell in such rapid succession one could not count them.

After we left Ypres, we heard still another fierce deluge of shell-fire fall on that spot late in the afternoon.

Such was the commencement of the fight for Hill 60, near Verbranden Molen, which was to be contested bitterly for many a day, costing thousands of casualties to friend and foe. The next day, the 19th, the Germans tried to win back the position at the point of the bayonet, and succeeded in gaining a foot-hold on the southern slope of the hill, only to lose it after a hand to hand fight that afternoon.

The Huns also gave Ypres and the Menin Road a heavy shelling for an hour on the 19th, just twenty-four hours too late to catch our "joy party." The day of our visit was the last one that found the Menin Road a safe place, for daily thereafter the 17-inch shells were busy with the terrible work that was to end in the utter devastation of Ypres—work which was to continue for the rest of April, through May, and well into June, with but little respite.

A couple of days later the West Surreys had a fight for Hill 60 that nearly swept away the battalion. The Germans brought up some field guns and hammered away at our parapets at close range. When the West Surreys came out, after gallantly holding the position until relieved, a subaltern was the senior officer left in command. The "Princess Pat's," too, were to leave the majority of their officers there. Hill 60 took toll of all but a remnant of that regiment.

We dropped "Algy" Court at his billets, then hastened to St. Omer, where a good dinner was awaiting us. St. Leger's mess was always a cheery one, having among its members Surgeon-General O'Donnell, Colonel Cummings, of the R.A.M.C, Colonel Warren, of the Army Post Office, and Colonel Thresher, the Camp Commandant. That night Colonel Father Keating and Captain Father Rawlinson were fellow-guests, two greatly beloved "*padres*," in either of whom was sufficient subtle merriment and quiet humour to cheer up a whole corps of pessimists.

A captured German order gave rather gruesome details of a liquid-fire thrower of sorts, intended, so the order said, for fighting in streets and houses.

The German official report accused the British at Hill 60 of using shells containing poisonous fumes.

Odd forerunners, these, in the light of subsequent events, for on Friday, April 23rd, came the first German gas attack.

The 23rd dawned bright and clear, a perfect spring morning. Soon after daybreak word came that the Germans had broken the French line between Bixschoote and Langemarck. The 1st Cavalry Division was ordered to concentrate between Ecke and Godawaersvelde, preparatory to being sent up in support.

The Germans had sprung their first gas attack in the grey of dawn, launching the asphyxiating fumes at a portion of the allied line held by the 78th French Reservist Division.

The success of the new manoeuvre had been extraordinary. That it far exceeded the most sanguine hopes of the Germans was clear from the fact that very few troops were available to take advantage of so great a hole in the allied line. No German cavalry was sufficiently near at hand to be utilised. That this point was brought well home to the Huns was made clear to us within very few hours afterward, for before the second gas attack the Germans had moved up a couple of corps of cavalry to a point within call.

But the opportunity had passed. Gas, when its use was unexpected, its effect multiplied by ignorance as to what it really was, and vague conjecture as to what it might be, and gas when our troops were expecting it and had been warned as to its objects and dangers, were very different propositions.

That the German gas attacks were for some time most demoralising, and often locally successful, was not to be denied; but some part of the line invariably held, and made the local enemy gain of less importance. Respirators assisted men to stay in their trenches in spite of the coming of the noxious fumes. Of far more value was the gradual realisation on the part of the men that gas could be withstood, and might or might not envelope them in sufficient quantity to produce a deadly effect.

Those French reservists who first were wrapped in the strange greenish-yellow mist that left them gasping for air and dying of strangulation, were not to be too greatly condemned for the general scamper that ensued. Under the circumstances, the indefinable and inexplicable horror would very likely have torn the line from the grasp of the most seasoned troops of either the French or British armies. Later I saw battalions of English veterans in utter demoralisation by the coming of the gas, and it was many a day before the sight of a gas cloud failed to bring great terror to many a soldier who had to face it.

By ten o'clock on the morning of the 23rd the situation seemed most serious. Back from the Bixschoote-Langemarck line the French had come to the line of the canal that leads south from Steenstraate to Ypres. At a point not far from Boesinghe the Huns had actually crossed to the west bank of the canal, were at the very doors of Boesinghe, and had taken Het-Sas and Lizerne to the north. Lizerne was well to the west of the canal, and on the main Dixmude-Ypres road.

Messages that reached the 1st Cavalry Division, explaining the situation, were addressed to the Cavalry Corps, Indian Cavalry, 2nd Army, and the new Northumbrian Territorial Division. All these units were to be engaged on that front before many days had passed.

General De Lisle ran to 5th Corps Headquarters in Poperinghe before eleven o'clock. We passed battalion after battalion of the North Country Terriers along the road, trudging sturdily Ypreswards, or lying in the fields for a breather.

Ambulances were continually arriving in Poperinghe, full of wounded and gassed Tommies.

I met Major Moore, of the Canadian Division, who told me the Canadians had been "at it hard." Another Canadian acquaintance, a wounded officer, came past, and told me something of the situation.

The Canadians had won laurels that morning by an action which showed clearly the great military value of individual initiative in the private soldier. That is the quality that made British generals think the Australian and New Zealand soldiers who were lost at the Dardanelles the finest men that had yet been produced in the Great World War.

In dugouts in front of Wieltje and west of St. Julien, some of the Canadians were unaware of the gas attack until the Germans had driven the French well back and come on after them to such close quarters that the grey lines were clearly visible to the surprised Canadian eyes.

Grabbing rifles and ammunition pouches, with no time for company or battalion formation, officers and men rushed toward the advancing lines of Huns, and seeking such cover as could be found, opened a fierce fire at short range. The natural, inborn individual fighting spirit of men raised in the open—men to whose hands a rifle was no stranger—met the situation with such instinctive cohesion of action that the Huns were driven back and the line saved.

A 5th Corps Staff officer told us the Canadians had actually saved the day and had established, during the early hours of the morning, a crescent-shaped line from the Canal south-east of Boesinghe to a point just north of St. Julien, the crescent bending southward as the line crossed the Ypres-Langemarck road. From this line they were gradually being forced south by heavy German attacks.

From one to two o'clock our divisional headquarters waited by the roadside in the western edge of Poperinghe while our three brigades came up, preparatory to a move toward the scene of battle.

That hour of inaction was crammed with scenes that told of the heavy fighting ahead of us. Lyne-Stephens, convoying a couple of dozen of the splendid Du Cros ambulances, full to overflowing with shattered men, hurried past *en route* for Hazebrouck. As a hospital train of twelve coaches, every available corner containing a wounded Tommy, steamed west, scores of motor omnibuses hurried eastward toward the sound of the guns, every khaki-coloured 'bus with its complement of the Lancashire and Yorkshire Terriers of the North Midland Division. Refugees laden with cardboard boxes, pushing loaded bicycles or pulling-carts groaning under tall piles of household effects, added to the roads congestion. Detachments of infantry marching on, guns rattling up, ammunition trains urging their claims to special facilities for a clear road, added to the *mêlée*.

Over this highway, jammed with two lines of traffic bound in each direction, the 1st Cavalry Division and its transport pushed its way, through Poperinghe, where railway trains were debouching long lines of blue-clad French regulars, and then on along the road toward Elverdinghe, to the eastward.

General de Lisle went first to Woesten, which we found full of French territorial troops. Shells had fallen in the village during the morning, but none were bursting near when we arrived.

We started down the road toward Elverdinghe but had not gone far when *Bang! bang!* just in front, then the whirr of shrapnel bullets, the sharp crack as they struck the *pavé* a few yards ahead, and spurts of dirt and dust, told us that the roadway was receiving attention at the hands of the Boche gunners.

I pulled the car up sharply, and as I did so two more shrapnel burst a few feet above the road in front of us, the missiles from the exploding shells singing past and striking all about with nasty smacks, as if in boasting evidence of a creditable amount of velocity and precision.

One regiment of our division was assigned duty as a reserve for the Belgian left, which was not far north of us. Another regiment was to act as reserve for the French in front of us. The remainder of the division was a sort of general reserve, to be utilised wherever and whenever necessity arose.

A run to Elverdinghe showed that it had been heavily shelled, the church being riddled with great holes. Our line was pushed to the east of the town. An ambulance driver who had been left in Elverdinghe told me he was sure "someone will get it in this hole soon," and he proved to be no bad prophet.

As dark closed we learned that the Canadians' line had been forced back, but the support line had held firm as a rock, and our men were counter-attacking most gallantly as the day ended. The *rumph! rumph!* of the howitzer shells increased in frequency, the cannonade swelling in volume as the night came.

A good sized *château* between Poperinghe and Elverdinghe housed our Headquarters Staff for the night.

A run to Cassel at daybreak was a maddening experience, the road from Steenvoorde to Poperinghe being packed and jammed with all manner of horse and motor transport. A big five-ton lorry belonging to the Canadians had broken down as it was being turned in the narrow roadway. Result, an immovable barrier across the *pavé*.

If ever in my life I longed to tamper with a job that was "none of my business," I did so on that 24th of April. Organisation of the traffic on that congested road could have been so easily done with a dozen assistants, and hours saved to all users of the road.

Thousands of light French *camions* were waiting at Cassel for train-load after train-load of French troops from Arras. The 9th Corps, which had so few days previously left Ypres, after a sojourn of there of many months, was being hurried back as fast as steam and petrol could bring it.

That morning I was given a message for General de Lisle from the French corps commander, to the effect that the British cavalry was required in the front line.

Temporary divisional headquarters had been established at the fourth kilometre stone on the Elverdinghe road, to allow messages from regiments or brigades easily to find it.

When I arrived with the message I transmitted it to Major Fitzgerald, then set off to seek de Lisle, who, "Fitz" said, was making a tour of the line, and could be found either in Woesten or Elverdinghe.

I chose the latter objective. The way was lined by great black French *spahis*, clad in variegated garb and wondrous head gear, for the first couple of kilometres. As we approached Elverdinghe, all signs of life vanished. An odd stillness brooded over the immediate vicinity, a sort of local lull in the maelstrom of sound the shell-bursts were making and had made throughout the night, a couple of miles to the eastward.

A half instinctive pause in the edge of the village, and a moment spent in tense listening, gave me an uncanny feeling of solitude. As I stood, undecided whether to push on into the town or circle back for Woesten, the silence was mashed to reverberating atoms by an 8-in. howitzer shell, which fell not far from the town.

Bang! rumph! r r r rumph! Bang! Shrapnel and high explosive seemed to come together.

Another and another shell followed, then a blinding crash as I was turning my car and a shell burst in the square not far away, showering bits of shell and debris over me.

The pieces slap-slapped resoundingly against the metal panels of the car, and one good-sized stone was hurled against my back.

As I raced away to safety towards Poperinghe, the shells still came into the village and around it, and followed the road at my back, urging me on.

Shortly afterwards I saw Captain Bertram Neame, the adjutant of the 18th Hussars, who had been wounded in the right hand and arm by one of the shells.

"An aeroplane marked with red, white and blue rings, but evidently a German flying false colours, circled round over the battery near us," said Neame, "and half a dozen German shrapnel fell there at once. Then the 'plane circled over the farm containing 18th Headquarters, and another farm which was sheltering most of A Squadron. Immediately afterwards shells poured into the two farms, and several of the men were hit."

Months after I read the diary of Captain T. O. Thompson, of the R.A.M.C., who was attached to the 18th Hussars.

His graphic account of the shelling in Elverdinghe that morning read as follows:

> A Squadron were in the next farm, and all their men sleeping peacefully in the sunshine against the wall of a barn, when, without warning, a 'coalbox' arrived and landed full on one man. They found only an arm and a leg and his head. The next arrived later and wounded two men. The inhabitants of the farm cleared at a run, and some French territorials, who had been in that farm for seven months, went like greased lightning.
>
> The colonel (Burnett), and adjutant (Neame), and Captain H. (Holdsworth), walked about thirty yards up the road, when a shell arrived and wounded the adjutant in the hand and H. in the back. It hit the colonel on the back, fortunately on the belt, and slightly wounded him in the thigh. It bruised the major, who was twenty yards away, on the shin.
>
> The Germans kept on putting shells along the road, and then started on the village. They were the beastly 8.2 high explosives, and were going just over us on to the Poperinghe road. Six horses were going up this road when a shell landed about fifteen yards short of it. One of the grooms was badly-wounded, one killed, being lifted into and left hanging in one of the trees by the roadside.
>
> Then the 4th Dragoon Guards came down the road on foot and passed into the village, but came out again as a shell greeted them in the square. They came off the road, and came along a hollow near the stream toward us. The rear squadron was marching along a ditch behind a hedge-row in two-deep formation when a beastly shell landed right in the ditch and hurled four

Damage caused by a 17-inch shell in Poperinghe, April 1915

of them sixty feet into the air. Two others were killed as well. Brown, a 4th D.G. Lieutenant, was one of the four; his hand was found in the stream one hundred and fifty yards away.

All things considered, I was lucky to get out of Elverdinghe unhurt that morning.

I found General de Lisle as he was returning from Woesten with Captain Nicholson; I then ran to Woesten with a message for General Briggs.

General de Lisle was faced with the fact that he was acting as reserve to the British left, and therefore suggested to the French commander that the French reserves should first be used, and the British cavalry only called upon to occupy the front French line when no further French reserves were available, a suggestion of which the French general at once saw the wisdom.

Returning from Woesten, Nicholson and I found we must make a detour, as the narrow country road was completely blocked by French horse transport.

Dashing into Poperinghe at high speed we were surprised to see the townsfolk running hither and thither in great fright and confusion. Six great shells had been thrown the long distance from the enemy line and landed in the town. They had come but a couple of minutes before, a scared Belgian told us.

I lost no time, swinging through the square and out on the Elverdinghe road at high speed. No sooner were we clear of the centre of the town than Hun shells screamed wickedly over us on their way toward the railway station, exploding not far behind us with tremendous concussion. Guns of large calibre were being used by the Germans.

First Cavalry Division Headquarters was moved from the kilometre stone to an *estaminet* nearby, as the inhabitants had brought up two great wagons and decamped therein with bag and baggage.

Tales of Canadian prowess and fine work by the 13th Infantry Brigade, which was sent to their support, were mingled with conflicting reports of the number of guns captured by the Germans. First, the loss of a couple of dozen was admitted by the French. Before a week had passed we knew the number actually taken by the Germans was much greater.

Ypres, we heard, had been so heavily shelled the day before that the entire town had been evacuated.

All the morning I watched ambulances full of wounded French

Red Cross Ambulances on the Coast

soldiers *en route* for Poperinghe, file past war-worn batteries of "75's" pushing toward the front. The begrimed French gunners, with their cheery faces, seemed to know the esteem in which we held them and their splendid guns, and to be keen to get into action and stem the advance of the Germans, which was slowly but steadily surging towards us though our men were fighting hard every inch of the way.

The Belgian refugees poured back, forced off the road by the lorries, ambulances and guns. Slight mothers with numerous progeny, one, or sometimes two, of the lesser units in arms, toiled by. Each person, young or old, capable of carrying a load, bore heavy burdens. Bicycles with huge bundles balanced on the saddle, were pushed westward haltingly, as road-space permitted. One lad passed on crutches, flanked by two grand-dames carrying blue buckets crammed tight with portions of the family wardrobe.

Most of the faces of the refugees bore a stolid, matter-of-fact expression. Some were quite cheerful. Many seemed stoically numbed to all feeling. The strong wind tossed their unwieldy bundles, and they stumbled awkwardly out of the path of hurrying traffic, their feet bruised against the loose stones that edged the *pavé*. Tired, dirty, buffeted by the gale, with strained and aching muscles and broken feet, fleeing from death or worse, and in their flight abandoning their worldly all, I wondered there were not more signs of heartsickness and despair on their thin faces.

Shells screamed over us and ploughed great holes in the British aviation park east of Poperinghe. After the first half dozen of such visitors, the Flying Corps packed up and took its departure for safer quarters.

A wounded Canadian said the 2nd and 3rd Canadian Brigades in front of us were wiped out as a fighting force. Their trenches, he told us had been literally blown to bits. A counter-attack by the Canadians, the 13th Brigade and the French 45th Division on their left, had started well, but failed to achieve much. German batteries and machine guns greatly outnumbered ours and were taking heavy toll as the battle surged backwards and forwards.

Before the day was over the French reported that they had recaptured Lizerne.

Night closed with an increasing din from the arms of all sorts and calibres on our front, never to cease for the whole night through.

I was sent after dark to G.H.Q. at St. Omer, a journey that meant many a long hour of tedious waiting in the midst of the tangled skein of traffic along the way.

Returning at daybreak on Sunday, the 25th, I planned a roundabout route from Steenvoorde to Poperinghe, circling well north of the main road. I had travelled but a few kilometres when I found the narrow, muddy road in front of me completely blocked by a train of French lorries, laden with troops. Some of the vehicles were mired, and the block bid fair to be immovable for hours. By sheer luck I stopped opposite a farmyard, in which I turned the car, and not far back gained a cross-road. A mile beyond the route was rendered, absolutely impassable by two detachments of British transport, which had met face to face on a road barely wide enough for one.

"We have been here a divil of a toime," said a cheery Irish driver at the rear of the column, "and from the look of it beyant there, we'll be slapin' here in the mud this night."

Nothing daunted, I turned, pushed by willing hands when deep mud made assistance necessary, and headed the other way. But fate was unkind. Again I found the road barricaded, this time by two signal lorries that had, like me, tried a detour. One had skidded sideways and stuck fast. The other was trying to pull his fellow back on to the roadway. Disheartened, I soon tired of what threatened to be a long wait, and returned toward Steenvoorde. A new convoy of French trooplorries closed this avenue of escape, but after an hour of floundering through almost impassable lanes, I reached Abele, on the main road, and was soon thereafter in Poperinghe.

Truly an ounce of prevention in the way of road organisation and route selection by some competent authority would have been worth many pounds of the condemnation poured forth with volubility by all road users in those days of tiresome traffic tangles.

Our headquarters moved to an *estaminet* just outside Woesten.

I learned, on arrival, that at midnight word had come from the French Commander, General Putz, whose headquarters were but a few hundred yards distant, to the effect that a mistake had been made in a previous report, and Lizerne was still in the hands of the enemy.

The roads were filled with French troops moving up, and relieved reservists coming back, while battery on battery of grey "75's" wheeled past.

"I don't know when; they are going to put any *more* guns," said Budworth, our Divisional C.R.A., "the whole country round is stiff with 'em now."

Fresson, the French liaison officer attached to the 1st Cavalry Division, sought at French headquarters an explanation of the situation on the extreme French left, where the Belgian right joined it.

Fresson, on his return said:

> Lizerne was attacked by French and Belgians, and Pilkem by French only. The mix-up in the report was due to the Belgians. The story of Lizerne is indefinite, except that the Germans were not driven out, as reported. As to the Pilkem attack, this failed utterly, due to wire, machine-guns, and general concentration by the enemy of the position they had captured.
>
> A further attack is to be made this morning at 10.30., when the Pilkem ridge is to be again stormed.

The Pilkem ridge was east of our part of the front, not far distant from the canal itself. The sounds of battle from the line facing it were continually in our ears.

General Smith-Dorrien drove by. One of his staff told me that at ten o'clock on the night before (Saturday night) 200 Canadians were still in St. Julien, though the line had been pressed back, leaving the little band cut off and surrounded by Germans. All night they had fought on, and were still fighting.

Some of our men had gotten up sufficiently close to hear the Huns call out to the gallant Canadians in a lull in the firing: "Surrender, Canadians! We are around you! You have no chance!"

"See you damned first! Come and get us," was the answer sent back in the night by a clear young Canadian voice, and Bedlam was again let loose.

That was the spirit of the men that Canada sent to France to fight for the Empire.

On the Sunday morning, said the Staff officer, a determined effort was being made to relieve what remained of the gallant 200.

All our attacks that day and those of the French as well failed. Lizerne remained in enemy hands, and the last of the heroic two hundred Canadians had evidently fallen in St. Julien before night, for all sounds of firing from that direction ceased. Strive as they would, our troops had been unable to reach and succour them, though costly efforts were not wanting. Weeks and months afterwards anxious ones waited for word from some of that noble little band in St. Julien, but no word ever came from German hospital or prison camp. They had fought on to the last man, to the bitter end!

At night the Germans attacked Broodseinde, east of Zonnebeke, with great ferocity, but were driven back by our 5th Corps troops.

What was left of the Canadian 2nd Brigade was holding Gravenstafel, just north of Zonnebeke, and not far to the south-west of Passchendaele. The Huns poured mass on mass against the depleted ranks of the Canadians, who were compelled to fall back, evacuating Gravenstafel, but stubbornly disputing every foot of ground lost.

The night of Sunday, the 25th, closed in, with little in the situation to cheer us, except the knowledge that the entire vicinity of the Ypres Salient and the line to the north of it was crowded with fresh French and British troops and battery on battery of guns.

By Monday night the London Sunday papers had reached us.

What was our surprise to see that the London press was greatly cheered by the meagre French and British official reports, and united in condemning the German official reports, which were flatly characterised as lying inventions.

The German official reports were, as a matter of fact, in that particular instance, more correct than either the French or British official reports.

The French report declared Lizerne and Het-Sas to have been taken from the Huns. The Huns had never been driven out of either town.

The British report was vaguely optimistic, evidently bent on minimising the German gains. It was so worded that 999 men out of 1,000 would understand from it that most of the ground lost on the 23rd and the days immediately following had been won back from the enemy. Certain it was that no one would gain the idea from the British official report that the Huns had been steadily forcing our line back, that our counter-attacks had failed, and that the Ypres Salient was then so threatened that no one but a madman would deny that further reconstruction of our line around Ypres, involving the giving up of a large section of our front line had become a military necessity, to be performed at the earliest moment such a manoeuvre could be carried out. Indeed, the section of our line to be abandoned must needs be far greater than that the enemy had won by his surprise gas attack against the French.

I do not wish to give the impression from the foregoing that the German reports were, as a rule, more correct than French or British official *pronunciamientos*. I think they were by no means so to be described. In matters of fact, as to captures of men or guns, or details as to bits of line lost or won, the Hun official reports were less often incorrect than some might think. Now and then, when dealing with some matter of conjecture, such as an estimate of our casualties, they were absurdly wide of the mark. The average French official report might err slightly as regarded detail, but was in the main most dependable. Our chief quarrel with the official reports as issued by the War Office to the British Press was that they were at times subject to more than one interpretation. Escaping actual inaccuracy, they did not always convey the impression at Home warranted by the facts at the Front.

On the morning of the 26th I ran toward Wieltje, and obtained details of the exact position of the lines.

The French left touched the Belgian right along the Yser-Ypres Canal north of Lizerne, where the German line was pushed to its further western point. The French line ran close to Het-Sas and crossed to the east of the canal a few hundred yards south of Boesinghe.

At a point a couple of thousand yards east of the canal the British left joined the extreme French right.

From that junction our line ran eastward through Fortuin, a village half a mile south of St. Julien, then north-east toward Gravenstafel, then south-east to Broodseinde.

At two o'clock that afternoon a grand attack was planned, all along that east-and-west line.

The 13th Brigade was on the left; two companies of the Rifle Brigade and the East Kents came next; five battalions of the 10th Brigade and a battalion in reserve were near Fortuin; on their right was the 11th Brigade; east of them were the York and Durham Territorial Brigades. The Northumbrian Territorial Division was in the Wieltje area in reserve, and the Lahore Division was coming up to the north of Verlorenhoek, on the right of the Northumberland Terriers.

Our forces, to be sent forward in attack, numbered over two score battalions, say, 40,000 men.

The Canadians had been withdrawn from the Salient to take stock of their battered remnants and fill their ranks with reserves from England. They had been tried in the fire and could be proud of having gained the name of one of the most brilliant fighting contingents that had been seen on the British front since the commencement of the war.

The French were again to attack the Pilkem ridge at two o'clock, when the British line, between four and five miles long, was to push vigorously northward in a desperate attempt to drive the Huns from the ground gained by gas attack three days before.

Our share in the show was small. The following order was issued to the brigades:

> At two p.m. today the French will attack Lizerne and Het-Sas. The 1st Cavalry Division are ordered to support the left flank of the French, acting in reserve. The division will be saddled up by two p.m. and the horses of the 1st Cavalry Brigade collected in the area south-west of Woesten. By two p.m. the 1st Cavalry Brigade will assemble, dismounted, north of the Woesten-Oostoleteren road, about the nineteenth kilometre stone, ready to support in the direction of Pypegaale, if required. The 2nd and 9th Brigades will remain in their present positions, ready to support the 1st Cavalry Brigade dismounted.

This gave vague promise of a bit of fun, as Pypegaale was only a mile from the coveted Lizerne, to which the Huns were holding so doggedly.

But our participation in the mill was only to take place in the event of the French attack ending in disaster or resulting in such extraordinary success that the Germans would be put to absolute rout.

The shells fell all about in those days, and rarely did I visit the support positions—which I did scores of times each day—when the air was not full of the droning shells of our own and the French batteries, pounding the enemy's positions on the canal.

Shell-fire; aeroplanes, British, French and German; anti-aircraft shells, both ours and those of the enemy, and passing troops and batteries became such common sights as the hours went by that one hardly bestowed on them a passing glance.

A Belgian woman was caught, near a battery position, flashing signals with a piece of bright tin to a Hun airman high overhead. The French took her away, one stout soldier to each arm, to summary execution.

Children were at play at the roadside. A dozen boys were engaged in a mock bombardment. A bottle served as the hostile town. Stones made good shells. All waited for the order, "Fire!" and then rained shots at the target with a will. Now and then one of the children would say, "*Rumph! rumph!*" mockingly, as a Black Maria fell near enough to jar them, but for the most part they paid scant attention to the fierce cannonade in progress all about.

In a field by the road a man was ploughing stolidly. A woman was hanging her washing on the line, singing as she worked. A 13-pounder anti-aircraft shell buried itself a few yards away, but she evinced no interest in it, and did not even allow its coming to interrupt her song.

Artillery work in modern warfare is carefully organised. It was difficult to realise in the midst of such an inferno of shell-fire that every gunner, who was so hard at work in those April days, had some definite objective when launching shells enemy-ward.

Major Budworth was directed to conduct the artillery attack on Lizerne. In other words, the guns of H and I Batteries of the Royal Horse Artillery were to pave the way for the French infantry attack.

General Putz was anxious to retake Lizerne and Steenstraate as well. The latter town was on the canal, a few hundred yards east of Lizerne, and astride the Dixmude Ypres highway, along which German reserves, to meet the attack on Lizerne, must be brought.

Budworth placed the batteries near Woesten, about 3,000 yards from Lizerne, which was surrounded by country so flat and so dotted with groups of trees that artillery observation was difficult.

A couple of gunners were sent into the French front trenches at 11.30 a.m. to observe the range-finding shots.

The Lizerne attack had been timed for 2.30 p.m. All watches had been most carefully synchronized. At 12.15 p.m., to the very second, H Battery fired three shots, then, after an interval, three shots more. Five minutes after the second trio had been sent Hunward, I Battery also fired six shots in groups of three. The observation officers on reconnaissance 'phoned back to the batteries from the French line, and gave minute details as to errors in range of the dozen shells, adding such information as would allow a more correct setting of the timing-fuses.

Errors in direction at such range—3,000 to 4,000 yards make an ideal range for the British 13-pounder and 18-pounder field-guns—were rare, in view of the fact that our gunners were provided with accurate large scale maps from which the range could be splendidly laid.

To get the guns closer to the enemy than 3,000 yards made it possible that the gunners might be subjected to hostile rifle fire, if the line should be forced back slightly. At such close range as 2,000 yards so low a trajectory was necessary that cover was rarely possible. Further, the supplying of ammunition to the guns was, under such circumstances, a most difficult problem. If an artillery commander could place his field-guns within 3,000 yards of the enemy position he considered himself fortunate.

Budworth was compelled to use shrapnel, as the 13-pounders at the Front at that time had not been provided with high explosive shell, although it had been repeatedly promised. Had high explosive shell been available, one battery would have sent it hurtling against the walls and houses in the little village of Lizerne and the Germans hiding behind them. The other battery would have simultaneously swept the streets and open spaces with shrapnel. With no high explosive, the only alternative was to use long fuses in the shrapnel, which then burst on percussion against the buildings behind which the Huns were sheltering.

The observation from the front line was chiefly valuable as a guide to the timing of the shrapnel that was to be used to scatter the hundreds of bullets over the open spaces. A 13-pounder shrapnel contained about 285 bullets, an 18-pounder, 365. The timing fuses burst none too accurately, at best. Atmospheric conditions frequently affected the burning of the fuses, and even the heating of the gun as it went into action sometimes did so.

H and I Batteries, having obtained the desired information from their observers as to the range and timing of their twelve shells, waited patiently until half past two o'clock.

At that hour, 400 shells were fired into Lizerne. For the first five minutes each battery fired four rounds per minute, then came a two-minute interval. For the next five minutes every one of the twelve guns in the two batteries fired five shots per minute. A second lull of two minutes was followed by still more rapid fire for another five minutes, six rounds per sixty seconds blazing forth from each of the dozen field-pieces, seventy-two shells per minute falling in the village. Thus they continued, the spasm of firing and the brief interval of stillness alternating, until the 400 shells had been fired.

That the work of the Horse Artillery was well done was apparent from the result. Its efficiency was confirmed later by captured Germans wounded in Lizerne, who termed the place "Hell itself" while the initial bombardment was in progress.

But the work of the guns was by no means ended. The salvo died down at the appointed time. The French Colonial Zouaves rushed forward, bayonets in hand, with wild cries, and then the gunners were set to their task.

They fired another 400 rounds at the road from Steenstraate to Lizerne, a second road leading to Lizerne from the south-east, and a third road connecting the two. These three roads were the avenues most likely to be utilized by the Huns for bringing up reinforcements to meet the attack. "Searching "the roads and a couple of special points, one just back of a rise of ground, where it seemed possible reinforcements might be gathered, kept the gunners hard at work.

Shrapnel rained over such spots, bursting from twenty to thirty feet above ground, and spreading death all about.

Watching the two batteries in action gave me a high opinion of their abilities. Nothing in modern warfare was so fascinating a study as that of guns in action.

France, with her faith pinned to low trajectory and high muzzle velocity as exemplified in her wonderful "75's," and Germany's gun-religion, centring on weight of shell, made a formidable contrast.

The making of a field-piece was ever a compromise between those two schools—a gun firing a light shell straight and fast, or a gun in which speed and direct line were sacrificed to gain weight of projectile.

A 35-pound howitzer shell and an 18-pounder shrapnel, such as that fired by the British field artillery, were sent on their mission of death from guns of practically the same weight. Thus greatly did an increase in muzzle velocity mean a corresponding increase in *avoirdupois*.

Thirty-eight hundredweight was generally agreed by gun-experts the world over to be the weight permissible for field pieces; this limit being imposed by questions of mobility and transport.

It was to gain those assets so great to the French military mind, low trajectory and high muzzle velocity, that the weight of the "75" shell was dropped to 15 pounds.

Howitzer against field-gun, with high explosive shell for both, was German practice against French practice. As one who became very tired of the continuous rain of big German howitzer shells, I must confess a wholesome respect for Hun theory in relation to questions of modern artillery. But no German gun, light or heavy, could, to my mind, compare with the wonderful "75."

A return to General Putz's headquarters found the French staff in possession of a report from the Front, to the effect that the Algerian Brigade had taken Lizerne, held all the trenches on the west side of the canal, and were preparing to cross the canal at Lizerne and Het-Sas.

Later developments showed the French officers in the fighting

A French "75" in the mud of a Flanders beet-field

An ambulance which was struck by a shell while carrying wounded from east of Ypres

line had again been optimistic to a point of inaccuracy in reporting Lizerne captured. The next day it was discovered that the Germans still held two houses on the western edge of canal, and had "dug themselves in "in an entrenched bridge-head on the canal bank. The French troops were in a semicircle, 300 yards distant, and were bringing up, under cover of the night, "75's" on either side of the miniature German fort, and preparing to batter it down by high-explosive shells fired at point-blank range.

The 1st Cavalry Division left the reserve line before Lizerne was finally wholly clear of Germans.

All day the din of battle on the long front had been maddening. Ear-drums became tuned to it for a time. But periods of acute sensitiveness would recur, in which the sound seemed to beat against one's brain with a dull ache, punctuated with sharp pain from the constant concussion.

An evening message from 5th Corps Headquarters told of the failure of the great attack at 2 p.m., owing to gas fumes from the German trenches. A later attack had been organised, in which the Northumbrian Territorial Division had won from the enemy some trenches south-west of St. Julien, and then pushed on and captured St. Julien itself. The Manchesters, too, had taken some German trenches east of St Julien.

But the good work was to be undone. That night the Huns won back St. Julien, and by daybreak on the 27th the line was practically where it had been twenty-four hours earlier, in spite of sad losses.

April 27th saw another strenuous effort by our gallant troops on that front. The southern edge of a wood, situated less than a mile west of St. Julien, was penetrated, but later the men returned to our original line.

The German official report said that the Huns fairly mowed down British troops when they advanced near St. Julien, and their artillery caught our men as they were retiring and inflicted frightful losses. Unfortunately, there was no exaggeration in that report.

Arriving at our headquarters *château*, east of Poperinghe, we found that half an hour earlier a dozen or more 17-inch shells had fallen in and about the town.

Poperinghe was being shelled daily, eleven townsfolk having been killed on the afternoon before. Most of the population had sought a more salubrious locality.

Of great interest to us was a huge shell-hole that had just been

View showing depth of 17-inch shell hole in the garden of a château between Poperinghe and Elverdinghe

made in the *château* garden, fifty yards from our sleeping quarters. It was over thirty feet in diameter and ten or twelve feet deep.

The big shell had shattered every window in that district, and the concussion had ruined most of the tiled roofs within sight. Great shell splinters, weighing from five to thirty pounds, still warm, were lying about.

That night, after eleven o'clock, when all were asleep, four more 17-inch visitors arrived in that edge of Poperinghe. All four shook the *château* to its foundations, one falling within 100 yards of it and smashing three dwelling houses into one mass of splinters, plaster and debris.

General de Lisle was sleeping on the floor of the *château* dining room. The first of the mammoth quartet so shook the building that a lustre chandelier, housed in a dust-covering and therefore unnoticed, became detached and fell to the polished floor below. Its myriad tiny pieces of glass jangled musically as they showered over the general, who was sleeping peacefully beneath. Fortunately, de Lisle was not hit by any of the heavier portions of the costly ornament, but his emotions on being awakened from deep slumber by the resounding smash of the shell, followed by the crash of the falling chandelier and the attendant rain of tuneful prisms, can better be imagined than described.

For the rest of the night, the headquarters staff—with the exception of de Lisle himself—repaired to the cellar in search of less interrupted repose. The general, having ascertained that no other lustre chandelier was suspended from the ceiling, stuck to his original pitch.

The next morning at daybreak, 1st Cavalry Division Headquarters moved from that chateau, in spite of its many desirable attributes as a habitation.

On the 27th, General de Lisle sent me to the headquarters of Major Pilkington, of the 15th Hussars, on an errand. The reserve Belgian line was hard by. In backing my car, to turn it in the narrow lane, a bank of a reserve trench or ditch caved, and the poor car stood on its tail, at an uncomfortable and astonishing angle. Colonel Burnett and one of his 18th Hussar officers passed, and with their help and that of a dozen obliging 15th Hussar troopers, we attempted to move the brute. It resisted our combined efforts. Then the Belgians near by saw what had transpired and came at a run. In a jiffy the car was out, but having been lifted with more zeal than discretion was strained in so many places that it ran more like a crawfish than a car, until a week

Staff officers at lunch

later, when time and opportunity allowed me to substitute an ample and expensive list of new parts.

Plodding through Poperinghe late that afternoon, the first of seven or eight 17-inch Boche "big 'uns" fell close behind me. I felt, rather than heard, a crash, the wave of sound deafening me. Missiles rained down sharply on roofs, walls and paved roadway. Lame duck though it was, the car lifted itself and sped at a touch of the accelerator pedal. I heard some of the other shells explode, but was well out of harm's way by the time they arrived.

On the 28th of April the division was moved back to a bivouac in the woods that lined the Poperinghe—Proven road, the main highway to Dunkirk.

Late in the afternoon, after a splendid day of lying in the sun, which was greatly appreciated by the whole division, billets to the westward were assigned to us, and we trekked off without delay.

Wormhoudt, a French-Flemish town on the main road from Dunkirk to Cassel, was selected for headquarters, and there we rested for four days before returning to our old home, the La Nieppe *château*, on the road from Cassel to St. Omer.

En route to Wormhoudt we passed the Indian Cavalry, coming up to relieve us as reserve. The Poona Horse, Sind Lancers, and Inniskilling Dragoons presented a fine appearance as they rode by.

Rest was welcome to the division. The troops had not been in the actual firing-line, but had been in continual occupation of reserve trenches for days, frequently under heavy shell-fire, and rarely with an opportunity for taking off their boots or sleeping elsewhere than in the open.

The villages and farms around Wormhoudt provided excellent billets for the troopers. Barns filled with straw and flax were warm and comfortable resting-places after the days and nights in cold, damp trenches.

So April ended peacefully for us, the Germans holding what they had won on the 23rd and closing the month with a vigorous bombardment of Dunkirk, a few miles north of us, which served no useful military purpose, but gave the Huns the satisfaction of killing a fair number of civilians, including a good bag of women and children.

Looking east over the Menin bridge at the edge of Ypres

Chapter 5

More Hun Gas

The first days of May found me with but little work to do. I spent some of my time running up into the Salient and hearing talk of preparations for a withdrawal of our line to a smaller horseshoe around Ypres. This was to be done as soon as all was ready for the move, and the utmost secrecy enveloped the operations.

I saw Rex Benson, of the 9th Lancers, who was acting temporarily as liaison officer with the French troops along the canal north of Ypres. Rex said the French had made but little progress towards the Pilkem ridge and General Putz had apparently decided to concentrate his position and give up open assault for the present.

The Hun howitzer fire was so fierce along the roads when I skirted Ypres on May 1st that I decided to desist visiting the Salient. In short, I got "cold feet" about the Ypres roads, and decided to do my joy-riding in other directions.

Romer Williams, of the 4th D.G.'s, and I went to St. Omer on the 2nd and brought out a couple of Romer's Red Cross friends, one a San Franciscan, named Sherman, at whose billet we had found marvellous cocktails. We all dined at General Mullens' headquarters, a gay party.

As we were feasting, the Huns in front of Ypres were up to more devilment. They let loose a heavy gas attack on the evening of the 2nd and made the British trenches south of St. Julien untenable. Our men retired, but the gas hung stationary for a few moments, and prevented an immediate German advance. This fortunate pause gave time for a concentration of all our guns on the spot. When the gas had dispersed sufficiently to allow an advance by the enemy, our gunners threw a *barrage de feu* across the German front as it emerged from St. Julien and the little wood to the west of it, and effectually stopped the way.

Meantime, our men had regained their trenches.

The 2nd Cavalry Division, dismounted, was called up as support during this attack. To reach the trenches into which they were ordered they found it necessary to advance across an enemy *barrage de feu*. The 4th Hussars and 5th Lancers were the regiments engaged. For a time it seemed they would be badly cut up, but luckily they got through the curtain of shells with only forty killed.

So *some* cavalry units had been thrown into the actual line, after all.

On the 3rd the 1st Cavalry Division moved back to its previous winter billets, the Headquarters Staff again repairing to the La Nieppe *château*.

The Huns attacked our Ypres line all day on the 4th, but with no success. That night the evacuation of the extreme eastern section of the Salient was carried out without serious casualty.

The enemy patrols that poked through the Polygon Wood at daybreak on the 4th, and discovered the British retirement to a line further west, must indeed have been surprised. The fighting of the previous ten days had cost the Allies over thirty square miles of ground and more than 20,000 casualties, but the British Army had undoubtedly gained in morale, nevertheless. Colonials and Territorials, as well as old line regiments filled with new reserve men, had fought shoulder to shoulder with the veterans of Le Cateau and the Aisne, every unit gaining strength unconsciously as each contingent rose in the other's estimation. Mutual admiration and mutual confidence had welded the army all the more closely together.

On a call at 5th Corps Headquarters at Abele, west of Poperinghe, I saw a couple of what appeared to be divers' helmets. These were loaded into a car, with a good-sized roll of rubber tubing and a homely pair of bellows attached to each of the grotesque pieces of headgear.

Curious, I asked a "Q" officer, standing near by, just how this paraphernalia was to be used.

He said:

People get strange ideas about fighting gas. These outfits were designed and forwarded to us to be sent up front, so up front I am sending them. They are provided to allow some of our men, say about 3 in every 10,000, so far as present supply goes, to stay in the gas-filled trenches while some pals with the bellows pump good air to them through a few hundred feet of hose.

If the gas area should be of considerable extent the chap with the bellows would soon be pumping chlorine into his fellow-Tommy, and die pumping at that, or else take to the woods and let the diver himself get what air he could find.

Many accidents might befall the tube. A Hun might sit on it. I hate to think of myself, squatting in a trench with one of those things over my head, praying for air, with the bellows man pumping his heart out trying to get ozone through a rubber tube on top of which some fat Boche had plumped, while he potted away at one or the other of us.

A shell, too, would have an interesting time with such a tube. Imagine the chap in the helmet hollering, 'Pump away, you lazy beggar, I'm not getting enough air to keep a flea alive,' and all the good old oxygen pouring out of a jagged hole in the bally pipe, hundreds of feet from him.

Then, suppose a man, coming up before daylight, got his foot caught in that length of tube—

But I realised I had started something I couldn't stop, and fled.

On May 5th I found E. F. Lumsden, of the A.S.C., an old friend with a passion for car repair of all sorts, who had charge of the lorries and motor workshops attached to the 7th Brigade Royal Garrison Artillery Ammunition Park. His lot were in Estaires. I turned my car over to them for rejuvenation while I hied myself to London to purchase an alarmingly large collection of parts with which to assist the somewhat extensive rebuilding Lumsden had gleefully planned.

I was back with a heavy load of hardware and empty purse by the night of May 7th, and by midnight on the 8th left Estaires with my chariot, which was in a greatly chastened mood.

While I was on leave in England the troopers of the 1st Cavalry Division had spent their nights in the Ypres Salient digging reserve line trenches and making barbed wire entanglements. Ypres on fire, the trench line alight with flares and the flash of constant shell-bursts, made this work more spectacular than pleasant. Once or twice a shell fell sufficiently near the troopers to wound one or two. One Black Maria unfortunately dropped among a squadron of the 18th Hussars, killing two of them and wounding a couple of dozen more.

Lunching on the 8th with a gunners' mess on the Laventie front, I learned of a big "push" ordered at dawn on the 9th. The Auber ridge was to be attacked from the southwest by two Indian Divisions, and from the north-west by the 8th Division and the 7th Division, with the Northumbrian Territorial Division and the newly arrived West Riding Territorial Division somewhere about. Something like 120,000 men were thus to be engaged. The Canadian Division was in reserve, in addition, and the 9th Division, the first of the "K" troops to reach the Front, was expected by rail that night.

The 6th Division, in the Bois Grenier area, was ready and eager to push forward toward Lille if the Auber ridge attack proved successful.

Instructions had been given, in anticipation of any misunderstandings which might tend to lead to another fiasco like the Battle of Neuve Chapelle. Orders were issued that troops in certain areas were to push on and not delay, because telephonic communication had not been established. The order of the day asked the troops to "break a hole in the enemy's line," and assured the attacking divisions that the whole army was behind, ready to deal sledgehammer blows on the broken German front.

My gunner friends confidently expected to sleep in Lille on the night of the 9th, and proceeded jocosely to mark on a map of that city the houses each one chose as his billet. Roads to Lille had been selected for the ammunition columns, and orders given which would ensure a supply of shells that far forward, in case the attack "got through."

All was excitement when I left that front in the small hours of the morning of the 9th, and greatly would I have loved to stay and see the Auber Ridge attack at daybreak. But at early morning light on Sunday, May 9th, the 1st Cavalry Division, placed under the orders of General Plumer, who had taken General Smith-Dorrien's place as the General Officer commanding the 2nd Army, was once more to be sent to Ypres.

Things had not gone well in the Salient on the 8th. The 5th Corps, then under General Allenby, who had been promoted from Cavalry Corps, was composed of the 4th, 27th and 28th Divisions. These troops had been driven from their first-line trenches by a strenuous German attack, and had fallen back to the next line with heavy casualties.

The 2nd Cavalry Brigade had been rushed early on the 9th into the reserve trenches east of Ypres, and were in readiness from Potijze south to the Menin Road. The 1st Cavalry Brigade and the 9th Cavalry Brigade were near Vlamertinghe, west of Ypres, waiting orders.

The Huns had begun a ferocious onslaught on that perfect Sunday morning, and the roar of battle around Ypres drowned, in our ears, the noise of the 1st Army attack towards Aubers.

That 9th of May was to see bitter fighting on many fronts. The enemy attack on the Ypres Salient, and our "push" against the Auber ridge, were pregnant with bloody work, but away to the south, in front of Arras, the French Army was commencing the second day of the biggest attack it had yet planned since the winter mud had limited the fighting to trench warfare.

Five hundred thousand men and 2,000 guns were hammering at the German front, in an effort to break through to Douai, and though it was too early to expect a detailed report of the onslaught, word had come that the soldiers of France had won through in three places.

On the Russian front the German arms were crowned with success on that day, in a gigantic conflict, and the day before saw the sinking of the Lusitania and the sacrifice of its load of women and children.

One seemed to live many hours in a few minutes in those May days. All-engrossed with the work in hand, we were none the less anxious to hear of the great movements about us, in which our interests were not less keen than in the fighting in our own immediate area.

The new British line around Ypres ran from the French right, 2,000 yards east of the Yser-Ypres Canal, and about the same distance north of St. Jean, east for a mile or so to a homestead dubbed the Canadian Farm, then south-east across the Ypres-St Julien road, and across another road that previously had served as a secondary route to Passchendaele.

From that point the trenches led south, passing to the west of Verlorenhoek, a town on the Ypres-Zonnebeke road. South again, and a little east, they crossed the Ypres-Roulers railway, skirted the western and the southern shores of the Bellewaerde Lake, took in the grounds of the ruined Hooge Château and the eastern fringe of the woods that surrounded it, passed east of Hooge, and thus reached the famous Ypres-Menin road.

On went the line, winding snakelike through the eastern edge of the Sanctuary Wood, south of the Menin Road. Here the Salient reached its furthermost eastern extremity.

Then began a south-westerly trend, less than a mile in front of Zillebeke, reaching Zaartsteen before crossing the Ypres-Comines railway and later the Ypres-Comines canal.

From the canal the trenches ran more west than south to St. Eloi, then still on to the westward, until they circled south, away from Ypres, in front of Vierstraat, Kemmel and Wolverghem successively. There they faced, then passed Messines, reached the Ploegsteert Wood, crossed the

River Lys and bent round Armentières, on their way through the Auber and Neuve Chapelle area, to the Festubert and La Bassée fronts.

Early morning on that eventful Sunday found me driving General de Lisle and Hardress Lloyd to Ypres, straight through the devastated old city, out of the Menin gate, over the Menin bridge and on up the Zonnebeke Road as far as Potijze.

From the railway crossing at the western edge of Ypres, past the smashed cathedral of St. Martin, round the ruins of the Cloth Hall, through the Grande Place, and down the Rue de Menin, dead horses and men lined the way.

Ypres, which I had seen shelled so heavily time after time without its semblance of a city being destroyed, was at last indescribably in ruins. The slender pinnacles at the ends of the Cloth Hall still stood, and the tower itself had not fallen, though it had been so riddled it seemed in imminent danger of collapse. The tall torn tower of St. Martin's, near by, was also standing.

I found great difficulty in picking my way through the square, past shell-holes, piles of paving blocks, and heaps of dead horses. At one end of the Grande Place a howitzer shell had burst directly on an artillery limber, the horses and men being piled indiscriminately together, every one instantly killed. They lay in a heap on the broken stones of the square.

Our previous brewery headquarters was levelled to the ground, and the house where we had slept when last in Ypres was smashed out of all recognition.

Shells were falling in Ypres as we went through it. Across the Menin bridge the road, once a broad highway, had been narrowed to a mere path by pile on pile of shell-strewn bricks and stones. The houses were one by one completely disappearing, as though the space they occupied was required for other purposes, and the demolition of each one of them was a preconceived part of a plan of extinction of all signs of habitation.

Dead horses in dozens along the way lay close to the wheel track. We passed an ambulance, its front portion torn away by a shell, and then the remnants of a supply wagon, smashed to matchwood.

As we sped on, as fast as the continual obstructions and deep shell-holes would allow, shells fell behind us, screeching overhead every few seconds with strange, weird, discordant notes, culminating in a reverberating *bang!* that seemed thrown back at us by the high walls across the moat.

The dozens of dead horses became scores as we pushed on. Some fields by the road were literally covered with them.

A signals corps man told me that at one point his orders for dark night journeys across those fields were as follows: "Go down the hedge till you reach the ditch, turn right, and go toward the big pile of dead horses until you come to the gap in the next hedge." Those instructions could be easily followed on the blackest night, if one's olfactory nerves were in working order.

Every breath of air seemed to our unaccustomed nostrils to be charged with noisome smells.

As we approached Potijze the infantry fire grew less in volume. The Hun onslaught, the first of five distinct attacks to be pushed home by the Germans that day, had failed, and the breathing space was the more heavily punctuated by the howitzer shells for half an hour, as if in a special spleen of disappointment.

Most of the British guns had been withdrawn from the Salient and to the west of the canal. Two batteries of 18-pounders left near Potijze were firing with the valour of one hundred as we came up. But field-guns of light calibre, firing shrapnel, have less voice in an argument than the heavy howitzers with their 6-inch, 8-inch, or 14-inch high explosive shells. The Huns' howitzers on that Ypres front must have outnumbered our heavy ordnance by at least twenty to one that Sunday morning.

Long straggling strings of wounded soldiers trickled past on the Potijze road, making their way painfully around Ypres to the northwest, for to linger long on the Menin road, over which we had come, was to court sure death.

General de Lisle stopped the car not far from the Potijze *château*, and he and Hardress Lloyd walked through a field to the dugout in which General Mullens had established 2nd Cavalry Brigade Headquarters.

I turned the car and backed it between two walls of what once were dwelling-houses. Sitting close to the bottom of the wall, beside the car, I counted shell intervals while waiting. From two to three shells burst near the Potijze crossroads every minute, but by far the greater number of Hun projectiles went on, over my head, to the Menin bridge and Ypres.

A good-sized bough from a tree above dropped on my head, and a piece of shell casing, quite hot, struck my foot as it fell, spent, beside me.

For ten minutes splinters swept the roadway continuously, and the stream of wounded ceased to pour by until the fury of the sudden bombardment had spent itself. The constant shock of concussion was nerve-racking.

After a quarter of an hour the shells fell less frequently, though odd ones struck the road at intervals.

Behind the Verlorenhoek-Hooge line was a smaller Salient, called the G.H.O. line. It served as a support position, and between it and the canal were whole colonies of dugouts.

Much of the G.H.O. line was so situated that a parapet of sand-bags, in full sight of the German observers, made it a frequent target. On some days during the fighting that followed the casualties in the G.H.Q. line rivalled those in the front trench It was never a popular resting place, and was often the subject of much vituperation.

General de Lisle and Lloyd returned to the car, and nearer Ypres made another halt to visit the reserve dugouts in the fields toward the St. Jean road,

"Take good cover, President," said the general, as he started across a shell-torn meadow.

Easier said than done, I thought.

The lee of a house wall sheltered an empty biscuit-tin, on which I perched, under a lean-to of rough boards. The sky showed a fairy blue through hundreds of holes in the sheet-iron roof of the rudely constructed shed, evidence that a bursting shell above had "scattered" splendidly.

In spite of shell interludes I had one or two interesting chats with passers-by. A hospital corps sergeant told me the Huns shelled the Zonnebeke road, beside which we were chatting, every time they saw a transport on it.

"They give it hell when something moves over it," he said impressively. "Just let us bring an ambulance up here in the daytime, and see them get busy, the devils."

"That's nice," said I. "Do you think they could see my car when it went up to Potijze?"

"Sure." he replied with conviction. "Sure. If they haven't shelled you yet they *will*, all right, don't *you* worry."

He left me cogitating, as he strode off whistling, evidently unaware he had put anything but comforting ideas in my head.

All those who came from "up there" agreed as to one thing—the storm of howitzer-shells made one's chance of living through a "turn in the trenches" extremely slim. Many men were undeniably demoralised by it.

A 28th Division subaltern told me:

> The few of my poor chaps that are left seem to have the idea their number is up. They keep saying that if they don't get it today they'll sure get it tomorrow. Hardly any of them have much hope of getting out alive. I keep trying to hearten 'em, but it's rotten work. Every time I rip out something intended to be cheerful along comes a Jack Johnson and blows up a whole bally section of trench, burying alive those it don't kill. Then the poor beggars alongside just nod at each other and say: 'You and me next, Bill,' and what in hell *can* I tell 'em?
>
> Why in the deuce we don't have more guns up here *I'd* like to know. It does get sickening to be shelled, and shelled, and shelled, day and night, and hear so little of the same sort of stuff going over *their* way. Damn the German guns, anyway.

I sympathised with him, and told him so.

"I would like to see what de Lisle would do if *he* was running the guns," I told him. "He would send some hell of his own making over to those Huns if *he* was doing it, from what I have heard him say."

Odd prophetic fragment of comfort, that. Three days thereafter de Lisle was given command of the whole Verlorenhoek-Hooge front and all the artillery east of the canal, a territory which he soon had "stiff with guns." In spite of the preponderance of the Germans in heavy ordnance our gunners gave the enemy good packages of the medicine with which our hammered troops had been dosed for so many weary days.

The run back over the Menin Bridge and through Ypres safely accomplished, we visited the headquarters of General Snow, commanding 28th Division. While waiting there a Hun howitzer shell ambled lazily over my head and exploded a couple of hundred yards beyond, throwing up a great cloud of black smoke.

"Enemy airmen spotted this little lot," said a passing "red-hat." "Warm time coming for Snow."

His anxiety was unnecessary, however, for the next shell went much further over us, and another two further still, as if searching for moving troops far behind the line.

The 3rd Cavalry Division troopers, loaded in motor-buses, went Ypres-ward during the afternoon. General Sir Julian Byng had taken

Allenby's place at Cavalry Corps, and General Briggs had been given command of the 3rd Cavalry Division in Byng's place. The British Army contained no finer soldier than Briggs. This left the 1st Cavalry Brigade without a G.O.C., as General Meakin, who had been appointed to that command, was in England on sick leave. Consequently Colonel "Tommy" Pitman, of the 11th Hussars, was placed in temporary command of the 1st Brigade. Pitman, like Briggs, was a born leader of men—a tower of strength in himself.

Once during the afternoon my work took me to Ypres, but not beyond it. A fresh attack was on, and the Boches were sweeping the Menin Bridge and the road beyond with shrapnel.

Even Macfarlane's intrepid motorcyclists could no longer go over it with their signal corps messages; but were compelled to dismount, leave their motorbikes in Ypres, and proceed on foot to Potijze by a roundabout route through the fields. Those cyclists generally used a road long after it had been given up as impassable by everyone else, and when they at last abandoned it as too dangerous for use it was indeed time, in their parlance, "to give it a miss."

Our 2nd Brigade troops were under intermittent shell-fire all that day, but came through with unusual good fortune. One shell lit in a group of 18th Hussars, killed five and wounded eight, but the other units escaped with extraordinarily few casualties.

At the headquarters of General Bulfin, Commanding 28th Division, Lord Loch, who was G. S.O.1, on General Bulfin's Staff, gave us a very welcome tea.

From one of the 28th Division Staff I learned that the 4th, 27th and 28th Divisions had been through a more terrible time in the Salient than we had known. Snow's division, the 27th, were terribly depleted in numbers. "Not many men left, and very few officers indeed," was the sober way Snow had spoken of his lot that day.

The five heavy attacks of the 9th, in spite of the battered condition of the heroic men who faced them, resulted in no real gains and the Germans suffered severe losses.

We sought eagerly for news of the British attack along the Auber ridge. Early in the morning word had come that the 8th Division had made a splendid beginning by taking the German first line trenches in front of them. In the afternoon we heard that the 4th Corps "got on" well, but the Indian Corps and 1st Corps were held up by machine-gun fire and had made no progress. A further attack was to be made at 4 p.m. on the 10th. On the 11th, the G.H.Q. information summary remarked laconically, that there was "nothing to report from the 1st Army Front." So the big attack, of which my gunner friends along the Fromelle Road had such hopes, had fizzled out.

Weeks afterwards I heard the full story from the lips of men who were in the front of the fighting, but our task in Ypres was growing hourly sufficiently absorbing, so that the whys and wherefores of Rawlinson's failure to break through were of less interest than the question of repelling the German attack on the Salient.

As dusk drew on the conflagrations in Ypres lit up the eastern sky. Our night headquarters were in a *château* not far west of the unfortunate town.

Wounded still straggled back in small groups, and ambulances arrived every few minutes at a dressing station hard by the gates of our *château*.

Watching those ambulances unload made me proud to be an Anglo-Saxon. The men were magnificent in their incomparable morale. Many a smiling face hid teeth set hard in pain. Many a Tommy knows not only the inestimable value of keeping a stout heart to help himself through, but the immeasurably greater treasure of an ample store of cheery words and light-hearted jokes wherewith to lift a comrade from pain-racked despondency.

Broken bodies, broken limbs, and many a broken head were there in plenty, but one looked far to find a broken spirit.

Before we went to sleep, good news came from the French. All the way from Loos south to Lens, it said, and on through Thelus to Arras, the German first-line trenches had been captured, save in two places. On the 10th, the French reported having taken 2,000 prisoners and ten guns. In spite of all, the succeeding days' reports whittled down the final result to a tactical success, not a strategical one. The break in the German line was made good by the enemy in short order, and soon Gaul and Teuton were facing each other much as they had done, previously, and the inch-by-inch battles of the Labyrinth were soaking the ground of France's black country with French and German blood.

The big French attack and the British "push" had equally failed to smash the German line.

On our front British soldiers were to continue to show that their line could hold as solidly as the Hun line had held to the south, in spite of the hell of howitzer-fire that was daily to be let loose in the Salient.

Rocked to sleep by the earth-tremble of bursting tons of high explosive, day-dawn on May 10th seemed to come the next moment after my head had hit the floor which served me as a pillow.

Before seven o'clock in the morning I was again in the Salient and once more under shellfire.

Taking Colonel Home through Ypres and over the Menin bridge, we were not long in reaching Potijze.

The weather was perfect, hundreds of small birds hopping about the roadways and twittering excitedly, as if protesting to each other against the continual coming of the shells.

Behind a ruined house near the Potijze crossroads, I made a lucky discovery. Someone had built a comfy little dugout, six feet by four and nearly three feet deep, into which I at once repaired. Its earthen walls were reinforced by heavy planks, and a roof of earth-covered timbers was edged with barrels and sacks of bricks and mortar. Ponchos lined the inside of the walls, and the floor was deep with straw. On a shelf stood the remains of a ham bone and a tin half full of marmalade.

With thirty to forty jarring explosions in the vicinity every minute, this habitation was little short of ideal, save for the smell, which was fierce in its intensity and persistence.

The earth of the open spaces near by was thrown into yellow and brown heaps by the hundreds of howitzer shells that had rained on them for days. Dozens of dead horses, scattered about, offended the eye and polluted the air.

A detachment of troopers, bent on rendering the trenches of the near by G.H.Q. line a more safe shelter, had been spied by the Hun gunners, who for hours sent a continual shower of shells over them.

I had not waited long before I found I was not the only occupant of my shelter. My companions bit me surreptitiously, leaving red blotches which burned irritatingly.

I sat in the open air for a few moments, deciding there was not sufficient room in the dugout for my small but persistent comrades and myself, but a big shell landed near and sent such a spattering horde of splinters all around that I ducked back underground and took my chance with the less serious wounds of the busy little dugout folk, who seemed half starved, in spite of the ham bone and marmalade that had been left to them.

A couple of worried, hungry mongrel dogs came nosing about fearfully, heads cocked inquisitively when they caught sight of me. I gave them the bone and was thanked by a series of tail wags from each.

A Hun shell set fire to a building not far distant, and soon immense clouds of black and saffron smoke were rolling heavenwards.

Many shells came close to where I was tucked away, one throwing a cart load of debris over my car, but none of them in the least disturbing the tranquillity of my snug quarters.

Returning through Ypres, we found the Menin Road and bridge had been further hammered since we had come over it. At one or two points it was almost impassable for a car. The carcass of a dead horse had been blown right across the path, so that I was compelled to pass over part of it.

Houses were smoking on all sides, and red flames rose skyward in several quarters of the town.

A solitary old woman in black was picking her way tortuously past the dead and over the tumbled piles of brick and stone. She was, we thought, the last survivor of the civil population.

General Adeney, of the 12th Brigade, called at 1st Cavalry Division Headquarters and told me of the heavy shelling on the front that his brigade had held. The signal wire from his. headquarters to that of his division was cut by shell-fire fifty-five times in one day. His men had gone through a terrible time, but had stood it magnificently. General Adeney had wide experience with the Hun gas, and assured us its effects could be greatly nullified if care was taken to follow out the instructions as to the use of the respirators and face-masks, which had been issued to each man whose duty took him into the Salient.

The 2nd Cavalry Brigade went from the G.H.Q. line to the front position during the evening, but were relieved by the 1st Cavalry Brigade before the next morning. The 1st Brigade spent the day in dugouts in a little wood near the Ypres-Roulers Railway, close to the trenches. Shell-fire had cost the 2nd Brigade thirteen killed and fifty-four wounded during its occupancy of the G. H.Q. line.

The 9th Cavalry Brigade reported itself "quite comfortable" in splendid dugouts near Wieltje, but the shells wounded four of its officers and eighteen of its men, nevertheless.

From the windows of our headquarters château the fires of Ypres could be seen burning brightly all night, a red splash on the inky black of the horizon. Bursting shells and the flash of our guns never ceased. Bright stars dotted the dark canopy overhead, and brilliant trench-flares rose and fell in graceful arcs. The wonderful, ever-changing sight and the continual diapason of the heavy explosives was awe-inspiring.

Early morning usually came with a lull in the gun-fire on both sides, unless an attack was in progress. We hurried through breakfast on the 11th, and lost no time in getting away for Potijze.

General de Lisle, Major "Bertie" Fisher, of the 17th Lancers, who had joined de Lisle's Staff as G.S.O. 2 (in place of Major Fitzgerald, promoted to G.S.O. 1 of the 2nd Cavalry Division), and Captain Hardress Lloyd were my passengers.

The *rumph! r-r-rumph!* of itinerant Black Marias told us that German hate still held against shattered Ypres. As we approached the town one or two heavy explosions were followed by a cloud of dust and smoke where the shells had fallen on a building already a heap of debris and scattered its remains high in the air.

At the railway crossing west of Ypres several newly made shell-chasms made me pick my path warily. All the way to the Grande Place shell-holes and gathering piles of rubbish and timbers made progress difficult.

The space in front of the cathedral was knee-deep in loose paving blocks and stones.

As we turned the corner of the Cloth Hall, and could see the battered square, our sight is arrested by brilliant sheets of scarlet flame edged black, that shot across the Rue de Menin ahead of us.

The bright morning sun and blue, cloudless sky above, the grey and white ruins on every hand, and the blood-red, leaping, straining, struggling patch of angry flame that roared in our faces as we drew near to it, made a picture that would have delighted the heart of an artist.

I stopped the car.

The general at first counselled rushing through the fire, but I dreaded the result. Even should we have dashed past unscathed, the thought of the petrol in the car made me hesitate.

Then, beyond the conflagration, we saw that a house at the western approach to the Menin bridge had been knocked over by a shell, and so fallen that it completely blocked the road. Half a hundred men must work for hours before the Menin bridge would once more be open for traffic, though fortunately the bridge itself was undamaged.

Reversing the car and regaining the Grande Place, I threaded my way past deep holes in the *pavé*, and cautiously clambered over piles of debris as we sought another route eastward. Along a street where desolation reigned supreme we went, until we reached the eastern moat wall. Turning north, we sought an outlet on the St. Jean road.

Pushing over great fallen timbers, nail-studded and threatening a puncture at every revolution of the wheels, over, by and into holes in the paved road, it seemed impossible the car could surmount and pass the mounds of wreckage and paving-blocks that filled the way.

Over the railway we crawled, and to the very northern edge of Ypres. Just as we were congratulating ourselves on having won through, in spite of apparently insurmountable difficulties, a monster shell-cavity, thirty feet in diameter, and so deep as to be absolutely impassable for the car, opened in front of us.

The road was wide, but the shell had fallen in its centre, heaping the earth and stone at the edges of the gaping crater until it blocked the street from side to side.

General de Lisle and his two companions dismounted and proceeded on foot, instructing me to "be careful and get home safely."

Heading the way I had come was a task of some magnitude Pneumatic tyres wire not made to traverse shell-torn roads covered with glass, nails, and sharp bits of iron and stone, trusty Dunlops did not fail me.

In the square I stopped to get a photograph of a fire that was enveloping the houses at the back of the cathedral. Every building in the district was burning, some smouldering and smoking threateningly, while the flames raged fiercely from top to bottom of others standing near.

As I pulled up, a fearful crash came from the Menin bridge not far behind me, the shock of the concussion almost throwing me down. Giving up all idea of procuring pictures under such circumstances, I ignominiously fled as fast as it was safe to go.

Passing the cathedral, I saw a fine collie dog, his tail between his legs, slinking along furtively. I called him, dismounting from the car and trying to induce him to come to me, but he was scared so badly he only ran the faster at my approach.

In the western edge of Ypres a worn, drawn-faced Belgian, with a hunted look in his eyes, was slowly and carefully shoving a wheelbarrow, on which was a rude pallet. Stretched upon it lay the wasted form of a frail woman, close-swathed in as much bedding as the method of conveyance would allow. Her skin was wax-white, her wide eyes large and lustrous. She had not sufficient strength to prevent her feet from trailing the ground. An aged crone shuffled beside the sick woman, on her face a picture of agonised fear painful to see.

Dragoon Guards resting in the huts near Vlamertinghe

Big Hun guns were searching for little British ones not far away, and at every detonation the poor old woman jumped nervously.

An offer of assistance met with no response, as if they were past all capability of communication. The horrors they must have gone through for weeks in some cellar in that stricken town baffle imagination.

They were undoubtedly the last of the residents of Ypres to leave the town alive. If others remained, it was but to be buried under the falling walls of their hiding places, or to meet a worse fate in the flames that were raging from one end of the city to the other.

Vlamertinghe received a sharp shelling that forenoon, and a few minutes afterward I took General de Lisle through the town to the headquarters of General Wilson of the 4th Division. As we ran through Vlamertinghe, Tommies were busy sweeping the roadway clear of debris thrown about by the shells five minutes before.

When at General Bulfin's Headquarters *estaminet* a quarter of an hour later, I saw Hun shrapnel again begin bursting in twos over Vlamertinghe, which was gradually becoming an unhealthy locality.

The clear air brought out dozens of aeroplanes, which kept the anti-aircraft guns busy. The Germans sent up a couple of weird "sausages"—anchored observation balloons of peculiar shape.

The amount of ammunition used in the continuous shelling of the trench line was stupendous.

On one run toward Ypres I passed the "Princess Pat's" (Princess Patricia's Canadian Light Infantry), fresh from the 27th Division trenches, and on their way to a rest in billets. They were indeed a sturdy lot. All forenoon the Huns shelled our front line from the Menin Road to the north as it passed the Hooge Château and circled the Bellewaerde Lake. Wounded men poured back through Ypres from the Front, marvelling that they had escaped death in the trenches, and wondering still more that they had not been blown to atoms as they trudged back along the deadly Menin Road.

A wounded trooper of the 11th Hussars reported his regiment unpleasantly situated in bad dugouts in a wood, between the Ypres-Roulers Railway and the Bellewaerde Lake. The dugouts were not of sufficient size to accommodate the whole of the 11th, and when a detachment of Argyll and Sutherland Highlanders claimed shelter therein as well, the congestion became dangerous. The Hun shells burst immediately over the dugouts, and some casualties had occurred before morning dawned. So little accommodation seemed available

Graves of Captain Annesley, Lieutenant Drake and Captain Peto, all of the 10th Hussars, in a graveyard on the Menin Road

that one squadron of the 11th had been sent back to the G. H.Q. line, where it had been badly hammered by howitzer fire for hour after hour as the morning passed.

Romer Williams and I walked from our *château* to a "Mother" gun, concealed under a screen of dry branches in a nearby farmyard. The big 9.2 howitzer was throwing its 290-pound projectiles, filled with lyddite, into the Hun trenches in front of Hooge, nearly 9,000 yards distant. The five-mile journey was accomplished by each shell in 35 seconds, a rate of more than 500 miles per hour. Dodging a shell which was coming at such speed would be something of a feat.

Yet, standing directly behind the breech, we could distinctly see the 9.2 shell as it left the muzzle and started on its sinister errand.

For so huge an engine of war its paraphernalia was simple. The howitzer stood on a platform built into the farmyard. Rows of shells, each a load for four men, lay in a ditch behind it. On a log, under a tall tree, sat the captain gunner, by his side a non-com. busy figuring out mathematical equations, and another poring over a large-scale map. With his back to the tree crouched a Royal Flying Corps man, his receiver to his ear, and an elaborate box of wireless telegraphic tricks beside him. Across the road a slender pole, a score of feet in height, completed his wireless installation.

"Fire" said the captain, sharply.

Flash! bang! "Mother" recoiled with a shock and returned leisurely. Not a big noise or a very trying one on the ears of those near by, unless in front of the "business end." The crew stood close at hand as each round was fired.

Before an unsophisticated onlooker would imagine the great shell had reached its destination, the wireless man, listening attentively to the message from an aeroplane observer high over the Huns, and out of our sight, sang out "150 yards over."

A cabalistic sequence of numbers was shouted in *staccato* tones by one of the non-coms, repeated by a man at the breech, and *flash! bang!* went "Mother" again.

"Well placed. Right into them," said the wireless operator, as the approving message was ticked from his fellow in the 'plane.

Flash! bang! the work went on, comforting the battered men in our own trenches, and harrying the Germans in theirs.

"Made nine direct hits on their trenches yesterday," said the captain gunner, "and have got the range pretty well today. Managed to get a couple into one of the German batteries this morning, too." And he grinned.

If the men who made the shells could have known how much heart every 9.2 projectile put into the brave boys that faced the Hun trenches, weary to distraction of everlasting German shelling, and little return thereto, they would have been justly proud of their handiwork.

A "Mother" shell was a fine tonic for those who were behind it, "when it popped."

On the night of the 11th the 1st and 9th Brigades "took over" the parts of the line held by the 27th Division and most of that held by the 28th. Up to that time the troopers had been only in reserve or support, yet so heavy was the Hun gun-fire in the Salient that our division had lost one officer killed and seventeen wounded, and the casualty list among the men was but few short of one hundred.

De Lisle was given command of a stretch of line reaching from near the Bellewaerde Lake to the Wieltje-St. Julien road, and 2,500 28th Division men and all the guns east of the Yser-Ypres Canal were placed under him. He at once planned to throw several additional batteries into the Salient, and gave orders which would result in a shell-surprise for the Huns. Every time the German gunners started to shell our trenches, the German trenches were to be deluged with a half an hour of concentrated shell-fire from all de Lisle's field batteries, his 6-inch howitzer battery, and the single 60-pounder gun that had been allotted to him.

The day closed with the repulse of the last of three sanguine enemy attacks that had been launched since morning, two of which had gained a foothold in the British line, only to have it, in each case, torn from their grasp by costly counter-attacks.

The Ypres-Poperinghe road was filled with troops marching westward. "To what lot do these men belong?" I asked General Mullens, as we stood watching the passing columns.

"They are of the Northumberland Brigade," said Mullens. "I am told that but 900 of them are left out of more than 5,000. Another brigade went into the Salient 5,500 strong a fortnight ago, and has come out today numbering but 950."

I went to bed by the bright light of burning Ypres, which made every tree cast flickering shadows to try the nerves of the men who tramped up in the cold darkness to share the morrow's battle, or trudged back to billets to sink into the torpor of extreme exhaustion, until in their turn they should again face the shattering shell blasts.

May 12th was comparatively a quiet day. The wind had changed, and Hun gas attacks were impossible until it again swung round to the east.

I told Captain Francis Grenfell, of the 9th Lancers, about the "Mother" gun not far away, and we strolled down where it was quartered just in time to watch it fire a score of rounds at a German battery which was in action at the bend of the Ypres-Comines Canal near Hollebeke.

A second 9.2 gun had arrived in the night and taken up quarters in an adjoining farm. It had been doing good work near Brielen, but was "spotted" by a German air-scout and "found" by the enemy's guns. One man killed and several wounded by a German shell decided the gunner in command to "make a get-away" from the discovered position.

The 3rd Cavalry Division troops were put under de Lisle's command in addition to those of his own division and the odd brigades of the 28th Division.

A slice of trench taken by the Huns on the 11th, and retaken by a British counter-attack that night, was rushed by the enemy on the morning of the 12th and captured, only to have another British counter-attack prepared for the evening. Thus the line of battle surged forward and backward day after day, each section of trench being fought over time and again with heavy losses to both sides.

Slowly the German circle was drawing closer to the stricken town. The second Battle of Ypres was in full swing.

At lunch time General Allenby and his chief of staff were guests of our mess. It was a source of great satisfaction that the cavalry, on the threshold of one of the hardest struggles it had been called upon to face, should be under a corps commander who had so long been at its head as the G.O.C. of the Cavalry Corps. No man that I saw in the months I was with the British Expeditionary Force inspired more confidence in his leadership than Allenby.

General Meakin arrived from England, but decided that the command of the 1st Cavalry Brigade, to which he had been assigned, had best be left in the hands of "Tommy" Pitman until its turn in the front trenches was done. Pitman knew the ground and had a wonderful grasp of the situation, and to no other one man was due more of the credit for the holding' of the line during the ensuing forty-eight hours.

On the night of the 12th, the tired infantry of the 28th Division

OFFICERS OF THE CAVALRY CORPS

was given relief from the firing-line, and before dawn the two and a half miles of front trenches, from the Canadian Farm, north of the Ypres-St. Julien Road, south to the western shore of the Bellewaerde Lake, a few yards from the Ypres-Menin Road at Hooge, was manned by the dismounted troopers of the 1st and 3rd Cavalry Divisions.

The 2nd Cavalry Brigade held the extreme left of this stretch of cavalry line. The 18th Hussars were furthest north, the 4th Dragoon Guards in the centre, and the 9th Lancers on right. South of them were the three regiments of the 1st Cavalry Brigade—5th Dragoon Guards, 2nd Dragoon Guards (Queen's Bays), and 11th Hussars. The 5th Dragoon Guards were on the left of the Queen's Bays, whose right rested on the Ypres-Zonnebeke Road near Verlorenhoek, a thousand yards from Potijze, where de Lisle so often took me each day. The 11th Hussars were in some trenches near the grounds of the Potijze *château*, The 9th Cavalry Brigade was in dugouts near Wieltje.

South of the Ypres-Zonnebeke Road came the 3rd Cavalry Division front; the 7th Brigade first, then the 6th Brigade, the 8th Brigade being in reserve.

Of the 7th Brigade, the 1st Life Guards formed the left, their trenches leading south from the Zonnebeke Road. One of their squadrons was in a reserve trench at the back of the line. Next on the right came the 2nd Life Guards, then the Leicestershire Yeomanry, whose right rested on the Ypres-Roulers Railway.

The 6th Brigade held the line from the railway to the Bellewaerde Lake, the 3rd Dragoons on the left, the North Somerset Yeomanry on the right, and the 1st Royal Dragoons (Royals) in reserve a bit to the rear, and but a few yards north of the Menin road.

The 8th Brigade, in reserve, was composed of the Royal Horse Guards (Blues), the 10th Hussars, and the Essex Yeomanry.

Each cavalry regiment had a fighting strength of about 300 men. The 1st Division numbered some 2,400 rifles, and the 3rd Division roughly 2,700, say, just over 5,000 men for the two divisions. An extra number of machine-guns made up for their comparatively small numerical strength.

The trench-line into which the troopers were thrown that night was in poor condition for defence. A foot of mud was the average bottom, and further attempts at digging only resulted in more water and mud. Parapets of sandbags and wire entanglements were sadly needed all along the line, and, at that, sandbag parapets were all too easily demolished by Hun shell-fire, which made short work of them.

A typical farm in Flanders, in which British Soldiers were billeted

A careful reconnaissance of the 3rd Cavalry Division trenches failed to reveal a stretch of 100 yards where more sandbags and more wire were not urgently required.

CHAPTER 6

The Great German Attack on May 13th

Dawn on the 13th of May was the signal for a howitzer bombardment of the cavalry front which surpassed in intensity and duration any previous gun-fire during the whole war.

From four o'clock in the morning until five o'clock in the afternoon it drifted from one section to another, without respite. During the entire forenoon the trench line north and south of the Zonnebeke Road, viewed from Potijze, a thousand yards to the rear, was covered continuously with a heavy pall of smoke, as if a well-fed conflagration was raging beneath. The flashes of bursting shells in that smoke-cloud were so numerous that no human eye could follow or count them, even in a most restricted range of vision.

The sound was one grand, incessant roar. All the thunderstorms of time, crashing in splendid unison, would not have made a more magnificent din. The ear could not intelligibly record so tempestuous a maelstrom of sound-waves, and the brains of those in the midst of its wildest fury became numb and indifferent to the saturnalia of explosion, save for one here and there which lost its mental balance, perhaps never to be regained.

Early in the morning General de Lisle sent me to Potijze with Captain Hardress Lloyd. General Meakin rode up with us on his first visit to the Salient since his return from sick leave.

Ypres was impassable. We took a roundabout course to the north, now dashing down a muddy lane, now over a turnip field where constantly passing traffic had worn a sort of path, over an improvised bridge across the canal, at last reaching the Ypres-St. Jean Road that led away to Wieltje and St. Julien. By a cross road of sorts we found our way to Potijze, thankful to have arrived safely.

Before we had traversed much of the way from our headquarters, west of Ypres, we were in a bad shell-zone. On the narrow road, ammunition limbers went up at a trot and returned at full gallop. The route was lined with red-bandaged wounded struggling rearward as best they could, and ambulances were always in evidence. As we turned a corner a Black Maria exploded with a fearful bang fifty yards ahead, right beside the roadway. A small piece of the shell hit General Meakin in the head, but luckily was so spent it did not cause a wound.

As we neared the canal blue ruin was spread everywhere. Battery on battery of our artillery, firing like mad, barked and roared from the fields at our sides, while Hun shells fell close and fast around them.

A car dashed towards us, the chauffeur holding up his hand to stop us. It was "Babe" Nicholson's car, empty except for the driver, whom Nicholson had told to "look out for himself," while "Babe" was showing the way trenchwards to a depleted battalion of York and Durham Territorials sent forward as reserve. Only 380 of their 1,000 remained from the fortnight's fighting and sixteen of their officers had been killed or wounded, but they trudged up as if arriving fresh from home.

"Stop, sir," said the scared chauffeur. "They are shelling the road beyond so heavily no one can get through."

"Did you just come through?" asked Hardress Lloyd.

"Yes," replied the boy; "but a couple almost lit on me. One of them blew the car into the hedge."

"Go ahead, President," said Lloyd grimly. "We have got to get there somehow."

We got there, somehow.

Once we ran through the ill-smelling shell-cloud of a coal-box that burst a few yards in front of us, and twigs from the trees fell over the car as the shells screamed above, but we dodged on, past shell-holes and around barricades, untouched.

Pulling up, I saw Nicholson's car behind us, the driver grinning.

"I thought if it was good enough for you it was good enough for me," he said. "But I'm hanged if I thought *anyone* could get over that road and not be hit. It's the first time I've been up here."

I introduced him to my tiny Potijze dugout, which he thought "smelled horrid." He was inclined to a preference for the open air until a great howitzer-shell lit fifty feet away, pieces from it knocking over some of the wall of the ruined house behind which the dug-out had been made. As he joined me in the cramped space below ground another Black Maria burst across the road from us, making the earth tremble and showering splinters on the roof of our shelter.

Fortunately for those whose work took them over the roads that morning the sky was leaden and rain fell at intervals, rendering German aeroplane observation impossible. Had a Hun airman caught sight of the traffic-filled road over which we had come the enemy gunners might have effectually closed it to traffic.

As we waited at Potijze the shells from the British guns behind us seemed to fill the air. Gradually the fire of the German howitzers concentrated on the trench-line in front of us, and the Boche gunners burst shrapnel all about the fields, searching erratically for the English batteries.

Budworth, of the artillery, was very much upset that morning by the target selected by one of the British howitzers.

Our divisional batteries H, I, and the Warwickshire Territorial Battery, were doing fine work and splendid execution.

Budworth's observers sent back word that some of our heavy guns were shelling a farm that he had instructed should not be shelled by his batteries.

Instantly he sent to the howitzer commander and asked him to "Please get off that farm."

"What's wrong with it?" asked the howitzer man. "It's in German hands, right enough."

Budworth said:

"Of course it is. But I've figured out that the Hun artillery commander would have his headquarters about there; very probably in that very farm. The old chap is peppering my batteries with shrapnel, which don't bother us, for we just get in our funk-holes and wait until it's all over, then run out and bang away. For that matter we don't even go in for it, if we are busy. If the old Boche chap who is running their guns should be killed by one of your big shells, and another German beggar, who decided to use high explosives on us, should take his place, we couldn't stay here long. Whatever you do, don't bother the old German gunner-chap. He is quite all right, from our standpoint, where he is at present."

Budworth's theory was proven sound by the fact that out of his three batteries of field guns he only lost eleven men and ten horses in a fortnight of fighting.

Standing in the Zonnebeke Road and looking toward Verlorenhoek, the shell-swept front line was plainly visible, a little more than half a mile away.

To reconstruct a fight on a two-and-a-half mile front such as the battle of May 13th, with official regimental reports to which to refer, would be sufficiently difficult. To piece it out while it was actually in progress was increasingly so.

I ran back and forth from our headquarters west of Ypres to the town of Potijze many times that day. By evening, when I left the Salient for the night, I had met with scores who had terrible tales to tell. The wounded made an unending stream westwards, and numbered many a familiar face.

Officers and men all declared the shell-fire was the heaviest they had seen. At no point in the line was the German shelling more fierce than on either side the Zonnebeke Road, near Verlorenhoek. The Queen's Bays were to the north of it, the 5th D.G.'s on their left. On the south of the road were the 1st Life Guards, and on their right the 2nd Life Guards, then the Leicestershire Yeomanry.

The Bays, under Lieutenant-Colonel "Algy" Lawson, formerly of the Greys, held on like grim death in spite of the storm of shell that burst over them at four o'clock in the morning and continued hour after hour throughout the day.

The Life Guards were driven back from their trenches with heavy losses, and the Leicestershire Yeomanry had to fall back as well.

This exposed the right flank of the Bays, but still they stuck to their position.

At about half past ten o'clock the commanding officer of the 5th D.G.'s ordered the retirement of his regiment, the men trickling back in two thin lines, one at either end of their section of front.

This resulted in the left of the Bays being uncovered as well as their right, but they put their teeth in and held on. The 11th Hussars came up magnificently on the left shortly after, and shared the glory, with the Bays, of saving the line.

Twice during the day the Huns formed for an infantry attack in front of the Bays, and each time our splendid guns were told of the concentration, and poured shell into the massing Germans with terrible execution, scattering the enemy detachments like chaff before the wind, and thus nipping the attack in the bud.

A strong enemy detachment came down the Zonnebeke Road and deployed to the north of it, immediately in front of the Bays. The Boches were lying in the open, but were protected from our rifle and machine-gun fire by a swell of ground.

A fat German observation officer obtained a place of vantage in a shattered farmhouse just south of the road. No amount of sniping could dislodge him, though the bullets chipped off bits of brick from the slender stack behind which he was sheltered. Up came a Naval Division armoured Rolls-Royce. Opposite the end of the Bays' trenches it stopped and opened fire.

The Hun officer in the farm noted the approach of the car, and fled up the road as fast as he could run.

"I had to laugh so much at the funny figure the little fat chap cut, with the tails of his long grey coat flapping straight out behind him as he ran," said one of the Bays to me that night. "I swear it did in any chance I had of hitting him. He got back to his own lot safe, I think, but he did made a holy show of himself doing it."

A large number of the enemy were seen concentrating in a wood in front of the Bays toward evening, and again word to our gunners was followed by a bombardment of the group of trees that made immediate evacuation of it the only alternative to sure death.

On the extreme left of the cavalry line, the 18th Hussars suffered more heavily than the other regiments of the 2nd Brigade, though the 9th Lancers had many casualties.

The trenches occupied by the 18th Hussars were blown to bits. Some of the regiment retired to the left into the adjacent trenches of the East Lancashire, and some went back over the open ground in search of the reserve trenches. Failing to find them, the troopers advanced to the ruins of their own line and dug themselves in as best they could, only to be blown out of some parts of the trenches a second time.

The Hospital Corps men could not reach the 18th wounded, as the Huns had a machine-gun trained on the only approach to the trenches. Consequently many men, unable to be moved to a place of safety, were killed as they lay wounded in trench or dugout.

The right of the cavalry line, from the Ypres-Roulers Railway toward the Menin Road, was in very soft ground.

The 3rd Dragoon Guards, North Somerset Yeomanry, and Royals, of General David Campbell's 6th Brigade, were literally picked up and thrown back by the howitzer shells, while the line was simply blotted out of existence.

The Royals, in reserve, made a charge at 7.30 in the morning that took them to the place where the original trenches had been, but all that remained of them, even at that early hour, were great tumbled piles of earth and mud without semblance of form.

Cecil Howard, Campbell's Brigade Major, was the only officer on the 6th Brigade Staff who was not hit, Campbell himself being slightly wounded.

The most spectacular manoeuvre of the day fell to the lot of Bulkeley Johnson's 8th Brigade, who were taken from reserve to counter-attack at 2.30 p.m. and win back the part of the line out of which Kennedy's 7th Brigade, the 1st and 2nd Life Guards, and the Leicestershire Yeomanry had been shelled.

The area to be won back reached from the Ypres-Zonnebeke Road to the Ypres-Roulers Railway. On the left of it the gallant Bays had stuck to their trenches On the right of it, David Campbell's men were holding on, though frightfully decimated; their left, resting on the railway, bent back slightly by the retirement of the 7th Brigade.

The British artillery opened the 2.30 attack in splendid style. Then up went the 8th Brigade, Blues, 10th Hussars, and Essex Yeomanry.

It made the pulses beat high to hear the story of that charge from the Bays, who had reserved seats for the show.

The lines swept forward with a cheer that was drowned in the crashing of the shells. The Blues reached the line of shell-holes that marked the position of the Life Guards' trenches. No cover was to be found. So on they went, a few of them actually penetrating the German trenches 400 yards beyond, but soon realizing that their numbers were insufficient to maintain their position, and slowly coming back with what was left of their regiment. The 10th Hussars went up invincibly, men dropping at every step. One big trooper was seen advancing some distance ahead of his comrades, those who had been in line with him at the start all down. He stalked along coolly, without waiting for the others. The big trooper made a gallant showing, standing for a moment and firing steadily, then tramping on, to stop and fire again. No one dreamed he would reach the Hun trenches alive, but he did so, and was the first of the 10th Hussars to disappear over the enemy's parapet.

Had the Germans stuck to their trenches the few of the 10th to reach them might easily have been wiped out. But the Teuton soldiers fled before that stern advance.

Like the Blues, the 10th Hussars were too few to be able to consolidate the small portion of enemy trench which they had won, so nothing remained but a retirement.

Back they came, the Hun supports quickly taking advantage of their withdrawal. Two armoured cars pushed beyond the Bays' trench, up the Zonnebeke Road, and poured a heavy machine-gun fire across the rear of the retreating 10th Hussars' line. Few of that regiment would have returned had this covering fire not protected their retirement.

Once a group of troopers took a few dozen German prisoners, but the captured Huns were nearly all killed by German shell-fire before they could be taken to a place of safety. No trenches existed in that area into which to put them, and English and German, captors and prisoners alike, were mowed down by Hun shrapnel as they crossed the fields towards Potijze.

Months after that memorable battle, I had sent to me by a friend, a distinguished officer in the 11th Hussars, some leaves from his war diary. His account of the operations of his regiment that day read as follows:—

Thursday, May 13th.—At about four a.m. a terrific bombardment began against our front line trenches. The fire was most intense, and heavier even than at Messines. At 7.30 a.m. Brigade Headquarters received a message from the 5th D.G.'s, saying that a great deal of their trenches had been blown in, and that their position was critical. The troops of C Squadron, 11th Hussars, under Norrie, were ordered up to support them. There was no communication trench to the front line, but by clever use of the ground they reached the 5th D.G.'s with very few casualties. The bombardment still increased. The Bays were holding on as well, but asked for more ammunition. A party from Renton's troop succeeded in getting some up, but had several killed in doing so.

About 12 o'clock a regiment of the 3rd Cavalry Division, on the right of the Bays, were shelled out of their trenches, and the Germans succeeded in getting a footing in them. General Briggs ordered a counterattack, which was launched at 2.30 p.m. Renton, who had been twice up to the front line to get information for the Brigadier, volunteered to lead the 10th Hussars up to the Bays' right, where they were to commence their attack. The whole affair was carried out like an Aldershot parade movement. The men screamed at the top of their voices, the officers making hunting noises, as they all charged across the open. It was a glorious sight. The Germans ran as if the devil himself was after them, our guns pouring shrapnel into them. The trenches were retaken, but in the excitement the attackers rushed on another half a mile.

The Germans then turned on all their artillery, killing their own men as well as ours. Confusion followed, and the attacking line, being broken up, withdrew about half a mile It was a pity they ever went beyond their original line, as the casualties were heavy.

To return to our own section of the line. The 5th D.G.'s reported that they had put Norrie's troop into their front line, keeping the other troop (Sergeant Lemon) in a support trench. Their casualties had been heavy, and the situation extremely critical. During the afternoon information came in that the whole of the 5th D.G.'s had been shelled out of their trenches, and were retiring. Shortly after this Lance-Corporal Watts came back from the front line with a message from Norrie, explaining the situation. He had held on with his troop when the 5th D.G.'s retired, and besides his own men had a troop of the 5th and one of their machine-guns, and was covering the left flank of the Bays—a grand piece of work. The line had to be held at all cost, so the 11th Hussars were ordered to advance and retake the lost trenches.

Lawson's Squadron (A) was sent in advance, with instructions to work up behind the Bays, and push in on their left. Later, another message came in to say that a squadron of the 19th Hussars, under Tremayne, had pushed up to Norrie and had been put on his left; however, there still existed a considerable gap of unoccupied trench. Divine Providence must have come to our aid, as the shelling practically stopped as the regiment advanced. Soon after 6 p.m. Brigade Headquarters heard that Lawson had successfully got his squadron up to the front line. B Squadron, Stewart Richardson, followed on, and by dusk the line was re-established.

Our casualties for the day were about fifty, the Bays had the same, and the 5th D.G.'s had over one hundred, a large number of which, however, occurred during the retirement. As the sun was setting the battle died down. It had been a nerve-straining day, full of gallant episodes.

Wires cut, messengers killed, and the inevitable and exaggerated and mistaken reports of the wounded, made the long day of fighting an anxious one at de Lisle's headquarters.

The day's casualties in the 1st and 3rd Cavalry Divisions were thought, until well into the following day, to exceed fifty *per cent*, of the men engaged.

Early in the forenoon came word that "Hardly any of the 3rd. D.G.'s and the North Somerset Yeomanry are left." At midday Colonel Burnett and Major Corbett, of the 18th Hussars, were reported killed, but two or three hours later we learned the news, while unfortunately true as to Major Corbett, was incorrect as to Burnett, who was sound and well.

At 4 p.m. General de Lisle sent me to Colonel Browne, the chief medical officer of the 1st Cavalry Division, to ascertain what was actually known as to officer casualties in the division.

Colonel Browne said:

> We cannot get the ambulances up yet to evacuate the wounded, the shell-fire so covers the roads. Thus far but eight of our wounded officers have been brought back.

Among the eight was Major Sewell, of the 4th D.G.'s. The 9th Lancers, Sewell thought, had suffered from the shell-fire even more heavily than the 18th Hussars.

As I was about to leave Potijze, at seven o'clock that night, a staff officer reported that General Kennedy had just told him but ninety men were left to him out of his fine 7th Brigade, and he greatly feared that a large proportion, if not all, of the missing were killed or wounded.

General Briggs, at Potijze, received report after report of heavy losses from the various 3rd Cavalry Division units, as dark drew on, until it seemed that the division had been practically wiped out. But 200 men were reported to be left to Campbell of the 6th Brigade. Kennedy's 7th Brigade mustered 120 at the close of the day, and Bulkeley Johnson's 8th Brigade was so shattered that to obtain an estimate of its numbers was most difficult.

In spite of the fact that the 6th, 7th, and 8th Brigades had, according to all military theory, ceased to exist as fighting forces, their remnants were gathered together as best the darkness of the night allowed, and put hard at work "digging themselves in," in preparation for the fight that the morning light would be sure to bring them.

The Northumberland Territorial Brigade, its numbers raised to 1,200, was sent up to help the tired troopers dig. Their general, Fielding, an old Aisne acquaintance, lunched with us that day. He had just taken over their command, as their former brigadier had been killed a fortnight before in the Salient. The transformation of that lot of Terriers from raw, untried troops to veterans of shell-warfare had not taken many days.

Captain Johnson, a French liaison officer who had been attached to General Briggs' staff since Mons, and who had won the respect and deep affection of all with whom he came into contact, was shot through the head and instantly killed that night as he was accompanying General Briggs on a tour of the trenches in front of Potijze.

Wilson's 4th Division, on the left of the 1st Cavalry Division, which had also suffered heavily on the 13th, had sent a message asking the cavalry to take over some of its line, but that night it found it possible to occupy a few hundred yards of the line held by the 18th Hussars. This proved a most welcome assistance. The right of the 3rd Cavalry Division front, from the Ypres-Roulers Railway to the Menin Road, was given into the hands of the Irish Fusiliers, of the 27th Division.

The line, thus shortened slightly, was the scene of feverish work all night long, that the importance of the small German gain might be minimised, and a further Hun advance blocked.

The actual ground gained by the Germans on May 13th was but 300 to 400 yards on a front of 1,000 yards. Our new line from the Zonnebeke Road across the Ypres-Roulers railway was in better terrain than the old position, and offered superior natural advantages for defence to the deplorable original line.

So we were far from disheartened when day broke on May 14th.

The German heavy guns had seemed at times during the 13th to number scores on scores. Though fire came from every direction into the badly placed and rottenly made British trenches, blowing our thin line sky-high all along the front, the net result of advantage to the enemy was extremely small.

On the morning of the 14th de Lisle said to me:

Bad as our losses have been, I have the situation in hand. The men have held the line, and will continue to do so. Every hour sees things get better.

The shattered, depleted, almost annihilated regiments of the day before were found by the grey light of that cold, rainy May morning to be fighting forces still, their moral undamaged, and their spirits undimmed.

By half past six o'clock I was off for Potijze with de Lisle, a heavy rain during the night having covered the road with slimy mud and made it terribly slippery. We found Hun gunners so docile that I could with impunity run the general to the G.H.Q. line on the Potijze road.

As I waited in the roadway two of the Blues came past. Mud-covered and battle-stained, they slouched along as if completely tired out.

"Good morning," I called out, cheerily.

"Good morning, sir," they answered, straightening, instinctively, as they spoke. Fine chaps they were, and soldierly from head to foot, in spite of the mantle of dirt in which they were wrapped.

Nerves and muscles relaxed, almost at the limit of endurance, steeped in physical fatigue, like a flash they could pull up, eyes clear, heads erect, voices firm, the look on their faces showing that they were just as good fighting men at that moment as they were thirty-six hours previously.

Over the smoke of welcome cigarettes we chatted of the charge of the day before. The rushing of the German trenches, the capture of a section of them, and then being overpowered and turned out by overwhelming numbers of Huns, was gone over, spiritedly, by the troopers.

"Only seventy of the Blues are left, though," said one of them. "That's the hard part of it."

"You are sure to find more when things get straightened out," I replied. "Casualty lists always grow smaller when the returns are all in."

They trudged on soberly, "Hoping so." Splendid men.

I was sent to search the houses in Potijze, or what was left of them, for a couple of wounded officers who were reported to be waiting to be evacuated by an ambulance that had not yet arrived.

An Essex Yeomanry trooper limped slowly passed as I started, and I gave him a "lift" for a few hundred yards. He had badly sprained his knee during the charge the day before. By morning it had become so swollen and painful he could only hobble along with great difficulty. No thought of coming back to have it attended to, after the charge, had entered his mind.

"We were told to hang on till dark," he explained, "and it took all of us that were left to hang on. I couldn't have come back very well, could I?"

Before the day was over some of the official casualty lists of the brigades were compiled, and we were greatly cheered to find the losses were less heavy than had at first been reported.

The 1st Cavalry Division casualties for May 13th numbered 523. In the 1st Cavalry Brigade two officers were killed and five wounded, and 164 troopers killed or wounded. The 2nd Cavalry Brigade had a casualty list of 249. Three officers in the brigade were killed and eleven wounded. Among the killed was Lieutenant Lunan, a very brave medical officer attached to the 9th Lancers. The 18th Hussars lost 160, the 9th Lancers 140, and the 4th D.G.'s thirty-five.

The 3rd Cavalry Division suffered more heavily. David Campbell's 6th Brigade had eleven officers killed and twenty-two wounded—thirty-three out of a total of forty-nine. In the ranks, the Royals lost 117, the North Somerset Yeomanry 105, and the 3rd Dragoon Guards sixty-nine. The total for the brigade was 330 casualties. The 7th Brigade lost over 450 officers and men. Seven Leicestershire Yeomanry officers were killed and five were wounded. In the ranks, the Leicestershires had 180 casualties, making a total of over 190, all told, out of a strength of 300. The 8th Brigade's list of over 300 brought the total of killed and wounded for the 3rd Division to more than 1,100.

A patrol of 15th Hussars, under Lieutenant Kenneth Maclane, while the regiment was holding a part of the line to the north of Verlorenhoek, went up to the German first line trenches during the afternoon and found a section of them deserted, which showed the Huns were little better satisfied with the strategical location of their line than we had been with parts of ours.

Visits to Potijze from time to time meant coming close to big shell-bursts, but the fury of the 13th had made the itinerant shell-fire of the 14th so insignificant in contrast that we paid little attention to even the biggest of the Black Marias.

That night the 2nd Cavalry Division, General Kavanaugh commanding, relieved the 1st and 3rd Divisions on a narrowed front, the infantry closing in on the sides. Before morning of the 15th our tired men were on their way back to billets for a well-earned rest.

En route from Potijze to our headquarters at dusk on the 14th, my despatch case fell from the car. I went over the road carefully at daylight the following morning, and only desisted in my futile search when the "morning hate" made it foolish to tarry longer in the vicinity.

Hussar's cook-house, Vlamertinghe huts, Vlamertinghe

Great was my delight during the afternoon to learn that a wire had been received at divisional headquarters, saying that, "amongst the debris on the battlefield had been found a despatch case belonging to Frederic Coleman." A gunner of H Battery, R.H.A., had spied it in a roadside ditch in the Salient, and thoughtfully taken it to Major Skinner, commanding the battery, who had at once advised us of its recovery.

On the night of May 15th and morning of May 16th, General Hubert Gough's 7th Infantry Division made a splendid "push" to La Quinque Rue, in front of Festubert, the report of which made cheery reading.

The men of the 1st Cavalry Division were housed in "huts" near Vlamertinghe. On the 16th General de Lisle addressed the contingents, one after another. He asked me to verify one or two details that had been reported, and this work gave me a most pleasant couple of hours chatting about the battle of May 13th with men of half a dozen of the different regiments that took part in it.

The evening of the 17th found the 1st Cavalry Division, after seventy-two hours' rest, again marching through Ypres to take a further turn in the trenches.

The Salient had been comparatively quiet since the last German onslaught on the 13th, but howitzer shells were daily falling over the lines with tiresome regularity.

I was sent by General de Lisle to a house near Ypres, where we had planned to have a "basket dinner" before leaving for night quarters on the Menin Road. A very young staff-officer, instructed to guide me, misunderstood that such duty was required of him, and went off about some business of his own before I had been able to learn the location of the house.

Meeting "Rattle" Barrett, I asked him if he could give me the desired information.

"I don't know about the dinner part of it," said "Rattle"; "but your headquarters for the night are well east of Ypres, on the Menin Road. Go to the house nearest the *château* that stands by the *Halte*, where the railway crosses the road, and you can't miss it if you try."

The general had disappeared on foot, the juvenile staff-officer was nowhere to be found, so off I went, in accordance with Barrett's instructions.

Darkness was coming on. I passed along lines of 2nd Cavalry Brigade troopers, marching toward Ypres and through it.

Group of cavalry officers at the huts at Vlamertinghe

No lights were allowed, though my car was secure from liability of offence in that particular, for the electric installation had gone wrong, a not infrequent occurrence, and no one but a master electrician could coax a glimmer out of the headlamps.

Bump! Bump! I jolted from hole to hole in the smashed roadway. The streets were crowded with the machinery of the divisional relief in full swing. Ypres seemed more smashed, if possible, than when we had last passed through six days before. From the Grande-Place down the Rue de Menin, to the bridge and Menin Road beyond, and well out past the fork, where the roads branched to Zonnebeke and Menin respectively, the path was narrow and tortuous. Piled high on either hand were heaps of debris, alternated with chasms, some sufficiently deep so that a fall to the bottom would put a car promptly *hors de combat*.

An unpleasant smell of burning flesh came from the smouldering mounds lining the way.

Star-shells and trench lights from the firing line made it possible to see the road. Save for their assistance I could not have made the journey without accident.

The house where we were to spend the next few days was easily found. The officers of the 80th Infantry Brigade were busy in it arranging reliefs when I arrived.

A house of stout brick, badly scarred and knocked about, covered a cellar, low roofed and filled with foul air, but reasonably safe from shell-fire.

In this underground sanctuary the flickering light of a dozen candles fell on crowded tables for signallers, around which the men not busy with 'phone or ticker were asleep, heads resting on their crossed arms. Officers pored over maps spread on other tables, or were engaged in close attention to the receipt or despatch of innumerable orders. Against one wall were three or four bedsteads, covered with mattresses that had borne the wearied forms of a long succession of British fighting men, from general officers to privates, and bore ample evidences of having done so.

A battery of British guns were firing from a position near by, and German shells were bursting close enough to cause an interruption of a conversation by their constant crashes.

No news could I find of General de Lisle until Captain Webb, of the Signal Corps, arrived.

"The general?" he said in reply to my query. "I think the general is in a house on the right of the road as you leave Ypres on the west."

I lost no time in getting under way. The return journey was like a bad dream. Shells fell in the vicinity of the road, but not so near as to damage the steadily flowing river of troops, ammunition and food transport, horse and mechanical; ambulances, motor-cycles, and once, another car.

A fatiguing house-to-house search landed me at the spot where dinner had been. Orders left for me instructed me to bring various impedimenta to the Menin Road; so, for the third time, I ploughed through Ypres and toward the *Halte*, where at last I found de Lisle. Nor was that by any means the last trip over that route that I was to make that night. But enough of motoring troubles.

On the 18th it rained with dour persistency.

The 1st Cavalry Division line ran south from the Ypres–Roulers railway, past the west shore of the Bellewaerde Lake. It dipped southeast around the ruins of the Hooge Château and to the east of where Hooge once stood. Crossing the Menin Road, the front threaded the Sanctuary Wood, on the eastern edge of which the enemy were entrenched.

The position in the Sanctuary Wood was the extreme easterly promontory of the Ypres Salient, and not many yards west of the line which the 1st Cavalry Division held in February and March.

General de Lisle's cellar headquarters were less than 2,000 yards from the nearest front-line trench, and Hooge itself was not much further distant.

In an adjacent farm, which had been abandoned for many days, dead cattle and chickens lay about the yard. The table in the living room showed the family had decamped at meal time, evidently hurried by a shell which shaved a corner off the house. They left without waiting to gather up any of their simple belongings.

The lonely cows ambled inquisitively toward me, and were evidently greatly appreciative of a thorough milking, though few cared to drink milk from cows pastured in that poisoned zone, where every inch of ground was septic.

On a dash through Ypres at daybreak I again saw the poor hunted collie. Many mongrels thereabouts were frankly glad of a kind word and a pat on the head, but the highbred, beautiful collie, his splendid coat matted and bedraggled, was so thoroughly frightened that all my efforts to get close to him were fruitless. It was wicked to leave him to death by a chance shell, and more than one of us risked carrying away a shell-souvenir in a vain attempt to save him.

At an early hour de Lisle said: "Find a shelter of some sort for your car, President. Don't forget that the Germans turn their shells down this road a bit at times."

A search resulted in the discovery of a maltster's, where some push-cyclists attached to a battalion of King's Royal Rifles cordially offered to make room for my battered conveyance. A passing ammunition train the night before had ripped off a front mud-guard, and a horse ambulance had crumpled one of the rear guards, while a transport mule had endeavoured to climb into the tonneau, to the sad detriment of my folded cape hood.

I never met a more cheery lot than those K.R.R. cyclists, who generously insisted on my sharing a tin of steaming hot tea and warming myself at their comfortable fire. They showed me a pump in the ruins of a house adjoining, enabling me to get a rare wash, and a still rarer shave, giving me a quite respectable appearance in comparison with my comrades of the 1st Cavalry Division Staff.

During the morning the general sent me to a riddled *château* not far distant, where General Mullens had placed 2nd Cavalry Brigade headquarters. An attempt to use the remains of the drawing-room as a more comfortable habitation than the cellar, was abandoned during the day, as coal-boxes fell with annoying regularity in the *château* yard.

A call at the headquarters of General Arbuthnot, C.R.A. of the 28th Division, in a house west of Ypres, found my lost despatch case had been sent there by Skinner of H Battery, to whom General Arbuthnot had kindly wired offering to keep it until I could call and reclaim it.

At Arbuthnot's headquarters I met a captain of his staff, who had been a military *attaché* in China before the Boxer troubles in 1900, and who knew many of the acquaintances I had made when campaigning with General Gaselee in the war with China.

In the course of conversation, I mentioned the prevailing belief in many quarters that unwritten truces existed between British and German gunners with regard to shelling certain areas. I instanced Dickebusch, a continual home of one of our divisional headquarters, which had been unshelled until our coins hammered a town in the German lines where Hun headquarters were thought to have been located, and thereafter was inundated with a steady rain of shell-fire for many days.

The captain said:

Some peculiar things of that sort have happened. The divisional headquarters to which I was recently attached, occupied, near the line, a *château* which for months had not been visited by a German shell. I became possessed with the idea, without any real evidence to which to attribute it, that so long as our lot did not shell the Hollebeke *château*, our house would be free from a Hun shelling. The Hollebeke Château was in the German lines, and while I did not, of course, know positively, I felt sure it contained some German brigade or divisional headquarters. Many a time our batteries fired at enemy batteries on all sides of the Hollebeke *château*, but not once was it made a target by our gunners.

For week after week this condition of affairs continued, and was often the subject of comment among us. Naturally, in the absence of communication of any sort between the opposing forces, all this may have been mere coincidence.

One day, returning from a walk, I entered the drive to our *château* just as Hun shells began to rain upon us. The shrapnel came thick and fast for several minutes, and the divisional commander and some of his staff officers had very narrow escapes. One shrapnel bullet passed through a wall only ten or twelve inches from the general's head.

None of our divisional guns had been firing for some hours, but another battery in the vicinity had been doing quite a bit of shelling that morning. Curious, I asked the aeroplane observer who had been directing the fire of that battery what target he had given them.

'I went up to direct their fire on some German guns reported to be near the Hollebeke Château,' the observer told me. 'I couldn't locate the described spot, so directed our battery to throw a few shells into the *château* itself. Our gunners at once registered one lyddite through the roof and four shells right through the face of the building. I'll bet we made it hot for any Boches that were inside.'

Comparing times, I learned that the Hollebeke Château received its shelling exactly ten minutes before our headquarters *château* was shelled by the Huns. What made the incident more curious was the fact that for weeks our batteries did no more damage to the Hollebeke Château and never again, at least until I left it, did our *château* have a German shell near it.

The rain softened the earth about the dugouts in front of Ypres, and soon an epidemic of caved-in sides and roofs was raging all along the line, assisted by Black Marias, which shook the moist ground until dugout supports fell and walls collapsed wholesale. A captain of the 18th Hussars was in a dugout roofed by an iron bedstead. A small landslide brought down the beams above and the bedstead fell, so striking the Hussar officer that his neck was broken and he was instantly killed.

The 19th, 20th, and 21st of May passed quickly, the three brigades of the division changing from front line to support dugouts and back again in relays as the days succeeded each other.

On the 21st the sun came out, bright and strong, and justified a few minutes' delay *en route* through Ypres to obtain some photographs. The town was sadly depressing. Earthquake and conflagration might produce as much ruin, but could hardly arrange it so fantastically.

In Ypres Madame Caprice came hand in hand with Devastation and Death. In diabolical mood she flung the shattered buildings of the staid old town hither and thither with an eye to the spectacular. The grotesque met one's glance on every side. Only a James Pryde could have done justice on canvas to such a scene.

After a thunderstorm of almost tropical intensity on the night of the 21st, the 1st Cavalry Division troopers were relieved, and soon after daylight were sleeping soundly in the huts and the adjacent farms near Vlamertinghe. The 22nd and 23rd of May they spent in resting, and on the evening of the 23rd again went back into the trench line.

General de Lisle returned for his rest to new quarters at Esquelbecq, in a thirteenth century chateau which boasted the honour of having once been stormed by Marlborough.

The 14th Division of the "K" Army was billeted near Esquelbecq, and had been placed in the newly formed 6th Corps. Allenby's 5th Corps then consisted of. the 28th Division, 9th Division (the first of the "K" Divisions to arrive in France), and the Northumberland Territorial Division. The 6th Corps, containing the 4th Division, the 27th Division, and the new 14th Division was placed under the command of General Keir.

On the evening of May 23rd, while the troopers of the 1st, 2nd and 9th Cavalry Brigades tramped through Ypres once more, and took

View of the 13th century *château* at Esquelbecq

over part of the sodden trench-line of the Salient, General de Lisle again took up headquarters in the big chateau not far west of the demolished town.

The Salient front trenches led over the line that was taken up after the reconstruction following the hard fighting on May 13th. Wilson's 4th Division reached from the French right, near the Ypres-Yser Canal on the north, to the Canadian Farm, then past the Ypres-Passchendaele Road to the Ypres-Zonnebeke Road near Verlorenhoek.

From the Zonnebeke Road south, across the Ypres-Roulers Railway, as far as the Bellewaerde Lake, troops of the 28th Division composed the firing line.

They joined the left flank of the 18th Hussars, who occupied a position on the south side of the Bellewaerde Lake and in front of the Hooge Château, the trenches at that point being about thirty yards to the east of the *château* ruins. The right of the 18th Hussars rested on the Menin Road, and close behind them in reserve were three score odd York and Durham Tommies who had been sent up to dig.

South of the Menin Road, in the Sanctuary Wood, came the 9th Lancers, 11th Hussars, Queen's Bays, and 5th Dragoon Guards, respectively.

The 4th Dragoon Guards, 15th Hussars, and 19th Hussars were in reserve in the G.H.Q. line.

The night was less disturbed by gun-fire than usual, and even the rifle fire and itinerant sniping were of less volume than for weeks past.

General de Lisle, noticing the strong westerly breeze die away, and the wind shift to the east during the course of the afternoon, sent a warning to the troops in the trenches to be on the look out for a German gas attack next morning.

At earliest light on Whit Monday, the 24th of May, the Hun gas came.

Before three o'clock in the morning, the yellow-green haze was drifting slowly on the light breezes that heralded the coming of the dawn.

Over the eastern front of the Salient the smoke-cloud came from near Wieltje to the Zonnebeke road, and on to the south over the Menin Road.

The 28th Division troops, from the Ypres-Roulers railway to the Bellewaerde Lake, were in the thick of it, and were driven back *en masse*.

"Jeff" Phipps-Hornby and Frederic Coleman comparing underpinning outside Ypres, May, 1915; the thinnest and thickest "supports" in the 1st Cavalry Division

The trenches of the 18th Hussars and 9th Lancers were also in the path of the noxious fumes; but the 1st Cavalry Brigade troops further south escaped them.

For an hour the gas rolled westward, accompanied by a cyclone of shell-fire, and followed by a determined infantry attack.

No part of the cavalry line felt the gas more than the left of the 18th Hussars, which was held by a squadron under command of Captain MacLachlan, who arrived at Vlamertinghe from England at seven o'clock the night before. MacLachlan, with some of the half dozen other officers and 130 men sent out to replace the casualties suffered by the 18th Hussars on May 13th, was tramping through Ypres within half an hour after he joined the regiment. New to Flanders and the Ypres Salient, his experience of a gas attack before he had been in the firing line twelve hours was a trying one.

MacLachlan was impressed by the warning to be on the watch for gas, and was in his forward trenches, awake and alert. His respirator was ready, and he repeatedly told his troopers to see that theirs were ready also.

The gas was actually upon the men before they could distinguish the poison-clouds from the early morning haze that frequently hung over the lake.

The first thick mantle of gas scattered the 18th Hussars somewhat, but enough of them remained in the trenches to hold on until a German machine-gun opened on them from their left rear. Seizing the advantage offered by the retirement of the 28th Division troops, the Huns came on as swiftly as the dispersing gas would allow, and soon were well behind the 18th line.

MacLachlan, later in the day, tried to write a diary of what happened to him during the early morning hours, but it contained little detail. To piece together a coherent story of such events was difficult.

"*3.15 a.m.*, gassed out. *3.30*, in again. *4.30*, some York and Durham Light Infantry officers showed up. *5.15*, twelve men left out of my sixty-one. *5.30*, six men left. *6.30*, 15th Hussars coming up." So ran the diary.

The Germans poured around the Bellewaerde Lake on either side of it, and drove the few remaining 18th Hussars out of the trenches by an outflanking movement with sheer weight of numbers. The troopers retired across the Menin Road and trailed over the shell-swept fields toward Zillebeke, and then on to the southern edge of Ypres.

While the trenches on the lakeside and around the Hooge Château were being torn from the grasp of the 18th Hussars, the 9th Lancers on the right, across the Menin Road, were fighting like mad.

The gas so filled their trenches that at some points the troopers leaped on the parapets into the clearer air above, in full view of the advancing Huns, and poured a fire into the German ranks that dropped dozens of the enemy like shot rabbits.

Captain Rex Benson, howling like a dervish to make his instructions audible above the din of battle, mounted a high bastion and so directed the stream of fire of his squadron that the oncoming rush in front of that trench was stemmed.

A rifle-bullet smashed through Benson's arm and badly shattered the bone, but he held on in spite of his wounds until the first fierce Hun attack was repulsed.

Major Beale-Browne, commanding the 9th Lancers, at once realised the danger to his left flank as the German bullets began to pour into it across the Menin Road. Down the south bank of the highway ran a communication trench, which Beale-Browne at once ordered to be transformed into a defence against a Hun attack from the position that had been won by the enemy from the 18th Hussars.

A small infantry counter-attack to recover the ground at Hooge failed, though two companies of the Buffs got a foothold in some trenches north of the Menin Road, and not far from Hooge Château.

Beale-Browne's headquarters were in the Louave Wood, behind the Sanctuary Wood, and not far distant from the Menin Road. He and Captain "Bimbo" Reynolds, the adjutant of the 9th, who had been twice wounded that morning, constituted the bulk of the garrison of the Louave Wood, when they saw three or four hundred Germans advancing from the north towards the Menin Road, preparatory to attacking the wood, and thus gaining the rear of the 9th Lancers' trenches.

At that moment some York and Lancaster Territorials, who had been sent up from reserve in a wood south of the 9th, arrived. Beale-Browne at once sent to the infantry brigade for more of them. Lining the northern edge of the little wood with the Terriers he waited until the Huns began to stream across the roadway, then swept them back with volley after volley at close range.

This move and the gallant stand made by the 9th Lancers in their front line trenches, ably aided by the York and Lancaster lads, saved the day. A couple of squadrons of the 15th Hussars also played a gallant part in saving our important position south of the Menin Road.

The cost to the 9th Lancers was heavy, Captain Francis Grenfell, Captain "Algy" Court, and Captain Noel Edwards were killed, the latter dying from the effects of gas poisoning after he had been taken to the hospital at Bailleul.

Four other officers of the 9th were wounded, several men were killed by the gas, and forty-eight hours later the number of casualties, including those gassed and missing, was still over 100.

While the strenuous struggle was proceeding in the front line trenches, little was known of the actual results of the German attack. Every man attached to Beale-Browne's headquarters, except "Bimbo" Reynolds, was out of commission, save the telegraphists, who hung on in the poisoned air of the signals dugout until all the wires were swept away by the German shells, and all communication with the rear rendered impossible.

General Meakin took over the field command of the division, and Colonel "Tommy" Pitman again took the 1st Cavalry Brigade.

The 4th D.G.'s, 15th Hussars, and 19th Hussars in reserve in the G.H.O. line, were as badly gassed as though they had been in the front trenches.

In spite of this, they pushed their depleted ranks forward in support over ground where shells were bursting in scores and hundreds, and formed a new line along a road that ran north from and at right angles to the Menin Road, about 1,000 yards west of Hooge.

Here they held the enemy from making further inroads into our territory, fighting fiercely every hour of the long day.

The 15th Hussars and 19th Hussars suffered heavy casualties, and the 9th Cavalry Brigade lost one of its most popular officers in Captain Griffiths, its brigade major, who was killed by a shell.

The 4th Division front line held well, in spite of the gas. The only 4th Division trenches lost were along a front of 800 yards from the Canadian Farm to the Ypres-Passchendaele Road. The East Lancashires south of that road hung on with a bull-dog grip until help came and counter-attacks could be formed and launched to retake the ground that had been lost.

My friend in the 11th Hussars, from whose diary I quoted a few paragraphs with reference to the part the gallant 11th played in the battle of May 13th, kept a most vivid series of notes as to what happened in front of the 1st Cavalry Brigade on that memorable 24th of May.

While the 11th Hussars were on the right of the 9th Lancers, and therefore on the fringe of the attack, a perusal of the following will give an idea of what it meant to be in the front line of the Ypres Salient on a bank holiday in 1915:—

3 a.m.—Heavy firing, guns, rifles, Maxims, on our left; faint smell of gas; just as dawn breaks.

3.15.—All quiet on our immediate front, heavy shelling going on all round. Every wire cut between Brigade headquarters and ourselves, and with the artillery.

3.45.—Still no touch with brigade headquarters, so messenger despatched. The headquarters of the 11th, Bays, and 5th D.G.'s are all close together in a wood behind the trench line. The Bays and 5th Dragoon Guards each have one squadron in hand; there are also three companies of the 4th East Yorks Territorials in brigade reserve in the same wood.

4.—The Bays send an officers' patrol to the left.

4.20.—Heavy firing still continues on our left. Telephone message sent to O.C. A Squadron:—

Try and get information of situation on your left.

4.35.—Answer received:—

Adjutant 9th Lancers just passed here. Reports their centre and left gassed. No attack so far.

4.45.—Lieutenant Milne's patrol of the Bays returned. Report 9th Lancers have been badly gassed, and retired from their trenches in places, leaving big gaps. Reinforcements have gone up, and line has, he thinks, been re-established.

5.—Captain Osborne, brigade-major, arrives from Brigade headquarters. They have all suffered severely from gas; the regiments in G.H.Q. line have caught it very badly. The shelling has been very heavy, great number of casualties, men streaming back from all parts of the line. When he left Brigade headquarters they were in ignorance of the situation in any part of the line. The only thing which kept their hopes up was that not a single man of the 1st Brigade had returned.

6.30.—Lieutenant Milne reports that he went to officer commanding 9th Lancers, who told him that his line was complete to fifty yards north of the Menin Road. He has had many men gassed, and has used up all his supports to fill up gaps in the front line. He is pushing reconnaissance to his left. Heard that the officer commanding York and Lancaster Regiment had his battalion in a wood about 600 yards east of us, so went over and saw him. He has 1,000 men, and is reserve to the section of the line from our right to Hill 60. Got him to send two companies to the officer commanding 9th Lancers.

7.30.—Lieutenant Hartman, 11th Hussars, returned with his patrol. He had worked up to the Menin Road, where he had found Captain F. O. Grenfell, 9th Lancers, holding on with a very few men, and asking urgently for reinforcements of 200 men to strengthen his line. As Lieutenant Hartman was leaving, three platoons of infantry arrived.

9.—Heavy attack on Hooge. All our glasses are fixed on that point. The village (now only a few ruined houses) is on a piece of rising ground which commands, at close range, the rear of our position. Withdrew one of the 11th Hussars' Maxims and laid it on the village. Can see our troops falling back. If Hooge goes, we are in the soup. 9th Lancers headquarters are in Louave Wood. Beale-Brown is in command. He has still got one company in hand.

10.—Still holding on at Hooge. Can see more of our infantry moving up from Louave Wood.

11.—Patrol reports "enemy have broken through 18th Hussars' line north of Menin Road, and are working down on the road in rear of Hooge." Hear heavy firing in that direction. Send Osborne to officer commanding Y. and L. to get him to send three companies to hold northern edge of Louave Wood, with machine-gun and detachment at farm west of it.

12 noon.—Message sent by runner to Brigade Headquarters: "Still holding on to Hooge, but Germans are astride the Menin Road. Could you push up counter-attack in that direction? My line of retreat is covered by German machine-guns in that direction. Several orderlies have been wounded going backwards and forwards."

12 noon.—First messenger returned from Brigade headquarters. Counter-attack is being organised. Messenger states that on his way up he saw about 100 infantry straggling back from the lines on our right, stating that their "'ole battalion had been coot oop." If there is any truth in their statement, we are in a nasty position, so send off at once an officer's patrol in that direction to clear up the situation, and a squadron of the 5th D.G.'s to support the patrol and form a flank protection in direction of Maple Copse. No firing has been heard at all on our right.

12.5 p.m.—Learn that there is a company of Royal Engineers in the wood near the York and Lancaster headquarters, so send them following order:—

> Proceed with Y. and L. guide to O.C. 9th Lancers in Louave Wood, and ask him if he can find work for your fifty men in consolidating the position on northern edge of wood.

12.15.—Germans attacking right of 9th Lancers' line and left of A Squadron, 11th Hussars, with bombs. They are reported to have broken the 9th Lancers' line at one point, but been driven out again.

12.30.—Captain Lawson reports that section of trench held by Territorials between his left and 9th Lancers has been captured by Germans. They are working down his trench with bombs. The captured section slopes up from the stream, and looks down on the A Squadron trench.

12.35.—Interview the officer commanding 4th Yorks, explain the situation, and tell him to take another company up, and with the one already in the second line form a barrier behind the captured portion, getting touch with the 9th Lancers on his left and the 11th Hussars on his right.

1.—Message sent to officer commanding 9th Lancers:—

> Have pushed up a support to form a barrier behind the captured trench. Endeavour to get touch with them from the switch trench. A counter attack is now taking place from Potitjze towards Hooge.

1.30.—The pressure on the Menin Road seems to be relieved. The Germans are still bombing down Lawson's trench, but A

Squadron are putting up a good fight with bombs. Lieut. Gunter has been killed.

2.25.—Message sent by runner to Brigade headquarters.—

At about 12.15 Germans captured portion of 9th Lancers' trench close to 11th Hussars' left. Company of East Yorks sent up to form barrier behind broken line. Switch on 9th Lancers' right is now held instead of advanced trench. Western edge of Hooge still held by mixed force of men. Send me information of counter attack, for if Germans establish themselves on Menin Road during the night, position of brigade becomes untenable. If it is proposed to retire from here it would have to be done at night. Please inform officer commanding 83rd Brigade that I have had to call on all the York and Lancasters except 250 men. Following is disposition of line at present as known to me:—1st Brigade line as taken over last night. 2nd Brigade—9th Lancers, weakened by losses, with left on Menin Road; right broken but being secured. Remainder of 9th Lancers, with York and Lancasters, have formed a line right along north edge of wood facing north. They have two machine-guns on their outer flank and patrols to the Menin Road.

2.45.—Message sent to Brigade headquarters:—:

Please arrange to send up tonight two dozen hand grenades per regiment, and detonators, most important; also two dozen rifle grenades per regiment and two dozen extra detonators per regiment, as the bombs here are without detonators; also as many gas-sprayers as possible. Ask 1st Cavalry Division to send up trench mortars with Royal Horse Artillerymen or Royal Engineers to man them, as our men don't understand them. They are urgently required.

3 p.m.—No further developments. Situation well in hand, but hope that counter-attack is developing on north side Menin Road. Lawson is holding on to the line of stream, but position is untenable unless 2nd Brigade can re-establish original line on their right. Make dispositions for holding new line from left of B Squadron down communication trench to the support trench; thence along to where it joins up with front line. The situation on the right down as far as Hill 60 reported all right. The trenches near Hill 60 visited by our patrol did not even know that there was a fight going on. They thought all the firing was a long way to their left.

4 p.m.—Situation unchanged. Have got majority of A Squadron back into communicating trench, moved up squadron of the Bays to complete the line and join up with 9th Lancers. Send following message to Lawson, who is still holding on at the stream:—

> Most of your squadron are now back in communicating trench. Squadron of the Bays and infantry are holding the second line. I cannot send you up any more support; doubt your doing any good by holding on to present line. If you cannot get away now, wait until dark.

4.—Message sent to officer commanding 9th Lancers:—

> Portion of front line marked with crosses on accompanying sketch, has gone; suggest your falling back and holding line marked with red dots.

Operations carried on without any further alarms till dusk. We saw the right flank of the counter-attack coming up towards Hooge. The Y. and L. co-operated in this movement.

5.—Following received from officer commanding York and Lancasters:—

> Our attack on the Menin Road has been successful. All the enemy have been driven back off the road as far as our left flank rests. The companies have withdrawn to Louave Wood after leaving a post on Menin Road, facing north. Patrols have been pushed on to the north to try and get touch with the counterattack, but these patrols will now be withdrawn, and the Oxford Hussars will be asked to send similar patrols. Some of the enemy have been killed. Have collected their papers and identity discs, and will send them to Brigade headquarters.

Soon after dark we received orders that the brigade would be relieved tonight, but it was not till past midnight that the relieving regiments arrived. During the hours between dusk and midnight the enemy attacked vigorously with bombs both B Squadron and A Squadron trenches. At midnight the 16th Lancers arrived to take over. It was obvious that it was going to be a tight fit to defeat daylight. Not a moment was lost, but it was nearly two o'clock before the last squadron was relieved. The squadrons moved off independently, keeping as far as possible on the low ground. A violent fusillade commenced on both flanks of the Salient, and "Spares" were fairly flying about over our heads. The Germans were making another gas attack, and C Squadron, which took a more northerly route, caught it slightly.

Our casualties were slight during the withdrawal, and it was quite light by the time we reached Ypres. We raced on through the town, as shells were falling about in a most unpleasant manner. We got back to Vlamertinghe at 4.30 a.m., the men absolutely dead beat, having walked seven miles across country at top speed. We dossed down to sleep, most of the men preferring the open to the wooden huts. Forty-eight hours without a check has been a bit more than tiring. The casualties for the 24th of May were two officers killed, twelve men killed, twelve wounded, and four died of wounds. Lieutenant Poole, who was only slightly wounded on the way back to Ypres, unfortunately succumbed to tetanus a few days later at Boulogne.

After sweeping over the firing-line and drifting past the G.H.Q. reserve line, on that Whit Monday morning, the gas still moved westward.

H and I Battery men, caught in their dugouts, had a liberal share, and still more of the poisonous fumes gathered in ruined Ypres, or floated on to our divisional headquarters further to the west. Some of the gas was carried as far back as Vlamertinghe, between four and five miles from the German trenches.

"Willie" Du Cros, running with his ambulance convoy from Vlamertinghe to a dressing station well west of Ypres, was sufficiently overcome by gas to be for some hours dangerously ill.

Hardly a member of the 1st Cavalry Division Staff, including General de Lisle himself, escaped the gas fumes. Red and watery eyes, a pale bluish tinge to the complexion, violent headaches, and continual coughing were universal for the greater part of the forenoon.

Gas shells continually burst over Ypres and the roads near it. More than once I ran through pockets of gas, apparently caused by these gas shells. Every one of us wore respirators or masks when near Ypres, though "Babe" Nicholson inhaled sufficient gas through his respirator to render him unconscious for five minutes after a "dash up front."

General Mullens, of the 2nd Cavalry Brigade, and Captain Paget, his brigade major, were brought in a dangerous condition to our headquarters. By night they were able to walk about, but for a time it seemed quite possible neither would recover.

That evening I asked General Mullens, who was looking very ill, if he thought he was free from the effects of the poisoning. "Somewhat," he answered. "No one could imagine what the experience is like. The helplessness and mental suffering of it are beyond description."

Ypres came in for another terrific bombardment that day. The Menin Bridge and the Menin Road proved such death-traps that they were "closed to traffic" before the day was over.

Romer Williams, of General Mullens's staff, came through Ypres with a message just as I was going up.

"You have a fine bruise on your forehead," said I, pointing to a raw bump the size of a goose-egg. "How did you get it?"

He answered:

I haven't an idea, unless a shell bounced off it. Some of 'em have come close enough, so I thought they *might* have done so. As I was coming back down the Menin Road, an ammunition limber passed me, the horses at full gallop. I watched them cross the railway metals at the halt. The limber jumped up into the air when it hit the crossing and the horses seemed to be skimming the ground, they were going at such a pace. Just as the limber bumped up, a flash came, right over it, and when the smoke rolled away the road led clean on eastward, absolutely empty. Not a sign of horse, man or limber remained. A big howitzer shell must have hit it squarely on the outfit, and swept it into the ditch like the wind would sweep away a leaf. It was a terrible thing to see.

Colonel Browne of the R.A.M.C. and his staff worked like Trojans. Browne had not slept since 7 o'clock on the previous morning, and had a bad touch of gas, like everyone else near headquarters.

At break of day the roads were full of panting, coughing stragglers from the front. Scores on scores staggered into the big front gates of the *château*, and sank exhausted and suffering on the deep grass that lined the driveway. The medical officers hastily gave such relief as they could and packed the ambulances full of the wounded and the worst of the gas cases.

By 9 o'clock in the morning 600 gassed men and 160 wounded

had passed through Colonel Browne's hands, more than four-fifths of them members of the 28th or 4th Division units.

The number of men who were wounded by shell fire when coming back toward Ypres from the gas-filled trenches was legion.

Five signal corps men, attached to the 2nd Cavalry Brigade, were badly poisoned, but managed to get back as far as the big square at Ypres. They were in such a sorry state that a passing officer advised them to lie down on the broken cobbles of the Grande Place until an ambulance could be sent for them. They stretched out in a pathetic row, and had not lain there long when a Black Maria lit at their feet, shoving them half a dozen yards over the stones still in line, every man of the five dead, killed before he knew of the coming of the shell.

All day shattered men were brought to the divisional dressing station near the chateau crates. The wounds from the shells were terrible.

A wounded sergeant of the Cheshires refused a ride from east of Ypres in an ambulance, cheerily saying that those who *could* walk should do so, and not occupy space required for those more severely hurt. He carried back his full kit, tramping sturdily along with a grim smile on his fine face. At the dressing station a nasty bullet hole in his shoulder was disclosed, which would have laid many a man flat on his back.

"Good man, of the old school. New ones can't touch 'em," commented a grizzled hospital orderly, as the Cheshire sergeant passed out of the room.

A Tommy, with bright eyes peeping from a purple bit of face all but hidden by a mass of white bandages, insisted on telling his story to anyone who would listen.

"He has told his bally yarn half a dozen times, sir," complained a hospital orderly to the doctor. "I told him he was not to talk, but he just can't keep his bloomin' mouth shut, he says."

"Nasty wound, too," remarked the doctor, as we watched the talkative individual. "Bullet went clean through his face, in one cheek and out the other, and carried away every one of his upper teeth."

But his injury had apparently increased his volubility. We could hear his tale as he poured it into the ear of a gunner, wounded in both legs and unable to escape.

"You see the ol' gas stuff got us bad, some on us," he explained. "But I got this ere bloomin' smash in the jawr, and that took up so much o' me bally time I didn't pay no attention to no gas, you believe *me!* I warsn't the only bloke lyin' there. They was a fair lot o' our chaps near me.

"The snipin' was cruel. Some o' the poor blokes that was bloomin' well shot already got 'it agin. I was jest thinkin' mine was comin' when wot oh! 'ere comes three big Prooshuns, tall as 'ouses. Good-day, Bill, says I to meself. You next! It'll be the butt for *your* nut from these 'ere lobsters.

"But not a bit. They ups with me and carts me over to a 'ouse. Leastwys it *wor* a 'ouse, wonct. An' wot do *you* think! Them Prooshuns give me a bloomin' fill o' cold coffee, like Christians!

"'Bout this time the Buffs was comin' on an' my Prooshuns had to skin out, rapid. They didn't do nothin' to me only say, 'Ta-ta!' in Dutch. The fire got so 'ot I crawled off down a crick-thing full of the stinkinest stuff that ever got called water. I rounded around, after a while, an' come up back o' them Buffs a little. They saw me and bloomin' near shot my 'ead off, so I lay still.

"Then I crawled more. I 'ad got in front of some more o' our chaps by then. Big 'uns was goin' orf right there, an' 'eads was down, you bet. I was gettin' closer, when a fat-'ead sees me an' starts shootin'. I 'ollered, an' the more I 'ollered the more 'e let off 'is silly gun. 'E 'it my pore ol' cap, 'e did. Then some cuss shuts 'im orf, an' they come out and gets me.'

"'Who are you?' says a officer chap. 'I'm damned if I know,' says I. 'I've been shot at by everybody I've seen all mornin', except three big 'Uns.'

"'Mad,' says a cove, short-like. 'Send 'im in.'

"An' 'ere I am, with no jawr much left."

"Humph," commented the doctor as he walked away. "Guess he could stand the loss of some more jaw and not kill him. He seems to have plenty left."

A more sinister story was told by a trooper shot through the thigh. He said the Germans got into one of our trenches, in which they found him and nine of his comrades. Five of the ten had been hit. The Huns told the wounded to crawl away to as safe a place as they could find, and they straightway wriggled off down the trench, as directed.

With a scowl on his face a big German said to the five unwounded men, "We don't want you. Go!" He pointed his finger to the shell-swept field that led toward the British reserve line. The five started on a run, but had not gone far when the *rat-tat-tat* of a machine-gun behind them commenced. In an instant the air was full of bullets. Four of the five men fell dead. The fifth was the man who told the story. He fell, he said, at the first sound of the quick-firer, and thus escaped with a bullet through his leg.

Counter-attack followed counter-attack as the day wore on. We launched a small one at 2.30 p.m., a larger one an hour later, and a still larger one was planned for 6 o'clock. This last was to win back the lost trenches around the Hooge Château, past the Bellewaerde Lake, and on to the north.

The British guns cleared the way splendidly for the 6 o'clock attack. "Mother" shells fell into a line of ruined houses near Hooge. The Germans had placed several machine-guns there, and as the 9.2 projectiles knocked the bricks about their ears they scampered out like chickens. A machine-gun not far away in the 9th Lancers' trenches poured a hail of bullets into the Huns as they left cover, and numbers were seen to fall.

The Royal Fusiliers were attacking, but when their line "got up," the advantage was lost, other enemy machine-guns had been brought into the German trenches, and the attack "fizzled out," no real gain having been made.

So night closed in. By 2 o'clock in the morning of the next day the fresh 2nd Cavalry

Division troopers had relieved the tired men of the 1st Cavalry Division, who were once more brought back to the Vlamertinghe huts.

The cavalry had lost heavily, and was still to lose before the second Battle of Ypres was finished, though the ground won by the Huns on the 24th of May marked their furthermost westerly advance.

The part played by the infantry in the second Ypres struggle was greater, numerically, than that of the cavalry, but the work done by the troopers was of inestimable value. Their resistance broke the back of the enemy's onslaught at its most tense moments.

The work of the Queen's Bays on May 13th, and the 9th Lancers and 15th Hussars on May 24th, will long live in the annals of the British Army.

The following officers were awarded the Distinguished Service Order, the task of selection for the awards from so great a number of instances of gallant conduct during these May days being a most difficult one:—

Major George Harold Abseil Ing, 2nd Dragoon Guards (Queen's Bays). At Ypres on May 13th, 1915, when the line was broken beyond the right flank of his regiment, he came out of his trench in the front line, stood on the road in the open under heavy shell-fire, stopped the retirement of forty men of another unit, and turned them into his section of the defence. The good results of his gallant action were far-reaching.

Major Charles William Henry Crichton, 10th (Prince of Wales Own Royal) Hussars. Near Ypres, on May 13th, 1915, showed conspicuous gallantry and ability in collecting and rallying men who were retiring under heavy shell-fire through the 10th Hussars' position. In our counter-attack he continued to direct operations, giving great encouragement to his men whilst he lay in the open under heavy shell-fire with his leg shattered.

Captain John Grey Porter, 9th (Queen's Royal) Lancers. On May 10th, 1915, when a very heavy attack was made on the front line near Hooge, Captain Porter went up to the infantry line there and brought back very valuable information regarding the situation. On May 13th he rendered the greatest possible assistance in taking messages under terrific shell-fire to various parts of the line, and reporting on various local situations. He set an example of coolness and total disregard of danger that was beyond all praise. He has been twice wounded previously in this campaign.

The following eight cavalry officers were awarded the Military Cross for their work in the Salient:—

Captain Stewart Graham Menzies, D.S.O., 2nd Life Guards. Near Ypres, on May 13th, 191 5, after his commanding officer had been wounded, displayed conspicuous ability, coolness and resource in controlling the action of his regiment and rallying the men.

Captain Edward Archibald Ruggles-Brise, Essex Yeomanry, T.F. For conspicuous gallantry and ability, near Ypres, on May 13th, 1915, when he held a position gained in a counter-attack, although entirely isolated, until ordered to withdraw at night. He had only fifty men under his command.

Captain Guy Franklin Reynolds, 9th (Queen's Royal) Lancers. For splendid work on May 24th, 191 5, near Hooge. When the headquarters of the 9th Lancers were gassed, he constantly brought reports from the trenches under very heavy fire, and helped to reorganise the defence of the left section. Also when the enemy attempted to enter Louave Wood, he was invaluable in helping to reorganise the defence. He set the finest possible example of calmness, coolness, and courage although suffering from gas and twice slightly wounded.

Captain Charles Joseph Leicester Stanhope, 15th (The King's)

Hussars. For gallant and skilful handling of his squadron, near Hooge, on May 24th, 191 5, with most valuable results. His squadron, having been badly gassed, he took forward the remnants, together with stragglers he collected, and on his own initiative, under very heavy shellfire, reinforced the front line. He remained in action all day, and when the line on his left gave way he doubled back his flank with great skill, and continued with the utmost gallantry to hold the position.

Lieutenant Kenneth Douglas Lorne Maclaine of Lochbuie, 15th (The King's) Hussars (S.R.). Near Ypres, for good work in command of his squadron under trying circumstances, on May 13th, 1915. For gallant and skilful leading of a patrol on May 14th, by which he gained information of great value. He volunteered to lead this patrol, and pushed forward by day, a mile in front of our line, and returned with a good report as to the actual line then held by the enemy. For coolness, determination and skill in handling his squadron under difficult circumstances near Hooge on May 24th, 1915. He had been ordered up with his squadron to reinforce the left of another cavalry regiment, when the line north of the Menin Road gave way, and the situation became critical. Lieutenant Maclaine showed great skill in taking up a new position, facing north and west to meet the new situation, and maintained his position under most critical circumstances until relieved at 2.15 the next morning. His action contributed greatly towards maintaining intact the line south of the road.

Lieutenant William Spurrett Fielding Johnson, Leicestershire Yeomanry, T.F. For conspicuous gallantry near Ypres on May 13th, 1915. Was with Major Martin, and continued the action until the squadron was reduced to thirteen men. Afterwards displayed great coolness in withdrawing to a flank and joining a cavalry brigade.

Lieutenant James Archibald Garton, North Somerset Yeomanry, T.F. Near Ypres on May 13th, 1915, showed great coolness and daring. Held his position throughout the day, notwithstanding that the trenches had been blown in, and inspired all ranks by his behaviour. After all senior officers were killed or wounded, he assumed command of the regiment, displaying great judgment and initiative throughout.

Lieutenant Nigel Kennedy Worthington, 3rd Dragoon Guards (S.R.). Near Ypres on May 12th, 1915, showed great coolness and daring. He took over a new line of trenches just before dark, and to get round the line in daylight, he had to cross several open and fireswept zones. On May 13th, at great risk, he came back several times to report.

From the foregoing list of honours it would be unfair to omit the Distinguished Service Order given for magnificent work a week after the fight on May 24th, to Major Philip Granville Mason, of the 3rd (Prince of Wales') Dragoon Guards. The official report read:

> Whilst in command of Hooge Fort and the adjoining trenches, he showed conspicuous gallantry and ability in holding the village and defence line allotted to him, notwithstanding a terrific bombardment for several hours every day from May 30th to June 2nd, 1915, in which practically all his trenches and dug-outs were blown in.

On the 25th the regiments took stuck of their losses and began the work of refitting. I called at the headquarters of Colonel Burnett of the 18th Hussars, hearing he was in a dangerous condition from gas poisoning. No one was allowed to see him, and fears for his recovery were expressed by those who attended him. Burnett was soon afterwards sent home, where he was compelled to spend many long months of convalescence before he was able to rejoin his regiment.

Acting Adjutant Hill, of the 18th Hussars, had not been able to make out any accurate list of casualties. Two officers of the regiment were known to have been killed by gas, and five others were wounded. The killed, wounded and missing totalled nearly 190 out of less than 300. Many of the missing, it was hoped, would prove to have been gassed but slightly, and be able soon to resume their duties.

As the sun went down that evening their comrades of the 9th Lancers buried the bodies of Francis Grenfell and "Algy" Court.

Court's face wore a smile, as though he was quietly sleeping. Grenfell, shot through the heart at the height of the battle, bore, too, a look of deep peace, as if at last he had cheerfully gone to a better country, to join his beloved brother "Rivy," from the shock of whose death, on the Aisne, Francis had never recovered.

Staunch friends and fine men, both Grenfell and Court.

Whatever Peace may bring us, it can never replace the ones War has taken.

But they have left behind them their example, and the memory of the clean, young manhood that England gave, without stint, to fight for the right. With that memory enshrined in the hearts of those they have left behind, victory lies not with the grave, for such lives are deathless.

At an early hour on the 26th of May, General de Lisle was apprised of his appointment to the command of the 29th Division, which had won splendid laurels under General Hunter Weston in the Dardanelles.

My long and pleasant association with de Lisle bade fair to close, much to my regret.

In the course of conversation I told the general how sorry I was that I was not to accompany him.

"I much wish that you were," said he. "I doubt if I can take you to the Dardanelles; but if you care to come with me to London and the War Office, I will do what I can to have you attached to my new division."

After a morning of racing back and forth between the front and St. Omer, we sped to Boulogne, arriving in time to catch the afternoon boat.

No one could have been kinder than General Long, the Director of Supplies and Transport at the War Office. In his office, next morning, I met General de Lisle; but General Long could only tell us that "it will very likely be a long, long time before motor cars will be required in the Dardanelles; and, as you know, Americans are not eligible for commissions in the British Army, even should you apply for one."

So back I went to General Headquarters in France, deeply sorry to say "Goodbye" to General de Lisle and his magnificent 1st Cavalry Division.

ALSO FROM LEONAUR
AVAILABLE IN SOFTCOVER OR HARDCOVER WITH DUST JACKET

DOING OUR 'BIT' *by Ian Hay*—Two Classic Accounts of the Men of Kitchener's 'New Army' During the Great War including *The First 100,000* & *All In It*.

AN EYE IN THE STORM by *Arthur Ruhl*—An American War Correspondent's Experiences of the First World War from the Western Front to Gallipoli and Beyond.

STAND & FALL by *Joe Cassells*—A Soldier's Recollections of the 'Contemptible Little Army' and the Retreat from Mons to the Marne, 1914.

RIFLEMAN MACGILL'S WAR by *Patrick MacGill*—A Soldier of the London Irish During the Great War in Europe including *The Amateur Army, The Red Horizon & The Great Push*.

WITH THE GUNS by *C. A. Rose & Hugh Dalton*—Two First Hand Accounts of British Gunners at War in Europe During World War 1- Three Years in France with the Guns and With the British Guns in Italy.

EAGLES OVER THE TRENCHES by *James R. McConnell & William B. Perry*—Two First Hand Accounts of the American Escadrille at War in the Air During World War 1-Flying For France: With the American Escadrille at Verdun and Our Pilots in the Air.

THE BUSH WAR DOCTOR by *Robert V. Dolbey*—The Experiences of a British Army Doctor During the East African Campaign of the First World War.

THE 9TH—THE KING'S (LIVERPOOL REGIMENT) IN THE GREAT WAR 1914 - 1918 by *Enos H. G. Roberts*—Like many large cities, Liverpool raised a number of battalions in the Great War. Notable among them were the Pals, the Liverpool Irish and Scottish, but this book concerns the wartime history of the 9th Battalion – The Kings.

THE GAMBARDIER by *Mark Severn*—The experiences of a battery of Heavy artillery on the Western Front during the First World War.

FROM MESSINES TO THIRD YPRES by *Thomas Floyd*—A personal account of the First World War on the Western front by a 2/5th Lancashire Fusilier.

THE IRISH GUARDS IN THE GREAT WAR - VOLUME 1 by *Rudyard Kipling*—Edited and Compiled from Their Diaries and Papers Volume 1 The First Battalion.

THE IRISH GUARDS IN THE GREAT WAR - VOLUME 2 by *Rudyard Kipling*—Edited and Compiled from Their Diaries and Papers Volume 2 The Second Battalion.

AVAILABLE ONLINE AT **www.leonaur.com**
AND FROM ALL GOOD BOOK STORES

www.ingramcontent.com/pod-product-compliance
Lightning Source LLC
Chambersburg PA
CBHW020939230426

43666CB00005B/80